T0115097

The Legacy of a Hero;
Life Lived from the Christian Prospective

Tribute to the Late Dr. Lwanga

Pastor Stephen Kyeyune

 authorHOUSE®

AuthorHouse™ LLC
1663 Liberty Drive
Bloomington, IN 47403
www.authorhouse.com
Phone: 1-800-839-8640

© 2013, 2014 Pastor Stephen Kyeyune. All rights reserved.

No part of this book may be reproduced, stored in a retrieval system, or transmitted by any means without the written permission of the author.

Published by AuthorHouse 02/18/2014

ISBN: 978-1-4817-1034-3 (sc)
ISBN: 978-1-4817-1035-0 (e)

Any people depicted in stock imagery provided by Thinkstock are models, and such images are being used for illustrative purposes only.
Certain stock imagery © Thinkstock.

This book is printed on acid-free paper.

Because of the dynamic nature of the Internet, any web addresses or links contained in this book may have changed since publication and may no longer be valid. The views expressed in this work are solely those of the author and do not necessarily reflect the views of the publisher, and the publisher hereby disclaims any responsibility for them.

About the Author

Pastor Stephen Kyeyune was born in Uganda but he has lived overseas for the last twenty years. He is a father. He is the current pastor of the Multicultural Family Fellowship Church in South Bend IN USA.

Pastor Stephen Kyeyune enjoys reading and writing life changing stories. He is the author of other books including: The New Generation of Worshippers; The Acts of the Apostles; A Miracle at Prairie Avenue; When God Calls a Man; Growing in the Spirit; Shaping the Societies (A series of books on culture and Christianity). You can order copies of these books at <Amazon.com>. Or contact us at <stephkyeyu@hotmail.com>

Dedication

THIS BOOK IS DEDICATED TO THE LATE DR JUSTINE KIBIRIGE KAWOOYA LWANGA.

Special Acknowledgement goes to the Widow Mrs. Christine Lwanga and the Children.

From my Desk

Although this book is written to acknowledge the fallen hero, it is good for your spiritual growth and general studies. We are social animals, and many people are extremely passionate about the things that define them ethically and ethnically. This book covers the faith of some of the familiar biblical characters and gives a compelling reason for our faith. I recommend it for personal devotions. This book can make a good gift to a family member whom you want to win to Christ or who is already a confessed believer but is yearning for spiritual growth. It is good for people grieving the loss of their loved ones. It is good for general study because it covers all areas of life. This book is not a substitute for the Bible. I encourage you to read the Bible regularly in order to nourish your soul.

After the death of Dr. Lwanga, I was approached by Dr. Vincent Kabuye, a brother to the deceased, with a proposal to write something in recognition of the late Dr. Lwanga. I was humbled by his offer and I accepted it graciously. I asked him to provide to me an outline of the late Dr. Lwanga's biography. Doctor Vincent Kabuye is currently a senior high ranking officer in UPDF (Uganda People's Defense Forces). He is currently the Head of the Radiology Department at the General Military Hospital in Uganda. He is based at Bombo, a place that Dr. Lwanga called home. It is the same place where he spent most of his youthful age. Nobody is in a better position than him to provide the biography of the late Dr. Lwanga. In this endeavor, he became an invaluable partner in communicating this message and a key narrator of this story.

The late Dr. Lwanga was a father figure to me. I knew him since my childhood. His clean-cut persona made him a popular practitioner, which was also carried over into his personal life. He was a vanguard of the physicians and the nation at large. He loved serving the community; retirement was not on his schedule. He carried himself with dignity his whole life. He was not connected with any scandal. He was a real pearl our country could not afford to lose! "Death is such a bad reaper, often reaping the unripe fruit!" as said by Elechi Amadi, in his novel 'The Concubine'.

It is tough to write a story of a person you love because some might discredit the story thinking that the profile story is inflated. Not to mention the fact that Africans have a habit of saying good things only about the deceased people. To put it in better words, seeking to cast aspersion on a deceased is un-African. I have tried to write out of sincerity without speculation. I am not trying to put the late Dr. Lwanga on a pedestal, but I believe in honoring those who deserve the honor. I am writing for good reason. You can prop up a paper tiger with all sorts of stuff and it may at some point pass off as a tiger scaring away little rabbits and hares but when push comes to shove, paper will always crumble. Like it or not the late Dr. Lwanga is not a decoy; he was a humanitarian with recognitions and a place in history to boot. He was and he will always be a hero, an inspiration to the poor and a symbol of strength to the oppressed. Not because of what we write about him but because of the life he lived. He was a voice to the voiceless. He echoed what many of us couldn't say. He was a silent voice that spoke louder in actions. Surely, the brightest star burn out soon (RIP).

Uganda is gifted with many talented and auspicious human resources. If one was to have a bird's-eye view of all the practicing doctors in Uganda, he would not fail to find the ilk of Dr. Lwanga. However, Dr. Lwanga's personality and service delivering were unusual given the selfish culture of today. He was of material help that is not easily replaceable. He may be ridiculed for not being obscenely rich, but you could not fault him on compassionate, credibility and intellect. His passing left most of us stunned.

It is tough to lose the people whom we love. As I was mourning the death of Dr. Lwanga another tragedy happened. Nalongo Nakintu, the mother of Derrick and my twin daughters passed away. It was double jeopardy beyond misery. The idea that lightening doesn't strike twice in the same place proved to be wrong. One writer said that tragedies never come single. He was right regarding my situation because within the same month I was mourning the death of some of the most important people whom I cared for. The tragedy in life is to lose your heart's desire. Both of them died an abrupt death without being sick. This was difficult to fathom; it was hard to believe that they are gone. Indeed life experience is like a swinging pendulum; it is hard to stay up there without coming down.

As I was mourning and contemplating on the situation of my kids who were left helpless without a mother, my late father appeared to me in a dream and delivered the following message to me: "Where there is a crown there is a shield as well". At first I did not take the message seriously; I thought it was an old proverb. But the next morning, when I woke up, I had a revelation that Jesus has a crown to rule and a shield to guide and protect us. The message was comforting. Jesus is the reason for our living. We can go through the trials of life with such conviction.

Christians can read the end of their story with such assurance that there is no more sin, no more sorrow, no more pain, and no more death; for the former things have passed away. And the kingdoms of this world will become the kingdoms of Jesus Christ as He destroys sin, suffering, and Satan, and as He claims the ultimate victory on our behalf! That's the kind of confidence we have in Jesus Christ. We pray believing in God the almighty and majesty who reigns now from heaven, and who will one day finish the story as the victor with the faithful at His side! As per now my soul can rest in the blessed hope.

Pastor Gram says that throughout the history of our faith, the question has often been asked, "Where is God when tragedy strikes?" But even deeper than that question is the concern by some that God is aloof when hard times hit. And as often as that question has been asked, there's been no shortage of answers put forth by Christians and non-Christians alike. I love what Corrie Ten Boom said. She was a Jewish Christian lady that went through the holocaust with confidence. She served the Lord faithfully during World War II and was a prisoner in a concentration camp. She was quoted as saying: "There is no panic in heaven; only plans!" What a perspective from a woman who knew what suffering and tragedy was all about! Has it ever sunk in your minds that nothing takes God by surprise? When tragedy strikes our lives and takes the wind out of us, God is not moved; He remains steady and sticks to His plan for us. When sickness and death seem like they're winning and we're tempted to panic, God doesn't flinch. You see, while we're often taken by surprise, nothing takes God by surprise. No matter how great the power of Satan appears to be in this world . . . no matter how it may appear that evil is winning, God's power is mightier than the power of our enemy. Earth has no sorrow that heaven cannot heal. God is in control. This is our Father's world!

God provided the way out of the misery of this world but the onus is on us to accept the way He provided. It would be injudicious for us to clamor for other ways. The Father gave up the Son, and the Son gave up His heavenly glory to redeem the world. Jesus reconciled the world by His own blood. Surely God will not withhold anything from us. God surrendered everything important to Him; likewise we should surrender what is important to us for the welfare of others. The onus is on us to make this world a better place. The vertical reconciliation must yield to the horizontal reconciliation. The reconciliation with God must result into the reconciliation with the neighbor. This is the divine plan to make this world a better place.

Perhaps the greatest need of Africa today is reconciliation. This is the serious predicament, haunting our continent. If we are going to save our countries to undergone a state of gross moral decadence our moral and spiritual "lag" must be eliminated. This problem of spiritual and moral lag, which constitutes modern man's chief dilemma, expresses itself in three larger problems which grow out of man's ethical infantilism. I refer to them as sectarianism (bigotry, tribalism & racial injustice), poverty, and war. Each of these problems, while appearing to be separate and isolated, is inextricably bound to the other. These factors serve a prominent role, arousing strife and preventing Africans from realizing their common interests.

African unity can be achieved beginning from grassroots. It must begin in individual countries before it is extended beyond our boundaries and then to regions (east west, central, south and north) before it is introduced to the continent level. As much as it is necessary to preach the spirit of African patriotism we should not ignore the role of individual tribes. True reconciliation begins with acknowledging facts. There is a need for us to open up and address the real issues causing division among us. Each case should be handled differently as we engage the situation proactively. A rush to judgment often produces wrong conclusions, especially when we depend on the scraps released by the partisan leaders, security officers and uncovered by the biased news media. We do ourselves a huge disservice when our idea of patriotism is blind adulation without criticism. In the real world where live, development is achieved by sharing ideas. The society's contrivances, (respect for elders, social castes, etc) are there to facilitate civility but we have built walls of myth and mystique around them, such that they may not probably outlive our civilization.

We study, scrutinize and analyze ideas to find facts. Reconciliation and tranquility require appreciating facts; it is from reading books about the biographies of others where we can apparently get facts. A biography involves the full course of life lived. The full course is definitely determined after a person passes away from this world. A tree is best measured after it falls down. Every person should care for the legacy he leaves behind. Yearn to build a good character worthy of emulation for that is what makes a man and that is what we leave behind when we depart. From his book 'My African Journey", Sir Winston Church Hill writes "My journey is at an end, the tale has been told."

God is organized and detailed; He sets the same opportunities before our eyes so that we can look at the big picture regarding our priorities. Community is important to God because God loves people and He knows that people need people. He created us to live in communities, giving and receiving support, which leads to generosity and gratitude.

Our hearts are right with God as long as we love to do what Christ did. Anyone, whose desire is to reflect the heart and nature of God, can enter His presence. There is absolute way of knowing and seeking God. His way is normally offensive to our ways. During biblical times people looked for ultimate peace in Jewish Legalism, Greek Philosophies and Eastern Mysticism. Ultimate peace is not discovered in the changed world but in the transformed heart. "True contemplation is not a psychological trick but a theological grace"— Thomas Merton

To change is to live and to live is to keep on changing. The individuals who seek to build the healthy communities in accordance to the morality of God enjoy the benevolences that come with His rule. They reflect the heart, character and nature of God. They strive to build bridges of understanding, goodwill and mutual respect. They are honest, truthful, trustworthy, reliable, loyal and unselfish. With words of encouragement and deeds of compassion they reach out to those who are struggling. They help those who have fallen to get back on their feet and protect those who are vulnerable.

Our relationship with others (fellowship) is the key to development. You have the need, but don't forget that others have it too. Receive it in anticipation of passing it on. What we give out has a way of coming back to us. Respect begets respect, Love begets love, Trust begets trust . . . The reality is that none of these principles has any meaning except the meaning we give it by virtue of demonstration. Jesus is our point of reference; He practically demonstrated in His life everything He taught.

Communitarianism is about the rights of the group or society. It seeks to put the family, group, community, and country before the individual. It sees individualism as selfish and short-sighted. They shun Individualism because it seeks to let each person grow or fail on their own, apart from others and sees group-focus as denuding the individual of their inalienable rights. There is a moral element in their views but the sour truth is that God fixes you in order to fix the community. He deals with community but He is a personal Savior. He saves and fulfills you (as a person) in order to fulfill others. He blesses you in order to bless others. The transformation begins with you in order to be extended to others. It is good to love all people but to discern whom we fellowship with. We must carefully choose the values that we embrace. God intended us to grow as a community of believers. Integrating brings godly ideas together to build the big picture.

According to C. Wright Mills there is no separation between the individual and society, they are not two distinct parts, but should be seen as one part with different ways of viewing and interpreting the function of both the individual(s) and society(s). The function can be open to interpretation and the perspective and societal-ethos must be considered and taken into account when using the sociological imagination, that is when 'we' are trying to distinguish the differences, similarities, anomalies and norms form each other, firstly what constitutes a social norm in one interpretation may not be a considered a social norm to another.

Although humans are biologically similar, the societies and communities in which they live are distinct by their geography, history, culture, traditions, products, language, etc. There are qualities and activities which make people Africans, French, English, American, etc. But the morality that is applicable to all regardless of their ethnic background is defined by the Moral God. God never changes and so are His values. The Bible says that, "For I the Lord do not change" (Malachi 3:6). Pastor Alistair Begg says that, "It is just as well for us that in all the variableness of life there is One whom change cannot affect, One whose heart can never alter, and on whose brow inconsistency can make no furrows. All other things have changed-all things are changing. The sun grows dim with age; the world is growing old; the final chapter of the worn-out vesture has begun; the heavens and earth must soon pass away; they will perish-they shall grow old like a garment. But there is One who only has immortality, of whose years there is no end, and in whose person there is no change."

In the arena of the living, we are like cheerleaders picking up their little pitches. Given the fact, it is not enough to look at others' achievements; there is the requirement of a profound mindset of self-awareness. Effective cultural transformation requires artifacts, ideas and champions. It is necessary to have pioneers to initiate and ensure quality performance. The required degree of efficiency is attainable by individual characteristics congruent with a quality-oriented culture. However, lack of congruence between creative people and their work context may inhibit their innovative performance.

I suggest that the culture of reading should be encouraged in order to get our country out of its doldrums. With older people dying and younger people taking their place, it's more important than ever before to preserve our heritage. Luckily, with modern technology, we have what our ancestors lacked: various ways of storing this knowledge. From hard cover books to electronic books, it is now so much simpler to bequeath onto our children and grandchildren what we inherited from our ancestors.

Reading and heeding the Scriptures must be our priority but we should not ignore the secular literatures that have the political, historical and anthropological academia; also the novels which have a philosophical bent. Fantastical and science fiction novels could stimulate imagination. There are benefits of reading poetry like opening up your mind to new ideas. One of the most basic reasons to read poetry is that it's a great way to improve your vocabulary. If your usual reading material consists of magazines, newspapers, and blogs, you're unlikely to be encountering any new words. Aristotle said that poetry is finer and more philosophical than history; for poetry expresses the universal, and history only the particular.

The Bible is written in literature form. Like any other book, it is filled with many kinds or types of language. It has Law, History, Wisdom, Poetry, Gospel, Epistles, Prophecy, and Apocalyptic Literature. The Bible is the cradle of civilization from where we can hunt for knowledge and wisdom but this shouldn't be an excuse of not reading other books. There is a misconception among some conservatives that reading other books (non-Christians books) leads to rational thinking, which is deemed by some fanatics to be irrelevant to the Christian faith. People with such mentality speak from a vantage point that limits their view. I think more exposure and open-mindedness would change their perception about Christianity.

Some evangelicals have bought into the idea that having one's heart in the right place is all that matters—that a passion for Jesus and the life of the mind are mutually exclusive. What this view misses is that burning hearts are not nourished by empty heads. It is up to the individual believers to free themselves from the negative beliefs and teachings that keep them from acknowledging their divine sound minds. We must develop our minds if we are to sustain our passion for the Savior and deal with the bias against us.

The same religious fanatics propagate relaxing the minds in neutral in order to be deemed spiritual. You hear them bragging that God told them to do certain things, even minor things that could easily be figured out by their natural brains, like choosing an outfit to wear. They replace their power of thinking with the Holy Spirit. They are knowingly or unknowingly against rational thinking. It is creepy and hard to be around them. I want to say without apology that, there is a fine line between decorum and stupidity, and it's about time some people in religious circles found it.

I believe that God can speak to us supernaturally, but He also created us with different body organs including the minds to use them for His glory. He gave us freewill to determine the things that are glorifying to Him. God wants us to love Him with our heart and minds. Jesus instructed us that: "Love the Lord your God with all your <u>heart</u> and with all your <u>soul</u> and with all your <u>mind</u>." (Matthew 22:37). The total man is involved in loving the Lord. A believer acquires the minds of Christ and uses the same minds for His glory. The Bible says that, "For who has understood the mind of the Lord so as to instruct him?" But we have the mind of Christ" (1 Corinthians 2:16).

Negative religious fanaticism is a result of ignorance of the Scriptures. Some of these fanatics end up doing more harm than good. They end up fueling the fire of our critics. Disregarding the power of the mind is dancing at the tune of the critics who portray Christianity as a religion of ignorance. Extreme Secular Atheism discredits faith to be in opposition to intellectuality. Atheists like Ben Franklin made this comment: "The way to see by faith is to shut the eye to reason".

I strongly oppose the idea that Christianity is a blind faith that disallows rational reasoning. We should not be deterred by such useless detractors criticizing our power to reason. In fact this is the crux of my epistle to you. The main collective argument of this book is that it is rational to believe in God. We must not be myopic in our reasoning and must not arrogate right reasoning as our sole prerogative. What makes reasoning right or wrong is the absolute truth as opposed to relativity. Biblical thinking is viewing things from the prospective of the creator, within an informed framework, so as to live morally acceptable life to God. Infinite realities exist that are outside the reach of our observation. We know this to be true. Yet, too often Christians are labeled as crazy for making assertions about the spiritual world, God, and heaven. Faith is not just closing your eyes and imagining things that down deep in your heart you don't really think are true.

The unwarranted and puerile vituperation of the ATHIESTS baffles me. You don't have to see God in order to acknowledge His existence. Everything that we see is a shadow cast by that which we do not see. I pay for the doctor's bill, even when I cannot read his prescription. I believe in the sun, even when it is not shining. I believe in love, even when I am alone and I believe in God, even when He's silent.

During biblical times people looked for ultimate peace in Jewish Legalism, Greek Philosophies and Eastern Mysticism. Ultimate peace is not discovered in the changed world but in the transformed heart. "True contemplation is not a psychological trick but a theological grace"—Thomas Merton.

Transformation involves the changed heart and mindset. The acquired faith must be manifested in practical values in order to change your destiny. The reality is that everybody is being changed by something or multiple things but the believers are changed by the grace of God. To change is to live and to live is to keep on changing. There is the need to be transformed and then the process of conversion.

Overcoming the world begins now, in the present, by embracing the divine plan for our salvation. We overcome the world by receiving Christ and by manifesting His life by perpetually surrendering our ego (dying to the old self or nature). Our power is instigated by our brokenness. Psalm 27:4 (NIV): "The sacrifices of God are a broken spirit; a broken and a contrite heart—these, O God, You will not despise." God uses life circumstances to instigate brokenness.

A dynamic life is always fired by vision; vision built on the word of God. The vision begins with embracing the truth. Truth is not something that can be gleaned from any book other than the Bible; it can be revealed by God alone. We (believers) may be belittled for our lack of sophistication but we know it is not lacking in the basic things pertaining to eternity. Certainly, we are not ignorant of the truth. When the truth is birthed in you it exposes and drives away the lies, allowing you to possess your heavenly inheritance. The birth of Isaac exposed Ismail as an illegitimate heir and drove him away opening way to the legitimate heir to posses his inheritance.

It is our faith that connects us to the revealed truth. Faith is not against reasoning but faith goes extra miles where reasoning can't go. Reason deals with logic with limitation but faith deals with expectations without limitations. Faith hears the inaudible, believes the incredible, and receives the impossible. Brother Jim says that, "Belief in God does not need to be a blind leap of faith; Christian Theism is a reasonable inference given the circumstantial evidence. No successfully prosecuted case is evidentially perfect or complete, but all successfully prosecuted cases are evidentially sufficient. While we may not be able to examine direct evidence related to the existence of God, we do have sufficient circumstantial evidence to believe that Christianity's claims about God are true."

One critic wrote that "A theologian is like a Black man in a dark room looking for a black cat that isn't there and he finds it". Unlike Moslems, Christianity accommodates all kinds of criticism. I think we do ourselves a huge disservice when our idea of rationalism is blind adulation without criticism. Great minds are open to discuss ideas. Paul Harvey says that, "A blind man's world is bounded by the limits of his touch, an ignorant man's world by the limits of his knowledge, and a great man's world by the limit of his vision ".

Philosophers need not fear to believe in God. There are evidences in contemporary form showing how philosophers have historically believed in God. For example Brian Leftow's "From Jerusalem to Athens" argues that he is a philosopher because he is first a Christian. Christian belief is a help to the intellectual life and it was Christianity, which brought him to philosophy. He shows that historically it has been common place for philosophers to base their philosophy on theistic belief. He seeks to return philosophy to its rightful place as being rooted in the Christian religion.

Some of the greatest philosophers (Plato, Aristotle, Plotinus, Augustine, and Aquinas) discussed about philosophical issues pertaining to possible worlds, epistemology, the existence and nature of God, metaphysics, ethics, and the nature of human beings. Most of them acknowledged the existence of God, although some of them were not practicing Christians. As we shall see later on, the kind of believing that yields to salvation is deeper than mere awareness and acknowledging of God; it is receiving Jesus Christ as a personal Savior.

Any philosophical ideas should be viewed in the lens of the Scriptures. It is improper to compromise one's theology for the sake of philosophy. Non-committed people have no backbone to stand up for the truth. Until you know where you want to go, you settle anywhere and end up going nowhere. The culprits are likely to renounce even the important material advantages which Christianity may confer upon a State. Relativism and liberalism readily acquiesce in any sham process aimed at facilitating fraud or falsehood. I suggest that emotions and feelings should never be placed over the divine revelation. True believers must be committed to the truth. They must confess it, live it and resist any intrusion of falsehood.

The justice of God reveals the truth to all people indiscriminately; it is not revealed to the intellectuals only: "Where is the wise person? Where is the teacher of the law? Where is the philosopher of this age? Has not God made foolish the wisdom of the world? For since in the wisdom of God the world through its wisdom did not know him, God was pleased through the foolishness of what was preached to save those who believe" (1 Corinthians 1:20-21). Commitment to the revealed truth is the niche of those who are sincere and faithful.

This book is about the legacy of a hero. Every person has a hero or heroes. All of us (intentionally or not) study the life style of others purposely to pick a leaf. One of the most valuable things any man can learn is the art of using the knowledge and experience of others. We have the tendency of tracking the achievements of the people that walked the same footpath we are walking objectively to be like them. We envy or admire their achievements and measure our progress by their standards. We grow up looking at them as role model whom we want to emulate. Some go to an extremity by adopting a comic camouflage and take it upon themselves to mimic their heroes in speech, gesture, and dress.

On the negative side, we envy their achievements and measure our progress by their standards. That is when the achievements of others become our yardstick and their goals become ours. We do everything to beat the odds of life in order to achieve the same goals hence limiting our chances to excel beyond them. Graham Bell insinuated that, "Never walk on the traveled path, because it only leads you where others have been" Real dreams and vision will become clear only when you look into your heart. Champions are made from something deep inside them—a desire, a dream, a vision, a goal.

Given the fact, in the real life, our goals may not be achieved single handedly; we need others and they need us. Success comes after a combination and coordination of multiple efforts. Goals are not one time achievements but come in sequences. "As a single footstep will not make a path on the earth, so a single thought will not make a pathway in the mind. To make a deep physical path, we walk again and again. To make a deep mental path, we must think over and over the kind of thoughts we wish to dominate our lives."—Henry David Thoreau

In the secular world, success is defined by the people around us. We work tooth and nail to blaze and be recognized by the society. We risk being judged by different standards of men. That is most probably the reason why in the free world people yearn to do what seems to be right in their eyes to triumph. Real heroes do not yearn to earn public approvals but seek most sincerely and devoutly, to be guided by the power of the Holy Ghost in bearing testimony of the truth and divinity of this glorious work in which we are all engaged.

Real heroes are champions of peace and are judged by their perseverance in tough times when adversity meets integrity. Tough times call for bold leaders who will eventually steady the ship to safe waters. One preacher told the graduates that: "Don't show me your honors (degrees) now but show me your achievements twenty years from now". He meant that the validity of their achievements depends on the impact their degrees will have on their lifestyle. People are watching us to see what we do with the acquired knowledge from collages and other training institutions. For those of us who are believers, they are watching us to see if we really walk the talk.

We (believers) are not biological substances but spiritual entities. Don't gamble on your future by trying to Change your life. Life isn't about creating yourself but finding your image in Christ. You are not the masterpiece of your own life but Christ is. The required change is exchanging your will with the will of God. The will of God will never take you where the Grace of God will not sustain you. God is our security; He is a strong tower where we take refuge at the times of trouble. This does not exempt us from the responsibility to uplift one another. The Bible instructs us that, "Bear one another's burdens and troublesome moral faults, and in this way fulfill and observe perfectly the law of Christ the Messiah and complete what is lacking" (Galatians 6:2).

There is a tendency within humanity to look at our heroes as remedy to overcome our insecurities and frustrations. In this case our heroes become icons inspiring us to develop feasible strategies to reach the most desired future. Thank God for the heroes who inspire us to step up and be what God created us to be even when the world had written us off, treating us as failures. Such become the restraining power for us not to slip away into the muddy stench waters. They encourage us instead of ripping us to shreds, which is heartbreaking.

Heroes can come in all shapes and sizes; think of the father who works 18 hours a day and two jobs so that his kids can get a decent education, or the people who do volunteer work for underprivileged. I don't think that people are born heroes; they just shape themselves into ones. They sacrifice a lot and expect their protégés to exercise the quality of lives they lived.

Whereas people are not born heroes, I think that our upbringing influences our characters. If you are talking about someone rushing into a burning building to save a trapped person, then that person must be someone who has been brought up to think of others more than he or she thinks of himself or herself. So that makes a hero made by upbringing. In fact Africa's biggest problem points to leaders with poor-up-bringing; uncultured manners defined by dictionary as deficiency of manners.

I want to warn that even our heroes are human beings with setbacks. It is wrong to adore and worship a human being. God alone deserves reverence. It is good to make our heroes our admired friends but it should not escalate into adoration. Worldliness is replacing God's love. Worldliness is the corrupt system and attitude that leads to absolute corruption (sin). It is the life of empty show, for selfish desires. It is the life that brings temporary satisfaction. The love of God eradicates worldliness (1 John 2:15-17).

Also, we should desist from falsely using the names of our heroes to cover up for our omissions, excesses and failures. There is no man that can save you from guilt. God alone can do that. We are not biological substances but spiritual entities. Don't gamble on your future by trying to Change your life. Life isn't about creating yourself but finding your image in Christ. You are not the masterpiece of your own life but Christ is. The required change is exchanging your will with the will of God. The will of God will never take you where the Grace of God will not sustain you.

Why do we need heroes? An ancient phrase says "Tell me who you admire and I'll tell you who you are." Heroes define what values mean and they show us those values in action. People have endless lists of heroes and their heroic traits categorized by their choices. Some of our heroes are living while others have passed away. There are heroes whom we have never met but we are encouraged by reading about them in the newspapers and magazines. We love to read their stories because they are sweet and syrupy and they make us feel good about the progress we made and provide additional materials for the next steps required.

It is important for us to use the moral standard when determining our heroes. The world has different standards of morality. A great example is Adolf Hitler. To the Allies, the Jews, the gypsies and others he persecuted he was known as the greatest villain of all time. But to the German people, at the time, he was the savior and hero of their country. A Moral Hero is not a hero of accident or impulse (such as a firefighter in a burning building, or someone jumping in the way of a bus to protect another). A Moral Hero must have intentionally and selflessly upheld a moral virtue, such as kindness, patience, justice, compassion, love, or peace. They act out of integrity knowing of the full risks and consequences of their actions. Only by having assurance of the morality of God can we move forward to have the leisure to distinguish right from wrong, to set a standard of living.

Today, people resort to the press to brainstorm lists of heroic and un-heroic traits. Since the press is the main source of information, poor reporting can be more destructive than constructive to our communities. It is disgusting when the people who are prone to media are misguided by the very people they trust. There is a lot of exaggeration in particular when the reporter has a political agenda or an ethnic axe to grind. The culprits try to gag those who have issues with their choices or who disagree with them. As one journalist warned that "There are people who think the journalists are untouchable; so, they have a license to offend other people, blackmail those in compromised situations and extort money in order to kill stories. Code of ethics in journalism has to be adhered to."

Brother J Ikuya made this brilliant comment: "There is a wry irony in life; he who tells a blatant lie, surprisingly also expects to be believed. The reasons why some lies may be more credible than others depend on their level of sophistication, the manner of their camouflage and appeal, usually carrying grains of plausibility that conform to existing general awareness in society". He warned that a habitual liar is likely to contradict himself disgracefully, "A golden rule developed since the ancient world was that a liar must possess a keen, long memory. A lasting lie demanded consistency so as not to contradict the one told earlier. But, lies that were based on a short memory could not be sustained for long without incurring grief and contempt to oneself".

Journalists should be reminded that as we put pen to paper, we are writing for generations to come and we owe them the truth. Telling an obvious lie is actually insulting people by playing on their intellect. It is offensive. Unfortunately most ideas we read in our magazines are concocted exclusively from private thinking and solely by individuals; they are either hallucinations or entirely inimical to society. Most articles are characterized by uncommon or pretentious vocabularies and convoluted syntaxes intended to lure the readers into vagueness and confusion. I am afraid we are losing a generation to complacency. Today's writers amuse me; instead of being the mouth piece of the public, they have chickened to self-censorship.

It is not accidental that today the fiction books with fiction tales and the magazines of the liberal mainline Protestantism are on the bestselling list. The reason is because we live in the culture where people have no respect for God; people see no need to consult God to solve their day to day problems. The Bible warned that in the last days, the love of many will wax cold. But the one who endures to the end, he will be saved (Matthew 24:12).

The media can intentionally be rude or critical, for the sake of creating a story, at the expense of damaging your brand and how people view you. The culture of today enjoys scorning others and making fun of them. That is why comedians attract multitudes. The names of the true Christian heroes of our century are perpetually being tarnished by the liberal news reporters for purely selfish reasons. The liberals sometimes exaggerate their claims for rhetorical effect, assailing the constant verbal onslaught on the conservative Christians. They look for a reason even if they have to make it up, to put down someone and to make him mad. As Pat Buchanan once put it, "Christian-bashing is a popular indoor sport." This is how far we have dropped; even the most revered literatures unintelligently indulge in gossip on personal issues. Most books have been reduced to boulevard websites rivaling the like, twitters.

I want to warn that the hype warranted or not, asked for or not, solicited or not brings us down. We do not do things to be noticed but to please God. Attention isn't something asked for nor appreciated in our quest to please God. Journalist should avoid looking for cheap popularity. Justice Kanyeihamba said that, "Whenever people threaten you, it means you are doing a good job exposing their weaknesses and ferocity."

Story telling in itself is a way to fight the apathy in this world. By simple interactions, we can understand each other and make this world more open and loving. But we should avoid the temptation of unnecessary criticism and exaggeration. It is disappointing to find so many writers and commentators giving a blinding view of the obvious. Our journalism has lost its former integrity that was rooted in nonpartisan reporting. Some newspapers are compared to political platforms set to promote certain characters regardless of the flaws. We must not ignore the fact that at times verbosity or logorrhea (verbal diarrhea) is employed [by politicians and crooks] to baffle and bamboozle the reader or listener. No respectable and independent journalist should knowingly embark on confusing a reader. There is a need to forget our cherished biases even when pursuing the attainment of equality in diversity as a fundamental principle in our political development. Journalist should avoid getting sucked into the partisan political quagmire and should only aim to reporting the factual truth rather than material based on personal sentiments.

Most writers are for the most part self-absorbed, self-aggrandizing pinheads of little value to society. Self-promotion may result into bias reporting. As much as it is appropriate to expose our readers to our early lives, the same experiences should "have no bearing" to our career as writers. Our primary concern should be to promote others. I mean promoting potential heroes whose records speak volumes in doing what's right, fighting for what is right, sacrificing for the sake of others and saving life.

Today's journalism influences our culture by promoting certain characters with moral turpitude. The reality is that readers are fed on what newspapers think they should consume. The media choose heroes of their own kind and their choices regularly flash on the front pages of their newspapers and commercial advertisements with devastating impact on our youth. This kind of manipulation could have attracted massive criticism from the public, yet, you read a kind of muted response in the public. The reason is because we are living in the times of moral degradation. The god of this age has blinded the people with the spirit of seduction. The Bible warns that people become like the gods they worship. On the contrary, the readers have the right to hold the writers accountable for their publications. The readers may not, for instance, have the opportunity to choose the stories published by the media but they have the right to question the choices and integrity of the writers.

It is the core duty of the press to disseminate information, debates and comments on society. This can be done meaningfully by allowing different views to be expressed. Whereas it is true that the world we live in is a gymnasium for competition, each trying to outdo the other, this does not mean throwing cold water on the achievement of others just because we envy them. It does no pay to go after somebody's legacy adamantly. Civilization means appreciating and celebrating others as they force themselves into the limelight and the history books. We should recognize those who have performed beyond our expectations instead of venting our unchecked anger on them by unnecessary criticisms.

I cringe whenever I come across poorly reported articles in our national newspapers. The political biasness influences most of the reporting today, typically juxtaposing political repugnance and journalistic naivety. When people who are expected to inform the masses and help shape public opinion juxtapose extreme mediocrity and blatant postmodern political ignorance, then you realize how doomed we are.

Intellectuals do not prove their intellectually through sporadic anecdotal utterances in the media. They engage in research and publish evidence based papers that contribute to the body of knowledge! Sophisticated people rebut with evidence rather that act like a drowning man who clutches desperately at every passing argument purposely delaying the inevitable conclusion. It is mind boggling that "mediocrity" and "low expectation mentality" are slowly killing Africa. President Kagame has more than once expressed his concerns about the grip of mediocrity on Africa. As much as I do not agree with some of his policies, I find no justifiable reason to disagree on this one.

Given the constructive criticism, we cannot underestimate the role of media. The media is the market of ideas. The proliferation of information from the lowest person in villages to the highest office is possible through the media. One of the former prime ministers of England when emphasizing the importance of media said that, he would rather stay in a country that has the freedom of press but without a working government than in a country with a working government without the freedom of press.

The media is the public's sharp eye that has the responsibility of making all of us accountable. But it must be good reporting, this being an aspect of quality befitting any national newspapers. One columnists complimented one of the leading newspaper in this way: "The media must be thanked for, among other things, fighting to extend the frontiers of press freedom, and inspiring and training generations of courageous men and women; these are journalists more interested in their obligation to speak the truth to power as a way to build a better country—rather than sticking to what power defines as truth." (*10, Dec, Uganda Weekly Observers*)

The press like music is an international language. It is the depth and wealth of the editors' use of the English language that fascinates us to not only to read and listen to what they are saying, but how they are saying it. In this case, the media falls in the category of socially conscious music, songs that go beyond the basic functions of creating a melody, to acting as a societal moral compass of sorts, as society's sense of right and wrong. As a form of art, music offers commentary, context, meaning and explaining consequence of the things that are going on in society, which affect people on everyday basis. The smacks of slapdash journalism and a cavalier attitude towards proper reporting are therefore spot-on.

Good press acknowledges the fact that people are inclined to search for the gist of the article/matter. The same thing applies to good composing of the lyric. John B. Abimanyi says that, "Music experts emphasize this importance, saying that music, all music even that which is waved off as bubble gum and empty entertainment, is a mirror, a tool through which a society can look to see what it looks like. And in the end, experts say, paying attention to what a society's music is communicating, both directly and indirectly, keeps one's finger on the pulse of that society".

As I said, media and music have the same influence on our communities. That is why various companies are scrambling for celebrities to sign advertising contracts. As I was writing this book Pepsi announced signing a 50 million dollar deal with American Rn B Diva Beyoncé. Pepsi's move is in line with a trend toward content creation as advertisers seek new inroads into the music business and labels' marketing budgets continue to decline. The consumer market is stimulated by our hip-hop culture. Certainly, the Marketers' messages today are increasingly reinforced by hip-hop culture. "An analysis of rap lyrics showed 64 percent of the most popular songs released from 2002 to 2005 referenced alcohol. This marked a steep rise; an earlier analysis of rap songs from 1994 to 1997 showed 44 percent contained alcohol references." (*Researchers at the University of California, Berkeley, reported last year*).

The heart of writing a story should be to promote the moral aspect of it so as to impart the same values to the readers. The Italian musical term crescendo (abbreviated cresc.) is an indication to gradually increase the volume of a song until otherwise noted. Like a rhythm of the song, a story should be written in progressive manner in order for the reader to get acquainted to the theme of the story. The composers of songs have a tendency of playing around with indirect messages in an art form, knowing that the meaning(s) can be tangled up in the sea of vagueness. Often, the meaning cannot be directly denoted from their lyrics but it is constructed by the person who is consuming the art. The people's expectation of the press is to report stories with direct moral innuendos. There is no need for the news reporters to beat about the bush, calling a spoon a spade. For the majority of people, you have to call a spade a spade in order for the message to get home. I applaud Ugandan news reporters for writing informative and educative straight forward stories but more work is still needed.

I want to say that with or without the press, we are ever in the public eyes. We must therefore portray the ethical values at all times. Values outside the mainstream are good and decent even when they make us the curio in the circus sideshow of public and media opinion under the microscope. The Christians in particular must be transparent. They should not be worried about publishing their stories. God opened up our lives for others to read and to learn from us. The people of the world (non-Christians) have a reputation of failing to own up to matters of accountability. But Christians must be known for their impeccable characters without the possibility of their integrity wanting. Christians must go an extra mile in pursuing morality. Our morality must portray the character of the moral God.

The Church leadership must stand firm regarding the biblical values and resist swimming with the tide. We cannot belong to the world and Christ at the same time. The Church is in the world but not of the world. The Church does not therefore look for cheap popularity, for example, by approving whims and fancies of this confused world. Perhaps the most significant problem that mankind faces today is the hustle for superiority. It is passionately engraved on the hearts of many and its pursuits often skip steps which always demand to be revisited. A Church is made up of people whose objective is to glorify God alone. The believers are challenged to live the gospel values faithfully. Failure to live by the divine standard might diminish our influence in the world. NB. The Church institution (body of Christ) cannot cease to exist; not even the gates of hell can prevail against it. But, her influence can diminish gradually in case we deny the Holy Spirit opportunity to guide us.

The kingdom of God involves the kingdom minded people. They are God's people, positioned in God, who are under God's rule and who submit to God's commandments. They are the people who have access to God's promises and blessings. They are the covenant people who call God the Father because they are born of Him (born again). They are recreated (regenerated) into the image of Christ. You may call them Christ-like (Christians). They are scattered among different denominations (Catholics, Greek Orthodox, Protestants, SDA, Pentecostals, Baptists, Lutheran, Methodists and etc.). They have the mandate to give opportunity to the people of the world (who are not God's people by virtue of the new birth) to become God's people (born of God in the image of Christ).

It is within human instinct to want to excel. We discussed that in the real world success is determined by different standards depending on whom you talk to. Among Christians, success is determined by our spiritual maturity. In course of keeping with the biblical goal of spiritual growth and greater levels of maturity, we find in the Scriptures the call to abound or excel in Christian character, especially in the various ways we can express love to one another. Spiritual maturity is a quest for character for which there will be little progress without the pursuit of the divine excellence. Without pursuing the divine excellence, life will remain bland, very vanilla and lukewarm at best (see Rev. 3:15-16).

You might need to look at the following scriptures in order to understand my point: Ecclesiastes 9:10—Whatever your hand finds to do, verily, do it with all your might; for there is no activity or planning or knowledge or wisdom in the grave where you are going.

Philippians 1:9-10—And this I pray, that your love may abound (i.e., excel) still more and more in real knowledge and all discernment, so that you may approve the things that are excellent, in order to be sincere and blameless until the day of Christ; 11 having been filled with the fruit of righteousness which comes through Jesus Christ, to the glory and praise of God.

2 Corinthians 8:7—But as you excel in everything—in faith, in speech, in knowledge, and in all eagerness and in the love from us that is in you—make sure that you excel in this act of kindness too.

1 Thessalonians 3:12—And may the Lord cause you to increase and abound (excel) in love for one another and for all, just as we do for you, 3:13 so that your hearts are strengthened in holiness to be blameless before our God and Father at the coming of our Lord Jesus with all his saints. Also, 1 Thessalonians 4:1.

The quest for excellence fuels our fire and keeps us from just drifting downstream gathering debris. Self-denial involves rejecting the corrupt ways of the world by embracing the love of Christ. Believers grow up in absolute poverty and strive to raise the standard high. They aim to become like Christ. The grace of God is given to cover their failures. They trust in God's abilities in order to create and carry out effective solutions to their pending problems. They grow up with massive privileges at their disposal and work hard to keep the standards high. Again, they are not saved (justified) by their own works but they must manifest good works after salvation (sanctification).

CHAPTERS

The Legacy of Faith

God chose for us the kind of life to live. Spiritually, we are required to manifest the life of Jesus Christ. There is only one man whose legacy we can emulate for spiritual fulfillment. His name is Jesus. He is our standard for living because the life He lived became ours to manifest. He lived the perfect life which we cannot live without His grace and He died the death that we should not die because of His grace. His three and half year's ministry impacted the whole universe. The destiny of over seven billion people living on the universe depends on this one man (Jesus).

The person, works, and life of Jesus Christ stand as irrefutable evidence against the secular world views and all the religions of the world regardless of their composition. No one else is qualified or is capable to meet the needs of a fallen man or restore his lost glory as a result of the fall of Adam. In the person of Jesus Christ, we have one so unique life that cannot be explained by any natural processes. His person and life defy the natural. The uniqueness of Jesus Christ presents evidence, as Josh McDowell has so well written "demands a verdict," that this Man is not only unique, but the Savior of the world.

God instructed Israel to sacrifice animals but such sacrifices were not enough to justify man. David desperately pleaded that, "For thou desirest not sacrifice; else would I give it: thou delightest not in burnt offering" (Psalms 51:16). Jesus became our perfect sacrifice and High Priest opening the new way of approaching God without guilt. We can now approach Him not as our judge but as our Father: "Behold, what manner of love the Father hath bestowed upon us, that we should be called the sons of God: therefore the world knoweth us not, because it knew him not" (1 John 3:1).

The Bible says that, "In Christ we have also obtained an inheritance, having been destined according to the purpose of Him who accomplishes all things according to his counsel and will, so that we, who were the first to set our hope on Christ, might live for the praise of his glory. In Him you also, when you had heard the word of truth, the gospel of your salvation, and had believed in Him, were marked with the seal of the promised Holy Spirit; this is the pledge of our inheritance towards redemption as God's own people, to the praise of his glory" (Eph. 1:11-14).

The Bible provides many biblical characters (Abel, Job, Noah, Abraham, David, Solomon, the Judges, Prophets and Apostles and etc.) as historical figures for us to study their lives. None of them can do us like Jesus because none of them can transform our lives. We can learn from their successes and failures in the same way we (believers) are called to be written epistles for the world to read. People should be able to look at our lives and know what the Bible says. When we take God seriously the people can take us seriously. This is how we can effectively impact the world.

Decent people desire to leave a legacy not only to their children but to the world. Everyone is entitled to run their own race, write their own story, make their own history, and inspire others through their journey and imperfections, handwork, focus and great attitude. God created man to reveal His glory and to leave a legacy on this earth. Our legacy involves the testimony of our faith in Christ. These are legitimate questions to ask: When your time is done here on Earth, what will be your legacy? What will others remember about you? What will those in heaven have to say about your legacy when you get there? Is your legacy pleasing to God?

I want the people to see the love of Jesus and His grace through me. The legacy of Christ reveals the love of God. The Bible says that God is love. The love of God is beyond reasonable measure. One writer said that if you used ink in your pen from the oceans of the world to write about the love of God in the sky, the oceans would be dried up.

The kingdom of God on earth is where God exercises absolute rule. In God's kingdom, God fully runs the show. There won't be any rebels in that kingdom trying to do their own thing. In His kingdom there are obedient sinners saved by grace who have come to realize that the sole means of obtaining maximized joy is to first sow into what is important to God. There is nothing more important to God than obeying His commandments. Believers manifest the sinless life of Jesus Christ that is not in contradiction to the morality of God. They are positionally as perfect as Christ but they still retain the sinful nature until glorification. Their past, present and future sins were covered by the grace of God. They are called to take their cross daily and crucify the old nature. In the same token they strive to live this life with a deep burning desire to love like Christ loves. I want to say that God commands all people to be perfect: "Matt 5:48 Be ye therefore perfect, even as your Father which is in heaven is perfect."

It is necessary for us to live faithfully without compromising the biblical values because we are going to be remembered for the things we say and do. What we are remembered for really counts. One Christian artist wrote in his song that, "I want to leave a legacy. How will they remember me?—Not well traveled, not well read, not well-to-do or well-bred Just want to hear instead, "Well Done" good and faithful one . . ."

Death is inescapable. Ensure that you don't go to the grave with unfulfilled potentialities. We normally remind people to choose inspiring words concerning their lives, which they want to be written on their tombstone (gravestone) after they leave this world. A script or font (an epitaph) must be selected, along with pictures and designs. Whether simple or ornate, give careful consideration to how you want to be represented after death. Billy Sunday suggested that: "Live so that when the final summon comes you will leave something more behind you than an epitaph on a tombstone or an obituary in a newspaper". I want to challenge you to choose the best words suitable to be written on Paul's gravestone, in case it was discovered. I would suggest the following words because they describe his life: "I have fought the good fight, I have finished the race, I have kept the faith" (2 Timothy 4:7). Do you expect people to say the same words concerning you after you leave this world?

We all leave a legacy of one form or another. The question is whether it will be a positive one that brings glory to God or a negative one that is quickly forgotten. Here is a quotation from Evangelist Bill Keller that describes what I am saying: "With the understanding that this is a brief journey we are on, we should be motivated to get the most out of each and every day. Our focus each day should be on fulfilling our reason for being alive, and this is to serve and glorify the Lord through our lives. The greatest legacy we can leave is the lives we have influenced for Christ throughout our journey."

We must be aware that people are watching us. There is always somebody behind you picking up something. Paul instructed us in this way, "Join with others in following my example, brothers, and take note of those who live according to the pattern we gave you" (Phil. 3:17). I have a conviction that something I've written, said or done, will have a profound effect on those who come after. And if I am to have a profound effect, I want it to be a positive one. At times it is not easy to live by the same standard but this is expressively my intentions. Writing is as good as talking; it is easy to offend some by the words we use. "If your foot slips, you can recover your balance. But if your tongue slips, you can never recall your words."

The Bible says that, "A good man leaves an inheritance for his children's children" (Proverbs 13:22). Every Christian believer is supposed to have spiritual children. All of us should be concerned about leaving a spiritual legacy, a spiritual inheritance, for those who come after us. Passing on to the next generations a legacy with eternal value is far more important than a temporal inheritance of money and property. God wants to invest in you, and keep investing in you so that you invest in others. God wants to see how loyal you will be in this life to what is truly important to Him so that He can entrust to you the eternal blessings that none of us can conceive of right now. Remember that the legacy that truly matters is the one that God is impressed with. It is the legacy of faith founded and centered on Jesus Christ. It is the legacy that this world is not impressed with.

It is appropriate to recognize those people whom God uses to impact the lives of others. Whatever legacy left behind by our heroes should enter in the records of Genesis and should be a lesson for others.

The following scripture supports what I am saying: "Remember your leaders, those who spoke to you the word of God; consider the outcome of their life, and imitate their faith" (Heb. 13:7).

The Bible gives some biblical characters that left a legacy behind. In the Old Testament from time to time we get glimpses and hints of Jesus who is to come, in events or people who are pointing the way to Jesus. These are ordinary men and women who sacrificed a lot to live the lives pleasing to God. The testimony of their achievements depended on their relationship with God. We read their stories as inspired scriptures in admiration. They are inspiring and motivating. Hebrews 11 gives example after example of true faith so that we may be imitators of those who through faith and patience (longsuffering/ endurance) inherited the promises of God. Remember that all of the promises of God are delivered to us in one package (Christ). We cannot be more or less godly than manifesting the life of Jesus Christ Jesus. The excellence and power is of God.

Hebrews 11:4-6—By faith Abel offered to God a better sacrifice than Cain, through which he obtained the testimony that he was righteous, God testifying about his gifts, and through faith, though he is dead, he still speaks. God was pleased with Abel's sacrifice because it was given with good intentions out of obedience.

Enoch holds a rare distinction in the Bible: He did not die. Instead, God took him away. "By faith Enoch was taken up so that he should not see death; and he was not found because God took him up; for he obtained the witness that before his being taken up he was pleasing to God." The Scripture does not reveal much about this remarkable man. We find his story in Genesis 5, in a long list of the descendants of Adam. Only a short sentence, "Enoch walked faithfully with God," in Genesis 5:22 and repeated in Genesis 5:24 reveals why he was so special to his Creator.

In this wicked period before the Flood, most men did not walk faithfully with God. They walked their own path, the crooked way of sin. But Enoch walked with God and did not keep silent about the sin around him. Enoch, who lived in the seventh generation after Adam, prophesied about these people. He said, "Listen! The Lord is coming with countless thousands of his holy ones" (Jude 1:14-15, NIV). Enoch walked in faith the 365 years of his life, and that made all the difference. No matter what happened, he trusted God. He obeyed God. God loved Enoch so much he spared him the experience of death. God made an example for us that you can walk with God and escape death.

The walk that pleases God is the walk of faith. The Bible says that it is only our faith that pleases God: "And without faith it is impossible to please God, because anyone who comes to him must believe that he exists and that he rewards those who earnestly seek him" (Hebrews 11:6). Faith is putting your trust in God; it involves trusting in the finished works of Jesus Christ at the cross for your salvation. The faith of the faithful ones is validated by their good works. The Bible says that faith without works is dead (James 2:14-26).

Abraham is the father of faith because he obeyed God. When God called Abram he was in a city in Babylonia, named Ur of the Chaldees. Ur was a very advanced city and was believed to have been founded some five hundred years before the time of Abraham. Ur, could be compared to a modern city, having libraries, schools, and a system of law. It was a rich city and many valuable treasures have been discovered including elaborate jewelry. The false religion of astrology which was begun at Babel was practiced there as it was in all Babylonia.

Abraham's father, Terah according to Joshua 24:2, worshiped idols. Jewish tradition refers to Terah as an idol maker. Ur was an evil and idolatrous city worshiping many different Gods such as the god of fire, moon, sun and stars. Sin was the name of the chief idol deity of Ur. Ningal, was the wife of the moon-god, Sin, and was worshiped as a mother God in many other cities. Every female in the city at some time in her life would have to take her turn in serving as a priestess prostitute in the temples. God instructed Abraham to live his birth place, its luxuries and his close relatives and go to the land which God chose for him. Abraham believed God and by faith followed God's instructions to the land unknown to him. From the time God called Abraham it took him fifteen years to move but he acted on faith and obeyed God's instruction to move. Hebrews 11:8, states that: "By faith

Abraham, when called to go to a place he would later receive as his inheritance, obeyed and went, even though he did not know where he was going".

Abraham lived a life pleasing to God by separating from the people who worshipped other gods. At times faith requires being radically exclusive. God separates us from the norms, cultures and religions which do not glorify Him to make us vessels of honor. The spiritual pruning is biblical. God calls every believer to be radical about serving God by serving others faithfully. We must radically follow God's way of doing things to the point where it begins to change things in the earth. This is what it means to have radical faith. It means taking a biblical approach in everything you do without the possibility of compromising. When something is radical, it means it is strongly rooted in something. Pertaining to the things of God, radical faith is that which is rooted in the fundamentals of obedience to God's holy commands.

The major purpose of God on earth is to bring His kingdom on earth. God reveals Himself to mankind to change him or her into His image. God changes us from inside to the outside. Nobody remains the same after knowing God. There is no one single person mentioned in the Scripture who after knowing God walked in the same old ways. We are not here to impress people by what we do and by what we know but to please God by our faith. Loving people begins by knowing God. Knowing God begins with knowing Jesus Christ intimately.

Abraham pleased God by obeying God's Word even when it did not make sense to him. By faith he obeyed to offer his son Isaac in whom he had the promises of God. God demanded the burnt offering involving burning Isaac to ashes (Genesis 22:2, 13). The rituals of human sacrifices (ritual murder and the drinking of human blood) dominating the pagan world is the work of Satan imitating God who sacrificed His Son. Jesus said that, "Very truly I tell you, unless you eat the flesh of the Son of Man and drink his blood, you have no life in you." (John 6:53).

Abraham had two sons but he obeyed God's instructions by offering the right sacrifice (Isaac). God asked him to offer Isaac but not Ismail as the Muslims believe. The Muslims use the argument from Surah 37.100-113, to say that it was Ishmael (Ismail in Arabic) and not Isaac (Ishaq) whom Abraham offered to God. They celebrate *Idd-al-Adhaha* in commemoration of Ishmael. They falsely accuse the Jews for altering the scriptures for their advantage: *"The Jewish tradition, in order to glorify the younger branch of the family, descended from Isaac, ancestor of the Jews, as against the elder branch, descended from Ismail, ancestor of the Arabs, refers this sacrifice to Isaac (Genesis 22.1-18). Now Isaac was born when Abraham was 100 years old (Genesis 21.5) while Ismail was born to Abraham when Abraham was 86 years old (Genesis 16.16). Ismail was therefore 14 years older than Isaac. During his first 14 years Ismail was the only son of Abraham; at no time was Isaac the only son of Abraham."* (Yusuf Ali, The Holy Qur'an, p. 1205).

Sarah had the promise from God of bearing a son to Abraham. The Bible plainly or explicitly says that Hagar (Hajira in Islam), the mother of Ishmael, was never the wife of Abraham but only his slave-woman. Her relationship with Abraham was a result of Sarah's idea. After she became impatient, she took her maid (Hagar the Egyptian) and gave her to Abram her husband as a concubine to produce a son (Genesis 16.3). It should be noted that this was common practice at that time as evidenced by the Nuzi documents of the time. (See Jehoshua M. Grintz's Yichudo V'Kadmuso shel Sefer Breishit, Magnes, Hebrew University, 1983 PPs. 51-55).

The expression clearly means that she gave Hagar to her husband to cohabit with him and not as a second wife as Muslims often claim the verse to imply. Rather, in all that is said before and after this text, Hagar is regarded as nothing more than the mistress of Sarah. "Go into my maid", Sarah urged (Genesis 16.2). When Hagar conceived and looked in contempt upon Sarah, Abraham responded, "Behold, your maid is in your power; do to her as you please" (Genesis 16.6). There is even the Muslim tradition confirming that Hagar was only a servant in Abraham's household whom Sarah gave to him solely to bear him a son: *"Then he called Hajar who was the most trustworthy of his servants and he bestowed her (Hajar) on her (Sarah) and gave her clothes; subsequently Sarah made a gift of her (Hajar) to Ibrahim who cohabited with her and she bore Ismail who was the eldest of his children"* (Ibn Sa'd, Kitab al-Tabaqat al-Kabir, Vol. 1, p. 41).

When Abraham was 86, Hagar gave birth to a son and Abraham named him Ishmael. In Genesis 17:23, Ishmael was 13 years old when he was circumcised and Abraham was 99 years old at that time. When Abraham was 99 and Sarah was 89, God reassured His promise to Abraham and Sarah that they would have a son born to them. Read Genesis 17:16-21. Abraham was 100 years old when Isaac was born, and Sarah was beyond childbearing years. Ironically, the Muslims have a problem with the virgin birth yet they have no problem in believing that Sarah, childless until the age of ninety, is the first matriarch of the Hebrew people. Abraham and Sarah Humanly, biologically, and physically there was no way they could have a son. In the same way the virgin birth was a purely divine act. Grace is the prodigious outreach of God based on God's instinct and act without the intervention of man whatsoever, on behalf of Man.

When he was 13 years old, Ishmael was circumcised at the same time as all other males in Abraham's house becoming a part of the covenant in a mass circumcision. His father Abram, given the new name "Abraham," was also at this time, at the age of 99, initiated into the covenant by having himself and the males of his entire household circumcised (Genesis 17). At the time of the covenant, God informed Abraham that his wife Sarah would give birth to a son, which he was instructed to name Isaac. God told Abraham that He would establish his covenant through Isaac, and when Abraham inquired as to Ishmael's role, God answers that Ishmael has been blessed and that He "will make him fruitful, and will multiply him exceedingly; twelve princes shall he beget, and I will make him a great nation." (Genesis 17).

So Ishmael was 14 when Isaac was born. As Ishmael grew up, Hagar started to mock Sarah. In His sixth of seven appearances to Abraham (12:1-7, 13:14-17, 15:1-21, 17:1-21, 18:1-33, here and 22:1-18), God said: Do not be distressed about the boy and your maidservant (21:12a). God told Abraham that his descendants would be named through Isaac. Elohim, the God of righteousness, made it clear to Abraham that He was not going to accept Ishmael as the son of promise. Within the two sons of Abraham were two conflicting lineages. It was not possible for the two families to live together.

Sarah demanded that Abraham send Hagar and Ishmael away: "So she said to Abraham, "Send this servant away with her son! This servant's son won't share the inheritance with my son Isaac." (Genesis 21:10). God instructed Abraham to do what Sarah demanded. God agreed with Sarah and instructed Abraham to send Ishmael and Hagar away. This was a difficult assignment for Abraham, but he obeyed. The word used in sending away Ishmael is a familiar word in the Scriptures. This same verb, *garas*, is used to describe Adam being driven out of the Garden (3:24), and Cain being driven out of the presence of the Lord (4:14).

Ishmael was Abraham's son and it was heartbreaking for Abraham to have to give him up. For about sixteen years he had been the joy of his life. Abraham was a very rich man but he gave Hagar the portion required to be given to an expelled slave in accordance to the Babylonian law of Hammurabi. The food and the skin of water was no doubt enough to enable them to reach another settlement, had they not got lost wandering in the desert of Beersheba (21:14b). When Hagar was in the wilderness and an angel appeared to her, he called her "Hager, maid of Sarai" (Genesis 16.7) and told her "Return to your mistress and submit to her" (Genesis 16.9). As Abraham's son, Ishmael would receive his own special blessings from God (17:18), but he would not, and never could have been, the child of promise.

Ishmael became the father of the Arabs. Isaac became the father of the twelve tribes of Israel. There should be no doubt that Abraham offered Isaac as he was instructed by God. God's lineage of producing the Savior is clearly seen in the Patriarchs of the Bible (Abraham, Isaac and Jacob). Isaac became the father of Jacob. Jacob became the father of the twelve tribes of Israel. The earthly lineage of the Messiah (Savior), who became a substitute sacrifice for Isaac and all humanity, came from one of the tribes of Israel (Judah) and from the house of David. Jesus came from the tribe of Judah and from the house of David.

The inheritance was passed on to Isaac because he was chosen by God to be right. Isaac as described in the Hebrew Bible and the Quran was the only son Abraham had with his wife Sarah, and was the father of Jacob and Esau. Isaac was one of the three patriarchs of the Israelites. Isaac was the only biblical patriarch whose name was not changed, and the only one who did not leave Canaan. Compared to those of Abraham and Jacob, Isaac's story relates fewer incidents of his life. He died when he was 180 years old, making him the longest-lived patriarch. He lived a decent life. No wonder the Quran complemented Isaac with these words: "We announced to him an upright boy (Surah 37.101); and we read further that Isaac was specifically promised to him by name: Fabash-sharnuahu bi-Ishaaq—We announced to him Isaac (Surah 37.112)". Nowhere in the Qur'an is it ever similarly stated that Ishmael was promised to Abraham.

Abraham became the father of all believers. Christianity, Judaism and Islam trace their religions in Abraham. They are called Monotheism. Although, I don't believe that Islam is Monotheist. For example Muslims are required to make a pilgrimage to Mecca at least one time in their lifetime to touch and confess their sins to the black stone. They believe that the black stone is from Paradise. They believe that this black stone will have eyes to see and tongue to speak on the resurrection day to testify the names of those who have touched it with sincere heart (Narrated by al-Tirmidhi, 961; Ibn Maajah, 2944) So, AL-BASÎR The All-Seeing: The Stone has one attribute of Allah? These facts prove that Muslims have elevated the stone as a deity which is an associate of Allah. Some believe that the black stone was Abraham's stone; they ignore the fact that God instructed Abraham to leave all the idols and move to a foreign land to worship one true God. Muhammad chose to worship one of the gods of Terah (the moon god called Allah). In ancient Syria and Canna, the Moon-god Sin was usually represented by the moon in its crescent phase. A temple of the Moon-god has been excavated in Ur by Sir Leonard Woolley. He dug up many examples of moon worship in Ur and these are displayed in the British Museum to this day.

Paul told us that these two women (Sarah/Hagar) symbolize two covenants. Hagar symbolizes the Old Covenant of the Law given at

Mount Sinai. She was a slave and symbolized earthly Jerusalem in slavery with her children. Ishmael was conceived and born according to the flesh, a natural physical birth. On the other hand, Sarah symbolizes the New Covenant of Grace—God's Riches at Christ's expense. The two mothers are symbolic of our relationship with God. Hagar is symbolic of your spiritual mother if you are trying to earn your salvation by an illegitimate means contrary to God's way. Sarah is symbolic of your spiritual mother if you accept the legitimate birth by God. That is when your faith depends on your relationship with Jesus Christ, the child of promise, the gift of God's grace. The question to you is: "Who is your mother, spiritually speaking?"

The sending away of Ishmael paved way for Isaac to possess his inheritance. Here is a lesson for us: When the truth is birthed in you it exposes and drives away the lies, allowing you to possess your inheritance. In the same way the birth of Isaac exposed Ishmael as an illegitimate heir and drove him away. Faith became an integral part of Abraham's character. He had great confidence that God would fulfill His promises. God viewed Abraham's faith as righteousness. All Christians invest their faith in Christ.

Now I want to tackle another biblical character called Moses. Moses lived 120 years: 40 years trying to be no body; 40 years discovering that he is no body; 40 years God making him somebody. He had the vision of faith. He was born as an ordinary peasant but lived as a prince. He was born in a hut but he lived in the palace. He was a shepherd; he commanded the national army; he was a statesman, an administrator, a genius, a soldier and a priest.

The writer of Hebrew identified Moses among the heroes of faith. By faith Moses made careful conscious decisions. Moses wanted something greater than Egypt could offer. By faith Moses, when he became of age, refused to be called the son of Pharaoh's daughter, choosing rather to suffer affliction with the people of God than to enjoy the riches, the prestige and the passing pleasures of sin in the palace of the Pharaoh of Egypt; for he looked to the eternal rewards of heaven (Hebrews 11:24-26).

Moses decided to pursue his calling. He was not ashamed to associate with His own people who were despised as long as it was pleasing to God. In the same manner we are not supposed to be puffed up by the worldly successes, and we should not be ashamed of the truth and the poor folks of the Church. We follow Jesus into the wilderness, bearing the cross with Him even when the persecution heats up. He owned us, in our poverty and shame; He is not ashamed to identify with us in spite of our fallen nature. When we were loathsome and self-abhorred, He received us as His children. Never be so treacherous to be ashamed of Him. Your soul must cleave to Him.

Moses is the mediator of the old covenant. The Law covenant instituted at Mount Sinai was not made with Moses, but with the people of Israel, as Moses declared: "And Moses called all Israel, and said unto them, Hear, O Israel, the statutes and judgments which I speak in your ears this day, that ye may learn them, and keep and do them. The Lord our God made a Covenant with us in Horeb. The Lord made not this Covenant with our fathers, but with us, even us, who are all of us here alive this day" (Deut. 5:1-3). Jesus is the administrator of it. Three times in the epistle to the Hebrews Jesus is called the Mediator of the new, or better covenant or testament, (Heb. 8:6, 9:15, 12:24) the same with the everlasting covenant.

The Bible says that God spoke to Moses face to face (Exodus 33:11). It does not mean that Moses saw the face of God but it means that God spoke directly to Moses instead of speaking to him in visions and dreams: *"With him will I speak mouth to mouth, even apparently, and not in dark speeches; and the similitude of the LORD shall he behold* (Numbers 12:8). God chose Israel to demonstrate His love to the lost world. God's goal is not to elevate one race or tribe above the other but to bring about His redemptive plan to reality. Matthew's account traces the line of descent from Abraham to Jesus, while Luke's account follows the ancestry from Adam to Jesus. The Bible says that we are all equally received by God through Jesus Christ: "There is neither Jew nor Greek, slave nor free, male nor female, for you are all one in Christ Jesus" (Galatians 3:28). Whosoever seeks Him finds Him; whosoever believes is saved—Jews/Gentiles.

Elijah is known as father of the prophets. At the transfiguration of Jesus, Elijah and Moses appeared with Jesus in His glory. In the Old Testament, no person performed more miracles than Elijah. Dr. James Kennedy made this comment concerning one of Elijah's miracles: "Examine all of history, sacred and profane, and you will never find a contest comparable to the one between Elijah, the prophet of the one true God and the false prophets of Baal. The religion of Jehovah was being overwhelmed by the false teachings and philosophies of Baalism, and this created an inner struggle for the people of the True God." Elijah was human, just as we are but his life was characterized with miracles because of his faith. His faith and patience was tested.

Another biblical character of faith I am going to discuss is Naaman. Naaman was commander of the army of the king of Aram who had leprosy (2 Kings 5). Jesus recommended the faith of Naaman: "And there were many in Israel with leprosy in the time of Elisha the prophet, yet not one of them was cleansed—only Naaman the Syrian" (Luke 4:27). Jesus used the healing of Naaman to explain our salvation. Leprosy is symbolic of our sins. A leaper was an outcast who was isolated from the burke community, in the same way we are isolated from God by our sins.

Naaman's healing is synonymous to our salvation. An insignificant servant like you and me heard the good news that led to spiritual deliverance. Naaman thought that he could buy the healing but it was not for sale; it was a free gift from God. In the same manner many people would readily pay their way or do everything within their own means to earn salvation; they consider it to be too cheap to be free. They would do anything to impress God but God needs none of it. God demands our faith. It is only our faith in Jesus Christ that pleases Him.

God sent Elisha to Naaman with the good news of deliverance. Naaman expected the prophet to perform some rituals for his deliverance: "But Naaman went away angry and said, "I thought that he would surely come out to me and stand and call on the name of the Lord his God, wave his hand over the spot and cure me of my leprosy" (2 Kings 5:11). But Elisha, the prophet looked for Naaman's obedience. He instructed Naaman to go and wash in the Jordan River.

In the same manner we are saved by our obedience to God's way. God instructs us to wash in the blood of Jesus. Our faith in Christ is the manifested obedience to His only way of salvation. It is either God's way or no way of salvation. Like Elisha, we are despised when we are carrying the Good News to the lost world. Yet, we have the only information leading to spiritual healing and fulfillment that the world needs. There is no shortcut to salvation apart from Christ. The Gospel must be preached in order for somebody to receive Jesus Christ.

Another biblical character I want to discuss is John the Baptists. John the Baptist appears on the New Testament pages but he is considered to be one of the Old Testament prophets. Jesus called John the Baptists the greatest among those born of women (Matthew 11:11). There are only two people (Adam/Jesus) whose lives did not begin in the womb of a woman. Adam was created a mature man. Jesus is called the begotten Son of God because He was born of a virgin. He existed eternally (John 14:7-10). Although Jesus was born by Mary, He was very God who existed before time and space; He put on the human body to save the world. John's mother, Elizabeth, was a relative of Mary, the mother of Jesus. The two women were pregnant at the same time. The Bible says in Luke 1:41, when the two expectant mothers met, the baby leaped within Elizabeth's womb as she was filled with the Holy Spirit. The angel Gabriel had already foretold the miraculous birth and prophetic ministry of John the Baptist to his father Zechariah. The news was a joyous answer to prayer for the previously barren Elizabeth. John was to become the God-ordained messenger proclaiming the arrival of the Messiah, Jesus Christ.

John the Baptist is remembered for baptizing the Jews. Originally baptism was reserved for the Gentiles who converted to Judaism. John the Baptist's life was so inspiring that people confused him to be the Messiah. Others called him Elijah. The Jewish people believed that Elijah must come first to prepare the way for their Messiah. Elijah was prophetically announced to turn the hearts of the children to the fathers. The fathers in this case are the patriarchs. The Israelites had departed from the faith of their father Abraham. Jesus Christ said that John the Baptist came in the spirit of Elijah preaching repentance (Matthew 11:14).

John the Baptist announced the coming of the Jewish Messiah in a unique way. He did not point at time but he introduced the Messiah by baptizing Him. Whenever an earthly king was visiting, there were men who went ahead of him announcing that the king is here. John the Baptist played the same role. He prepared the way for the coming of the King of kings (Jesus Christ) by preaching repentance. Jesus (our Messiah) came to do what Jehovah purposed, to make a kingdom of kings and priests (1 Peter 2:9).

John the Baptist is the greatest because he was the humblest. He lived the despised sacrificial life in the wildness; he wore wild-looking clothing, lived in the desert wilderness, and ate strange food (locust) in preparation for his ministry. He was humble because he did not envy Christ; he desired to decrease, allowing Jesus to increase. Jesus gave His manifesto of the kingdom of God in the sermon at the mountain. He instructed His followers to carry their cross and crucify themselves daily. It means dying to the old corrupt desires so that the life of Jesus is manifested. The kingdom of God is God's virtues invading the earth.

Of course we cannot forget Peter the man of faith. Peter is the only human being who ever walked on the water. But it was when things looked the most ominous. And Peter, stepping out in faith, walked on the water with Jesus, rising above the chaos and fixing his eyes on the Lord! Peter made the first confession that, Jesus Christ is the Christ: "And Simon Peter answered and said, 'Thou art the Christ, the Son of the living God.' And Jesus answered and said unto him, 'Blessed art thou, Simon Barjona: for flesh and blood hath not revealed it unto thee, but my Father which is in heaven" (Matt. 16:16-17). Greek word translated "Peter" is petros, meaning "pebble" or "small stone," while the word rendered "rock" is petra, meaning "big rock" or "huge boulder."

Peter's words brought a word of commendation from the Lord. Peter was blessed because he had come to a correct conclusion about the person of Christ. Jesus told him that it was the revelation of God that opened his mind to such confession. Jesus promised to build His Church with people who had the same revelation. The Church is made up of people who confessed or who will confess that Jesus is the Christ. Our confession must come from the convicted and sincere hearts. Jesus warned that calling Him Lord without a sincere and obedient heart will not give you access to the kingdom of God. Those who call Him Lord must do the will of His Father (Matthew 7:21).

We cannot be good enough to please God unless our goodness is of Christ. We cannot seek God outside Christ. Those who seek Christ find God. Those who find God must be in Christ. Jesus said that no one is good but God (Mark 10:18). The goodness acceptable to God is the manifestation of the works of Jesus Christ in us and through us. Peter instructed that: "Grace and peace be multiplied unto you through the knowledge of God, and of Jesus our Lord" (2 Pet. 1:2). Peter lists the virtues or moral excellence virtues that each believer needs to add to his faith: knowledge, self-control, patience or steadfastness, godliness, brotherly kindness, and of course Christian love. The Bible warns of the danger of our good works which are done outside our faith in Christ: "For unto us was the gospel preached, as well as unto them: but the word preached did not profit them, not being mixed with faith in them that heard it" (Hebrews 4:1-2).

Jesus Christ must be the reason we do all things. As Pastor Alistair Begg says, "When the soul can clearly see this oneness between itself and Christ, the pulse may be felt as beating for both, and the one blood as flowing through the veins of each. Then the heart is as near heaven as it can be on earth and is prepared for the enjoyment of the most sublime and spiritual kind of fellowship."

The Kingdom Agenda shows in practical terms how God provides the authority and the dynamics to spiritually synergize every area of your life. Unfortunately, most times we keep God on the fringes of our lives, accessible if we have a need, but far enough away that He doesn't interfere with our own private agendas. The result is segmented, compartmentalized lives with a narrow focus on nothing but our own fulfillment. I consider this one to be spiritual suicide.

Briefs on the Life of Dr Justine Kibirige Kawooya Lwanga

(By Dr. Vincent Kabuye Kawoya–Young brother)

Doctor Justin Kibirige Kawooya Lwanga (JK Lwanga) was born on the 18th August 1938, probably in Mulago Hospital. His parents; Mr. Paulo Musoke Kawooya and Mrs. Gladys Nabulo Kawooya had a home at Kyabando village, just North of Kampala town then. That is where he spent his early childhood. He was the third born in a Family of 17 known siblings from five co-wives.

As a child he was very well behaved, hardworking and self-motivated. He would work in the gardens; digging, picking cotton and coffee without waiting to be told. He would help the ladies to collect food and firewood from the gardens and fetch water from the well. In other words he became a responsible person at an early age. He was a very obedient child and respectful to his parents and seniors in society. He was a humble person and hated self exaltation.

He went to school; first at Bukoto Moslem Primary School, at Nsimbiziwoome village. This was just a few miles South East of Kyebando. He was then staying with his Senga (Paternal Aunt), called Njereka Nazziwa. Their home was near the mosque of Nsimbiziwoome at Bukoto. Next he attended Makerere Anglican Church Primary School, on top of Makerere Hill. He was then back to Kyebando with his parents, probably in the mid-1940s.

From Makerere, he was taken to his Paternal Uncle's home at a village called Nyenje near Mukono trading center then. He went to Mukono Demonstration Primary School in company of his cousins. He studied up to primary standard six and sat for his Primary Leaving Examinations, which he passed very well.

The young Lwanga was subsequently admitted to Mengo Junior Secondary School in 1953. He was then around 15 years old and studied up to 1955. He had returned to Kyebando for the second time, but this time his parents had migrated to a village called Kiyagi in Kyaggwe County (just off Kayunga road) and had left the home to a relative called Kopoliyamu (Cyprian) Maseruka Sebowa. This is the gentleman with whom Lwanga briefly stayed while studying at Mengo.

Before the end of 1955, Lwanga moved to Naggulu and stayed with maternal relatives. He sat for his Junior Secondary school leaving examinations at the end of 1955, and again passed with distinction. He was subsequently admitted to the prestigious King's College Buddo. He studied his senior Secondary School from 1956 up to 1958 when he wrote his Ordinary level Cambridge School Certificate Examinations, passing with four distinctions of class one and four credits of class three, with an aggregate of 10 in 6 subjects and 16 in 8 subjects!

Before 1959, practically all the students who excelled in their Cambridge school certificate exams were admitted to Makerere University College to do what was called "Intermediate". This was a two year pre-university study, after which they did university entrance exams before they were admitted to do university courses proper. In 1959, Higher School Certificate (HSC) level studies (Cambridge Advanced School Certificate) were proposed in Uganda and tried in 3 pilot schools, namely; King's college Budo, St Mary's college Kisubi and Mbale Senior Secondary School.

Mr. Robinson the Headmaster of King's College Budo at that time, decided to push Lwanga to Makerere for the "intermediate". This did not go down well with the student, who wanted to go back to Budo to do the newly introduced HSC level studies. But he had to comply with the decision. Theirs was the last "intermediate" before HSC fully took root in Uganda.

Lwanga did his "Intermediate" from 1959 to 1961, then wrote his University entrance exams, which he passed very well as usual. He got admitted to do Medicine, in the Medical school (faculty of Medicine), a course leading to the award of bachelor of medicine and bachelor of surgery degree and lasting five years. All the Seven years at Makerere, Lwanga was a resident member of Northcote hall, room number 3. Makerere University College was at that time affiliated to the University of London, which controlled the curriculum, set the exams and marked them. By the time Lwanga graduated in 1966, the University was called University of East Africa, having become autonomous from University of London. The newly qualified Dr. Lwanga did his one year internship in 1966/1967, residing in the old doctors' mess behind the nurses' hostel.

In 1967 the medical school decided to introduce a three year postgraduate master's degree program (Masters of Medicine), instead of sending postgraduate students abroad for membership studies. Dr. Lwanga with a small group of colleagues was selected as pioneer students. This first intake consisted of distinguished doctors like Professors; C L Olweny, Stanley Tumwiine, Lobo among others. Unfortunately Dr. Lwanga didn't complete his first year as he got embroiled in a professional disagreement, with a few of his colleagues in the dialysis unit of the Department of Internal Medicine headed by a European boss. He quietly left academics and government service aided by the permanent secretary Ministry of Health (a great friend of his Dad!).

In 1968, he worked at Kiswa dispensary of Kampala City Council. Towards the end of the year he got employed by a Catholic missionary hospital of Naggalama from where he extended services to Nkokonjeru Convent hospital and at times to the small hospital of Kayunga Sisters convent. Around this time he met his future wife Christine (Tina as he fondly called her). Tina was herself a nurse at Nsambya hospital from where she resigned to join her husband.

Towards the end of 1969, Dr. Lwanga started setting up small private clinics. One was in Nakaseke, another one was in Semuto, in late Mr. Batesaaki's house. Subsequently he set up a clinic at Bombo where he also settled and resigned from the missionary hospitals. The clinic was in late Mr. Mukayanyi's commercial house on Kampala road, while he resided in Late Mr. Khemis's estate. Tina's first baby (Harriet Naggayi) came in that same year in July. From Bombo, Dr. Lwanga used to drive and visit several other clinics he had set up, including; at Kibibi Butambala (in late Mr. Sekamatte's premises), at Bweyogerere and at Wobulenzi among others. In Bombo Clinic, he set up a General Practitioner's Surgery. It was through this surgery and his generally humane methods of work that he made his name.

In the 1980s, one of the first three African doctors in Uganda, Dr. Bamundaga passed on. He was known to Dr. Lwanga and his sons requested Dr. Lwanga to take over his clinic. He supervised Bamundaga medical center into the early 2000s. Around the same time he took on and supervised clinics at Kiboga and Wakiso, where he did some surgery. Dr. Lwanga stayed and worked in Bombo most of his life, even throughout the turbulent times in Uganda up to his last moments on Wednesday the 18th of April 2012.

I think several personal attributes combined to make Dr. Lwanga such a wonderful and extraordinary human being. First of all he was an extremely intelligent person as demonstrated by performances at all levels of his studies. At times he was made to skip classes and proceed to the next level. He had a very good memory combined with a highly analytical mind and a brain rich in abstract thinking. He was capable of remembering a lot of facts, figures and events. As adulthood he was full of wisdom and prophetic in whatever he said.

He was a humorous person, always cracking jokes and making others laugh even in desperate situations! He had an equable personality. He was kind and considerate of others. He was sometimes abstract and often misunderstood just like most geniuses are. He was selfless towards others, always considering others first before self. Professionally he was ethical. To him, humanity always came first then worldly things like money, later. A day before he passed on he operated on a patient despite being obviously in ill-health! He was not a perfectionist but was always fond of doing things right. He was a staunch believer in the truth and in God, though he confessed to being "non-religious". He had earlier shown interest in the Bahia faith which subscribes to the universal truth of all religions and was not an atheist. He was always upright and believed in extreme honesty, an attribute which he always liked to pass on to others especially the juniors.

Justin was an inspirational man and a role model to many. He touched many lives and made many of us what we are through financial, moral and psychological support in addition to constant counseling. He was able to deal with anyone at his or her level and status; children and adults, women and men, illiterates and learned, elite and the lowly in society, sane and insane, religious and non-religious and so on and so forth.

Lwanga loved his Kiganda culture and roots; He loved his extended family, his Ngeye clan, his Buganda nation and his country Uganda, although at one time he wondered why he was born among a persecuted Baganda people.

Dr. Kabuye Second from the Left/ Dr. Lwanga on the Right, in the Kiganda Traditional costumes

Dr. Lwanga was a social man, who socialized with friends. He loved cinemas especially "drive in" cinema then located in Ntinda. He loved music and had a wonderful music system at home which was looted in the 1979 war.

Lwanga loved games and sports. In his university days he played Karam, table tennis and was an astute chess player. In addition, Dr. Lwanga enjoyed and played Owes, a widely played game in many parts of Africa. He played the game in Bombo up to the end of his life. He loved watching soccer and supported the local Bombo teams. He appeared to have played the game in his primary school days. While at King's College Buddo, Lwanga did some athletics. In additional, Dr. Lwanga loved motor rallies especially the East African Safari Rally. He would drive to strategic points along the rally route and enjoy the racing cars, then drive off after some time to several other sittings.

Dr. Lwanga was an avid reader. He loved books and he read them. He also wanted others to read them. He read all sorts of literature and believed that only the one who is widely read is better suited to understand the world. He loved discovering different points of view on numerous issues and always cultivated an open mind through reading. He taught himself Greek, Arabic, and Hebrew through reading various "teach-yourself" books. He read theology, philosophy, psychology, anthropology and many other arts and science disciplines. He read the Bible, the Koran, Torah etc., and could discuss religious issues with believers of the various religions at a highly informed level, often leaving them in great amazement! Professionally he read many textbooks and journals pertaining to all disciplines of Medicine up to his death. Indeed when his property was collected when he passed on, the bulk of it was "books"!

Dr. Lwanga was a political animal, interested in and analytical of events (past and present) taking place in his country and the world at large. He enjoyed political discourse at the highest intellectual level. He had much interest in politics based on principled issues. He campaigned as a Constituent Assembly candidate for Katikamu South constituency in the early 1990s, and for Member of Parliament seat for the same constituency, on a DP ticket in 2001.

Lwanga was an accomplished business man despite some rare and nearly disastrous miscalculations in his later life. He ran private clinics and did some farming. He was involved in transport sector with an Israel company known as Soleh Boney in the late 1960 and early 1970s before Idi Amin expelled the Israelis in 1972.

Lastly Lwanga was a family man, a loving husband and a caring father. Polygamy was and is not unusual in society. Although the biblical marriage is monogamous, I believe polygamy should not be unduly criminalized. Dr. Lwanga had 15 children from different wives.

As a postscript, Dr. Lwanga survived death on several occasions. Between 1971 and 1972, Amin's henchmen attempted several times to ambush and murder him but he was able to miraculously escape, probably with God's protection. He subsequently gave up everything; he sold all his cars, started footing to his clinic, reduced his outings including visiting his peripheral clinics, gave up suits and resorted to khaki clothes etc.

Another attempt to take his life was in 1977, that dreadful year when there was a lot of state instigated mass murder in Uganda. The last time was towards the end of the regime in 1979. Amin's blood thirsty thugs nearly cornered him as he approached his clinic. He was warned in time by his nurses before he reached the clinic and he fled to his Uncle's home deep in the villages in another county of Kyaggwe. There were several other attempts on his freedom which were less serious but scary all the same.

During the Obote II regime he was on several occasions arrested and taken to be murdered in Bombo barracks but each time was miraculously bailed out by sympathetic officers. On another occasion he was summoned to the District Commissioner's office in Luwero, 20 miles from Bombo, on allegations of supporting NRA guerillas. Again he survived by God's grace.

Rest in Eternal Peace Dr. J K Lwanga, till we meet again in eternity. We shall sadly miss you till then. (*This biography was written by Dr. Kabuye Kawoya*).

*Dr. Lwanga with folded arms upon graduation at
Makerere Medical School*

The Dr. Who Impacted My Life

(By Stephen Kyeyune)

My dad introduced Dr. Lwanga to me for the first time during my early childhood when I was in elementary school at Bombo Common School. He insinuated that the late DR. was my uncle. Not because we were blood relatives but most probably because my uncles from Semuto village (Gabriel/Santo) were standing next to him. They were his close companions, equivalent to his brothers. They spent most of their times at his house.

Dr. Lwanga was a family man who loved his wife dearly but at the same time valued his responsibility to the people highly. He was a people person; his home was a people place. The love of people was engraved deep in his blood and was one of the fundamental values he yearned to inculcate in his children. He had many friends hanging around him and accompanying him to various social activities. At his house, there were always people sitting in the compound, seeking advice on various matters or just whiling away the time. Of course some people befriended him for their advantage but the majority of them maintained a healthy relationships. Dr. Lwanga loved people and accepted them the way they are. As one writer said, "When you stop expecting people to be perfect, you can like them for who they are".

Dr. Lwanga was a very close friend to my father (RIP). In spite of their closeness, the two men did not have much in common. My dad was deeply involved in politics in the 1960s but during the regime of Idi Amin, he took a political sabbatical and turned his passion to business. Dr. Lwanga was fully devoted to the medical field. By the time my dad was abducted and killed, he was fully devoted to the

Church work and he had immortalized himself as 'defender of the faith'. My dad was for a long time the chairman of the board of elders at the parish level in Anglican Church. Dr. Lwanga was theistic but he was not a regular Church attendant. He had little interest in the Catholic religion in which he was raised. Still, he believed in a greater power and an afterlife, and he instinctively avoided any activities he thought harmful for his soul. He believed in miracles. He insinuated that strange happenings do occur; some of these are attributed to God. What is not in question is that there are phenomena that science, psychology and other human branches of knowledge cannot explain.

Although the two great friends (the late Dr. Lwanga/my dad) had different interests, their lifetime friendship was built on strong relationship as opposed to an ambivalent relationship. They were committed to their friendship. The experts of communication say that all relationships contain opposing desires at times; this is the essence of conflict. A chronic pattern of ambivalence typically generates a dynamic in any kind of relationships, including friendship, where one friend is identified as 'uncommitted' and the other as wanting commitment. One thing the two men shared in common was their integrity. They were open to each other. There was no anxiety because each partner did not withhold aspects of himself from the other. They did not have up their sleeves trump cards about each other. They were transparent to each other. Openness involves honesty by admitting your shortcomings and confessing where you fall short. Transparency is the key to avoiding hypocrisy.

The reality is that we are all vulnerable to hypocrisy. No matter how long we've believed or how spiritually mature we are, we're never too advanced to be hypocrites—people who cover up who they really are. Hypocrisy simply means acting to be something you are not. In the same way Hollywood actors are paid acting to be something they are not. One thing I've learned to practice in my own spiritual walk is to ask God to search me and remove the veneer and the vestiges of hypocrisy in my own life. I recommend this prayer to all believers who want steer completely clear of hypocrisy in their Christian walk.

Their relationship was based on principles as opposed to emotions. The characteristics of a principled person are ones that reflect the classical virtues: faithful, hopeful, loving, prudent, just, temperate and courageous. Remember that unprincipled great friends can make great enemies too. Unprincipled activities involve self-interest, narrowly understood and un-guided acts beyond any sense of classical ethics.

Genuine love for the good of the other should be the basis of human relationship. To be fully committed to any relationship is to accept the fragility and imperfections that comes with it. The solid relationship is built on the good and the bad as well. Friends who expect others to be perfect at all times end up with undesirable consequences.

I have known the Kawoya family for a long time. Mr. Paulo Musoke Kawoya (RPI) often stopped over at my dad's retail shop to talk to my dad. The late Paul Musoke Kawoya was a decent, quiet, passive and laid back person (easy-going). Unlike his sons, he was a man of few words. He was friendly but very self-sufficient when it comes to interacting with other people. He was a very private and restrained man.

Mr. Paulo Musoke Kawoya was a family man. He was a traditionalist who believed in polygamy. He however raised his children in an admirable way. I want to pause and talk about the acceptable marriage. Our ancestors were tenacious in getting problems solved. Marriage was used to establish covenant relationships between rival groups. Polygamy was therefore widely practiced. Polygamy was practiced in the Jewish culture as it is practiced among Africans. Personally I think that every man is polygamous in nature, his predatory instincts would make him so; it only takes extreme discipline and commitment to stay monogamous. Polygamy may not be necessarily an unforgivable sin but it is not the perfect will God. God's will is for a man and a woman to be joined in lifetime relationship (monogamy).

God created a man and a wife. Marriage is a covenant relationship representing our relationship with God. God was a husband to Israel. Christ is the bridegroom, the Church is His bride. Jesus came to fulfill the Law by rightly defining it. He said that: "Have you not read that He Who created them from the beginning made them male and female, and said, 'Therefore a man shall leave his father and his mother and hold fast to his wife, and the two shall become one flesh'? So they are no longer two but one flesh. What therefore God has joined together, let not man separate." (Matthew 19:3-7). The word man (husband) and woman (wife) are given in single form as opposed to plurality.

Marriage is not man's idea. God is the author of the institution of marriage. Marriage is not only a lifetime covenant between a man and a woman to which God is a witness, but it is the creation of a new blood line or a new family line. The term "one flesh" is used to describe a blood relationship created between the married man and woman. Adultery is not about sex. Adultery is about ego-satisfaction and betrayal. Any time a person decides to marry another wife, he violates the vows he made. It's about a person making life-changing decisions based upon promises that ultimately prove empty.

All biblical characters that practiced polygamy ended up in a chain of family problems. We know that the Middle East problems we have today were a result of the mistake of Abraham taking on a concubine (second woman) Hagar with whom he fathered Ishmael who became the father of the Arabs. Later on, Sarah gave birth to Isaac who became the father of Jacob. Jacob became the father of the twelve tribes of Israel. The hostility between Isaac and Ishmael has spilled over today's generation (Israel/Arabs). The houses of David and Solomon who widely practiced polygamy were full of family conflicts. Just to mention a few examples.

Mr. Musoke Kawoya's children earned public respect because they had a very healthy relationship with their dad. Children who respect their parents make good leaders. As one coach said that before he picks a player he must check his relationship with his father. If he did not respect his father he could not consider recruiting him. He went on to say that a person who does not respect his father cannot respect any other authority.

The late Paulo Musoke Kawoya was a World War II veteran. Like my dad, he used to brag about his past military services in the Kings African Rifles. After retiring from the army, he worked in hospitals. No wonder his kids followed the same trait. There is no doubt that parents will mostly want to influence their children to take on their trade, whether lawyers, doctors, soldiers or politicians, and mostly children would want to do the same, because parents are the greatest influences a child can have, the primary role models.

Mr. Paul Musoke Kawoya and his Family

Dr. Lwanga was the magnet that held the Kawoya family together. He did the family's donkey work over the years, allowing a unified and functioning family. He acted as a shock absorber for all the excesses of the family. He did everything for the benefit of the family rather than unjustifiably and cunningly couching his personal interests into the family. He always exhibited a positive attitude in everything he did.

Dr. Lwanga was a proxy family friend and mentor. I met him for the first time when I was in elementary school. My dad introduced him to me for the first time. At the first sight, I freaked out to meet him because of his status. You know, most educated people in my country seem to stifle any association with people of the lower classes. Upper class people who are secure in their status have the luxury of occasionally declassing themselves, and selectively choosing who they associate with. Doctors in particular are very tenacious, arrogant and are generally known to be vertically challenged, but Dr. Lwanga was a pleasant exception. A chance encounter with him did therefore not immediately suggest that he was an elite and a very successful businessman in the town, playing in the biggest league.

Dr. Lwanga always adorned a nicely pressed shirt and khaki trousers, a neat fit. He was always smartly dressed man and maintained his casual style throughout the years. Interestingly, unlike his peers, he didn't care about fancy suits; he valued family and friends and tried to live modestly. He dressed casual but his deportment (posture) was in a business and social setting. By deportment, I mean the manner he carried and conducted himself. He always projected a positive image, walking with poise and confidence without arrogance and inferiority complex.

When he saw me, he was extremely excited. Within a moment of time I was used to him as if I had known him for a long time. I began to sound like someone that had stayed with him for some time—even speaking off-cuff (speaking my mind). He was a good exemplar too. Ever since then, I have been a keen admirer of his personality and the way he articulated issues.

The more I got to know him, the more I admired him. Dr. Lwanga was polite, kind and down to earth person. Listening to him, you got to appreciate the inner man, away from his professional. He sounded very affable, a man who knows how to keep a conversation going with a cheeky laugh and wacky anecdote out of nowhere. He was not forceful but firm and articulately making his point very softly. He spoke with a deep voice with such confidence; his voice exuded nothing but strong will and determination. He was consequential, serious, joking around and laughing even while saying cheese. He was ever simple, soft-spoken, humble and concise—conveying volumes of meaning in fewest possible words. He was never haughty. Whereas he was an accomplished physician who would otherwise carry himself with pride and self-importance, he carried himself with simplicity, and accessing him was not as hard as it is with some elites in town. The only outstanding physical mark of being a doctor was his stethoscope that normally hanged around his neck to listen to or to auscultate a patient's heart, lungs, various pulse points and abdomen. People of various statuses made clear their admiration of his qualities, which they say was a far-cry from what most professions exhibit.

There is saying that beauty lies in the hands of the beholder. I can testify that Dr. Lwanga's decency depended on his personality. The career just added a new angle to him. The reason I testify with such confidence is because he was always the same man; he did not fake it and he did not change with time. He is the only person I know whose reputation remained intact and whose record unblemished until his demise. He remained a simple man right to the end. He never took people for granted. He associated with everyone. He wanted to see everyone happy. It was very hard to see him with an angry face even! Certainly, he had bad days like any other person but he did not rub it in the face of others. He was ever generous, flexible, and extremely polite flashing a smile on his face.

The old adage says that, "Tell me your friends and I will tell you who you are." Dr. Lwanga never wanted to associate with people of egoism but wanted to associate with happy, enthusiastic and fulfilled people. He did not prejudge people depending on what they have or their education. He respected even the people of the lower class, even those who have the moniker of "homeless", living on the streets, rummaging through dumpsters for food and using a puddle to take a bath. He did not act self-important. For that reason he was not impressed by people who considered themselves to be self-important. "You can agree with me that, the only people who are impressed by your stuffy, pretentious, self-important self are other stuffy, pretentious, self-important people. The rest of us aren't impressed. We're irritated, put off, and uncomfortable."

We live in a culture where vulgarity is in charge. The Country is dominated by a bunch of greedy fellows who only care about themselves and would do anything to become rich. But Dr. Lwanga was far apart as humanly as possible. His attitude was that of feasting on minnows rather than gunning for the big whale. The endlessly bragging about ill-gotten wealth as if they toiled, sweated and shed blood for it does not hold a candle to the man of his ilk. He was a man who carried a big stick without a hint of shouting or boasting about it!

Dr. Lwanga is a much celebrated physician and statesman. He was exuberant and took obvious pleasure in his work. Besides, he was always available when needed. He was not a kind of man if his wife summoned him, would leave a patient unattended and run home in fear of reprimand by wife. He valued life and he would do anything to save life. He was not the ilk of the lazy doctors who choose to amputate the whole leg instead of removing the jigger.

Dr. Lwanga's job was very demanding. He had to stay motivated and focused. His typical day began with morning breakfast and then preparations for long hours to work at his clinic. Not to mention that he treated some patients at his home before leaving to work at his clinic. He had to work over 20 hours a day, seven days straight, at his local Health Clinic. Because the patients in flow being high all day long, even in the afternoon, he never took his lunch break. He did surgical operations at night. He did not maintain a fixed schedule because he normally received emergency cases like accidents. In addition to treating patients he had to do the follow up and monitor their progress. Also, he had to study to be current with modern medicines and treatments. He had to be up by 4.00 and most days slept past midnight. No weekends, very short holidays, high levels of stress etc.

Dr. Lwanga did not have time to go to the gym but regularly took nature walks for physical fitness and to walk away from things when they got too much for him. He had a hectic day such that sometimes the hours in the day were not enough for him but as a family man he reserved time for his family.

His enthusiasm was stimulating, infectious and attractive to many people. For that reason people loved him and wanted to be around him. Generally speaking, he was a man of the people. His priority was the personal stake of others. He never focused on what he could get but on what he can provide. Giving was the only way that helped him to establish a real connection and relationship with people. He was able to win the hearts of the people because he cared about their needs.

Some people took advantage of Dr. Lwanga because they were fooled by his outsized easy-on-the-eye character into thinking that the doctor was soft. But those of us close to him know that, although he was flexible, he was a strong willed and principled man. Nevertheless, he loved all people despite their weaknesses. He believed that you catch more flies with honey than vinegar.

Dr. Lwanga was fond of people of different classes. He wanted to get acquainted with their problems in order to help them better. But he knew his limits. He was not nosy; he was not the type who always thought of how his neighbor's grass was growing. He was too civilized to muddle up in other people's business. In fact he disdained rumor-mongering.

Dr. Lwanga was ever attracted to success and desired to succeed. He nursed an irresistible quest for knowledge and ideas. As Oliver Wendell Holmes, Jr. said that, "A mind that is stretched to a new idea will never return to its original dimension". The late Dr. was a passionate advocate of learning. He was acquainted with a variety of careers. This enabled him to be a multi-skilled professional and therefore fit to advice many. Basically he had various knowledge and skills and he made the same skills available for public use. He had a passion of training others and passing on skills to others. He wanted others to excel and he would encourage them to do better. He was always a mentor to many, innovative and inspirational. To put it in plain language he was naturally unselfish leader. "If your actions inspire others to dream more, learn more, do more and become more, you are a leader"—John Quincy Adams.

Dr. Lwanga enjoyed nature. He supported the good work of environmentalists, conservators and preservators. He believed that there can never be a better tomorrow without the awareness and action to promote the kind of governance that will ensure the climate we want to live in. He was an exemplified epigraph of resolve to work with nature and celebrate the cycle of life. J. Ikuya said that, "Those who do not care about nature are least likely to care about other human beings as well. By caring for all other life forms, we also radiate the spirit of affection for the place of our people in society." He goes on to say that, "Our interest in restorative activities for nature is not merely from a casual heart for the pulse of life. The satisfaction of the presumed economic needs of man has been only extracting from nature what man enjoys without giving back to nature what sustains life, leading to accumulated deficits that halt further possibility of nature's harmony."

It is the love of nature that attracted Dr. Lwanga to agriculture. Most of the people in our locality were local farmers. However they lacked entrepreneurial knowledge and skills enabling them reap big dividends. What seems to stagnate agricultural development is mainly lacking in risk taking, social, and cultural behavior. The inconsistence was partly because the government did not espouse an efficient definitive educative policy. Dr. Lwanga advised the folks regarding increasing their agricultural produce by tapping into modern farming on a small scale (peasant level). At his home town, he demonstrated modern farming skills behind his yard in his fruits and vegetables Pot farming. In the village, he embraced large scale farming in agricultural produce, primarily pineapples. It is believed that pineapples cannot be grown without using pesticides. Whereas their side effects on human health are not established, there are clear signs that these pesticides are washed off into open water sources.

Although his agricultural produces were supposed to be marketed in order to supplement his income, his households' food security was not destabilized because his priority was to have enough food for their nutritional needs. His family's food security was paramount. He ensured that they had sufficient food for themselves. It is the surplus that was sold off to his customers. Farming was not the primary source of his income. Remember that in those days, farming was not what those seeking to make money did; most people were stuck in the antebellum days aimed at having white collar jobs. Moreover, he never did things to accumulate wealth. He maintained that Money has never made man happy, nor will it; there is nothing in its nature to produce happiness. The more of it one has, the more of it one wants. Success is not in fame and material possessions but in the lives you touched positively.

African leaders have failed to prioritize agriculture. Agriculture continues to receive more lip service than the funding and strategic thinking it desperately needs. The sector employs 70 per cent of the population but receives on average less than 8 per cent of the budget allocations in most countries. Ironically this is the sector which could turn Africa into the largest exporter of food if it received appropriate investment. Any money invested in supporting farmers should not be seen as a donation, but as the building blocks of a thriving economy of tomorrow. Unfortunately, most African governments carry out their planning to concentrate development in the cities at the expense of the majority of ordinary peasants in the rural areas. Consequently, agriculture is in steady decline. According to the statics of Uganda production, in the 1990s, agriculture's contribution to GDP averaged 37 per cent annually. This has continuously declined. In 2001/2, agriculture's contribution to GDP stood at 39.9 percent and dropped to 23.7 per cent in 2008/9. More recent figures show that the trend has not changed; with agriculture's share to GDP standing at 21.8 per cent for 2011, and at 23.4 per cent for 2012. Yet Uganda still considers herself an agricultural country!

Dr. Lwanga was normally rankled by the obvious ignorance of the people, who are indolent dependants waiting for handouts. He encouraged people to help themselves even with the minimal resources in their reach instead of waiting for help from outside so that they can pounce. "The whites say 'pray to God but row towards shore' meaning whenever someone is in problems, they can seek external assistance but they should also be able to try and help themselves. It takes just to have the will and charisma to work towards a certain goal." I recall him reprimanding them. He was not a sour critic as such but with humor he managed to capture the attention of many people. Such credentials demanded sustained intelligent combinations of brawn and strategic thinking.

Dr. Lwanga encouraged self-sustenance through communal works. To reduce unnecessary expenses and exploitation by middlemen, he propagated an arrangement of associations whereby the producers could be the consumers as well. He was naturally creative. I remember he insinuated that we could make a lot of money even by starting businesses that did not need capital to commence. He suggested the bee projects can help the youth sustain themselves without having to spend any penny. Also, mobilizing people into an association called "Musu Consumer Association". The association could register members who were interested in hunting and buying their hunted meat on regular basis. Unfortunately, he died before implementing most of his constructive ideas. Perhaps if our policy makers did more thinking first before acting, like Dr. Lwanga did, we would not have too many expensive white elephants.

Keeping professionalism and working on other projects was challenging but Dr. Lwanga had unique capabilities and dedication. He had determination to do what is right and complete a task or workload without being prompted. He had the capability to deliver work on time. Above all he was faithful to endure by being persistent in overcoming difficulties that arise in pursuit of a goal. In him was a giant that could not be deterred by opportunists and mediocre(s).

Dr. Lwanga attracted the attention of the youth. Today's young folks are incompatible. They ignore the old folks viewing them as having no swag. Dr. Lwanga associated with the youth and engaged them in serious thinking. In this way he bridged the gaps between generations. He was concerned about the success of all people. "When we seek to discover the best in others, we somehow bring out the best in ourselves"

He believed in African potentiality. "Our people must be taught the knowledge of self. Then and only then will they be able to understand others and that which surrounds them. Anyone who does not have the basic knowledge of self is considered a victim of either amnesia or unconsciousness and is not very competent. The lack of knowledge of self is a prevailing condition among our people here in Africa and other black people all over the world. Gaining the knowledge of self makes us unite into a great unity. Knowledge of self makes you take on the great virtue to learning."

Dr. Lwanga had good influence on the young folks. He challenged them: "Don't seek to be like me. Be better than me. That's the goal". He was fond of giving a stern lecture to the young people. He gave constructive criticism and shunned destructive criticism. He helped them discover what they could do best. He was not afraid to tell that you are not talented to do certain things. I know some of you consider it to be arrogant to tell someone that they don't have talent or they're pursuing the wrong dream for their life. It is like dashing ones dream. We've been wrongly taught that all it takes is a dream, and you can accomplish whatever your heart desires. Dr. Lwanga emphasized the need to discover your talent; he helped many to discover what they were born to do. He insisted that it is much easier than most people think to actually determine the real "one big thing" that we were born to accomplish with our lives. The compelling truth is that people succeed whenever they do what God created and called them to do. "Everyone is a genius. But if you judge a fish by its ability to climb a tree, it will live its whole life believing that it is stupid."

Some people are talented to do more than one thing. But you must try everything that comes your way in order to figure out what you can do best. Remember that passivity and poverty are inseparable twin brothers. The future belongs to those who see possibilities before they become obvious. Be an intelligent person that sees inaction in action, and action in inaction. "A pessimist sees the difficulty in every opportunity; an optimist sees the opportunity in every difficulty"— Winston Churchill.

Choosing the right thing to do goes hand in hand with timing. If you are aware of the importance of timing, you are likelier to attain success. But if you ignore the importance of timing, success is an uphill struggle. Timing is the state of affairs that determine whether you will be able to reach your goals or not. When the times are against you, everything you do is akin to swimming against the current. A great blessing is worthy a great sacrifice. Never give up on your goals. "When it is obvious that the goals cannot be reached, don't adjust the goals, adjust the action steps" ~ Confucius

Dr. Lwanga was so intellectually stimulating that your brain came alive every time you were with him. His counseling was ever pregnant with wisdom. I am one of many young people who benefited from his wisdom. His observations and support are still precious in my life. The best friend isn't someone who's just always there for you; it's someone who understands you a bit more than you understand yourself. The late doctor helped me to watch carefully before leaping and jumping into the gallery, saving me a lot of problems. He encouraged me to try doing what seemed to be impossible. He insinuated that, "Determination, initiative and persistence are the foundation of success. Cowards never start, the weak never finish, winners never quit—Try and fail, but don't fail to try".

He accentuated that if you want to receive the best from life, you will first have to give it your best. Life is a journey that never stops no matter how bad things seem to be. Always live life and look forward for a better tomorrow because the happiest people don't have the best of everything, they make the best of everything. What comes easy, won't always last. What will last, won't always come easy. A gem cannot be polished without a friction nor a man perfected without trials.

Dr. Lwanga's intellectual debates unlocked the retarded mindset. He liked debating issues without putting you down. He would listen to you and give you the benefit-of-doubt. He was a kind of person that would instantly make you feel important and special. He provided you an intimate space without being judgmental. I was always energized by staging a debate with him, although I was not his equal intellectually. "It is better to debate a question without settling it than to settle a question without debating it" (*Joseph Joubert*).

He was my inspiration and mentor as well. As a young man, there are some things which I was not comfortable to discuss with my dad but which I freely discussed with him. He was trusted and a man of integrity. He addressed most of my insecurities that I was plagued by during my early teenage life. He always turned my worries into a "Wow" feeling.

His favorite subject to discuss was education. He encouraged the young generation to study. I remember him drawing comparisons between the graduates of the past and the current ones. He promoted critical thinking and innovation. He insisted that knowledge is not a preserve of classroom; it is a preserve of readers and researchers. Having the education and professional background about a specific topic is a tremendous asset. But being able to come up with alternate solutions based on the creativity of your brain is also truly rewarding.

"You can't use up creativity. The more you use, the more you have"
~ Maya Angelou

School education should be nothing but mental gymnastics for the young, a means to exercise the brain like a marathon runner trains, building the endurance a mile at a time for the real "26 mile race" that will be your life. Dr. Lwanga castigated the current education system, saying it's more about cram work to pass exams rather than being investigative and research work giving room to student to think about issues and get solutions. He believed this to be the contributing factor to the scenario of having more job seekers than job creators. He wondered why every now and then the curriculum is being changed. School committees need not reinvent the wheel every time they try to improve the curriculum. He warned that the ministry of Education and the National Council for Higher Education (NCHE) had better pick interest in this matter lest students and their parents are fleeced of their hard earned money. He saw the need to groom a formidable force that can articulate from the point of research issues of national nature.

Dr. Lwanga had a magnetic way of making you feel "warm and fuzzy". He was the same at his house and on highways. Unlike some homes that are gloomy and tense, Dr. Lwanga's place was saturated with quality moments of cheerfulness coming from his heart and his attitude. He could easily strike up conversations with people. According to psychology, the most distinguishing mental qualities of a healthy male are autonomy and resourcefulness. Dr. Lwanga beat the logic of psychology because he had everything admired in life but he always wanted to be in the company of people. In real life people do not care to know how much you know until they know how much you care. He focused on loving people rather than harassing them into harmonious beings.

Dr. Lwanga's wisdom was coupled with a sense of humor. He cracked jokes as if he was a teenager. Not hopeless jokes but jokes to cruise you from your worries. He was the kind of person whom you always wanted to talk to. Whenever I talked to him my morale bounced back by leaps and bounds. He never dropped his intellectual hat even when cracking jokes. He respected others and he was respectable. I applaud him for always thinking upright in a logical manner without being verbally reckless and insensitive in the process of cracking jokes. One writer termed loose talking as "Disoriented thinking laden with verbal diarrhea".

Dr. Lwanga was such a humble man. He was never afraid to share his screw-ups. He always admitted his mistakes. He never minded to be the cautionary tale, and to laugh at himself. While he never made fun of others or laugh at other people, he was comfortable to laugh at himself. By doing so, he made it easy for us who looked up to him for leadership to openly confront and acknowledge our own weaknesses and failures that were way worse than his.

The late Dr. Lwanga was a good role model with a sense of humor. He enjoyed life and made it enjoyable for others. He cracked jokes even during the last minutes of his life. I am going to share a couple of his sense of humors that never escaped my memories. When I was a teenager, there is a time when I suffered from constipation. I knocked at the window of his clinic and asked him for medicine to ease my bowl movements (for diarrhea). He responded with a sense of humor saying that somebody just walked out of his clinic suffering from diarrhea. He insinuated that this is another way of asking him to help me to be sick! After the humor, he advised me to drink more water and to change my diet on the basis that my stomach needs fiber (fiber) to function well. Green vegetables and fruits provide plenty of dietary fiber. This fiber helps the contents of the bowels to move smoothly along. That way you get to visit the toilet at the normal rate (1-2 times a day), and passing soft stool.

I had a girlfriend who was a Munyankole by tribe. One day I was in romantic mood with my girlfriend in the late hours of the night and she was bitten by a snake. I took advantage of the moon light to kill the snake. After which, I ran to Dr. Lwanga's house to seek medical assistance (first-aid). After I told him of the tragedy, he asked me the kind of snake involved, but I could not tell because it was night time. He dressed up, got his flash light and came with me to check on the dead creature (snake). After examining it, he concluded that it was a non-poisonous snake. But because the girl was very hysterical, he whispered to me these words: "Give her two Aspirin tablets to calm her down but don't mention to her that it is Aspirin". His prescription worked psychologically to heal the girl.

Of the 3,500 or so known species of snake—only about 600 species (or 11 percent) are venomous. Most snakes are non-poisonous, and even if they were, chances are that they do not have any venom in the fangs. Not all venomous species possess sufficiently potent enough venom to kill a human. 70 per cent of the bites are by non-venomous snakes. Another 50 per cent of these bites are described as dry bites, meaning that they do not have poison in their fangs. There are three major families of poisonous snakes; Elapidae, which includes the mamba, cobra, king cobra and the coral snake; Viperidae family, which consists of vipers; and Hydrophidae family which includes sea snakes, commonly found at sea coasts.

Snake venom consists of four broad categories of toxic components, enzymes, polypeptides, glycoproteins and low compounds of low molecular weight. They produce toxic effects by destroying or altering normal cell functioning. Elapid snake bites are neurotoxic, they damage the nervous system leading to respiratory failure caused by paralysis of the muscles that aid in breathing. Respiratory failure can subsequently lead to death. Viper snake bites are primarily vasculotoxic. This means that they damage the blood components leading to severe bleeding, thrombosis, and ultimately renal failure which is the common symptom before death. The toxicity of the venom varies from one snake specie to another, but generally fatality is dependent on the amount of venom injected into the victim, the location of the snake bite, and most importantly, the time taken by the victim to receive medical attention.

Julie Mendezona, a head zookeeper lectured to me that the most venomous snake is fatal. A bite will effectively "start shutting down the function of messages going to your brain, to your vital organs, your lungs and your heart and even your muscles," she said. "So, paralysis is usually what happens with the patient. Because it can act so fast, being a neurotoxin, that's what makes it such a deadly animal. It can kill someone within 45 minutes. There have been reports of people experiencing effects of venom within half an hour as well." Barry Martin, a veteran snake catcher identified the inland taipan, as the most poisonous creature in the world. He said that, "It's known as a "fierce snake." They [used to be] called the 'two-step snake' as when it bites you, you take two steps and you're dead." In case you are bitten by a snake it would be helpful if the snake that inflicted the wound is carried to the hospital, as this will aid the health workers to choose the most effective antidote. However it is advisable for the victim not to waste time seeking to kill the snake but to run immediately to the nearest hospital.

I am still discussing the humor of the late Dr. Lwanga. He told his humor in exiting manner, his face shinning and his body shaking with happy corpulence. Even during times of sorrow, he shared jokes that elicited laughter, lightening up the emotional atmosphere albeit momentarily. I remember asking Dr. Lwanga why we donate blood to hospitals and yet we are charged exorbitantly at the time when we need blood transfusion. He answered that there are things which money can't buy. He said that money isn't everything because there are many people out there with lots of cash who miss the essentials of life like the right group of blood and they end up dead; their money cannot save them. The main issue is not how much money you spend but that you can get your type of blood at the time when you need it.

Another sense of humor that I am going to share was connected with spiritual matters. Before I was born again, I had the religious conviction that I was heading to heaven because of my religious background. I mentioned to him in course of our discussions that I was among the chosen ones going to heaven. Dr. Lwanga replied with humor that, "You are the only person whom I know that can be cocksure that you passed the exams before the grading process". He meant that there is no need of bragging that I am destined to heaven since we are still doing the examination and the grading will take place at the judgment day.

Dr. Lwanga used lots of humor to discuss local and international politics. For example he used to call Al Gore, the former vice president of America "Gowa"—the name given to one of the types of sugarcanes in Buganda. He used humor to predict the outcomes of various elections locally and internationally. I remember that he predicted that African Americans will soon rule USA, even before the current President Obama was in limelight. Back at my home country, despite the odds, Dr. Lwanga metaphorically said he chiseled for a president from the central region. He however cautioned that nothing comes on silver plate without sacrificing. I like this quotation: "Profound strength in human unheralded hereafter can be begotten out of fear to confront the notion of demurrer, vengeance, inflation, tariffs, wars, inoculation, but also affirm all mankind with pragmatic themes and recognize those who have tried their best to enlighten others . . . ."—Ben Odeke.

There's a thin line between being sarcastic and humorous, and being down right insensitive and borderline naivety. Dr. Lwanga used humor flamboyantly to throw around words but he never engaged his mouth without engaging his brains. He aimed first before shooting rather than shooting first and aim much later. He had some etiquette training to handle himself in public as a public figure.

Psychologists say that when we regularly talk to someone who is depressed it may make us feel depressed, whereas if we talk to someone who is feeling self-confident and buoyant we are likely to feel good about ourselves. Anon made this prayer: "Give me a sense of humor, Lord, give me the grace to see a joke, to get some humor out of life, and pass it on to other folk!" Humor is good for happiness but true joy comes from God; it comes from a fulfilled heart. Happiness depends on some external factors but joy is a decision you make. And you cannot afford to entrust it with events, people or moods. A fulfilled heart has permanent joy and contagious happiness.

Dr. Lwanga was a politician. Since childhood, Dr. Lwanga says he has been a political enthusiast. Although he flirted with politics from his youthful age, it was after the liberation of Uganda by NRA that he cut his political teeth—in the local council (LC) politics. He did not seek politics as a full-time job but he dreamed of representing the downtrodden people and advance the issues pertaining to their welfare. He identified with the poor and was anxious to forcefully push for popular causes. He was like a bridge that connected the elite class and the peasant majority. He was a good mobilizer too; he had the capability of bringing the masses on board. Above all, he played clean politics.

Although he did not make it to the apex of party politics, he was elected to serve at the town and district councils. He strongly believed in democracy and the power of voting. That freedom is worth fighting for and voting for. He believed that true democracy should be practiced on principle. He admired the democracies in the developed countries where politics is played by the rules and where there is no shortcut to success. He admired political debates in developed countries when they were campaigning. Dr Lwanga was one of the finest brains this country had and there was no way any of his opponents could have beaten him in an interview or debate.

Good politicians are good communicators. Good communicators are good listeners. Dr. Lwanga would lend his ears even to the despised of the society. He was not a picky listener. Choosing whom to listen to and not to listen to is the highest level of expressing intellectual stunting and an inferiority complex. It is proper to listen to all people with a discerning heart before engaging them into arguments.

The late Dr. Lwanga was remarkably charismatic. His charismatic qualities were contiguous. He spoke with an authoritative voice and calm demeanor. People in their everyday encounters, tend automatically and continuously to synchronize with the facial expressions, voices, postures, movements, and instrumental emotional behaviors of others. When people are in a certain mood, whether elated or depressed, that mood is often communicated to others. People liked to talk to him because he was ever feeling self-confident and buoyant.

In some people, unfortunately, natural charisma quickly loses its impact. Dr. Lwanga was naturally charismatic. He was more naturally persuasive than most people I know. He was good at persuading and convincing other people to accept his suggestions. He knew how to appeal to the people's emotions without compromising the basic values. He used his charisma to determine the mood of the social encounter. Unlike some politicians who use their acerbic tongues to cower their opponents, he interacted in a civilized manner with his peers.

Dr. Lwanga did not speak to be seen but objectively to impact the people. He built and maintained great relationships with all people around him; he consistently influenced (in a good way) the people around him; he consistently made people feel better about themselves. Above all he was a man without a flawed strength of character. He was very respectful and hugely modest—virtues many of our leaders are lacking. It was very difficult not to like him. He rode on his societal perceived "neutrality" to promote his political agenda. He was initiative; I admired his level of authenticity and honesty. His greatest strength depended on his impeccable record. He was the choice of the people; the track record speaks for itself. For the same reason he never launched vigorous campaigns. His popularity did not depend on people's manipulation. Rarely have so few words created so much acrimony in the rival camps as seen in his past campaigns.

Dr. Lwanga spoke the truth in love. Politics is not for the faint hearted! I never saw him speaking with a quivering voice. He was a fearless and impetuous, a man with a strong and generous heart, but one that was also sensitive and loving. Dr. Lwanga was outspoken. He was not afraid to stir up a hornets' nest even in hostile unfavorable environment. The problem we have today are people who don't like to hear the truth, people who don't like to debate issues, and people who will take anything at face value. They are gullible enough believing all kinds of lies. The false politicians hated him for his stand for the truth. Michael Parenti once wrote, "The first atrocity, the first war crime committed in any war of aggression by the aggressors is against the truth".

Dr. Lwanga had all of the qualities of a good leader. During his short time in office, the community benefited from his steely management skills. Although he had the potentiality of acquiring the best the world could offer, he decided to live a simple life. His excellence service at the local councils became a launch pad for even loftier political ambitions. He refused to jump on bandwagon of pilfering public resources in order to accumulate unexplained wealth. It's a pity that most politicians have been compromised by brown envelopes and frequent State House dinners. One wonders who then will fight for the common man!

Dr. Lwanga was a political animal but he kept a low profile. He pursued politics as means to an end but not as an end. Although he was privileged to be political elite, he chose not to turn politics into a career. After a stellar performance at local councils he whittled down into oblivion. He decided to drop out of elections after a fractious campaign fraught with acrimony. I know the reason why he was pushed to that end. In the politics of today, any goon with a sufficient minded and muscled outfit can break into the limelight of leadership, regardless of lack of track record. Politics has degenerated into personal mud-slinging. Most of the politicians of today are opportunists, fond of smear campaigns and riding on sympathy votes. To them the great thing about winning is that there is no such a thing as a "moral victory." It is so sad that there are so many low quality politicians across the Ugandan political divide!

Dr. Lwanga chose to opt out of elective politics because he could not afford to handle the above lifestyle. He reluctantly decided to bow out of the rough and tumble of elective politics in order to avoid being at loggerhead with other politicians who would do anything to win. His knee-jerk reaction to complicated situations has always been to shake the dust rather than stick around to the bitter end. This does not mean he was feeble; on the contrary, he was a kind of person that was ready to roll and be rolled in the mud to protect what he believed. He simply melted down to a rather reluctant candidate, still "agonizing" over whether to challenge his opponents in high political office. Definitely, he was supported by the leaders of the firebrand peasants' groups in his home area. Unlike others who did not see life outside politics, he believed that even outside politics, he would be still positioned to speak for the down trodden.

The other sharp sword that cut his political career short is that the ruling party had a lot of support in his home district. President Museveni described his support in Luweero in this way, "Luweero has the 'Mecca' for NRM and so the NRM's Mecca cannot forget the ruling government". The president expected NRM to sweep all the elective posts in Luweero district where Museveni begun his guerilla war that brought his government to power. The people ignored any kind of politicking and they largely voted the pro-government candidates because they thought they were closest to Museveni—a viewpoint they held thinking that was a sure guarantee that goodies would automatically flow from State House to their village paths. It was not easy to win election in this area outside the ruling party.

The leading parties targeted the leading and popular candidates. Dr. Lwanga joined neither of them because he cared for his reputation. It is for the same reason he shunned being hoodwinked into taking on a prominent role in what he considered to be a failed regime. Dr. Lwanga rode on his societal perceived "neutrality" to promote his political agenda. He did not wobble in his position in order to win favors. He joined politics not to shine in the limelight but to speak on behalf of the oppressed. He wanted to go to parliament purposely to air out the grievances of the majority of the people. He was vocal against any injustice. He never sounded like a broken record shrouded in sycophancy. Despite of his neutrality stand, he kept friends across the political divide. One lesson we can learn from Dr. Lwanga is that while politics is a contest, it does not have to be a matter of life-and-death war, and political opponents do not have to be enemies to be destroyed. Even at his late age, grievers talked of a rising star nipped in the bud by the cruel hand of death before the country could reap from his repertoire of attributes. The country missed the contribution of a dapper, meticulous and canny political operator like him.

In Uganda, most politicians have no conscience left. The hunger for votes has turned most politicians into grumpy and disgraceful persons who cannot inspire pride. They use false accusations to tamp down enthusiasm for their opponents therefore suppressing the votes. Suppressing is acceptable practice in African democracy. The online reference Wikipedia defines it as tactics that "can range from minor 'dirty tricks' that make voting inconvenient, up to blatantly illegal activities that physically intimidate prospective voters to prevent them from casting ballots." The culprits shamelessly accuse others of the very characteristics that epitomize their personality. The political intrigues and illicit love within the parties and between different parties are most probably due to the people who are lacking in sophistication that are recruited to man campaigns.

False politicians are self-serving and self-important. They are worse than open enemies. They are like hyenas stealing from lions in the wild. They cheat and they end up fighting for the loot. They can become anything for money and instant fame. They heap praises on those who side with them and on a whim bash them when they do otherwise. They are responsible for robbing the future of Uganda. That is why most youth shun politics. They opt to be educated in leaderships and shared skills to manage public entities not politics. The devastating consequence is granting men with indecent brains power over men with decent brains.

The political maniacs propagate that it is fair to use politics to make money and to use money to buy politics. The failed politicians have a reputation of selling out. Inevitably, only those with the fattest wallets make the greatest political sense. Most politicians have accumulated wealth judging from the manner they dish out money in campaigns. I think they ought to lead by example by explaining to the nation the genesis of their humongous wealth. No wonder Napoleon said, "The surest way to remain poor is to be an honest man".

The Lwanga model will be Uganda's savior if we constantly reminded our people of the dangers of electoral bribery. The majority of the people bribed are not elites of high breed but ordinary poor Ugandans, who use ropes designed for tying goats as belts. They need to be educated that when you accept a bribe to vote someone, you will have surrendered your sovereignty and ability to hold them to account. You will also have licensed them to pillage national resources to pay themselves back. A man who cannot vote his conscience has no conscience.

Dr. Lwanga was always graceful and civil. He served faithfully when he was elected in political offices. He refused to be a sycophant at the cost of basic service delivery. He showed us the characters of a true statesman. He was a populist, good with crowds and with some noted success. His personal doctrine of immaterialism appealed to the structural edifice that was deeply rooted within peasantry utopia. Many expected him to bring dignity to the high political offices. The truth is that Dr. Lwanga hated mediocrity and being a quick thinker, he wanted things done quickly rather than cheap talking. Although by the time of his demise, he was not vying for public office, he was actively involved in politics by educating the masses how to vote. Dr. Lwanga emphasized the need of voters to analyze carefully all those vying for public office in search for quality. We need politicians who act out of convictions but not convenience like many are.

Dr. Lwanga gracefully accepted defeat and moved on with his life instead of whining over spilt milk like the sore losers. Different people react differently to defeat. Some react with negative frustration like taking on suicide missions whereas others compete at another angle (positive frustration). It is like when one is thrown into water, he/she has to struggle to survive by swimming or learning to swim. You either swim through or be drowned. Dr. Lwanga was ever positive even after losing. He was good at concealing his emotions. He played politics as a clean game with a possibility of losing and winning. A man doesn't adopt a confident posture because he knows he'll succeed. He acknowledges that failure is a likely option. When the odds of success are clearly against him, he still exudes confidence. Hitler once said "Anyone can deal with victory but only the mighty can bear defeat".

Our up-bringing affects our judgments. The major reason why Dr. Lwanga did not compromise his integrity and values is because of his home up-bring. As an adage says charity begins at home. The conservative Catholic values rubbed on him even though he was not a practicing religious person. Dr. Lwanga lived by his conscience and beliefs. I admire his courage and firmness amidst the world of hypocrisy and pretence.

We need more people with moral values to serve in offices at all levels. Corruption is on the rapid increase in Africa because of the immoral people occupying offices. In a situation where there are limited resources, we need people with clear conscience that put others first and who acknowledge that success doesn't come over night. Dr. Lwanga proved that with patience and hard work plus determination, you can beat your challenges and make it. He pointed to his own achievements that depended on nobody but himself. He said he had a lot of huddles to overcome to be what he is. Yet his past hardship did not deter him from making such a huge difference in our community. Every person without biased attitude can agree with him.

Dr. Lwanga loved local and international sports. I remember him travelling from our local trading center to distance places to watch wrestling matches and other sports. He would come back and share his experience, whether it was fun or not. It was impressing listening to him because he spoke with humor. It was as good as attending the game. He had a natural knack for pulling out the punch lines from his favorite sportsmen, making funny of them, even when they wouldn't have been interesting.

One story that never escaped my minds was when Dr. Lwanga attended the world champion wrestling match between Ali Baba from the Middle East and Black Power from Nigeria. He came home disappointed. I asked him why he was disappointed when his man won the title. He said that as much as he wanted Black Power to win, he did not expect it to be so quick. He said that the people who braved the late-night chill did not have to wait for all the set rounds of the battle to see their 'savior'—Black Power—take out his rival. He said that he went to support his man and to enjoy the game but he missed the later. When it comes to humor, the sky is the limit; Dr. Lwanga would take the moment to grab your attention. He was always current with the news concerning the best sportsmen. He was a hobbyist. A hobbyist learns a great deal about their hobby or hobbies in the process of devoting time to them.

His favorite indoor game was chess. He competed in the game on the national level. He always put his team in the prime position to contend for the championship. He liked the game and he liked to win. But he will go to the history books because his career wasn't just about winning matches; it was also about mentoring others.

Most probably, he was attracted to chess because it involves a lot of reasoning and it shapes a person's behaviors. The Chess players have the characteristics of the supreme ruler. They are normally honorable, true to their purposes of living. Killing is not the way of winning for the Chess player. No. If they want to win something, anything, it is a question of strategy. A question of the mind. Four moves could lead them to victory if they were cunning enough. Or, they could annihilate the whole army to gain victory.

The reason why the Chess players used to be the highest in the hierarchy is because of their nature. In the Masterworld, one who is familiar with the game of chess would know that the shortest game would only take four moves to checkmate the King—two moves for each side. It would require no sacrifice at all, and yet, winning is possible. It shows that when playing Chess, the most careful planning, the awareness of chances and danger, would have the highest possibility of winning.

Dr. Lwanga introduced the game to many people in our neighborhood, most notably the youth. I remember that some of the youthful characters like Kabuye, Sempala and Muyomba benefited from his training at relatively young age and some of them excelled to play at the national level. Dr. Lwanga will always be remembered in Bulemezi as a man of exemplary kindness and a man who always looked after the best interests of the game. He also promoted local indigenous indoor games like *Omweso*. Now, that Dr. Lwanga is dead, a new, living legacy for his indoor games talents is expected to emerge.

Dr. Lwanga was experienced, wise and knowledgeable in a wide range of fields including outdoor sports. Not to mention the various corporations and Board of Companies he sat on and chaired. To put it in black and white, he was a jack of all trades. Death robbed us of the promising entrepreneur and future leader. The challenge of those of us who are still living is to catch and disseminate that encyclopedic knowledge that he left with us before it disappears. T. S Eliot's quotation: "We had the experience but missed the meaning", comes to my mind as we contemplate continuing his manifesto.

Dr. Lwanga was primarily a physician. This is what he was born for and what he was qualified to do. He operated a couple of 'charity clinics' mostly in rural areas. Uganda is still predominantly rural; the 2002 census reported only about 12 per cent of the population lived in urban areas. According to the report by the Uganda National Bureau of Statistics (UBOS), women in poor households are with the highest fertility rates in the region as compared to their wealthier counterparts. The report says that women in poor households produce up to nine children compared to four produced by those who are financially well off. The survey was conducted to provide policy makers in the health sector with information to plan future interventions, especially in its health sector reform activities.

In the past turmoil and tough economic environment, the Private-Not-For-Profit (PNFP) health facilities, known to most people as missionary hospitals, lost large numbers of skilled and experienced staff, who rushed for greener pastures elsewhere. Others overcharged their clients, yet the government gave them free essential drugs through JMS. But Dr. Lwanga did the opposite in spite of his cash-starved pocket. For him to leave a formal job where he was entitled to a salary and a house (bungalow) with water and electricity and start renting a two-bed roomed house in Bombo was challenging. Starting a clinic up-country was kind of going for gambling, because in such situation you can never be sure of many things. Not many elites can choose to take the same path. As Brother J Ikuya said that, "The attitude happily chimes with the feeling of being classy and elegant by our elites who enjoy snobbery of the seclusion of utilities for themselves in an apartheid-like clasp".

Dr. Lwanga's social consciousness can be traced back in the 1970s and 1980s during the most turbulent times in the history of our country. I mean during the vicious regimes of Idi Amin and Milton Obote. The dictatorial rules featured a lot of violations of human rights. Multitudes of civilians were denied access to freedom and social justice and many others massacred in cold blood. I look behind and I cannot imagine a human being surviving in such hostile environment. I give credit to Dr. Lwanga for enduring and persevering to work in the same environment. He maintained that the grass is greener on the other side because you aren't watering your side enough.

Dr. Lwanga desired to appropriately apportion available limited resources to address the health sector. He established various clinics to take service to the peasants. He finally settled and established his clinic in my home town (Bombo). This is the very place where I grew up. It is also a historic home place of Idi Amin. As we shall see later on, most of us, our past history was shaped and influenced by the brutal regime of Idi Amin. It is impossible to discuss our past history without discussing the dictatorial regime (between 1971 and April 1979), which was due to the tyranny exercised by Idi Amin. Tyranny involves centrally-directed force; anarchy entails decentralized violence. The two processes could reinforce each other. Amin's regime involved the worst tyranny, military/police totalitarian dictatorship of the worst kind in modern history. In Uganda under Amin, the moral lights went out and norms and values cultivated over generations came abruptly to an end. The consequence of which was sheer anarchy and normative collapse. Because of the primitive arrogance of Idi Amin, Uganda relapsed into primitive barbarism.

I call Dr. Lwanga's clinics 'charity clinics' because people of all classes had access to affordable and excellence services with or without money. Dr. Lwanga was a family friend and doctor as well. We were regular customers at his clinic but I do not remember any person from our family paying a penny for his services and medicine. Yet his services delivered to us were classic. He always showed extremely courteous readiness to assist us without irritation.

I grew up during the tough times of economic war when the country was on its downward spiral. The donor countries like the US had suspended any financial aid to Uganda. This was another way to express their unwilling accomplice in the perpetuation of death and sufferings of the native people of Uganda. Ironically, the sanctions increased the suffering of the peasants rather than hurting the regime. Most local people lived in viscous cycle of poverty. The harsh economic times continued to bite so hard that for an average man to enroll his child in a good school, access good medical care and afford the most basic ingredients of life was next to impossible. Not to mention that the state of most of the government hospitals, infrastructure and schools was devastating. Apart from the occasionally visible army boots on the ground, military hardware scattered everywhere and the Migs that made jaw-dropping maneuvers in the air, leaving some people almost scampering for their dear lives, you couldn't feel that the government existed in nearly every facet of life in Uganda.

The absence of government in hospitals was noticeable in the shortage of medicine, equipments, medical doctors and personnel to attend to you, filthy wards, the total lack of order in the health sector and the nonexistence of ambulances; patients used wheelbarrows as ambulances! The surgical tables became 'death theatres'. Patients littered all over the floor due to lack of beds. The acute care wing functioning was disabled by insufficient incubators, lacking oxygen concentrators, room for the mothers with children in acute, to rest close by as well as a bed and beddings for mothers doing Kangaroo.

Most hospitals didn't store safe blood due to lack of testing kits; Refrigerators in horrible state exposing risk to anemic patients who urgently needed blood transfusion. The situation deteriorated with no intravenous fluids in the health units and the patients unable to supply them. To live or die for many Ugandans was reduced to a question of probability. These were symptoms of the failed state.

We grew up in tough times with no definite healthcare program in place. People who paid their money to go to hospitals and health centers didn't get a service commensurate with what they spent. During the time of Idi Amin, Uganda was basically a failed state. Our country lacked medicines, well remunerated health professionals, quality and well equipped health facilities. Even in the government Referral Hospitals the beds could not accommodate the inpatients because of the enormous overflows that tripled. Not to mention the inadequate staffing. Each doctor in government hospitals attended to more than one hundred patients daily. According to the director of the hospital, a doctor on a daily basis is supposed to attend to 30 patients. People lost hope in the government because there was no immediate plan to renovate the dilapidated hospitals and re-equip them.

The private clinics and hospitals were too expensive for the local man that was not engaged in operating businesses *Magendo* style to access. Such prestigious facilities were reserved for the *Mafuta Mingis* (fatty fellows) who were allowed a leeway to amass wealth and enjoy life in the most luxurious ways. To be specific, special privileges were extended to only a small coterie of military officers and government official together with their hangers-on who wallowed in stinking wealth out of their loyalty to the regime while the vast majority of our people remained condemned in penury and deprivation.

During the military regime, the government employed non-qualified human resources on merits of royalty. The situation escalated to ambiguity due to poor management in all government institutions, workers' apathy, poor remuneration and lack of utilities. There was intensive poverty at a time when material wealth increasingly proved challenging for many and made the living conditions unbearable.

The people were caught between a hard and rock place (dilemma); they could not access the modern western medicine, and, when they went for herbal medicine, the religious and educated people would ridicule them, calling it satanic because of the pagan rituals attached to it. The tragedy concerning African medicine is that everybody who picks herbs, and builds a shrine calls himself a doctor! Although some African herbs are effective in healing, the majority of the traditional healers ignorantly attach the herbs and healings to witchcraft. Witchcraft or magic if you prefer to call it are part of the lives of many Africans. However most people wholesomely believe that what is thought to be magic or intervention of the spirits is actually tricks and gimmicks to fleece people. (*Concerning traditional healers read my book 'Shaping the Society' volume II*).

I said that in the developing countries the real problem with health staffing is hemorrhage because of poor remuneration in an environment that remotely attracts new scholars and hardly motivates extant ones. During the time of Idi Amin, the poor pay coupled with bad security caused acute shortage of health personnel, which appalled us. Most obstetricians and gynecologists took off for South Africa, Canada, Europe and other countries. They left for the green pastures where they could practice their profession in peace without fear plus with good pay. Well educated professionals were lured out of the country to apparently do domestic work in countries they thought would earn better. We were left with very few experienced doctors, nurses and midwives to treat our pregnant wives, daughters and sisters. Many expecting women from outlying areas couldn't make it to the government wards; others did not see it beneficial to go there and resorted to using traditional birth attendants. There was high mortality rate in the country.

Dr. Lwanga's vision was to establish an out-patient clinic but at times it served as a maternity ward. He ended up helping expecting women to deliver and save them from the excruciating labor pains. Dr. Lwanga in this way lent a hand in curbing the high infant and maternal mortality. All of the poor people in my neighborhood and far away turned to Dr. Lwanga for help. His clinic became a bigger health facility (in our catchment area) providing obstetrics, surgeons and laboratory services and etc. Dr. Lwanga's story is not unique in a situation where the doctor to patient ratio is beyond the expected average. These conditions largely sum up the story of health services in the rural areas—from the doctors to midwives, they all grapple with the same kind of predicament as they execute their professional duties across the country.

Dr. Lwanga handled patients from all disciplines of medicine. He said that, it is holistic so every case is new and challenging. Given the nature and critical condition of most of the patients, some cases were critical within a thin line between life and death. Dr. Lwanga was gifted because he had a clean record of treating patients. Most of his clients were convinced that they would be healed if only he touched them.

I asked him the reason behind his success. He admitted that doctors do not have all the answers to people's illnesses. However, they have responsibility to save life. Therefore saving life is his priority. In case things go wrong, he consults other doctors and get together with his team to do an evaluation and establish if there is something else they could have done to save the person or if it was beyond their control. He said that death should be due to natural causes rather than negligence. He gets tormented whenever a person dies when there was an opportunity to save that life.

He believed that there is no Mecca for medicine. The best surgeon in the world can only prolong life. This is what they were trained to do. It is important for any physician to make quick assessment and judgment. He said that quite often there are cases which are beyond his control. He makes quick judgment to send those patients to Intensive Care Units or other professional specialists in that area rather than wasting the patients' time and money.

Dr. Lwanga emphasized that successful treatment depends on the information supplied by the patient. It becomes challenging when some patients fail to explain their illness. With this they end up getting treatment that is not appropriate. Doctors know a lot about a lot of things, but they don't always know everything about you or what is best for you. Providing information to your doctor and other care providers can improve your care. Talking with your doctor builds trust and leads to better results, quality, safety, and satisfaction. He said that not all people trust doctors. But he is privileged because all of his clients have confidence to open up to him. With such openness they can disclose any information without fear. As one doctor said that, "Confidentiality is a very strong human rights principle that should only be ignored in uniquely specific circumstances".

Spiritually, we encourage people not to keep on citing the past because it is of no relevance to the future. But it is not the case with health care. According to Dr. Lwanga, any Doctor worth the qualification must know (diagnose) the patient's illness by looking into his/her past so that he can treat the patient (future) with the right medicine. He insinuated that doctors and patients ought to have a mutual relationship if patients are to get good services since 75 per cent of the diagnosis is made from the history of the patient, through effective communication.

It is easy to treat a patient that believes in his physician. He gave the example of one patient who had a deep cut on his small toe and lost his nail. He prescribed to him aspirin but the patient ignored it because it was not a spectacular treatment; he expected injections. The situation deteriorated forcing him to refer the patient to Mulago hospital, only to be given the same prescription. He reluctantly took it and the situation improved within the following weeks. People should stop being villagic because doctors know which will cure your sickness better and faster.

I believe that many other reasons contributed to Dr. Lwanga's success in particular his experience and his positive attitude. Most doctors become irritated after working long hours (overworked) and also have personal problems. Not to mention that some clients are often rude and bossy making it difficult for doctors to attend to them appropriately. But Dr. Lwanga's attitude towards his clients was ever appealing regardless of the fatigue. The things doctors say to the patients can have serious impact on the patients. "We are taught that even an unconscious patient can hear so we should mind what we say when around them because what we say might encourage or discourage them from fighting to heal".

The fact that Children form a big chunk of clients in rural areas cannot be ignored. The quality of relationship between mothers, who are usually the primary careers, careers and nursing and medical staff is central to the process of healing and their experience of coping with chronic childhood illness. Dr. Lwanga was open and accessible to all his clients. The way he communicated with families was therapeutic in nature adding quality to his services. He gave proper explanation on what tests he did on the patient and explained how it would benefit the patient. He identified with the pain of his clients who had terminal sicknesses allowing them coming to terms with the uncertainty of their deteriorating conditions.

Study shows that the relationship between those living with chronic illness and the doctor may influence the degree of healing. The way the medical staffs communicate with families has been identified as one of the mediating processes through which quality service is determined. Of course I am talking about terminal sicknesses like cancer with predictable trajectory. Once cancer reaches the terminal phase, the slope of the trajectory shifts from a relatively stable course to one of rapid decline. At the same time, there is a marked change in the treatment plan from one of active treatment to comfort care or end-of-life care.

As a physician, Dr. Lwanga had much to offer but he realized that he could give nothing better than himself. This reminds me of Zig Ziglar's quotation: "If you aim at nothing, you will hit it every time. Attitude, not aptitude, determines altitude. Among the things you can give and still keep are your word, a smile and a grateful heart. There are no traffic jams on the extra mile. Be grateful. Believe. Try," Ziglar said over and over again.

Dr. Lwanga did not trespass into a career but he was naturally created to be a doctor. Dr. Lwanga loved and enjoyed his work. According to experts, when you are choosing a business you should choose what you love doing; that is, what rhymes well with your talents, passions and purpose in life. This is most probably where God is calling you to serve. Choosing the right business is the first step to success.

Dr. Lwanga was a very good administrator. Inside his clinic it was business as usual; he darted in and out of his office (the examination room) to supervise his nurses like a choir master putting his charges into perfect shape before a big concert. I learnt from him to balance and realize when I need to give my staff lee-way and when to try a little bit of micro-managing.

His medical crew consisted of impressive employers with great attitude and interpersonal skills. He had a couple of nurses in his clinic whose core task was to keep the clients happy through amazing customer service and service delivery. He believed in perfection and high quality, and he was never satisfied till his clients were happy. He empowered his staff such that they were able to develop and represent the best interests of the clients. They worked together to set up a medical facility to reckon with in the town.

Dr. Lwanga was not materialistic. What mattered to him is leaving behind a good name rather than properties and a fat bank account. He charged the most reasonable fees in town and made sure the services to his clients were premier class! Therefore he had the moral authority to preach frugality, given his record. Although his clinics were commenced in form of business entrepreneurship, he invested shoves in charity. According to the economists, investing is a venture no person should avoid in the process of pursuing wealth. Well studied entrepreneurship challenges the misconception of capital in form of money and assets. They consider the biggest capital one ought to have is his head and brains.

Dr. Lwanga was primarily focused on delivering services rather than making profits; it was pay-as-you-can. His philosophy was built around the concept that you can have everything in life you want if you will just help enough other people get what they want. I actually wondered how he sustained his businesses without making profit. In economics, this kind of balance sheet would automatically call for peremptory shutdown due to losses. According to him maintaining perfect relationship with his clients was perceived as net gain. No wonder his clinics were ever congested with clients. It is his passion for the welfare of his clients and his generosity that kept his clients on their toes. It is the same thing (generosity) which his competitors lacked.

Charles Ocici says that, "Good business entrepreneurs are risk takers. Nauseating though a cliché it may sound, it still stands out as the cardinal trait anybody venturing into business at any time and level must possess. It takes courage, resilience and at times tear, but, "You must be ready to do what you have not done before from the start of business till forever".

All prospective business men have to know is that business is all about taking risks. But they have to calculate the risks very carefully otherwise it (risk taking) can be very dangerous and a big problem. They should not go for all risky ventures, but have to calculate before they venture. Risks come in different colors. The bottom line is—you have to break the egg to make an omelet. It could be recruiting staff whose ulterior motives you are oblivious of. It might take the form of sinking your first profits to establishing another branch or taking a perilous path into the jungle of partnerships.

Dr. Lwanga operated his clinics in unfavorable conditions as we shall see in the coming chapters. In order to get acquainted with the tough economic situation in which Dr. Lwanga operated, we are going to look at the testimony in Vali Jamal's book on 'Uganda Asians features'. His family delivered medical services at the same time and in the same areas where Dr. Lwanga had his clinics. His father, Dr. Mukhtar Ahmad, is one of the Asians who remained in Uganda when the Asian were expelled by the former President Idi Amin in 1972. The president recognized that his services to the country were far more useful than his citizenship, and exempted him. His wife is currently a social organizer whose contribution has been commended by even the First Lady Janet Museveni, and their children are doing as much in US and Pakistan.

Based on a number of interviews and written submissions in September and November 2007, Dr. Lal Din Ahmad said that his father came to Uganda in 1926 and embarked on his medical practices almost immediately. They were a medical family, with two of his brothers and a sister qualifying as doctors. They practiced in the jungles of Bulemezi. They spent most of their time treating patients in nearby villages (Bombo, Nandere, Goma, Wobulenzi, Luweero and Nakasongola). These are all very familiar places to me. He say that, "Most patients I treated gratis as they were simply too poor. Malaria was very prevalent then, but also dudus (earth worms) that bore into your skin and caused you acute discomfort. In the absence of the doctor, the houseboy would know how to dig in with a needle that had been sterilized over a flame!" Dr. Mukhtar Ahmad died last November (*Daily Monitor Sept. 27th 2012*).

We need more doctors to get involved in activities such as contributing to the humanitarian causes like helping the poor, orphans and the widows. They can work under different missionary groups, even if it is not necessarily a Church group, this would qualify as a major feather in the hat of any man who wishes to make an impact. The appeal is not limited to doctors only. Everybody can contribute to the development of our communities by joining hands with charity organizations like Habitat for Humanity, an international charity going around the country constructing houses for needy communities. One resource such organizations can never get enough of is labor. There are young men out there who have taken their university breaks to go upcountry to build houses. Even without the promise of payment, such activities have been known to help build lasting friendships, not to mention strong résumé.

Humanitarian workers are humble but their achievements are not. Africa accounts for 10 million of the 26 million people worldwide who were driven from their homes by conflict or human rights-related violence in 2011. Last year alone the humanitarian teams of the European Commission have touched the lives of 140 million people affected by conflicts and disasters around the world. It is to these teams and to our fellow European citizens who help fund their work we owe a debt of gratitude.

Getting your children involved with charitable activities is a great way to help them learn important values and feel good about themselves and their world. Psychologist Eileen Kennedy-Moore, co-author of Smart Parenting For Smart Kids says that, "Volunteering and charity work . . . (allows) them to experience a 'helper's high' [while] fostering genuine self-esteem, caring, and responsibility for the greater community."

For those of you who are believers, God calls you to serve wherever you are. Your priority should be to manifest the love of Christ in everything you do. A believer serves with conviction that he or she is saved rather than to become saved. We serve God from a point of salvation rather than towards salvation. Serving is manifested fruit of a saved person. If there is something we strive for, it is to be as benevolent and giving as our fathers of the Christian faith were. They had the ability to see the good in everyone they encountered, and they trusted in God who created humanity for provision. The world is eagerly waiting to witness the same values in action.

The spirit of servant-hood is a spirit of self-denial. Materialism is the giant killer that is chocking the spirit of servant-hood. Materialism is the cancer eating up our people causing all kinds of corruptions. In an era where materialism and all other isms that come with the territory seem to rule the lives of the modern man, most doctors, increasingly are not concerned with the legacy they would like to leave. The business of clinics have grown into what nearly all other businesses grow into, a trade where many doctors stick so many straws at different points of their clients, siphoning off their share wherever they can.

In the materialistic culture, people give in to the free-for-all. After all everyone is doing it, they say. Others dishonestly grab whatever they need regardless of the authentic means of acquiring them in bid to reach the highest of the heights even when it means abandoning their moral compass and diving into the cesspit. Intriguingly, they might scrap the bottom of the barrel, but yet have many more admirers to inspire with their material gains like houses and fleets of cars. Such regard them as their heroes!

Health Care is the first Casualty of Africa's chaos:

The Government's responsibility to protect and advance the interests of society includes the delivery of high-quality healthcare. Nobody should be denied quality healthcare because it is the right of every citizen. Unfortunately in most African states health-care is already in sorry state. We have managed to train many doctors but our healthcare is pathetic.

The well managed and prosperous economy should contribute to high quality healthcare. Prosperity for all means good health for all. For example in America, because the market alone cannot ensure all Americans' access to quality health care, the government preserves the interests of its citizens by supplementing the market where there are gaps and regulating the market where there is inefficiency or unfairness. Healthcare and security are the two most important aspects which American citizens consider in general elections.

The ultimate goal of achieving high quality healthcare will require strong partnerships among the sister states of Africa and the commitment of the individual African governments. Translating general principles regarding the appropriate role of government into specific actions within a rapidly changing, decentralized delivery system will require the combined efforts of the public and private sectors.

We need to borrow a leaf from the developed countries like United States that have the best healthcare systems. A framework is provided for understanding the 10 roles that government plays in improving health care quality and safety in the United States. Examples of proposed federal actions to reduce medical errors and enhance patient safety are provided to illustrate the 10 roles: (1) purchase health care, (2) provide health care, (3) ensure access to quality care for vulnerable populations, (4) regulate health care markets, (5) support acquisition of new knowledge, (6) develop and evaluate health technologies and practices, (7) monitor health care quality, (8) inform health care decision makers, (9) develop the health care workforce, and (10) convene stakeholders from across the health care system.

Good healthcare involves using the nation's resources effectively. The challenges to achieving a good health-care system are numerous, as evidenced by the many paths to an amicable solution. A number of long-term initiatives, therefore, need to be undertaken to build an efficient health system for Africa. Building capacity of personnel, rehabilitation of the physical infrastructure, better record-keeping and provision of timely information, equipping of health facilities and ensuring access to medicines are the key. We can work within our limitations. If at all we used our resources faithfully, we could get so much done with so little over here. But we must do things the right way.

All people must have access to quality health-care including access to medicine. Even good economies in Africa are lacking quality healthcare. For example Dr. Theobald Hategekimana revealed that despite Rwanda's progress in the medical sector, there is only one qualified surgeon in the country of more than 11 million people. Dr Hategekimana is a urologist and director of University Central Hospital of Kigali (CHUK). He goes on to say that there are only three specialists who also handle cases that include urology and only two neurosurgeons. Current statistics show that the country has only 725 medical doctors making the ratio one doctor to 16,000 patients. This is above the World Health Organisation (WHO) recommendation of at least a doctor to 10,000 patients. (*Daily Monitor Oct. 3, 2013*).

Life begins at conception. There is a need to give quality health care to all people including the pregnant mothers and a fetus. In Uganda, maternal and infant mortality and morbidity although declining, remain relatively high. The current maternal mortality rate of 438 per 100,000 live births translates to about 6,000 women dying every year due to pregnancy-related causes. At the moment, a Ugandan midwife delivers between 350-500 babies per year, twice the 175 recommended by the World Health Organization. The 2012 study shows that 106 infants die every day before making one month, while another 41 die on the day they are born. About 39,000 children under the age of five die annually in Uganda within the first 28 days of life, a study by Save the Children has revealed.

According to the United Nations Population Fund (UNFPA) country representative, Esperance Fundira, abortion is the fourth killer of women in Uganda and a total of 297,000 abortions are done every year. About 7,200 mothers die yearly and more than 144,000 survive death but develop serious complication in the process of giving life including obstetrics fistula. Fundira said out of these 140,000 occurred among girls between the ages of 15 and 24. At least 2,464 women are dying in Ugandan from cervical cancer annually. Over 3,577 more are diagnosed with the disease that has become Uganda's leading killer of women. People most at risk of cervical cancer are those who start sexual activity early and those with multiple sexual partners.

There is a need to recruit more personnel in all health centers. I mean more medical officers, midwives, anesthetics, clinical officers, senior nursing officers, health inspectors, laboratory technicians and assistants. Rt. Hon Zziwa made the following remarks when she officiated over the unveiling of the AAR Arusha Health Centre this year: "I am aware that currently, the doctor to patient ratio in the East African Community is low. In the United Republic of Tanzania for example, the figure is pegged at 1:25,000 which is way too low and falls short of the World Health Organisation's (WHO) recommended guidelines of 1:1000 by the year 2015. The entire region has similar challenges."

We are heading nowhere in the modern world without healthy populations. Sadly, the healthcare including healthcare technology has had difficulties rising above the fray. The reality is that growing health technology is symbiotic with improving health. There are a number of problems facing the rise of healthcare technology in the developing world. For one, problems like government mistrust, lack of reliable power and poor infrastructure get in the way of innovation, especially when regarding modern healthcare technology. The lack of development among African nations forces them to import much technology, which then leads to a lack of expertise, spare parts and required consumables for repair of these machines.

The reason we have failed states in Africa is because of the corruption and incompetence of African leaders. Incompetence plus mismanagement equals to underdevelopment, diseases, ignorance and poverty. At least 200,000 Ugandans are affected by various types of disasters each year, the World Bank has said. According to the World Bank, the high incidence of disasters occurring in Uganda every year has a negative impact on both the economy and people. The mess in Healthcare like any other government sustained programs stem from poor funding from Government. The outcome is increased infant mortality, child morbidity, incidence of diseases like malaria, etc.

It is common knowledge that malaria is the number one killer disease in Uganda. Malaria is caused by a parasite carried in the saliva of mosquitoes and kills hundreds of thousands of people a year, mainly babies and children under the age of five in Africa. According to WHO data, the disease infected around 216 million people in 2010, killing around 655,000 of them. Robust figures are, however, hard to establish and other health experts say the annual malaria death toll could be double that.

Ondoa agrees that malaria remains one of the greatest public health problems in Uganda. She says that in terms of the burden to our health system, clinically diagnosed malaria is the leading cause of morbidity and mortality, accounting for approximately 30-50% of outpatient visits at health facilities, 15-20 of all hospital admissions, and 9-14% of all inpatient deaths.

Prevention is better than cure but the government has so far not made much effort to protect its citizens against these killer insects, despite the existence of chemicals like DDT that can decimate them. The WHO's World Malaria Report, published on Monday, found the number of long-lasting insecticide-treated mosquito nets delivered to endemic countries in sub-Saharan Africa dropped from 145 million in 2010 to an estimated 66 million in 2012. This means that many households will be unable to replace existing bed nets when required, exposing more people to the potentially deadly disease.

The Nodding disease terrorizing the people of Acholi is preventable by spraying the Nodding Syndrome areas in Acholi Sub-region to kill and combat the multiplication of black flies, which are partly suspected to be behind the mysterious disease. Embracing chemical aerial spraying of the black flies could be very effective in combating the disease.

It is intriguing and shameful that in this century of digital era our people are still being terrorized with bugs like cockroaches, bedbugs and jiggers. Many parts of Busoga have been colonized by the same bugs. Today, the jiggers have jumped Lake Victoria to extend their territory by attacking the Baganda in Mpigi as I read of recent. In Nyeri (the home district of some of Kenya's leading middle class including President Kibaki) jiggers are such a big problem; so much to the extent that the man who has spearheaded the fight against those jiggers has gained international recognition and was recently moving around several countries trying to drum up support for the crusade against jiggers. Do we really need foreign interventions to get rid of jiggers? I think it takes just massive education on hygiene in order to eradicate the jiggers.

The outbreak of strange new diseases emerging today could have been prevented simply by improving on the living conditions of the people, limiting deforestation and encroaching on wild life reservoirs. According to the Centers for Disease Control and Prevention (CDC), the Old World fruit bats of the family Pteropodidae, are considered to be natural hosts for the Ebola, Marburg and Sars viruses that can be spread to human beings. Dr. Joaquim Saweka, WHO Country Representative to Uganda, believes increased exposure of humans to secretions from virus hosts like bats and monkeys makes us more susceptible to Ebola. "In some areas, people eat fruits and foods that have already been part-eaten by bats, which is very dangerous".

In their study published in Nature Communications, the researchers say the fruit bat is a reservoir for Lagos bat virus and henipaviruses, also considered deadly if transmitted to humans. They also say another disease similar to rabies is widespread in a species of fruit bat found in Africa. Bats have also been implicated in the spread of the deadly Mers virus. The researchers tested more than 2,000 bats. They found that 42 per cent were harboring henipaviruses, which can be deadly if they spread to humans, particularly in the form of the Hendra virus.

Dr. Denis Lwamafa, commissioner for National Disease Control in the ministry of Health, blames the depletion of wild animals' habitats, such as forests, for the outbreaks. "Where we have had Ebola, the monkeys were coming into people's homes and sharing food, and the bats were even staying in some houses after their habitats were destroyed and bushes cleared for farming in the cases of Luwero, Kibaale, and Bundibugyo, among other areas." Dr. Lwamafa says. Our forests are destroyed mainly by cutting down trees and use them for cooking (firewood\charcoal). We can save our forests by embracing Biogas energy. It is not only used for cooking, it is also used to light up homes.

Dr Makumbi, the head of disease surveillance department at the Ministry of Health has warned that Uganda will continue experiencing deadly hemorrhagic fevers like Ebola, Marburg because it is located in a hot spot for killer viruses. The country's vulnerability is facilitated by the geographical location, climate change, environmental degradation and encroachment on forest cover as well as the country's porous borders. "We are in a major hot spot where there is a pool of new and old viruses multiplying at a terrific speed. The climate change has also facilitated the multiplication of these viruses and this makes us vulnerable to outbreaks of this nature".

Most African countries like Uganda have no adequate strategies for infection prevention and control at the community and health facility level. The government should step in to restrict the culture of frequently interaction between animal reservoirs and humans. More education is needed regarding the eating habits of the natives. The report by the UN Food and Agriculture Organization says that eating insects could be more beneficial than eating wild animals. It could help boost nutrition and reduce pollution. The ammonia emissions associated with insect-rearing are far lower than those linked to conventional livestock such as pigs, says the report. Insects are regularly eaten by many of the world's population, but the thought may seem shocking to many Westerners.

Meningitis causes an inflammation of the membranes that protect the spine and brain. It can cause deafness or paralysis and can be life-threatening. Several species of bacteria can cause the disease, but the most prevalent strain is called serogroup A. An outbreak in 14 African countries in 2009 caused more than 88,000 suspected cases and at least 5,000 suspected deaths.

A new vaccine being rolled out in the "meningitis belt" that stretches across north-central Africa has reduced cases of the potentially fatal disease by 94 percent, doctors reported on Thursday in The Lancet. Researchers monitored the spread of type A meningococcal disease in Chad after the new vaccine, MenAfriVac, had been approved by world health watchdogs in 2010. Three regions of Chad where around 1.8 million people had been vaccinated by December 2011 were compared with the rest of the country where the vaccine had yet to be introduced. In the vaccinated regions, around 2.5 cases of meningitis of any kind, and none of meningitis A, were recorded per 100,000 people, compared to more than 43 cases per 100,000 in the unvaccinated areas, a fall in incidence of 94 percent. The risk of transmitting the germ was reduced by 98 percent among those who had been vaccinated, according to throat swabs and other evidence.

Cholera is an acute, diarrheal illness caused by infection of the intestine with the bacterium Vibrio cholerae. Cholera causes a large amount of watery diarrhea. Cholera has been very rare in industrialized nations for the last 100 years; however, the disease is still common today in other parts of the world in particular Africa. Poor sanitation is the major cause of the epidemic. For example lacking of proper use of toilets. In Uganda, 10 out of every 100 homes have no toilets. New Vision reported that In Uganda the beaches around Lake Victoria have turned into large toilets: "Kakyanga Island in Lake Victoria is littered with human waste in a manner similar to commuter taxis parked in Kampala's Old Park. I had never seen such widespread open defecation. I held my nose as questions boggled my mind." (*New Vision Apr 25, 2013*). Another shocking story appeared in one of our daily newspapers indicated that 1, 200 patients of Princes Diana Memorial Health Centre lV in Soroti district are using polythene bags to dispose off their droppings (faeces) because the facility's only surviving pit latrine is filled up. (*Red Pepper October 4, 2013*).

Typhoid fever is a bacterial infection that can develop after a person eats or drinks contaminated food, milk, or water. Outbreaks of typhoid fever sometimes occur when drinking water becomes contaminated with sewage. Symptoms of typhoid fever include fever, chills, cough, red rash on the abdomen and watery diarrhea. Some of the public referral facilities in Africa have been grappling with numerous challenges, including lack of water and better equipment. In Uganda, the water systems at some hospitals have been dysfunctional and other water pumping plants were disconnected from electricity power supply.

HIV virus was transferred from animals (chimpanzee, baboons and monkeys) to people. It is believed that the first cases of HIV appeared in the Congo basin where a vaccine against Polio (when using the bone marrow of chimpanzee) was tested for the first time. African leaders should not allow Africans to be used as guinea pigs by the Western countries to test their new drugs. HIV is a retrovirus that causes AIDS by infecting helper T cells of the immune system. The most common serotype, HIV-1, is distributed worldwide, while HIV-2 is primarily confined to West Africa. When HIV enters the blood of a new host, it takes three to 12 weeks for the body to develop antibodies against it, which can then be detected by the HIV test you have been doing. This is the so-called window period, during which someone who is infected may test HIV-negative and yet he or she has HIV, yet he or she can infect others. HIV can, however, be detected during this period by using another test known as the RNA-PCR test, but not all testing centers can do this test.

In the past years, Uganda was doing well in fighting Aids. Until recently, HIV prevalence rates had stagnated at 6.4%. The UN Aids indicator survey figures for 2011 show that HIV prevalence among adults has risen from 6.4% five years before to 7.3%. Ministry of Health figures indicate that new infections rose by 11.5% from 115,775 in 2007/8 to 128,980 in 2010/11. With questions being raised as to where Uganda went wrong, the blame game is on.

I applaud the government of Uganda for its commitment to fight AIDS but still more education is required concerning the subject. Also behavioral and biomedical interventions must be implemented in such a sufficient scale that they must have impact. In Uganda most hospitals lack CD4 machines. We have our own factories manufacturing ARVs. But it seems that we are losing the battle against AIDS due to peddled immorality and massive corruption. In dealing with behavioral change patterns we need more behavioral therapies and more evangelism. About 85% of Ugandans confess to be baptized Christians but the majority of them are not transformed, converted and committed to the Christian faith. They have the head knowledge of God religiously but without experiencing spiritual transformation and conversion. People need to be educated that abstinence is the best cure for HIV. Thank God for Jennet Museveni for sticking to the same message of abstinence. Without adhering to morality we risk more scourge of AIDS. The devastating consequence is because of our failure to prevent and actively rally against permissiveness (promiscuity, homosexuality, pornography, kimansulo, prostitution) and witchcraft that now pervade our country.

The myth that circumcision prevents contracting the virus should be ironed out. President Museveni put it in good words, "When you are circumcised, you don't become metallic and therefore immune to HIV/AIDS." People should be educated instead of being forced to control themselves. The recent proposal by the government to carry out mandatory testing has stoked fierce controversy, in a country where, despite being a leading killer, HIV/Aids remains a largely private matter, even rarely cited in cause-of-death conversations.

There is a need to control other diseases like TB which is the leading cause of death among people living with HIV in Africa. We need to import the Tuberculosis (TB) diagnosis equipments which offer a significant advance in the capacity of TB and HIV programs to diagnose TB quickly and help reduce its transmission. The equipment includes a Cepheid Xpert, an advanced device that can detect mycobacterium, the organism that causes tuberculosis, directly from sputum in less than two hours. An estimated 14 million people, mainly young adults worldwide, are infected with active TB, according to the WHO.

According to the World Health Organization, nearly 50 million people world-wide have been infected with HIV and AIDS since the first cases of the scourge were recorded about two decades ago. There is not yet a cure but there is medicine capable of extending life. A recent study has shown that preventing HIV infection among sero-discordant couples has been successfully attained by consistently following their anti-retroviral pre-exposure prohpylaxis commonly known as PreP. However, PreP may not work in groups where one of the partners is involved in extra marital affairs or in polygamous marriages. People need to be educated concerning the proper use of ARVs and their side effects. According to HRSA Care Action (August 2008), oral health is critical to an individual's overall health, but antiretroviral drugs can contribute to mouth dryness and tooth decay. Also, there reports of people who were allegedly treated with a combination of expired Nevarapine, Davodine and Namovadine tablets, causing their body immunities to weaken. Polio vaccination has registered noticeable success.

Polio vaccination has registered noticeable success. Two polio vaccines are used throughout the world to combat poliomyelitis (or polio). The first was developed by Jonas Salk and first tested in 1952. Announced to the world by Salk on April 12, 1955, it consists of an injected dose of inactivated (dead) poliovirus. An oral vaccine was developed by Albert Sabin using attenuated poliovirus. The United Nations World Health Organization (WHO) claims that there is an urgent need to improve vaccination supplies and to better communicate the health benefits provided by vaccines, noting that up to 22 million children are not being immunized against preventable diseases. Vaccination averts an estimated 2-3 million deaths every year, according to UN figures, from preventable diseases such as diphtheria, measles, whooping cough, pneumonia, polio rotavirus, diarrhea, rubella and tetanus.

Trachoma is the leading infectious cause of blindness, and also one of the neglected tropical diseases. Health minister, Dr Ruhakana Rugunda has said at least eight million Ugandans are at risk of suffering from Trachoma.

Africa's major problem is corruption. We lost decency and dignity. Dignity is like virginity, once lost, it can never be regained. The culprits progressively steal without any sense of shame. The money that was supposed to be invested into researches, education and medications acquired legs and walked into the wallets of the corrupt officials; the same legs should be amputated, if at all there is any hope of doing better.

Statisticians calculated the mortality rate for the world to be roughly at .833 percent. It means that 1 out of every 113 people died last year. Statics shows that over 153, 000 people die every day in the world. 1.78 deaths per second. 107 deaths per minute. 6390 death per hour. 56.0 million death per year. Of course these numbers are based on inductive generalization and therefore are not reliable. World health organization (WHO) estimates that Non communicable diseases (NCDs) were responsible for 63 percent of the deaths in 2008 and 80 percent of these deaths occurred in low and middle-income countries including Uganda. About 1,064, 000 million people are estimated to have died of NCDs in 2010 alone. According to the recent studies by the ministry of health in Uganda, an estimated 43% of the deaths in the country are caused by NCDs due to poor lifestyles (poverty). It is pathetic, that the people that drink alcohol from morning to sunset do it out of frustration because they have been robbed of their future and ambitions.

In Uganda it is estimated that about 2 million people live with diabetes, unfortunately 80 percent of these are not aware and will present later with serious complications like blindness, impotence and strokes among others. A strong law should be enacted to control the consumption of unhealthy foods. It will be very expensive for the government to treat such diseases, worst still losing the young population to what can be averted.

According to the United Nations Children Emergency Fund (UNICEF), Uganda is among 15 countries including Afghanistan, Angola, Burkina Faso, China, the Democratic Republic of Congo, Ethiopia, India, Indonesia, Kenya, Mali, Niger, Nigeria, Pakistan, Tanzania, which account for 53% of total episodes of diarrhea and 56% of severe episodes, and 65% of total episodes of pneumonia and 64% of severe episodes. Pneumonia is the leading cause of death in children worldwide. UNICEF says in 2011 the highest number of childhood deaths were in sub-Saharan Africa. Pneumonia is caused by a number of infectious agents, including viruses, bacteria and fungi. Streptococcus pneumonia is the most common cause of bacterial pneumonia in children, followed by Haemophilus influenzae type B (Hib). Respiratory syncytial virus is the most common viral cause of pneumonia.

According to the Country Director Water Aid, more than 10 million Ugandans consume contaminated water, putting their lives at risk from water-borne diseases like cholera an infection in the small intestine caused by the bacterium Vibrio cholera. Also skin diseases and worms.

Tapeworms: These worms are flattened like a tape measure and mainly result from eating half-cooked meat such as pork, beef and fish. Usually one may not be aware he is hosting the worms, but symptoms may include tiredness, abdominal pain, weight loss and diarrhea.

Pinworms: These commonly occur in children and are spread by close, crowded living conditions. They are transmitted through contaminated hands, surfaces or bedding and swallowing airborne eggs. The worms usually come out at night to lay eggs and deposit them around the anal opening in the skin folds. Many people with pinworms have no symptoms, however, itching around the anus at night is common as well as Irritability, loss of appetite and abdominal pain.

Hookworms: These are caused by coming into contact with soil or water where the worms reside. This parasite lives in the intestines, where it feeds on blood. Hookworms can cause severe anemia and diarrhea.

Roundworms: These are caused by coming into contact with infected soil, food or stool. Children are more susceptible because they tend to stick their fingers in the mouths without washing them first. Roundworm eggs can find their way from the intestines to other organs, causing damage.

Liver flukes: These make their home in the body where they attack the liver and make holes. They are transmitted by eating contaminated foods.

Worms can affect any one, though children are more prone because they tend to eat anything they come across. One should deworm at least once every six months. Common symptoms: Because worms usually infect the digestive system first, causing problems such as loss of appetite, stomach ache, abdominal discomfort, bloating, diarrhea, bloody stool, vomiting, constipation and gas accumulation.

The two main types of intestinal parasites are helminthes and protozoa. Helminthes are worms with many cells. Tapeworms, pinworms, and roundworms are among the most common helminthes in the developing countries. Conventional medical treatments can get rid parasites very quickly and with fewer side effects. Eat more raw garlic, pumpkin seeds, pomegranates, beets, and carrots, all of which have been used traditionally to kill parasites.

Worms have a life cycle, so they have to be killed at every stage. For instance if you kill the adults, but not the eggs, the eggs hatch and the cycle will continue. If you kill the eggs, but not the worms, they will lay more eggs, thus the vicious cycle. It is easy for every person to get rid of these parasites. Easy as it is, people shun the treatment. Even some members of parliament are deliberating in our highest legislature with worms in their stomach!

It is disturbing when our people die from the negligence of the government like lack of medicines and oxygen in hospitals. Neglecting the Intensive Care Units (ICU) has mostly affected patients of pneumonia, head injuries, kidney and heart failure. Most of the ambulances are broke down, others are hanging by stone. The hospitals cannot run them because they cannot afford fuel, tyres and maintenance.

Because healthcare is not cheap many ordinary people have found themselves in critical health conditions that they cannot manage financially. These conditions include the rising cases of heart complications or cancer, which are very expensive to manage. Essential things have turned out to be luxurious for ordinary peasants. For example very few people can afford to go to the gym to exercise. Visceral fat, which is what causes a pot belly even in thin people, is far more menacing because the fat is packed in-between the inner organs and is strongly linked to heart disease. Genetics, a high-fat diet and a sedentary lifestyle all contribute to visceral fat.

Mental health is one of the components in the health service delivery that is given less attention at all levels. There is by far less trained health workers compared to the demand. In Uganda, currently the country has only 30 psychiatric specialists and the majority of them are based in Kampala. There are increased mental cases with less Psychological facilities. Dr. Fred Kigozi, the director Butabika Mental Referral Hospital in Uganda says that, "Mental health is still underfunded because we have failed as stakeholders to put it in the mainstream health care system", he said. Butabika hospital alone receives a total of 52,000 general patients a year and between 30,000-35,000 regular clients per year. The majority of the patients end up in the shrines of the witchdoctors. Some of the commonest medical conditions that could cause disability are epilepsy, mental retardation and cerebral palsy. It is estimated that there are over one million disabled children in the country. The World Health Organisation estimates that the figures of people with disabilities could be double and perhaps even rise to 10%.

Most deaths in Africa could be averted. For example Kwashiorkor, a childhood disease of protein-calorie malnutrition that is, for the most part an economic disease. Indelible Skelton images of malnutrition kids in Africa flash on the front pages of our screens. Little kids scraping the bottom of saucepans, a futile hunt for morsels of food. It is impossible to capture in words the indictment that the images pass on our society. Such images are boring until one discovers that the lifestyles of the rulers have a direct bearing on the survival of African children.

Consider the preventable tragedies like shortage of electricity in hospitals. The State Minister for Health Dr. Elioda Tumwesigye and MPs were recently shocked to find midwives at Kiryandongo Hospital using a charcoal stove to sterilize delivery and surgical equipment for use in the labour ward. The electrical autoclave machine containing boiling water, delivery scissors, forceps, cord clamps and retractors was placed over a charcoal stove due to lack of gas and electricity needed to heat it. (*New Vision, Dec. 28, 2013*).

The scourge of lightning is inflicting terrible damage in terms of lives and property to various regions of Africa. Yet prevention costs are minimal with traditional lightning protection. Copper or other conductive rods, called "air terminals" provide set points that terminate a lightning strike, and then carry the current safely to the ground through a combination of grounding cable, wire and clamps connected to ground rods.

In Uganda, according to the Police Bi-Annual Traffic Accident Report 2012, some 1,500 people have been killed in the first six months of this year due to road accidents. The deaths statistic includes 578 pedestrians. According to the report, road traffic accident deaths were highest in March and lowest in June. The total number of accidents amounted to 10,261, of which 1,266 were fatal, 4,787 serious, and 4,208 were minor cases. We have many accidents because our roads are in sorry state. Nearly 75% of Uganda's 20,000 km road network is in dire need of refurbishment; it is partly contributing to the 2,500 lives lost in road carnage annually. The Government needs to undertake a new contracting mechanism to keep roads in good condition.

The national road network has been in steady decay in urban and rural areas. There is a need to allocate local contracts to companies to maintain paved/ tarmac roads as well as undertake periodic maintenance of murrum ones. Successful bidders should be under contractual obligations to ensure a full-time presence on the allotted roads, sweeping, clearing bushes, opening-up drainages and re-graveling roads during the contract period.

There are no bulbs in the street lights, no signposts and no reflectors. Some of these things are regularly installed and stolen. Once such social services come our way, it's incumbent on us to guard them jealously. It's a civil obligation to do so. Any public property stolen as we watch is like shooting ourselves in the foot because we are all losers. The public has a right to good infrastructure; road maintenance should not be portrayed as a reward conferred in exchange for loyalty to the ruling party.

Improving road safety has to start with the individual. Attitudinal shifts are required to inculcate a culture of safe road usage. We have the ability to stop the road carnage if there are tough laws in place and if people are willing to comply. The government cannot afford to cherry pick on certain offences, while ignoring others. Intriguingly, in Uganda, speed governors policy died a natural death, safety belts policy went to the limbo just to mention a few things that need to be implemented by the laws. Road safety campaigns are launched only after a fatal accident and there after ignored.

Most accidents are caused by motor bikes (*bodabodas*), mini-bus taxis, buses and trailers. There are reckless drivers out there putting the lives of innocent people at risk. For example there are bus drivers who switch jobs after being involved in bad driving incidents. We need to subject these drivers to rigorous tests and whoever is found to have abused drugs should never be licensed to drive passengers. Why doesn't police keep records of bad drivers and even blacklist some of them? We need to regulate the hours for which bus drivers are allowed to drive these vehicles on long routes across the country. Do we need the UN to come and address parliament about Mabira accident hotspots? Do we need international donors to lecture us on road safety signage? Come on!

African governments should regulate the selling of prescription drugs by unprofessional pharmetics personnel. Also drug companies aggressive marketing of prescription drugs directly to consumers, a practice that is prohibited in most other countries. There is no reason why chloroform is sold on the streets of the cities. A chill runs through my spine whenever I hear of people murdered by using chloroform. This is the liquid criminals pour into people's houses so that it evaporates and the vapor puts the occupants into a deep sleep. The thugs then break into the house to rob, rape or kill the occupants. An anesthetist estimates that 10ml of chloroform can make someone sleep either through inhalation or in a drink. And it can be fatal. According to the US agency for toxic substances and disease registry, 100ml of chloroform can kill. But the report says some people have died from drinking doses as small as 5ml, while others have survived after drinking much larger amounts.

The spokesman of Uganda police Mr. Ibin Sekumbi says that the police is aware that chloroform is sold on the open market in pharmacies and clinics, which gives opportunity to the wrongdoers to access it. "As Police, we have no mandate regarding the custody and trading of such chemicals. They are sold in pharmacies, clinics and laboratories. But other people buy them for personal use. So we still have a challenge on such drugs as Police," Ssenkumbi notes. (*New Vision Dec., 29, 2012*).

The medicines and health delivery monitoring unit should carry out proper screening in order to eliminate the quack surgeons. There are so many such properly recorded practitioners plying their trade in different towns and their environs who appear to have long forgotten whatever they learnt in the medical school. We are told many of them never attended medical schools while others maneuvered their way to graduation.

Generally, the problems of Africa are initiated by the economic and political instability. Poverty is the cancer eating up all institutions. Africans are left to the vagaries of a poorly-regulated private sector, which exploits many of our people. Unemployed people are vulnerable people. Unemployment means there are many people that are hungry, homeless, unwell yet unable to pay for quality health care. African Governments have often been reluctant to set minimum wages, claiming this would affect investment prospects for the countries. Bad governance brought influx of refugees from one country to another. Epidemic diseases are rampant in war zones and refugee camps. Today Europeans are fed up with the nonstop influx of refugees and the rise in Nationalism in member countries cannot be brushed away by crying that they are racist! They are simply defending the country-freedom-social system they fought to build as nations.

Lawlessness coupled with the sorry state of hospitals, poor remuneration and poor administrations encourage the ills of our countries. Poor healthcare is compared to homicide. As one politician lamented that, "When the thugs of the dictators don't kill you on streets, they would send you to hospitals which were bereft of drugs or close an intensive care unit at the country's main national referral hospital and you die from there helplessly." The poor communication, muddy roads, potholes, broken bridges, flooded streets, traffic congestion, insecurity and etc. make even the poor medical facilities available inaccessible. The greedy politicians and their families fly overseas to access classic medical services or use flights to referral hospitals to leapfrog over the stinking and untidy muddy roads and bridgeless rivers.

In Africa, we have failed states, where public health policy and mechanism have collapsed, as our leaders are per-occupied with looting the treasury than serve the people who fill the very treasury they loot. Frank Habineza lamented that "Uganda's health sector is rotten to the core thanks to the vile corruption tendencies by the bureaucrats and the politburo".

Gaddafi was in power for 42 years yet the sewage and road systems in Libya dated back to the Italians education system and healthcare system whereby it is free but decayed to a level that made both worthless. Libya has some 50 Billion Dollars a year in oil income with approximately four and half million native population, enough money for the citizens to have quality health-care. Yet the local population have been living in poverty, some under $50 a month.

Natural resources has the largest value creation potential to mobilize own capital, but profit often ends up elsewhere. Africa has enough resources to ensure a decent life for everyone, not just the few who have stolen more than they will ever need in their lifetime, while the majority live in the sordid environment. Corruption is well orchestrated from the high offices. There is a saying that 'a fish rots from its head' (*"Ekyenyanja kivinda kuuva ku mutwe"*). Very pathetic, the same people whose resources are looted are always eager to beg these thieves for funeral contributions. Shadowy figures usually creep out, competing to corner attention to themselves with generous offers during funerals, as demonstration of mature sense of service delivery. Ironically, it is their fleeced money that could have saved their lives that is reserved to pay for their burials! Accepting their money is like accepting *amabugo* from a man who killed your father, son or wife. It is like belittling the poorest of the poor (*"kukudaala"*).

Not to mention that there are strings attached to every penny donated by our good politicians. Brother J. Ikuya says that, "Undoubtedly, the heart of giving alms or doling out donations in philanthropy is commendable. But genuine offertories are normally made from one's volition. It is obscenely inhuman for an ostensibly sprightly person to give a lift to a cripple on condition of being granted a personal favor from the disabled person."

In those countries with the high rate of corruption, donors are feeding the wealthy and healthy, while the poor and sick listen to irrelevant excuses and stories. Investors invest at their own peril. The corruption scandals involving donated money intended to improve on health-care projects are a breach of trust between the country and its development partners.

Corruption unfortunately knows no class, religion or tribe. It is like an epidemic. In a corrupt country, everyone has a price and being caught in a corruption scandal will not scathe them especially since they will find someone else to bribe. The anti-corruption nets can only trap small fishes. The big fishes end up stealing with impunity. Intriguingly, a peasant in the rural areas who steals a chicken is lynched whereas a cabinet minister who embezzles millions of dollars of donated money for Aids patients walks away scot-free!

Ironically, the insatiable greed for more money and more stuff is not quenchable by acquiring more money and more stuff. But corruption has been accepted as a normal way of life in Africa! In fact most people in Africa have this illusion that the more one steals or embezzles, the happier one becomes. Those who steal keep on yearning to steal more. One of the biggest mistakes that many Ugandans make, when they first read or hear of a major financial scandal involving the swindling of hundreds of millions or billions of shillings, is to instinctively feel envy at the corrupt official in question. Envy, not disgust, is the initial reaction that most of us feel (if we will admit it). The corrupt officials are envied for their fat bellies because in Africa, obesity is equated with wealth. But health experts say that fatness is associated with sickness. Health-wise, the bigger you are the more pathological you will be. As you grow fat, everybody organ especially the heart, brain and kidney start screaming for help.

The situation in Africa is alarming. We are witnessing an institutionalized corruption, exacerbated by revolving the same thieves in juicy posts and even drafting all known head of state relatives into the theft racket. The corrupt officials should not be handled with kid gloves by switching them to other ministries because the expression "once a thief, always a thief" is true. Pastor Fred Bahati, has proposed radical solutions to check graft, including expelling the corrupt from churches and mosques. "The level of thieving in Uganda is beyond corruption and can be termed as terrorism, robbery, murder, kidnap, rebellion and devilish. We should find new measures to discriminate and make life hard for the corrupt," Bahati suggested.

African leaders who came to power in the shadows of liberations are prone to corruption than the democratically elected leaders. The culprits wash their mouths by blaming the past regimes for their current errors. They keep reminding the masses that they are entitled to the meat of the hunted animals by virtue of their participation in the liberation struggles. I compare it to a member of the European octogenarian army veteran or leader mentioning their defeat of Hitler and Mussolini where never they were challenged with Justice.

According to the editorial of the Observers, any poor remuneration of critical officers needs to be looked into in order to register maximum success in fighting corruption. From police officers, military, Auditor General and IG staff to state attorneys, magistrates and judges, the government can't attract and retain the best when the pay is so basic. Not all who endure it can be relied on to withstand temptation. As Justice Irene Mulyagonja, the IGG, succinctly remarked, "The best brains prefer to use their acumen in defense of the corrupt rather than prosecuting them on behalf of government." It is not difficult to see why.

The press has done a good work as whistleblower to fight against corruption. They also act as the political watchdog of the people. We ought to hear the truth as painful as it is and take steps to address the basis of those concerns. Except that some corrupt regimes are set to muzzle the press. I recall that way back in the late 1990s to the early 2000s, some Rwandan journalists belonging to the Umuseso publication disclosed the procurement of junk helicopters and the wanton looting of the DR Congo resources orchestrated by the then RPA top brass, they were persecuted but later managed to escape into exile. The above stern action was a harbinger for any one with hopes of openly condemning corruption tendencies by the political elites as such would be translated into subversion and or dissent against the state. The fight against corruption starts with the independence of the institutions that are able to detect and divulge the vice including the freedom of the freelance reporters.

I mentioned that downsizing (slashing expenditure) is the right direction for our governments to take. African governments need to revise their priorities. I want to recognize some of the patriotic leaders of Africa who worked hard to uplift the standard of the peasants in Africa by shunning the luxurious life that come with the office of presidency. One of them is the former president of Ghana Mr. Rawlings. He set a good example regarding leadership and stewardship.

I was touched by President Yoweri Museveni's ten point program that was read by President Y K. Museveni after taking oath of the office of presidency. Yoweri Kaguta Museveni came to power in 1986 to clean up the place and set Uganda on the road to permanent peace, security, democracy, prosperity and happiness. I can recite by heart one of the most inspiring statements in his inaugural speech as President of Uganda on January 29, 1986. Uganda would become an industrial state within fifteen years and transformed from subsistence to commercial agriculture. A middle class economy and society would be realized. He articulated his agenda in the ten point program which was expanded to fifteen in 1998.

President Museveni, in one incident practiced what he preached (As reported by The Observer 2/12/2012). In April 1997, Museveni had been travelling from Bundibugyo in his chopper and when the visibility became horrible, the pilot made an emergency landing at Mwera (six miles from Kakiri, off Kampala-Hoima road). His helicopter was forced to land along Hoima road due to bad weather. President Museveni did the unthinkable. He hitched a ride in a Matatu, leaving behind his motorcade that had been put on standby.

According to the driver of the Matatu, Hamidu Musoke, he was approached by an army man who deceived him that his car had developed a mechanical problem. However when he reached Mwera, the soldier told him to stop. There was a long convoy of cars and after a few minutes, he saw Museveni disembarking from the bush and shockingly entered his Matatu with a bodyguard. On the way, Museveni chatted with him. Musoke said the president asked him where he hailed from and who his parents were. Along the way, Musoke's car almost ran out of fuel and he was only saved by the fact that a service station was not far away. After refueling for Shs 10,000, Musoke drove Museveni up to State Lodge Nakasero. For his services, he was given Shs 100,000 even though he had asked for Shs 40,000. I think that we can do better in the current situation by revisiting the ten point program.

We should borrow a leaf from some European presidents. Much has been said about the Uruguayan President Jose Mujica, who donates up to 90 percent of his $144,000 annual salary to charity. In terms of actual wages, Mujica's salary actually compares favorably to that of other leaders but he is considered to be the poorest president.

It is important for our leaders to be less extravagant. African leaders must acknowledge that every life is valuable. A person in Africa is as important as one in USA. Unfortunately, we live in a world now where if a person lives in a poor country, it's okay that their health is not as good. We need to find ways so that health and survival are equitable around the world. Every person must have the same access to quality health-care. All people must have health insurance. Each regional referral hospitals must be well equipped with essentials like the heart equipment, oxygen and breathing equipment, clean blood, ample beds, drugs and stand-by health workers. The health workers must be well remunerated. In addition, the doctors must be well facilitated with transportations like motorbikes to reach the inaccessible regions of the country. Not forgetting the air ambulance consisting of helicopters. Again, quality health-care is the basic right to every citizen.

Many patients with terminal sickness are sent home to die without any medical assistance. There is a need to provide necessary help; physical, psychosocial and spiritual on a weekly basis. There should be a computerized system that captures biometric data of a patient

86

and keeps track of the patient from the time of arrival at a health facility to the time of his departure. There should be medical officers, who deliver medications at their doorsteps. The World Health Organization (WHO) recommends Palliative care as an approach that improves the quality of life of patients and their families facing problems associated with life threatening illness, through prevention and relief of suffering by means of early identification, impeccable assessment and treatment of other problems, physical, psychosocial and spiritual. In Uganda, the need for Palliative Care is gradually increasing as cancer and HIV/Aids continue to eat into the health of our people. Hospice Africa-Uganda is one of the few medical institutions in the country accredited to offer such treatment but this is a drop in the bucket; much more services from various institutions are required to meet the demand.

Health inequalities remain a major public-policy challenge worldwide. It is not only a moral issue; health inequalities carry significant economic costs. According to Clare Bambra, the prevailing explanation for health inequalities is rooted in the social determinants of health—that is, the environments in which people work and live. Affluent people have better access to health-promoting environments, such as well-maintained schools that offer a good education, high-quality housing, and stable jobs in secure, safe settings. The poorer you are, the more exposed you are likely to be to health-damaging environments. Various theories draw on this basic framework—and each competing explanation suggests different strategies for reducing health inequalities. For example, the "cultural-behavioral" approach explains health inequalities in terms of differences in individual behaviors, asserting that poorer people have worse health outcomes, owing to a higher propensity to smoke, drink alcohol, and eat less healthy foods. This view naturally underpins interventions like targeted smoking-cessation services or health-education initiatives.

I want to conclude by saying that the importance of a good healthcare system cannot be overemphasized. Healthcare is one of the most important components of a person's life as diseases or illness can ruin one's life. Healthcare covers all goods and services that are produced to improve health, including curative, preventative or even palliative solutions. The biggest asset one can have in life is good health. To be prosperous, one needs ability or strength, and as the saying goes, 'health is wealth'. As I said, healthcare is a human right issue and a country can't be developed without basic healthcare facilities.

It is the responsibility of the governments of Africa to do serious sensitization on all hygienic aspects and to regulate productions and consumptions of certain foods, drugs and herbs. The squandered resources should be used to provide clean water and improve the drainage system. In spite of the poverty and diseases, our governments must prove that they are in charge and in control of the situation, rather than acting like a theoretical model, which when tested may not work or even be near the optimum result.

<u>Preventing terminal sicknesses like cancer by healthy eating</u>: The best way to combat cancer is to ensure your diet always has groupings of foods and nutrients that are well-known to not only prevent but also to treat cancer. Eating healthy (fibers, fruits and vegetables) can help in preventing cancer.

Vitamin C: Vitamin C enables the body to fight cancer naturally. Vitamin C is found in many citrus fruits such as oranges, lemons, limes and grapefruit, but can also be found in mangoes and papayas. Vegetables such as broccoli, green peppers, cucumber, tomatoes and greens like kale are also good sources of Vitamin C, among others because some of these have a compound with good anti-oxidant properties. Presence of oxidants in the body makes one susceptible to cancers.

Vitamin C cannot be stored in the body, therefore, one needs to include it every day in one's diet. Green tea and cacao: Green tea contains high levels of catechins, which can block the growth of many cancers. For many cancers, there is a direct relationship between the amount of green tea consumed and the reduction in cancer risk. One study suggests that one should consume at least five cups daily. Green tea contains high levels of catechins, which can block the growth of many cancers. Honey can be a powerful immune system booster. It has both antioxidant and anti-bacterial properties that fight toxic oxidants.

Cocoa is the raw form of chocolate that is rich in highly absorbable antioxidants. Cocoa is the raw form of chocolate that is rich in highly absorbable antioxidants. However, do not get too excited and load up on chocolate bars. Most chocolate is loaded with other additives like processed milk products and sugar that have the opposite of cancer-fighting qualities.

Cruciferous vegetables: Broccoli is one of the best cancer-fighting foods on the planet. It is loaded with various nutrients that have been found to prevent breast, prostate, skin, colon and rectal cancers. Sprouts of broccoli have been found to be the most beneficial. A direct cancer-inhibiting nutrient can be found in greater concentrations in the sprouts than the full mature plants. Cabbage and cauliflower have similar qualities.

Dark, leafy greens: These vegetables are high in carotenoids and antioxidants, which inhibit the growth of certain types of cancers. These vegetables have incredible levels of vitamins, minerals and fibre. Dark leafy greens are a nutritional powerhouse that should be a regular part of everyone's diet.

Curcumin and spices: Found in turmeric, curcumin has anti-tumor and antioxidant properties. Curcumin is a popular Indian spice in the ginger family. It is quite possibly the most powerful anti-cancer spice. Curcumin has also shown to have both chemo protective and chemo-sensitising-properties. This means that it will both enhance the positive cancer-killing effects of conventional chemotherapy, while at the same time protect healthy cells, which may be susceptible to being harmed by chemotherapy.

Garlic—the more you eat, the more you benefit. It contains compounds that activate factors in our cells that control cancer-fighting processes. Other beneficial spices include ginger, dill and parsley.

Carrots and tomatoes: High in beta carotene, carrots fight many forms of cancer, including lung, stomach, intestinal, bladder, prostate, breast, throat and mouth. It is better to eat them raw rather than cooked and in moderation due to high sugar content. Tomatoes are one of the anti-cancer super foods that contain lycopene and antioxidants that attack the cancer-causing elements in the body. Lycopene is known to kill cancer cells in the mouth and is linked to reduced risk of breast, prostate, pancreas and colorectal cancers. It is actually more effective if cooked rather than raw.

Avocados: Avocados are perhaps one of the best foods. They are loaded with healthy fats and are high in antioxidants. It is now believed that they may be useful in treating viral hepatitis, which causes liver damage and liver cancer.

Vitamin D and cancer: Vitamin D acts more like a hormone than a vitamin. Like a hormone, it has a huge impact on how genes express, or fail to express themselves. In fact, one in every 25 genes in the human body interacts with Vitamin D. This means that deficiencies may weaken the genetic infrastructure of our body and place us at risk for diseases such as cancer. Without Vitamin D, our immune system is incapable of producing certain antimicrobial substances, leaving our body unable to fight bacteria, viruses and cancer. A vitamin D deficiency will prevent the body from killing precancerous cells before they turn into full-fledged cancer. Besides preventing cancer, Vitamin D is also needed for strong bones and calcium absorption in the body. The good news is that Vitamin D can also be generated by exposure to the sun. However, if you are looking to supplement Vitamin D, understand that not all Vitamin D is created equal. Research demonstrates that vitamin D3 is the most powerful form.

Omega-3s and cancer: Your body cannot produce omega-3s like it can Vitamin D. This means that you need to make sure that you are consuming them. Greater intake of omega-3s has been associated with a reduced risk of cancer. The primary way that omega-3s help is the ability to stabilize the immune system and reduce inflammation in the body. The good news is that omega-3s are in a tonne of foods such as beans, certain oils and vegetables as well as fish and meat products.

The Root of Africa's Post-Independence Problem:

One of the notorious dictators and racists said that, "The fact that blacks look like human beings and act like human beings do not necessarily make them sensible human beings. Hedgehogs are not porcupines and lizards are not crocodiles simply because they look alike. If God has wanted us to be equal to the blacks, he would have created us all of a uniform color and intellect" _P.W Botha (Former Apartheid President of South Africa), August 15, 1985. His words reinforced the need of liberating every inch of our continent. But on the contrary, Africans have degraded themselves, at least judging from the manner the leaders treat their subjects.

We need leaders that can initiate fundamental changes—to fundamentally change the African colonial states and remove the bottlenecks of Africa. Nkrumah at his maiden speech said "The Independence of Ghana was meaningless unless the whole of Africa was free". In the 1960s, we were hopeful that Africa's independence would usher in a new era of dignity and social prosperity in our lives. Unfortunately, several years down the road, Africa is faced with a pendulum situation, swinging from democracy to absolutism then democracy.

President Museveni attributed African's malaise to leaders who overstayed their welcome. Ironically, Uganda has the distinction of the longest living oligarchy second only to Zimbabwe. If you intend to take lessons in how power compels people to contradict themselves, you have African leaders as an ideal sample. But, that's not all; you will also discover that the trend has survived through decades simply because there are those who worship these wicked African angels, and they are many, for that matter. Some, with fringe benefits.

President Guebuza of Mozambique said that peace and security are the corner stone of development. Lack of peace and security are due to dictatorship. It is for the same reason the majority of the people of Africa are still living under poverty in form of poor health, unemployment, sustained hunger and malnutrition, and today's environmental decay. In order to sustain peace and development, citizens should be empowered to scrutinize the government on all fronts. It is therefore essential to build a bridge of trust between the people and their leaders. This in turn eases governance of the country.

Ethnic violence is a living experience in most parts of Africa; genocide has become a tourist attraction; military coups have become a traditional phenomenon of changing political power; foreign aid projects have collapsed; and there is widespread evidence of large scale corruption in most of Africa's social, political and economic institutions.

The UN, a new body founded in 1945 as a successor to the weak League of Nations, put at the centre of its charter and policy a new Universal Declaration of Human Rights in 1948. Mankind was one and the UN believed in creating a world of dignity of all regardless of creed, colour, gender or race. The only thing that separated us was the fortune or misfortune of social, economic and political circumstances. The African states are obliged to ensure protection of human rights and guarantee freedom and dignity of individuals and groups as stated by the Universal Declaration of Human Rights. All African governments are accountable to the same international decrees but they deliberately violate human and peoples' rights. There is lip service everywhere, double standards and selective application of laws and international instruments. Compliance with international human rights instruments and national laws remains generally discretionary and subject to the vagaries of political expedience. The Holocaust during the World War II was a watershed event in the 20th Century. A shaken western world sought to banish forever the extreme nationalism and racism that they believed had caused such catastrophic human suffering.

Hypothetically, I believe that the Africans are feeling more insecure now than before independence, with thugs terrorizing the masses with impunity. Black dictatorship has proven to be worse than the tyranny of White colonialism. Most African leaders who fought for independence (post-independence leaders) did not want to quit. Their system was similar to that of "elected monarchs". People like Mugabe fall in this category. The system which sought to reward charismatic post-independence leaders is an outdated pre-independence fashion.

New wine deserves new wine skin bottles. Nations are perpetually faced with different challenges which need fresh ideas, competences and timelines. Political leadership is not simple technical or bureaucratic twaddle. It is inspiration of society on the main levers of governance. Leading a nation is not a joke—it is serious business requiring sleepless nights, and after two terms, a honest leader should quit without being begged or coerced.

Most African leaders come to power as liberators. Ironically, most of them used to be lynchpins of the past regimes they fought. They have been a mere change of guard without bringing fundamental change. They have proved to be no different or even worse than their predecessors. Sometimes one wonders whether the past rulers have come back in the soul of the current one. Liberators claim to have the right of the lion's share after the hunt. It is like they went to the bush to look for an animal to kill and eat. Moreover the buffalo that is killed has no rights to complain when it is being slaughtered and eaten up. The so-called liberators kill in order to access power and often kill to stay in power indefinitely.

Nelson Mandela left the legacy of a true liberator. He was a committed freedom fighter and selfless leader. He sacrificed his personal life so that the majority of Africans can be free. For a young man to leave his wife, young children and take up the struggle not knowing the consequences and having to spend 27 years in prison was a big sacrifice which he did wholeheartedly. Mandela inspired mankind whose humility and simplicity was over riding and transformed South Africa as a revolutionary. After liberation he resisted the temptation to super glue himself in the revered presidential seat. To him, power was not about self-aggrandizement or compensating one's suffering. Unlike most African leaders, Mandela retired early to give space to others to rule. Pius Katunzi complimented his leadership in this way: "He didn't feel like he did a favour to South Africans and therefore they owed him, whereby he had to pay himself by overstaying his welcome. It is not that he didn't have a vision. He was a visionary but his approach was that South Africans could still benefit from his wisdom even if he was not the captain of their ship."

Beno Oluka applauded Mandela's capability of checking his ego: "Few public figures are as glorified as Mr. Mandela is in South Africa and, arguably, around the world. In South Africa, his name and images are almost everywhere, although, unlike in the cases of African presidents of a bygone era, he did not impose it on the country."

Even the leaders who claim to be democratically elected have turned into vultures that remorselessly rip their prey. Africans peasants have become the wild beast, whose carcasses the leaders of the dictatorial regimes have devoured continuously at their will.

Our leaders lack the charisma of the African Heroes, great generals and icons in the likes of the great Mansa Musa (the most benevolent emperor and wealthiest person of all time taking today's exchange rate into account), Shaka (revolutionary, and forward thinking king); Mutesa I (the visionary king of Buganda who opened way for the Christian missionaries to come in); Kabalega 'The Defiant' (Bringing pride to Africa by opposing & resisting European/white supremacy). Born on June 18, 1853 Kabalega was Bunyoro's Omukama from 1870 to 1899. Kabalega's fame started back in 1894 when the British declared war on Bunyoro and was able to engage the mighty British forces for a period of five years. It was not until 1899 that he was captured together with Kabaka Mwanga of Buganda by the British forces. He was eventually exiled to the Seychelles Islands where he stayed for 24 years. In 1923, Kabalega was given permission to return home, a journey he did not complete. He fell sick on his way back and died on April 6, 1923 in Jinja before reaching his kingdom. What happened to the patriotic spirit of Kwame Nkrumah, Lumumba (African republican) John Gideon Okello who led the 1964 revolution against Arabist supremacy in East Africa, among many others?

The chaotic situation that characterizes the history of Motherland is not coincidental. When there is a state of repression, people react differently; there are those who sit back hoping that things will get better; others decide to collaborate; and others decide to resist. As one retired General said, "But in a state of injustice, even if you are not affected yourself, there are times when you say that wrong is wrong and it must be resisted".

I am justified to say that Africans have proved to be incapable of managing their own affairs. This is most probably what is inciting the former imperialist countries to exhibit new ambitions of re-establishing hegemony over the Third Word—Africa, the Middle East, etc. The former colonialists legally intervene into our affairs because they have a soft heart to the oppressed people and show full solidarity with the struggle of those seeking freedom and justice. The German ambassador to Uganda, Klaus Dieter Duxmann, said that his country would always stand by those who call for, and defend, freedom: "Freedom is more than just freedom of thought. It is freedom to express one's own opinion. It is freedom to voice public criticism".

The critics see the Western interventions marred by hidden intents. President Museveni has been quoted many times as saying outsiders cannot be expected to solve African problems because they lack the correct appreciation of them both politically and culturally. I agree that we need to liberate our minds from the thinking that the west has a solution to our problems. The former colonial masters pay more attention to their interests as opposed to ours. They are mum regarding human right abuse as long as the Africans dictators are credible allies. The African dictators can overstay in power, can arrest the opposition every other day, can pass draconian laws and let their countries wallow in poverty, as long as their troops are available for United Nations whenever they are needed to go on peace keeping missions. The former colonial masters are likely to turn a blind eye as long as the dictators vote on their side whenever the [UN] Human Rights Council sits. The dictators can go scot-free as long as they sign as many human rights treaties as required.

The whites tend to use our inadequacy (self-resignation and resorting to criminality and other social ills) as their social political punch to outweigh black potentials. I wish all black would understand the psychosocial effects of this thinking that the whites themselves are keen to keep in order to maintain their self-made superiority.

Some critics blame the colonialists for Africa's post-independence turmoil. They say that Sub-Saharan Africans have long complained about the artificial boundaries which the colonial powers made of their continent. The Africans are given three choices: acceptance of the injustices, unification e.g. Tanzania or secession e.g. Sudan and South Sudan. South Sudan gained independence in July 2011 after a bloody decades-long struggle for independence from Sudan but in December 2013 violence erupted. The unrest took on an ethnic dimension, pitting Kiir's Dinka tribe against Machar's Nuer. The problems going on in the DRC is another example.

I want to say that the problems of Africa are caused by political instabilities. The current political fever in the countries of Africa is caused by the greed of some politicians. Instead of unity we are engaged in grand scheming and positioning ourselves ahead of each other the way grasshoppers (*nsenene*) locked up in a bottle jostle to come on top of the other, definitely they lose their strategy of getting out of the bottle. African politics has multiple faces. The overt fact is that economic development and democracy are mutually exclusive but equally important. We need both concurrently.

History is in large part the record of human achievement, of endeavor and creative action. The African past provides many splendid examples of such achievements. How did the patriotic African spirit, which offered tentative hope and promise at independence quickly degenerate into violence and a breakdown? Real power in Africa is in the army. Dictatorship in Africa is enforced by military rule. The dictators created a misleading impression that the army is beyond the scrutiny of ordinary folk (civilians), the taxpayers, whose money is used to pay their salaries. Security personnel no longer respect their civilian masters. Insulated from the daily struggles of life, they approach constitutional civilian unrest with live fire, recklessness and impunity. In most parts of Africa, there is no security guarantee for the all; the *wananchi* are no longer safe at the hands of their protectors.

Successful military commanders have been the frontrunners for political offices. We ignore the fact that good military commanders do not necessarily make good presidents. As one writer said, "The army, by its nature, is an autocratic institution which demands absolute and blind obedience. Anyone without any skill could actually become *afande!*" One retired army officer insinuated that,

"The work of the army depends on command and order from above, there is no negotiation yet democracy is all about negotiation and consultation which is not the case in countries where leaders are soldiers". President Museveni angrily said in a radio message, one Saturday, while announcing the action taken against the senior air force commanders that he was "tired of businessmen who are pretending to be commanders in the army". (*Observers Sunday, 14 October*).

Although there is some truth in all of the above suggestions, I think it is erroneous to generalize soldiers as dull and cruel who are incapable of rendering civil services. Soldiers are normal people with skills and emotions like everyone else. The calling of a soldier is as noble as that of a doctor or a religious leader. Ideally, soldiers have a constitutional duty to protect the country, her citizens and their property. They need to be educated and polished regarding their civil obligations. The danger of soldiers joining politics is that they are more likely to be used as rubber stamps for the commander in chief. In the same way it not right for civilians to serve on the Army High Command—no value addition will be realized as the army is a highly specialized sector and we civilians could easily misconceptualize things and end up not rendering the desired effect.

In most African nations, elections are in place in order to give people an illusion that they have freedom of choice, yet they really don't have choice. All the other institutions like the parliament and Judiciary are just symbolic and are there just to create a semblance of democratic governance. Even the democratically elected civilian presidents of Africa are not angels. People are aware of misplaced priorities. Any confidence in their ability to rule has been irretrievably lost to self-indulgence. Most of the democratically elected civilian presidents of Africa mutate into something akin to military governments. All dictators are hypnotized and they all crawl out of the same ditch. All of the dictators are self-imposed rulers with authority to kill with impunity. In African countries ruled by dictators you can be killed anytime. All dictators ride on the backs of their armies to procure long and cumbersome tenure in power. They are good at making empty promises and intimidations to the masses which is a fallacy. A dictator has the alpha and omega mentality; it is one person dictating and destroying the whole country. "No man is good enough to govern another man without the other's consent"—Abraham Lincoln.

African dictators use the loopholes in the constitutions of their countries to blatantly abuse the moral integrity of the office of the Commander-in-Chief. Reading from Oxford Dictionary of English, Commander-in-Chief for this purpose means "a politician or head of state in supreme command of a country's armed forces" where command means, "give an authoritative or peremptory order; be in a strong enough position to have or secure; be in charge of; dominate from a superior height; control or restrain", etc. Fountain of Honor means, "guarantee eternal honor to anyone who drinks from it" implying being devoid of mischief or any semblance of it where honor means, "high respect, great esteem; the quality of knowing and doing what is morally right", etc.

Mustering the dynamics of the gun has contributed immensely in the political careers of African leaders. In Africa, the real power is with the military. That is why the dictators promote only loyal cadres to key posts. Government jobs are segmented for cadres and not professionals. The dictatorial governments are not about building institutions but instilling the cults of personalities. There isn't much meritocracy learnt from cadres than loyalty. The major parties should bravely educate the masses that gun-trotting leaders are backward and mean no good for the nation-but want all power and resources for themselves. We need a nation that has respectable institutions not the one-man show type of thing that stifle all opposition and good national progress for all.

Human rights are God given but not bestowed to us by any man. Mark Twain made this comment: "It is by the goodness of God that in our country we have those three unspeakably precious things: freedom of speech, freedom of conscience, and the prudence never to practice either of them".

In a Democracy, the minority have their say, and the majority have their way. Democracy is not perfect but it is the best system the world could offer as per now. Remember that some of the worst dictators like Adolf Hitler were democratically elected. "Dictatorship naturally arises out of democracy, and the most aggravated form of tyranny and slavery out of the most extreme liberty."—Plato.

Democracy in Africa does not go deep enough into the skin. Paul Kagame insinuated that, "The democracy we believe in is not about copy and pasting from contexts that are not our own". Any political pundit (a rational one, that is) will tell you that there is no dictator in the whole world and worse still from a cursed African continent who organizes elections to be defeated. It is almost impossible to defeat the incumbent in election because most of the Constitutions of Africa heap authority on the presidency, creating fertile ground for dictatorship. The Constitution has become for us, a document, which our leaders are willing to violate at every turn, not caring that in so doing, they are actually committing a crime. The presidents of Africa have power to undermine the parliaments and the judiciary. They have power to appoint the political and civil employees in all sensitive offices including the electoral commissions. Democracy in Africa rarely produces the most competent candidate. The incumbents have no concrete and credible challenges because the electoral commissions have no credibility. Africa is in dire need of electoral reforms. Thank God for recent reforms in Kenya. Kenya achieved change through the 2010 referendum. Henceforth, the Chief Justice, electoral commissioners, Inspector General of Police, Central Bank Governor and all public officials except Cabinet, apply for jobs when advertised and submit to an open, competitive process.

Africa is continent where campaign messages rarely influence voting choices; many cast their ballots based on tribal, ethnic, social or regional ties. The incumbents dish out sacks of money to people to buy votes. Yahya Jammeh is no stranger to controversy. Most politicians in Africa are self-centered. They do everything to be elected not because they want to serve people but for their selfish ends. The moment they get elected they forgot the local diehards who gave them power. As Puis Katunga lamented over Ugandan politicians that, "The country has failed to sync with the politicians, because their interest is to run us like their chattels. We only matter when it comes to giving votes. And once we vote them into office, then we cease to matter and they can do whatever they want with us, including choosing whom to protect and whom to abandon."

Most African leaders falsely use democracy to cover up for their greed, omissions, excesses and failures. They consider themselves authentic democratic leaders simply by learning to croon the chorus of democracy without practicing what they sing. The endless monotony of oppressive policies and intentional blunders of most African governments simply numb the democratic institutions. I think most politicians in Africa take on a communist approach (they are ideogically communists). It is not coincidence that the former Soviet union (Russia) has been the vanguard of assisting most freedom liberations in Africa. Not because the communists cared for the Africans but because they wanted to promote communism by minimizing the influence of the capitalists.

The Soviet Communist International (Comintern) was founded in March 1919 at a congress in Moscow by Vladimir Lenin. The international objectives of the Comintern were self-evident from its title. By 1920, Lenin had left no doubt that he envisioned the Comintern as ". . . a branch of the Russian Communist Party, organized on its model, and subject to its orders." They imposed "iron military discipline" upon party members in their countries, ensuring fealty to and "the fullest comradely confidence" in the headquarters in Moscow. They resolved to eliminate any future opposition to ideology before finding a common ground in order to consolidate. Stalin did it against his fellow Bolsheviks revolutionaries. Stalin eliminated 20m peasants in the early Soviet era. When Boris Yeltsin was being sworn in, he began his oath thus: "I, the people of Russia, do solemnly swear . . . ." Yeltsin did not see a Russia beyond himself like all African dictators.

Some African leaders opt for socialism. "You don't have to be a Communist to see that China has a lot to teach us in development. The fact that they have a different political system than ours has nothing to do with it."—Julius Kambarage Nyerere. Unlike the West, China, continues to face criticism for dealing with African governments without paying any attention to local governance issues, especially in respect to human rights abuses and democracy. "The Socialist Party of China is using the cloak of a political party in order to conceal its evil designs. These demagogues would coerce the government and flatter the people for their own evil ends. They are a danger to peace and law and order. They advocate violence and assassination . . . ."

Certainly, most African dictators do not represent the cream of African elites. We have mediocres masquerading as intellectuals in Africa. They cannot escape becoming victims of bringing out half-baked data in areas they did not research well. It is disgusting when every clown in Africa introduce themselves with such titles as Doctor, Professor, His Excellency, etc. In course of their performance they have more than vulgarized their respective titles. Generally, this sarcastic self-styling is a ridicule of those academicians and intellectuals, and leaders whose thinking is neither dignified nor elevated.

Africa is a continent in dire need of true leadership but could offer illiterates in the person of Idi Amin and his ilk. There is no known vitamin that could have boosted Amin's thinking. Perhaps he needed a Brain Stabilizer to step up his understanding. President Museveni, in June 1999, while meeting district leaders in Mpigi, insinuated that Dr. Milton Obote, who led Uganda twice, was only fit to rear goats, not to dabble in politics. (*The Observer Sunday, 09 December 2012*).

Central African Republic dictator Jean-Bedel Bokassa was overthrown after a student revolt that ended up with the massacre of 100 of them in 1979. One of the most ruthless dictators in post-colonial Africa, Nguema's country only enjoyed independence from Spain for 145 days in 1968 before the founding president became a "cross between Pol Pot and Mobutu", as Martin Meredith writes in The State of Africa. The son of a witchdoctor was gifted with low intelligence and failed exams to qualify for a civil service posting three times. He was to despise academics with a twisted passion. During his reign, the use of the word "intellectual" was treasonable, and Macias Nguema thought it a sign of scholarship to wear glasses, so the bespectacled were detained. In 1974, the pot-smoking Nguema chased all teachers, alongside a third of the population, to exile, banned newspapers, and closed all libraries and schools. During his 11-year rule, all that children learnt were political slogans.

Africa could only offer buffoonery in the person of Jammeh and serial lovers like Zuma or Mswati. I mean leaders who are often attracted to diversity, power and uncertainty, and tend to have strong sexual drives and high-octane energy to cope with their demanding itineraries and strenuous diaries. "President Idi Amin liked women. He was the proverbial fisherman who cast his net far and wide to catch good fish." Physically striking, intelligent and hardworking ladies would not escape the Big Daddy's eye. Idi Amin and Macias Nguema kept a herd of women and ordered all former lovers of their current mistresses killed.

We are led by many rubber stamp heads of state that have not made any real change on this continent. The best Africa could offer are delusional revolutionaries forever in search of colonialists like Mugabe, believers in luck like the aptly named Goodluck Jonathan. The Nigerian leader recently gave a lecture concerning his theory that wearing a hat of a certain style consistently, and meditating on what it represented, could change one's personality: "You can tell the character of a man by the hat he wears, and how he wears it—A hat worn low over the brow could denote a Casanova or wicked character; a bowler hat expressed self-assuredness or arrogance; a cowboy hat—such as Jonathan himself wore—was a mark of confidence and boldness." Really?

The best Africa could offer are fake pharmacists like Jammeh who claimed to have a cure for all sorts of ailments including HIV/Aids; leaders like Thabo Mbeki aiming at defeating non-African science and challenging us to go back to our African sophistry. Puis Katunzi made this comment concerning Africa's post-independence leaders: "By some strange coincidence, many of these immediate post-colonial rulers were not known for their wisdom. If they didn't become stooges of the West or East or pawns in the Cold War between these blocs, they were outright brutes who killed their subjects without a flinch as they lined their private pockets with public resources."

Most African presidents are accused of wielding an iron rod on their subjects to intimidate them so that they just follow their rules like sheep following cattle whilst grazing! African leaders have a reputation of being obsessed with power for their own glory. For example the ordinary people referred to the former president of Tanzania as Ndugu [brother] Mwalimu Nyerere but at times he couldn't resist the temptation of being worshipped as Baba wa Taifa (father of the nation). If I am allowed to quote Puis Katunzi, "There was one particular leader at that time who relished in the prowess and skills of a cock and decided to name himself, Mobutu Sese Seko Kuku Ngbendu wa Za Banga (A cock that leaves no chicken untouched). In Kenya, we had Baba Daniel Arap Moi, who was without any doubt referred to as Mtukufu (his holiness, his Excellency). On the periphery of Great Lakes region, in Malawi we had Kamuzu Banda, who enjoyed being referred to as Nkwanzi (the lion). Intriguingly, most these leaders were a product of coups or guerilla struggles."

Such were leaders determined to rule their countries in form of monarchs. By either a stroke of bad luck or otherwise, the wind of change that swept across Africa in the early to late 1980s, carried with them many of these first generation leaders. Those who weathered the storm like Moi and Kenneth Kaunda are enjoying their retirement. There is spectacular thread that ran throughout the control of these countries.

Dr. Myles Munroe called upon African leaders to emulate former South African president Nelson Mandela who ruled for only one term and relinquished power: "Politicians are concerned about the next election but true leaders are concerned about the next generation. Leaders relinquish leadership positions for others—Referring to Nelson Mandela as the greatest leader Africa has ever produced, Dr. Munroe said, "Mandela spent in prison more than 24 years but ruled for only one term. He did not use power to protect himself from people but used power to empower people." Munroe advised leaders to always create strong institutions as foundations for national visions bearing in mind that whereas visions are permanent, leaders are temporal.

Moses Khisa diagnoses the problems of Africa as dictatorship: "It is that the president violates the Constitution and gets away with it. It's not that we don't have checks and balances against the president, it's that many counterbalancing constitutional mechanisms are either unabashedly ignored or blatantly undermined—Arguably the most cited provision of the 1995 Constitution is Article 1: "Power belongs to the people . . ." But without credible mechanisms that allow for free and fair elections, through which the "people" can exercise their power, that provision is inconsequential, making elections a routine ritual that merely legitimizes the exercise of real (de facto) power."

General elections in most African countries are stage managed *katembas* (dramas) used to hoodwink donors. Under the prevailing circumstances, we have constitutions that give overwhelming and pervasive powers to the incumbents, the biased electoral commissions and bogus electoral laws, the partisan coercive police administration and military involvement in elections; it is like chasing phantasm to imagine that elections can be free, fair and transparent.

The democracy of Africa is a system where numerous elections are held at great cost without issues and with unchangeable leaders. The incumbent has advantage of using state apparatus against the citizens to win elections. What is the use of staging election when voters continued to be disenfranchised and the election marred by irregularities? Even courts settling election disputes are impartial.

Democracy in Africa works only at the lower level. The topmost positions are fenced off from competition and openness. This kind of ring-fencing of certain positions is not without costs. Kenya once had a powerful party, KANU, ever led by the professor of politics (as he has often referred to himself), Daniel Arap Moi. When he finally relaxed the grip of power and passed the mantle to his protégé, Uhuru Kenyatta, the latter crashed the party with such a resounding thud that no one has ever succeeded to lift it up again. Even Uhuru himself has since quit the party and formed his own, The National Alliance (TNA). African political parties should make the top positions open for competition in order to avoid the KANU bug.

Constitutionally, MPs belong to the legislative arm of the state. They also act as the political watchdog of the people, expected to represent the general population by holding government to be responsive to their needs. "The Constitution makes us not rivals for power, but partners for progress" (John F. Kennedy remarks to congress). This is a great statesman views about separation of powers between the executive and Legislature. Unfortunately in most parts of the continent the constitution makes the two institutions rivals for power.

Most African parliaments serve the interests of the members of parliament as opposed to the interests of the people. This is the place where Draconian laws are being formulated and some even passed. Saddam Gayira made this comment concerning the parliament of Uganda: "When Parliament once refused to pass the national budget, the executive just withheld MPs' salaries and they quickly succumbed because these salaries also service bank loans. Parliament is just another impotent appendage of the state, and it has apparently sold its soul. It, therefore, goes without saying that the Uganda Parliament has lost respect and is slowly becoming a laughing stock".

In Africa, the incumbent disorganizes the opposition with money and patronage on the one hand, and on the other, we see greedy politicians who have no values and principles to protect. Most of the African Members of parliament are greedy and corrupt. They are real hyenas feasting on the carcasses of the poor. Uganda MPs are already well-facilitated at the taxpayers' expense—with a large salary, interest-free car loans and more recently, iPads, now the parliament agreed to spend over Shs 80 million on a day care, something that rubbed many Ugandans the wrong way. As one columnist wrote: "— the increasingly venomous creature commonly known as the African Member of Parliament contains a standard gene for greed, whichever part of the continent you are in".

Poverty is not restricted to one part of the world but corrupt ignoramuses that our leaders are, should be questioned and opposed and not supported. It is unfortunate that some of our MPs are useless parasitic, good at cheering and applauding the executive instead of asking questions and playing their overseeing role of the executive. They are akin to the nodding disease victims because they nod their heads at every bill presented. The other vice is the politics of patronage. Some members of parliament have lost their conscience; they refuse to express critical views in the hope that they will be appointed ministers. They defend the dictators because in order to live the high life, they have to sell their souls to the devil to stay afloat.

They end up compromising in exchange for comfort. In private lives, it is called a bribe but in politics, it is called "concessions".

All over the continent, parliamentarians from Kenya, Malawi, Uganda and Namibia have been agitating for better pay, with their avarice conveniently having little regard for party lines. In Uganda, each MP is paid Ugshs 15 millions minus allowances. We have 333 MPs in the parliament. Kenyan lawmakers, already among the highest paid in the world, recently also hatched a sneaky plan to raise their exit allowances from an already out-of-touch $18,000 to $118,000 in a move that had the majority of citizens wrinkling their noses in disgust.

The question of "moral certitude" should be of concern to the peace loving people in Africa where the majority of people are faced with the choice of how to contribute to socio-political and economic transformation without being run over by the powers that may not necessarily have the moral authority but have the most political power, the most cash and the military might to instigate violence.

Africans need to be educated regarding voting. Not all democracies are really fully functional. In Africa, tyrants are still more likely to be elected into office; because those are the kind of people that current African culture allows and has respect for. Here is one way to differentiate. In functional democracies, National Problems are expected to become the Personal Problems of the elected representatives. However in corrupt dysfunctional democracies (democracies that exist only in constitutional theory), it is the exact opposite; the Personal Problems of the elected are made to become National Problems of the citizens, who already have too many crushing problems of their own to bear with.

50 years since independence Africa has been unable to rid itself of colonial structures. Africa's post-colonial era has been characterized with the brazen thieving typical of the high noon days of Amin, Mobutu, Boigny, Bokasa, Gadhafi, Kamuzu Banda, Gnasingibe Eyadema, Siad Barre, Haile Silasi, Hosin Mubarak and the likes; a trait that sent the economies of most states into a tailspin of destruction—sacrificing institutions at the altar of a powerful

presidency. The presidents of the countries control the executive, judicially and Parliament. Dictators have a problem of concentrating power around themselves, which has affected everything, including decision-making

Freedom of press is always the first casualty of all dictatorial regimes. They gag the most vociferous and critical journalists. It is absurd that those few who genuinely ask pertinent issues are gagged. They are harassed by stereotyping them as rebels. Thomas Jefferson said that, "To preserve the freedom of the human mind then and freedom of the press, every spirit should be ready to devote itself to martyrdom; for as long as we may think as we will, and speak as we think, the condition of man will proceed in improvement".

The freedom of press as enshrined in article 19 of the United Nations Declaration of Human rights, the Media is guaranteed freedom to be able to work in an environment that is independent, transparent to promote a democratic society. But press freedom in Africa remains fragile as journalists continue to be attacked by security agencies. The reason of infringements on media freedom is to suppress critical view points. The dictators are offended whenever the media exposes them. What the dictators ought to know is that; freedom of speech does not exist without freedom to offend. Human mouth is not only for eating; its other use is also for defending human race from institutional abuse. "Woe to that nation whose literature is cut short by the intrusion of force. This is not merely interference with freedom of the press but the sealing up of a nation's heart, the excision of its memory"—Aleksandr Solzhenitsyn.

Great opinions about Media censorship: "A popular Government, without popular information, or the means of acquiring it, is but a prologue to a force or tragedy, or perhaps both. Knowledge will forever govern ignorance, and a people who mean to be their own governors must arm themselves with the power which knowledge gives" James Madison (former U.S President).

In journalism, governments often pay moles in media houses to dilute key issues in news headlines. Apartheid regime did it, Eyadema did it and Mugabe does it. In dictatorship a state is responsible for everything, and no one is responsible for the state. The dictators or their ruling parties participate in daily businesses and control the economy with big monopoly and wining government tenders every time. The supposedly custodians of the countries' resources end up looting their countries dry.

Renowned Africans dictators, in the heydays of their reigns, these great helmsmen managed to bask in the hero worship and to build a personality cult around their presidency. They chose to play the hard ball, simmering tribal tensions and bigotry. Have you ever wondered why the people's political leanings in most countries of Africa is holistic rather than instrumental, egalitarian or altruistic, etc? The dictators and their minions are the extreme end of the negative and nasty, unnecessary libido.

Africa as a whole suffers from what we may call state patronage and tribal hunk stars. Wily politicians stir up conflicts between tribes as a means of cementing their hold on power. Some put as many people as possible from their own tribe into the public payroll. The African dictators fashion their States in their own image, such that every individual that holds an important job in their governments—whether in Parliament, Judiciary, Cabinet, Public Service, statutory bodies, public enterprises, Army, Prisons or Police is personally directly or indirectly appointed by them to the offices. Most of these appointees remain loyal all the way to the end because they depend on the appointing figure for patronage. The public service ends up suffering from what Chinua Achebe called the cult of mediocrity.

In Africa, nepotism is naturally normal. After all, there is no law that prohibits someone filling up all public jobs with relatives! Otherwise, your own relatives might accuse you of discrimination. Nepotism makes a country a family business; they run the country compared to the CEO running 'their' company. The African dictators are comfortable to deploy blood relatives in key administrative posts because your brother, sister, wife, husband, child, uncle or aunt are more likely to remain royal more than those with whom you have no blood connections. As one of the leading politicians said that, "If you needed top secrecy and royal officers to help execute a mission; you do not go far from your village. Surely you look close to those with whom you grazed goats, those you went to school with and those whom you know will never oppose your thinking".

The close relatives and friends of the dictators become the anointed ones of the inner circle who get the benefit of knowing how things are done for the better of the country. For example Mswati staunchly resists government reforms, and is free to choose the prime minister, other top government posts and top traditional posts—though he takes special advice from the queen mother and other special counsel. The close relatives advise on the best international spin-doctors to whitewash the tainted image of the leaders. They become the untouchables. Sectarianism is a recipe for alienation, conflicts, resentment, implosion and/or explosion. Such are dysfunctional governments based on divide and rule.

According to Orwell, the book 'Animal's Farm" reflects events leading up to and during the Stalin . . . The Soviet Union he believed, had become a brutal dictatorship, built upon a cult of . . . . "All animals are equal, but some animals are more equal than others". Orwell's quotation fits the description of African dictators. We live in the situation compared to animal farm whereby some animals are greater than others; some are squirrels and yet are given better treatment than the others. Our politicians are the major cause of bigotry. One philosopher insinuated, "All men are by nature equal, made all of the same earth by one Workman; and however we deceive ourselves, as dear unto God is the poor peasant as the mighty prince." Plato.

Africans peasants have been faulted; they have seen the destruction of the sense of self-esteem, being the consequent of one person wielding superiority of force over others, when the stronger appropriate to themselves the prerogative even to annul the injunction that God created all men and women in His image.

So far five presidents in Africa have been fathers to future presidents. Three of these have been succeeded by their sons immediately upon their death. They include Joseph Kabila in DRC, Faure Eyadema in Togo and Ali Bongo in Gabon. Two other sons have succeeded their fathers but only after a long period of time, with two other presidents in between. This latter category came to power through a constitutional process where their father's name played a decisive role: Ian Khama in Botswana and Uhuru Kenyatta in Kenya. They leveraged their fathers' legacies to stake their claims. I think every citizen (including the family members of the presidents) have the right to run for the highest office as long as they do not manipulate the democratic system to climb up.

Not all of the dictators have been lucky to get away with bigotry. For example the dictator, Papa Francisco Macias Nguema of Equatorial Guinea was overthrown by his cousin, Colonel Teodoro Obiang Nguema Mbasogo, the current president, in September 1979 and sentenced to death, at the age of 55. Teodoro Nguema Mbasogo has made the same mistake of his predecessor. He has pumped his regime with members of his family: His son is the Vice President, another son is the Commander of Special Forces, his brother is Minister of Defense etc. Recently, the Senegalese police arrested Karim Wade, the son of former president Abdoulaye Wade, on suspicion of illegally amassing some $1.4 billion during his father's 12 years in office.

Other dictators like Gadhafi perished together with their family members when power slipped from their hands. He loaded his sons with promotions forgetting that a tree with heavier branches will fall harder. David made this comment: "There is an archetypal curse upon first-borns and father's favourites. Beginning with Esau and Isaac to the present, first-borns have never fared well. They normally gender unnecessary rivalry because they are often put on a pedestal for all the Ruebens, vultures and hyenas to gaze upon. And if they are as naive as their progenitors, they also are often fooled into thinking and believing that the world is their oyster."

A good father under a normal circumstance would shield his son from harm's way. But dictators like Gadhafi use their sons as a human shield. Their sons become their personal body guards or armors to defuse arrows from adversaries; their sons become their political vanguard; their sons are gloomed as their successors to continue their illegitimate establishments. The sons are positioned to inherit all of the enemies accumulated throughout the decades their fathers have been in power. Underneath the inherited power is a volcanic rumbling, which awaits to be vented out to their sons as soon as they assume leadership. What a package of inheritance dictators want to bequeath to their sons!

When public men indulge themselves in abuse, when they deny others a fair trial, when they resort to innuendo and insinuation, to libel, scandal, and suspicion, then our democratic society is outraged, and democracy is baffled. Intrudingly, those who have plundered and accumulated enormous resources in the past are free to rove about and use their stolen wealth to influence events in the country. Looters of yesterday become heroes of today and are elected in the highest offices.

Human right observers are not wimps who turn their backs on blatant human rights abuse. Panic sets in when the repercussions and consequences also known as censored moments manifest. It is the same panic that led so many Nazis including the fearless Germany Fuehrer to commit suicide rather than be tried for their crimes.

Dictators are allergic to justice. The early sign of dictatorship is overruling the justice institution. "Knowledge without justice ought to be called cunning rather than wisdom"—Plato.

African dictators carry on with their atrocities well aware of their invulnerability to prosecution when they are out of power. Baptized with immunity from prosecution for life, they wreak havoc on the hapless citizens. The supporters of immunity from prosecution suggest that the reason why leaders overstay in power is because they fear to face the law for the crimes they commit as leaders and at times such crimes are inevitable. They suggest that some dictators would readily relinquish power if they were assured of immunity after they leave the highest office. I think such is really slippery slope and hallow reasoning because it has helped in creating criminal and tortuous leaders. With such insulating from prosecution, the leaders are prompted to think that the countries do not deserve to get back what was stolen from them. What impudence!

Most of the victims of the dictatorial regimes are civilians. In Africa the ones with guns are more afraid of the ones without guns. The dictators have no respect for the constitutions: According to them, a crime is not defined as an act of violating the constitution but any act perceived to be against their governments; the government is basically the law. The Dictators create monstrous, moronic and ludicrous laws and institutions to keep them in power. They forget that, they too, can become vulnerable to the same instruments after they are forced out of office. It is like choosing to ride a tiger and then you become scared to get off! African dictators should be aware that there is an appointed time to lay in the bed that you made. You will one day be accountable to the same oppressive laws that you established. The very thorns that you set up to trap others might become your nightmare tomorrow!

All dictators have the same mother and share the gene: They all have skeletons in their closets. African dictators have one thing in common: killing streak always in the background. They rule with iron fists, regularly purging those showing the slightest sign of dissent. Most are executed or sent to prison camps. Most dictators came to power at the expense of taking innocent lives. They are guilty of Scorched Earth Policy. Scorched Earth policy is a brutal military strategy which is usually deployed by dictators while advancing towards enemies or retreating from rebel zones. It involves destruction of assets, food, animals, shelters, vegetation/forests and innocent lives in those areas. The aim is to deny their enemies of useful resources/assets, potential manpower, or sometimes used by government forces for propaganda purposes. It is intriguing how we Africans could commit such atrocities against our own for the sake of power. It baffles me that in my country Uganda, during the past regimes, the streets of Kampala and the swamps of rural areas were strewed with dead bodies.

Dictators are intoxicated with power. The naked truth is that nobody rules forever. Mahatma Gandhi once wrote, "When I despair, I remember that all through history the way of truth and love have always won. There have been tyrants and murderers, and for a time, they can seem invincible, but in the end, they always fall. Think of it—always."

Africa is the richest continent with rich oil reserves and mineral mines. But such riches benefit a few anointed ones. Our greedy leaders have looted all of the natural resources to stuff their bank accounts. They have turned our beloved countries into limited companies which they rob at their will with impunity. They would do anything to hold on power. For example when issuing contracts for the excavation of our natural resources, they opt for the financers of their election campaigns instead of going for the highest bidders.

Basically, the African dictators have mortgaged off our natural resources. For example the DRC has vast mineral wealth including diamonds, copper, oil and gas; one estimate puts the value of these resources at $24 trillion. However, it is pretty much the poorest country in the world. Mobuto Sese Seko, the former dictator sold the mineral resources in advance by talking loans which he deposited on his person accounts. 'Repayment' of loans made to the corrupt Mobuto Sese Seko has proved an important means of draining the DRC's wealth. Mswati, has a personal fortune of roughly $200m (about Shs 500b), is a controversial figure in Swaziland, where up to 70 per cent of its 1.2 million citizens are impoverished.

According to Weekly Observer, "One significant policy, which drastically crippled the economic potential of almost all African countries, was privatisation. This called for the transfer of public parastatals into the hands of the private sector. In Uganda, for example, entities we sold included Uganda Railways, Uganda Transport Corporation (UTC), Uganda Airlines, Uganda Commercial Bank. The same reforms saw the collapse of the cooperative unions, which were the cornerstones of the agriculture sector." The government of Uganda mooted adopting the same policy on recently discovered oil reserves.

African leaders have a reputation of divesting and privatizing the economy to the whims of the market forces rather than vesting authority in political decision-makers. President Kaunda used his cabinet minister to mortgage off all the mines in Zambia. Capitalism has eaten the revolutionary credibility of our leaders. The opportunity cost is unbearable to the peasant class Africans. Privatisation was a strategy by the IMF and the World Bank to promote foreign investments by means of guarantees or participation in loans and other investments made by private investors. In other words, the interests of foreign giant corporations were pushed in the name of privatisation. The consequences of this have been extreme levels of poverty which are becoming chronic; and this has become a distinguishing characteristic for low and middle-income countries.

Robert Mugabe has been the President of Zimbabwe since December 1987. He was once seen as a hero after leading guerrilla forces against the then-white rulers of Rhodesia. He took power in 1980 as Prime Minister before becoming President in 1987. He has been involved in a number of controversies, specifically the plunder of neighboring Congo in the guise of helping the latter's government. His land reform program has also been characterized by violence as he seeks to redistribute land that was inequitably distributed during his country's time as a colony of the United Kingdom.

Kenya's independence offered opportunity for those with, or close to power, to also primitively accumulate wealth on a grand scale. It is estimated that Mzee Jomo Kenyatta accumulated up to 200,000 hectares of productive land while in power! Land that was bigger than Kenya's Nyanza province, or a collection of Ugandan districts. Fortunately, although the Kenyata family had capitalist instincts, they wisely invested their 'loot' into the production and service sectors. They minimized reliance on imported goods. There is no known big economy in the world which built its capacity on imports.

African countries have the most favourable natural endowment and possess virtually all the conditions required for economic development. What is needed is a mindset change, concrete action or implementation to take advantage of these conditions. As Brother J Ikuya said that, "The quarrel with the colonialists was not that they had not built railways, airports, schools, etc, but that their design of these amenities met the interests of their domination instead of positioning our people to be free. During the re-assumption of power by the Uganda People's Congress (UPC) in 1980, Dr Milton Obote's stirring catchphrase was to "fight poverty, disease and illiteracy". We scoffed at these as empty hogwash because we believed the rhetoric did not embrace really crucial political issues intended for resolution at the time. It also did not define any political principles on the obtaining social situation or how to address them."

During the times of Idi Amin sustainable wealth creation was only possible under the clique of loyalists. The Amin regime murdered people for being successful in business, notably through the murderous struggles over Mafuta Mingi properties. The success of the famous entrepreneurs like Kabali Kaggwa, the pioneer doyen of African enterprise led to his murdering by Idi Amin in September, 1971. Before Amin murdered him, Kaggwa routinely exported horticultural produce to Kenya and Europe! Had Uganda had a stable government and rational political and economic policies, he and others, would have transformed into our industrialists, etc. Consequently, conspicuous consumption became the norm. Also, stifling macroeconomic instability and political uncertainty were commonplace, right through Obote II. We are kept behind because of the bad leadership characterizing our century, forcing the visionary pioneer entrepreneurs to go underground or in exile.

Africans are rotting in poverty which leaders exacerbated to prop up their dictatorship. I mean that Africans are languishing in poverty because of the deliberate plans of their leaders. African dictators use poverty as a tool to keep them in power. The dictators have the mentality that it is easier to rule poor people than rich people. For example Idi Amin barred all of the Christian denominations in Uganda from getting financial assistances from the western countries. The dictators want the religious and cultural institutions to depend on government handouts in order to control them. The dictators continue to dole out financial hand-outs in order to ensure that people look to none other than them as a fountain of survival. As Prof. David Todd put it, "their aim is; to achieve a systematic scheme to make everyone a beggar. They want to remain the sole provider of bread, so that everyone listens to their lies and worship them."

Africa is paralyzed by the dependence syndrome. Privileging an economic analysis, and working through neo-Marxist models developed some time ago by exponents of the "dependency school," the authors highlight the mechanisms fostering the dependence of "peripheral" countries to the world capitalist system. Such a perspective conceives of Africa as having been placed in a position of dependence during colonization and then "under-developed" within the international capitalist order. As Samir Amin puts it in his Unequal Development (Harvester Press, 1976), the partition of Africa in the nineteenth century enabled the colonizing countries to obtain inexpensive export commodities, while Africans were forced to adjust to the external exigencies of mercantilism on terms convenient to the forces of global capital.

In the twentieth century, African leaders are still obsessed with aids from the western donors as it was the case before independence. Mwenda says that, "A major reason democracy is problematic in poor countries is this attempt to realise it as an external pressure and imposition. Local elites, realising the support they get from western capitals, begin to disregard the necessity of internal political negotiation and compromise. Instead, they seek to rely on external actors to achieve that which domestic political negotiation is supposed to deliver."

The African leaders need to rethink their overreliance on aid for budget support. The aid the West gives to African countries is another form of neocolonial domination and imperialism, and this aid is actually paid back in one way or another. There is actually no foreign aid that is 'free.' Western powers design aid policies for poor countries which are only symbolic in nature. For example, many of the donor-funded projects in Africa come with the so-called expatriates who are highly paid and enjoy an affluent life in African countries. We need support for humanitarian causes, similar to the United States' approach whose support is directed at project assistance such as in the area of HIV/Aids. But we may not need, let alone deserve, budget support when we are busy stealing it and squandering locally-generated revenue.

There is evidence to suggest that Uganda would be capable of funding her entire budget if the money collected by the Uganda Revenue Authority was not stolen or used extravagantly. The money stolen from public coffers could be much more than what is donated to Uganda. Ironically, other countries have thieves, Uganda is for thieves.

One commentator lamented that "Africa has been turned into a desolate and destitute continent. Without foreign aid, our economies can cripple in a blink of an eye. Let us get back to the drawing board and logically analyse what went wrong and what can be done." It is a shame that we should be pleading for aid instead of utilizing internal resources frugally. It is time for us to start cutting our coat according to our cloth. "Never stand begging for that which you have the power to earn."—Miguel de Cervantes.

We need to downsize the number of cabinet ministers, the number of districts, number of president's advisors, the fleet of presidential luxury cars, private jets and etc. in order to balance our budget. We need an austerity plan. President Joyce Banda decided last year to sell the jet, bought by her predecessor Bingu wa Mutharika for $22 million, due to the cost of running it. Malawi will use $15 million from the sale of the country's presidential jet to feed the poor and grow crops to fight malnutrition, an official said. Since taking office, Banda has introduced a host of cost-cutting measures and uses commercial airlines to travel outside the country.

One economists said that the problem with most Ugandan rich elites is having no long term investment strategy, they never give to charity, for social corporate responsibility reasons and neither do they create hedge funds or make profits through arbitrage even though, given the advancement in technology it has become extremely difficult to profit from mispricing in the market. Many traders have computerized trading systems set to monitor fluctuations in similar financial instruments. Any inefficient pricing setups are usually acted upon quickly and the opportunity is often eliminated in a matter of seconds. It's important that this breed of Rich Elite learn the importance of long term investments in infrastructure, Leverage can be created through options, futures, margin and other financial instruments.

The following commonsense habits can deliver us from being a begging society and country: Working on being a good custodian of Uganda's wealth, not spending beyond our means, creating a level playing field whereby all Ugandans have equal chance of succeeding through hard work and Getting rid of corruption. African governments have not been serious about fighting the cancer of corruption. The strict laws spare the big fishes as the small fishes (*mukene*) get munched away. Not to mention that the big fishes have advantage of using the swindled cash to bribe their way out. In some countries south of the Sahara the laws against corruption are very lenient. There is no possibility of freezing the accounts and assets of the culprits to compensate for the stolen money. On one of the many social networks I subscribe to, there was this posting: "Many States in the World have corrupt Officials. In Uganda, the corrupt have a state."

As much as the donors have a soft spot to help African countries, there is no way that these countries can continue to ask their citizens to fork out higher taxes to pay for spurious aid projects, which never materialized, when they themselves are facing economic challenges. There is no sense in spending their money onto what tomorrow won't be noticeable.

The lawlessness we see on the streets of most cities of Africa is caused by poverty. As the cliché goes, a hungry man is an angry man; the poor are hungry, dehumanized, frustrated and dejected gallant sons and daughters of Africa. They cannot uphold law and order when their own human rights are violated by the very state they serve. If nothing is done to save the situation, surely, we will continue reaping incompetence, corruption and a kind of Acquired Integrity Deficiency Syndrome (Aids).

Ultimately, we (Africans) are the sole architects of all our problems. Intrudingly, we end up blaming our miseries on the colonialists. As Brother J. Ikuya says that, a failed huntsman blames his intended quarry for its making a successful escape. Consequently, the amount of curses one hurls at a prey for its flight bid signals the level of deficiency in one's hunting skills. Good hunters rarely swear during their hunts, always drawing from their experience to ensure unfailing catch.

When the Union Jack was lowered on the October 9, 1962, the new Uganda flag went up and has stayed since then. And on that auspicious occasion, several speakers lauded the Queen's government for its efforts in combating the triad of evils, namely: Poverty, Ignorance and Disease. Fifty years after Independence, Uganda is still grappling with the 80 percent youth unemployment rate. At 50, we are still struggling with creating comprehensive policy frameworks to manage such crisis unemployment levels. We have yet to secure a prudent, visionary, innovative, creative, pragmatic, responsible and progressive government capable of establishing conducive economic, social and political conditions.

Uganda has had eight heads of state from the time of independence: Mutesa II, Milton Obote, Idi Amin, Yusuf Lule, Godfrey Binaisa, Paul Muwanga, Tito Okello and Yoweri Museveni, besides Benedicto Kiwanuka, who held the position of Chief Minister between 1961-1962. President Museveni has ruled the longest time and he is the only one still living of all Uganda's presidents since independence. With the exception of a few, the majority of the former Uganda's presidents were carried away with greed for power. As the old adage goes, "power corrupts, but absolute power corrupts absolutely". Changing leaders has not helped because the more we changed the more we remained the same!

The ideals that inspired the struggle for independence died. The constitution that had given the country a semblance of hope lies in tatters. We have been ruled by governments in which injustice, impunity, dictatorship, greed, corruption and incompetence reign supreme. Civil wars have characterized our post-independence period. We must not ignore the fact that Uganda has occasionally fought various political and military wars leading to multiple liberations with less impact to the development of the country. Most of them are inept leaders in the name of liberators. The pearl of Africa has seen bloodletting with dictators taking the country at intervals and instilling terror among innocent Ugandans.

The squatting regimes of self-imposed liberators are bellicose and frantic for any opportunity to lay their hands on lootable wealth within and beyond their territorial boundaries. The fruits of liberations are yet to be noticed because the country is still bleeding in misery from an entrenched system that keeps our people dispossessed in the economy and disempowered in politics as it was before the armed insurrection. We have failed even to maintain the little opportunities which were extended to us by the colonialists. Take the example of

Mulago hospital. It was given to us by the colonial rulers in 1962. By now we should have at least one big public hospital in each Division of Kampala and in each district upcountry. However, money goes to 'ghosts' of all types. It is a shame that we are not able to maintain even a health center. Shame indeed! The peasants lie dying in hospitals, whose lives would have been saved by a fraction of what these already wealthy, "freedom fighters" continue to hoard! Even their children's nests are feathered for umpteen generations!

One of the leaders of opposition in Uganda said that, "The guns used by the colonial government to subjugate Ugandans are still the source of power for today's tyrants. Without real power, our people have no say in what happens to the country's resources. That's why official mega-corruption, plunder, opulence, and dispensing of "favours" by ruling armed gangs go on with impunity."

Thank God that the people are waking up to realize 'the power of the people' to expose and reject the dictators, the corrupt regimes and to denounce the politics based on regions, ethnicities and militarization. African activism is becoming meaningful activism as of Gandhi type. Activism, in its real meaning, is reaction to a wrong, driven by a cause. At last there is gleam of light predicting the bright future for Africa. Concerning the corrupt regimes and for those who continue to support them, the future should be abundantly clear: "The sand is running out of the hourglass."

Strong economies for individual states of Africa should be in place before bidding for a united Africa. Although the road ahead is demanding and challenging in many aspects, it is not too late for our continent to shine. There is a saying that Rome was not built in a day. We should borrow a leaf from Europe. A continent which had consumed itself in war for centuries has become a continent unified in peace and democratic values, and one of the stronger supporters of peace throughout the world. Former enemies are now united in a common endeavor to ensure long-lasting peace. We must work hard to promote democracy, peace and high respect for human rights.

I am going to end with the following quotations: "In politics, nothing happens by accident. If it happens, you can bet it was planned that way."—Franklin D. Roosevelt, 32nd President of the United States.

"We must be prepared to make heroic sacrifices for the cause of peace that we make ungrudgingly for the cause of war. There is no task that is more important or closer to my heart". Albert Einstein.

"Patriotism is not short, frenzied outbursts of emotion, but the tranquil and steady dedication of a lifetime." ~Adlai E. Stevenson.

Dr. Lwanga Served in Hostile Environments:
Obote I, Idi Amin, Tito Okello, Muwanga and Obote II:

In order to celebrate the life of Dr. Lwanga, it is important to reflect on our past history. As I said, it is impossible to discuss the story of Dr. Lwanga without the backdrop of Idi Amin, Obote and civil wars. In all civil wars whichever were fought, some people would die on either side and all these were Ugandans. The innocent citizens who died can be described as the legendary grass that suffers when two elephants clash.

This year we are celebrating fifty years of independence. There is a raging debate as to whether the 50 years have been fruitful or wasted. Some say that the slow progress is necessary; it is the reality of the notion that a child will crawl before he/she runs. The fact is that Africa is years away from its desired state. The one million dollar question is that, "What went wrong and what should be done in order to avoid history repeating itself?" All answers point to political turmoil.

It is therefore necessary to understand the geopolitics of our country and what suites it best for it to stand as a country. The cure to the fracas lies in understanding why the politicians became the animals they are and the people became unruly. The most poignant insight into the dictators who have ruled our country is made by scrutinizing the word 'narcissism'. The Concise Oxford Dictionary of Current English defines narcissism as a "tendency to self-worship, absorption in one's own personal perfections". It is derived from the name of a Greek youth Narkissos, who fell in love with his reflection in water.

The name Milton Obote will remain a gigantic image in the Ugandan mind and cast a shadow over Uganda's history for at least another generation to come. Many in central Uganda shudder at that name. Like Mr. Hare and Ichuli in the Nile English Course book, Obote was a trickster and a professional schemer. A deep political crisis arose in Uganda in the early part of 1966 after he tricked the Kabaka of Buganda into accepting a ceremonial presidency. Uganda became a parliamentary democracy headed by a powerful prime minster (Obote). The Kabaka responded by asking Obote to remove his government from the soil of Buganda. This was the drop of water that made the vase overflow.

Idi Amin, working on Obote's orders led the Uganda Army to attack the palace of the king of Buganda, the late Kabaka Fredrick Walugembe Muteesa II (affectionately known as King Freddie) on May 24th. The army had intent of capturing and killing King Freddie. After a day long battle in which the army deployed tanks and heavy artillery, it became evident that the Kabaka and his defenders with their small arms could not hold the palace against the attacking force. Fortunately, the Kabaka was able to elude capture and with the help of several loyal supporters was able to escape into exile.

Obote ignored the fact that the Kabaka is the embodiment of Baganda. This will forever be a blemish on his legacy. To any Muganda, be it a man or a woman, the issue of attacking the palace and sending Muteesa into exile annoyed them. They detested it and they would not easily forgive and forget. Remember that it was the colonialists' action of sending off Mutesa into exile that initiated the spirit of independence. The Baganda people could not tolerate the foreigners to humiliate their king; they started pushing for independence.

Obote used his power to dismantle the cultural system that formed the backbone of stability in Uganda. Whether you like it or not, the Baganda are, together with the Zulu, Ashanti, Yoruba, Banyankole, Basoga, Banyoro, Batoro and etc., classified as 'centralized' people, where the kingship institution is the fountain head of societal/organizational endeavors. In the 'decentralized' societies such as the Acholi, Ibo or Maasai, the clan is supreme—just as the king in the 'centralized' peoples is.

In her book The Land of Promise, Mary Stuart writes concerning the kingdom of Buganda: "The early European travelers who came first to Uganda did not fear strangeness; in fact, they went in search of it. What surprised them was to find a people whose dignified sense of order seemed so like their own." No wonder monarchs and their rites of passage are of greater interest to westerner tourists; even greater than gorillas or birds which have top tourist billings.

Culture is very important even more so in today's homogenized and globalized world. The history of any given ethnic group is rooted in the cultural institutions. You cannot know yourself unless you know your history. Arthur Bagunywa made this comment concerning the cultural institutions of Uganda: "First and foremost our indisputably rich cultural diversity dictates a logical choice of corresponding political structures to match God's predetermined ethnic design. No amount of political engineering can change the cultural mosaic of Uganda".

Yoga Adhola says that, "As an identity, the Baganda had been a dominant identity in that region since 1600 (to grasp this read). This position of dominance imbued them with the ideology of a dominant power. They feel they are superior to other identities and deserve a special position in the affairs of Uganda. When the colonialist came, they accorded them that superior and special position in the affairs of Uganda. Their treatment by the colonialists was to reinforce their superiority complex . . . . It is this Obote who led the Buganda removal from a position of dominance or what Professor Mazrui once called a status reversal. They are not going to forgive him for that."

When you deprive a 'centralized' people of their king, they have nothing to fall back on. Obote's agenda of eliminating the kings in the name of establishing a republic did not project astute political acumen. Intriguingly, Obote and the dictators thereafter ruled as absolute monarchies, replacing the constitutional monarchy with the rule of tyranny. They acted like even greater monarchies coercing all people including those who do not agree with them into paying allegiances to a political institution they disagree with. It is like they are playing on people's minds! The sour truth is that dictators hate federal (fedro) because they cannot afford to have another bull like them in the kraal. That is why the opponents of our king allow the mushrooming of the nonexistent kingdoms with aim of suffocating an institution which had existed for over 600 years.

Obote is responsible for the untold sufferings of the majority of the people of Uganda. He was enthusiastically welcomed by the Baganda people but he turned around and portrayed himself like a pauper who was invited for a meal but instead of saying thank you, he goes on to chase the hosts away. The 1966 attack on the Lubiri was the peak of the souring relationship between Mengo and Obote. Months after the attack, an attempt on Obote's life was made at Luzira when the president was on his way back to preside over the pass out of prison warders at Luzira prison, only to hit his deputy John Babiiha. Dan Kamanyi was the brain behind the first attempt on a sitting president's life in Uganda. He confessed that, "I organised a group of six people, four of them—John Obo, Henry Kyeyune, Capt Mugarura and Katabarwa—were cadets just dismissed from the army and were bitter. Others were Dan Kiwanuka and me—We started planning on how and where we could hit Obote from. Ambushing him was the easiest option." (*Daily Monitor Sept. 16, 2013*).

The politics of intolerance in Uganda was initiated by Obote. He turned out to be a pathological liar who only spoke the truth by accident. After the 1966 crisis, after forcibly abolishing the constitution of Uganda that he had pledged to protect, Obote debased himself before Ugandans beyond reprieve by trying to destroy the history of Buganda. In political science, they call such habits—officiating history, where a regime thinks history starts with its coming to power.

J. Ikuya quoted President Yoweri Museveni, in the late 1960s, when he was a student at the University of Dar es Salaam displaying an imprint of remarkable fervor in the cause of agitation against the Obote regime: "He would lambast the effrontery and arrogance of UPC rule, using acerbic imagery for his student audiences. He compared the UPC haughtiness to a man who slays another's father, takes over the widowed mother for a wife and then demands that the orphaned children should respect him as their dear father!"

On March 2, 1966 Obote the then prime minister, abolished the offices of president and vice president and assumed all executive powers. Then on April 15, 1966 forced parliament to adopt a new constitution which they had not read that came to be called the 'pigeon-hole' constitution. With military planes flying over a parliament surrounded by the military, Obote was sworn-in as executive president. Obote's action opened a window for dictators to come in without restraining. Since then, the country has been led by common thugs and highway robbers camouflaged under the guise of expensive suits. The window that Obote used to become a leader should be shut otherwise we might end up capitalizing on alleviating the symptoms rather than curing the disease.

Betty Kamya said that, "Uganda's Constitution creates dictators. Dictators are arrogant, work for self-preservation and believe in own invincibility, the outcome of which are human rights' abuse, patronage, corruption and electoral malpractices. Like maggots and flies are consequences of rot emanating from a compost heap, these vices are consequences, not the cause of dictatorship! Until we deal with the Constitution, dictatorship is here to stay, no matter who occupies State House."

Obote diverted the power that belonged to the citizens of Uganda to the hands of the President, who exercised his sovereignty through the army. The 1995 Constitution places soldiers below civilians and that is why Article 1 is clear that power belongs to the people. After dismissing the constitution, the power of the gun and the military force used by the executive overwhelmed the Parliament and the Judiciary creating the facade of democracy. Uganda's constitution ceased to be worth the paper it was written on. Lawlessness is apparently seen in the brutality of the police and other security agencies. The security agencies degenerated to opportunistic murderers and are the genesis to our social and political problems. They ceased to be nonpartisan.

Milton Obote and Idi Amin were cut and sewn from the same piece of cloth: illegitimacy, cruelty and dictatorship. The former (Obote) only happened to be more cunning whereas the latter (Idi Amin) was more authoritarian and murderous. But Obote blamed Amin for the same mistakes which he created. Introspection is something the vast majority of us can't do. All we know is to blame somebody else. To the people of central region Obote is as culpable as Amin. It would be sheer mockery for one to criticize the other. These two dictators remind me of the Luganda proverbial saying *"Obukookolo bugeyana"*; both lepers (*Obukookolo*) tease each other (*bugeyana*) forgetting they all have missing fingers (*engalo empaanvu*).

Idi Amin, a man of little education, even less sophistication, and with a brutal streak, became the instrument that Obote relied on to amass his own political power. Obote lived to curse the day he promoted Idi Amin to command the national army. It was a matter of time the rabid dog that he trained to bite turned against his master. Amin attracted the attention of Obote's foes. As the late Achebe said; "When you bring ant-infested fagots into the house, don't complain when lizards begin paying you a visit." Soon, Amin became the 'blunt tool' that the British and the Israelis turned to when they decided to get rid of Obote in 1971. A man who was not mentally fit to be a group leader or even a local LC chairman became a president! He could have been a good soldier but the presidency was too long a shot.

Obote's woes internationally began after he openly pursued to become an African activist. Obote clearly saw the dangers to Africa emanating from the attitudes towards our continent from outsiders. For example, once while speaking about the challenges to our continent, he said: "When we come to Africa, we find a situation where the rest of the world appears to be saying in unison that they have a natural right to come to our continent and share with us our natural heritage. I say that we Africans must rise up and exert our rights."

In pursuit of African unity and regional integration, Obote proceeded to build close friendships with Nkrumah, Gamal Abdel Nasser of Egypt, Julius Nyerere of Tanzania, Kenneth Kaunda of Zambia and Sekou Toure of Guinea. These were the giants of Pan African unity. In pursuit of the liberation of all oppressed peoples, Obote build close friendships with leaders outside the continent like Indian then-prime minister Indra Gandhi, and Marshal Tito of Yugoslavia. He became a major player in the Non-Aligned Movement and a powerful voice in the OAU. He was a passionate critic of white minority governments in Angola, Mozambique, Rhodesia (now Zimbabwe), Namibia and Apartheid South Africa. In 1965, Ian Smith made the Unilateral Declaration of Independence (UDI) of Rhodesia. Progressive African opinion was outraged. It is Obote and Nyerere who offered Nkrumah the strongest support to push Britain, which was the colonial master, to discipline its rebel clients in Salisbury (now Harare). The former colonialist hated him for his stand and hatched plans to eliminate him.

The Western countries saw Idi Amin as an answer to Obote's aggressive activism. They joined hands with Idi Amin to pull the rug out from under Obote. They ignored Amin's bad record and focused on getting rid of Obote. Journalist and historian Mark Curtis notes that the British were all too aware of Amin's murderous ways, even as they supported his coup in 1971. Curtis notes: "Amin was 'corrupt and unintelligent', Harold Smedley wrote two days after the coup. There was 'something of the villain about him and he may well be quite unscrupulous and indeed ruthless', a Foreign Office official wrote six days after the coup. Richard Slater managed to convince himself, however, that 'despite his limitations, he [Amin] has considerable dignity and more the air of a leader than Obote'."

Internally, tension was building and Obote's problems were mounting. Obote had successfully mobilized the allied tribes of the north (Northerners) into his party (UPC). He successfully used tribal sentiments to play on people's conscious. At the beginning of his regime, Obote had a cozy relationship with Idi Amin. However, things started to fall apart. The relationship of the two staunch members of UPC became wobbly; apparently a quiet storm was burbling under the radar. Treachery for treachery. They both had up their sleeves trump cards about each other; unprincipled great friends can make great enemies too. It was a matter of time that Ugandans saw a face-off-cat-fight between the two. And the ripple effect touched the tribal feud button, which set the UPC into self-destruction mode.

After being shot at during a Uganda People's Congress delegates' conference at the Lugogo Indoor Stadium on October 19, 1969, Obote started suspecting everyone, particularly Amin, of having been involved in the assassination attempt. In Luganda there is a saying loosely translated "the destitute dog you natured, is the one that bits you". The panic caused Obote to hit at every moving object. This state of affairs went as far as causing the ban of all political parties in Uganda.

Idi Amin was groomed for power despite his unclean record. For example Idi Amin had masterminded the murder of Brigadier Okoya and his wife on 24, 1970 at his residence on Gulu-Kampala Road in Koro Village. Idi Amin used Guwedeko and Kasule, the air force technician in his nasty scheme to kill Brigadier Okoya. The two officers were arrested, detained and taken to Luzira Prison by Obote. On January 16, 1971, Amin convened the press to announce that Obote planned to have him arrested. This public appeal sealed the destiny of Amin as he was now in open and obvious conflict with President Obote. Obote now wanted Amin out of the way. Indeed, Obote had just reshuffled the army and kicked Amin upstairs and was trying to consolidate his position in the military.

Idi Amin increasingly became a hard nut to crack. Because of the internal disputes, Obote had decided not to travel to Singapore to the Commonwealth meeting. However, Nyerere, Kaunda and progressive opinion in Africa felt that his voice would be important in bolstering the pressure on Heath to back down on selling arms to South Africa. It was in response to this need to help South Africa that Obote placed his presidency at risk and travelled to Singapore. And his travel was tragic as it gave Idi Amin legroom to engineer a successful coup. In fact, when Obote went to Singapore Commonwealth he left orders to his royal military commanders to the effect that he wanted Amin's head on a silver tray upon his return from the Singapore Commonwealth meeting that was held from January 14 to 22, 1971—orders that his lieutenants were unable to carry out in a timely fashion.

It is believed that Britain worked with Israel to topple Obote's government. One intriguing moment that Obote recounted before his death was that the then British Prime Minister Edward Heath stated during the Commonwealth conference that "those who are condemning the British sale of arms to South Africa, some of them will not go back to their countries."

Apart from the master mind (Amin), Obote had successfully arrested the officers who were involved in the murder of Brigadier Okoya. When Amin took over the government, the duo (Guwedeko/Kasule) were released and promoted. Guwedeko was promoted to the rank of Brigadier and Kasule promoted to major. Later on, the same officers and all people who were involved in the investigation of the murder of Brig. Okoya were killed by Idi Amin in bid to suppress any possible witness against him.

Some historians say that Obote himself forced Idi Amin to overthrow him while the West looked on with relief! Others say that Idi Amin became a leader by chance. James Tumusiime in his book called, "Uganda's Presidents" wrote that, "All leading bookstores with all that we have been allowed to know about President Idi Amin, it is hard to imagine he had refused to take office as president after the 1971 coup. It could even be doubted whether the coup was actually his work! And that it took one junior officer, Juma Oka—nicknamed Butabika—to put Amin at gunpoint for him to accept the presidency. Idi Amin appeared just as Captain Charles Arube was volunteering to become president. Amin accepted to become president on January 25, 1971. Of course, the transformation that he underwent thereafter is amazing—and has been sumptuously recorded."

In his inaugural speech, Idi Amin seemed to be a reluctant leader. He announced that he was a soldier, not a politician, and that the military government would remain only as a caretaker regime until new elections. Why didn't he quit thereafter? G L. Binaisa has the right answer; he used to say that '*Entebbe ewoma*' (literary meaning that the highest office is addictive).

As I said, it is impossible to write our history, even the biography of Dr. Lwanga without discussing Idi Amin. From the time of His regime of terror, Uganda began a steady journey of moving from progress to regress. Yet Amin is the most known person internationally, more known than the Olympic gold medal holders.

Who was Idi Amin? His childhood real names were Idi Awo-Ongo Angoo. He was born on May 17, 1928 at about 4.00 a.m. in a police barracks at the present International Conference Centre in Kampala. He was of the Adibu clan of the Kakwa ethnic group. His father was initially Andreas Nyabire, a Catholic who converted to Islam in 1910 and became Amin Dada. Andreas Nyabire Amin Dada was born in 1889 and died in 1976. He was a Kakwa from Adida in Southern Sudan. The mother of Idi Amin was called Assa Aatte. Born in 1904, she died in 1970. She was daughter of a Lugbara Sultan (Chief) at Leiko Iruna in the present day Democratic Republic of the Congo.

In 1933 Idi Amin lived with his mother's relatives at Mawale near Semuto in the present Luwero district. There he reared goats from 1936 to 1938. He then moved to the home of Sheikh Ahmed Hussein in the present Semuto town from 1938 to 1940 where he started reciting the Koran. In 1940 he came to Bombo to live with his maternal uncle Yusuf Tanaboo. He tried to register for the equivalent of Primary One but Nubians were not admitted in schools. As a twelve-year-old Amin participated in the Nubian riots against discrimination and was injured by Makerere College students at Wandegeya. In 1941 Amin joined Garaya Islamic school at Bombo, and again excelled in reciting the Koran under Mohammed Al Rajab from 1941-1944. Amin and Abdul Kadir Aliga won honours in reciting the Koran in 1943. At the end of 1944 Amin and fifteen other students at the Bombo Garaya were taken for conscription into the army. However, Amin and five others were released for being underage. He then went to the present Kiyindi zone at Kalerwe near Bwaise and started doing odd jobs in 1945. He got a job as a door hat and coat attendant at the Imperial Hotel at the end of 1945. Later in 1946 a British army officer was impressed and offered to recruit Idi Amin in the army. Amin served at Magamaga Barracks in Jinja as a laundry and kitchen army staff as he trained until 1947 when he transferred to Kenya for real military service.

He served in the 21st KAR infantry brigade at Gilgil, until 1949 when his unit moved to Somalia at Belet Uen to fight the Shifta animal raiders. In 1950, Amin's unit returned to Fort Hall in Kenya. There he trained in the Scottish military band. In 1951 he returned to Jinja but went back to Kenya the same year. In 1952 his battalion was deployed against the Mau Mau. Amin became corporal the same year. In 1953 he became a sergeant for his role in starting the mobile foot patrols in the forests occupied by the Mau Mau. While fighting the Mau Mau, Amin had a son and a daughter with two Kikuyu women.

Amin's name appeared on the list of those soldiers who performed best against the Mau Mau. He was also nominated for promotion to the new rank of *afendi* (that is, warrant officer equivalent). He returned to Jinja, Uganda in 1954 where he was selected best in the parade for Queen Elizabeth. In 1955 Sgt. Amin again led the guard or honour to welcome Kabaka Edward Mutesa from exile.

He moved to Lango district in 1956 and successfully defended the Langi from the Karimojong raids as head of a platoon. He got a child with a Langi woman. The same year 1955, Amin's unit was deployed to quell a military mutiny in southern Sudan. He again performed well by the standards of the time.

In 1957 Amin led requests for salary increment. It was denied. Amin also failed the intellectual (written and oral) tests for promotion. He was posted to the KAR band. In 1958 Amin again failed promotional exams but passed field exercises in 1959 and was promoted in December of that year. In July 1960 a British officer called Ronald Cedric Weeding was defeated and killed by the Turkana in Karamoja. Amin was sent to Karamoja. The army spokesman described Amin as having "restored the prestige of the forces of law and order in the region of Karamoja". Subsequently, Amin was commissioned to Lieutenant in July 1961 by Sir Frederick Crawford. The same year Amin and Daudi Ochieng were assigned the duty of negotiating with Sir Edward Mutesa for a political compromise. He convinced Mutesa that the Uganda army in which Amin was part, would never move against the Kingdom. The mission was a success.

Idi Amin then moved against the Turkana in 1962 with two convoys of the 4th KAR. Using the threat to cut off their penis, Amin disarmed the Turkana without a fight. He was again part of the initiative to placate the unhappy Mutesa when in 1963, he proposed that the Kabaka becomes Major General and Commander-in-Chief of the army. Ironically, the same year, Amin prevented the recruitment of Kabaka Yekka and Uganda People's Congress youths into the army. He instigated complaints about the drive for educated people to take over army leadership. The few of them who managed to join dropped out due to the deliberate tough training intended to demoralize them and discourage them. Not because Baganda people could not fight, taking into account that 99.99% of officers in the 2nd World War were Baganda.

Early in 1964 Idi Amin complained that the army was doing all the heavy work of the independence government of the Rwanda where it was helping to keep law and order. He said that they were also working in the Rwenzoris and on the Sudan border but had not benefited from Uhuru like the civil servants and the politicians. The British army commander Lt.-Colonel W.W. Cheyne blocked Idi Amin's request for a salary increment. Idi Amin instigated the February-March military mutiny. Idi Amin was proposed for the role of mediator between the mutineers and the UPC-KY government for the mutiny he had started. The end of the mutiny saw the British officers lose their jobs to Amin. He also got a salary increment, the promotion to Major and the command of the First Battalion.

Idi Amin who in 1962 had been discontinued from a platoon commander course at Wiltshire in the U.K and who in 1963 failed to complete a paratrooper course nevertheless became a deputy Army Commander in 1964. In 1965 Idi Amin was given the task of supporting the Congo nationalists to resist the foreign supported government of Mobutu Sese Seko. Idi Amin benefited financially and invested in a bus company called Trans-Nile. At the end of 1965 the Congo mercenaries defeated the Idi Amin-backed rebels in the Congo.

In Uganda Amin was identified with Prime Minister Obote who was being pressured to leave office. Idi Amin on February 22, 1966 resisted the military coup to oust Obote and helped execute a counter-coup to give Obote absolute power. Amin led the assault on the Lubiri but contrary to orders from Obote seized only one side instead of encircling the Lubiri. Mutesa escaped. Idi Amin was promoted to Colonel and became the Army Commander replacing Brigadier Opolot in 1966. In April 1968, Obote promoted Amin to Major General—a reward for his loyalty during the Republican Monarchist crisis.

His long military career took him to the very top of the Ugandan armed forces as Army Commander. It was from that position that he staged a successful coup in 1971, deposing his benefactor, President Milton Obote. Many thought the Idi Amin takeover was a short term thing, and what was initially taken as a happy turn of events for Uganda turned into resentment and later a nightmare. His eight-year reign of terror belongs to the annals of historical infamy, often mentioned in the same breath as Hitler, Stalin and Pol Pot.

Outside its borders, Uganda is synonymous with the image Idi Amin. Even someone who might not locate this country on the world map will say they know Uganda because of Amin. Amin earned the image of a "monster" ruler, such that the mention of Uganda tends to elicit all sorts of wild imaginations. Surprisingly, by his external appearance, you could hardly notice that he was a killer. He was a jovial, sociable and burly figure who liked to entertain his audience. But behind a grinned face was a well calculated monster. He was a kind of guy who would kill you when smiling. He was a celebrity too. He was a former heavy weight champion and a good swimmer.

Obote was unscrupulous leader shadowed by political myopia, pragmatism, untold greed and insensitivity to the common man; this was punctuated by primitive acquisition of wealth, extra judicial killings, personalization of state property, press censure, rape of the land's supreme law (constitution) and extermination of people criticizing him. The people of the central region had no choice but to welcome Amin because they wanted leadership. In the absence of genuine leadership, they would listen to anyone who stepped up to overthrow Obote's regime. They were so thirsty for it such that they would crawl through the desert toward a mirage, and when they discovered there's no water, they would drink the sand.

At first people liked Idi Amin and welcomed him as a liberator. But soon the people realized that his public assertions should be taken with a pinch of salt. "You can fool some of the people all of the time, and all of the people some of the time, but you cannot fool all of the people all of the time"—Abraham Lincoln.

People welcomed Amin because they wanted to break from their past. They probably asserted that they would be better off with the Angel they didn't know than the devil they knew. They were inclined to trust the Angel they didn't know because the devil will always remain the devil: cunning, deceptive and angelic in appearance.

After Amin absolutely consolidated powers, he started to act arrogantly, oblivious of any cares because there were no consequences. He became intoxicated with power and he saw no life in future without power. Eventually he became a thorn in the flesh of every peace loving Ugandan and it was tough for us to untangle from our predicament or even to look for help from outside! The Western powers were not the beacon of hope either. In the first place they groomed Idi Amin to power well knowing that he was a murderer and a nihilist at heart.

Amin restricted the rights of law-abiding Ugandans. Instead of revamping a system that Ugandans could be proud of; he unleashed terror against innocent people. Even after Amin showed his true colors and began butchering the innocent citizens, the countries that brought him to power did not swing into action to remove him. Apart from the anti-Amin sentiments hyped by the Western countries and economic sanctions, which ironically were more oppressive to the local people than to the dictator, they did nothing to attenuate or even eliminate the massacres and to cater for the victims of the regime. Historian Prof. Phares Mutibwa argues that Amin could have been toppled any time during his first few days in office if a military invasion from the outside had materialized. But the Western powers and our African neighbors did nothing about it.

The British government was running circles defending the indefensible. Their policy and approach to pull the plug on the rising tide of dictatorship continued to be unimaginative and moribund. The British High Commissioner Slater made the following astonishing remark concerning Idi Amin: "So long as he stays in power, Ugandan reactions to controversial British policies in Africa will be containable and the influence of the moderates in the OAU [Organization of African Unity] will be strengthened. It remains therefore a British interest to see his regime consolidated."

The British government was preoccupied with securing British interests when Ugandans were dying like leaves falling from a tree, something that rubbed Ugandans the wrong way, at least if moral aptitude is anything to go by. The foreign media outlets turned a blind eye to the early signs of the brutality of the military regime, allowing Amin to get away with murder. They were busy selling

Amin's image to the world by showing how unpopular Obote and his policies were in the country. They instigated that Amin assumed power in a mood of moral righteousness after abuses of power and political excesses under Milton Obote. The lurid errors by foreign journalist were enough to misinform the world. The 'information gap' was playing games with both the obscenities of an African tyrant and the credulousness of the rest of the world. The more the Western countries ignored Idi Amin's rule of tyranny, the more he entrenched himself and the harder it became to uproot him. "Things may come to those who wait, but only the things left by those who hustle"— Abraham Lincoln

Amin was cunning and manipulative. As one editor commented "Amin was not an unwitting beneficiary of the situation but quickly demonstrated political cunning that would resuscitate several times in the years to come." Three days after his coup, he released all political detainees, some 55 in number, many of whom had been arrested during the 1966-67 political standoffs. Abubaker Kakyama Mayanja, who had fled to exile in Britain in 1966 during the attack on Mengo, and who had been a minister of Buganda, was gushing in his praise on his return from exile after Amin's coup. He said that the new revolution of the coup is the country's resurrection. "My pleasure is beyond words and is really not expressible, just leave it at jubilation." Prof. Mutibwa notes that even prominent members of the Indian business community were glad to see the back of Obote and his nationalization policies.

Amin, would, however, score the biggest goal when he had Edward Mutesa's body brought back from exile for a state funeral. The Kabaka had died mysteriously in exile where he had fled the 1966 attack on his Buganda Kingdom. The return of Mutesa's body, announced just a day after the 1971 coup, would serve to not only cultivate confidence in the new government, but raise hope among Ugandans, that a 'savior' had come to rescue the country from its past woes. Beneath Amin's 'good' gesture was an intention to reap political capital and to enter the good books of Buganda, who were still hurting from the exile, death and burial abroad of their king.

Obote had shifted power from the ruling party to the army. He had recruited the royal army. The military leadership was handed over to the fellow tribesmen and his cohorts. The children of those in the clique were given power in the day to day running of the government and controlling almost the entire economy. Amin's priority was to reverse the situation. He (Amin) was not a sleeping dog. He launched a systematic recruitment drive which attracted 10,000 men, mostly loyalists, in three months, doubling the size of the army in the process. Mamdani notes: "The core of the new recruits included some 4,000 Sudanese ex-Anyanya fighters, along with a sprinkling of former Zairian freedom fighters. The bulk of the remainder came from Amin's own West Nile District; 40 per cent of these were Muslims".

In sum, the new army was primarily a mercenary force. The greatest care was taken to ensure that the condition of their survival was the continuation of Amin's rule. The massive military recruitment drive by Idi Amin was an answer to earlier attempts by Obote to populate the army with his own tribesmen (Langis/Acholis) and isolate Amin. Thus the army now had two factions: the remnants of the pro-Obote faction, and the new pro-Amin recruits. There was a contradiction that had to be resolved. It was a contradiction that gave very early glimpse of who Idi Amin Dada really was; a not-so-gentle giant whose primary tool of political persuasion and control was violence.

Idi Amin Dada's military regime in Uganda was launched with a systematic slaughter of military officers of Acholi ethnic identity and those officers suspected to be loyal to Milton Obote's government. Kasozi noted in his book, The Social Origins of Violence in Uganda: "While Obote used the 1967 Detention Act to lock his opponents in prisons where they were 'well treated', Amin killed them." Such was the fate of various high-ranking officers known or perceived to be his opponents. There were mass killings of members of the [General Service Unit], the Special Force, police, prisoners and civilians." In fact two thirds of soldiers, out of a total of 9,000 men, appeared to have been executed in Amin's first year of power, according to accounts. This massacre story only acted as a spark for a stick of dynamite that had lain idle. An avalanche of allegations of executions was yet to follow.

In September 1972 at Simba Battalion Barracks, Mbarara after the attempted invasion of Uganda from Tanzania had been thwarted by the Uganda army, there was massive slaughtering of Langi and Acholi soldiers. During that same week, the US president, Richard Nixon, referred to Idi Amin as a "pre-historic monster" (an ape without education) and instructed Henry Kissinger, the secretary of state, to support the British, who had planned a military intervention to stop the bloodshed in Uganda. Nixon's orders were a result of a New York Times front page story on September 21, 1972 of a photo of Simba Barracks displaying the military brandishing rifles on a pile of corpses. The plan of invasion never materialized because Kissinger never followed through.

Kasozi notes, chillingly, that many people looked the other way in the early days of the Amin's regime despite the rising body count: "What is upsetting about Ugandans is that while the Langi and the Acholi suffered, many laughed, thinking their turn would never come, just as they had laughed at the Baganda in 1966. But wherever violence occurs in the state, it eventually overflows to everyone. By 1971, the fires of political violence that had been lit at Nakulabye were spreading into the rural areas of Apac, Lira and Gulu. Soon they would scorch all the land."

This reminds of Martin Niemoller's quotation. He was a German preacher with an acerbic tongue, who later turned into a social activist. He once worked with the then notorious German Chancellor, Adolf Hitler. He fervently backed Hitler's sinister plans of keeping Germany unadulterated, most especially by the Jews. But later Neimoller fell out with Hitler. He was on several occasions detained without trial on Hitler's orders. His poetic quotation goes like this: "When Hitler attacked the Jews, I was not a Jew, therefore I was not concerned. And when Hitler attacked the Catholics, I was not a Catholic, and therefore, I was not concerned. And when Hitler attacked the unions and the industrialists, I was not a member of the unions and I was not concerned. Then Hitler attacked me and the Protestant Church—and there was nobody left to be concerned."

Idi Amin's next victims were the Jews, the very people who planned the coup that brought him to power. The Jews are known for their earliest contribution to the development of Uganda. They completed the building of Entebbe airport, the Uganda Commercial bank headquarters now called Cham towers, the Bugolobi flats and Malire barracks Bombo.

After Amin failed to secure a deal of arms sell with Israel and the Western countries, he turned to His Arab friends. The fallout led to an animosity between the Muslim leader (Idi Amin) and the Jewish nation, one could be tempted to think that the two have never seen eye to eye. Obviously, Amin had wider grievances against Israel, the US and the Western world in general, and the failed arms deal was just another drop of petrol on a simmering fire. Perhaps the most combustible issue between Muslims and the Western world has always been the plight of Palestine and Israel's continued domination of it with tacit Western approval.

In October 1973, Syria and Egypt attacked Israel. As a fledgling state, Israel was surrounded by powerful hostile nations including Jordan, Egypt and Syria that were keen to break the newcomer apart. In bid to demonstrate his loyalty to the Arab world, Amin hurriedly formed the African Liberation Force comprising 300 officers and sent them to the Golan Heights to fight Israel. The Six-Day War in June 1967 and especially the Yom Kippur War in October 1973 underscored why the world needed to support Israel against the aggression of Arab neighbors eager to destroy it. Israel fought valiantly to beat back the aggressors, and in the process seized strategic pieces of land as guarantees for its security.

Within a moment of time, in his own incoherent and naive flamboyance, Amin turned into a fanatic African activist, preaching the song of greater equality in global terms and speaking in hammer and tongs against Zionism and imperialism. As one writer put it, "The role of Idi Amin helped to erode the legitimacy of Western hegemony by challenging it and defying it in a variety of ways. First, the myth of Western invincibility was receiving severe knocks from Amin's sustained strategy of irreverence—Amin converted the whole world into a stage, trying to force some old imperial myths through the exit door, and to bring in new defiant myths of black assertiveness. The biggest act of defiance still remained the expulsion of British Asians and the nationalization of some British firms and property."

Amin adopted God as a convenient ploy after taking power. He misused the Almighty's name to back his sensitive crusades. For example on August 4, 1972, Idi Amin announced that he had a dream in which God asked him to expel the Asians from Uganda. It has also been argued that Amin was emboldened in his action, at least in part, by his newfound friendship with Libya's Col. Muammar Gaddafi who had also engineered the expulsion of Italians from their former North African colony. The majority of indigenous Ugandans looked at the Asian community with indifference at best and, at worst, hostility, partly fuelled by jealousy over the wealth the minority had accumulated.

On August 9 Amin signed a decree revoking entry permits and certificates of residence of non-Uganda citizens of Asian origin, including those from India, Pakistan and Bangladesh. If I am allowed to quote the Ugandan newspaper: "The citizen Asians, asked to queue in order to confirm the validity of their citizenship, found their passports and certificates torn up. Eventually all Asians were expelled. Neither citizen nor professional remained." They all had to leave Uganda in ninety days. Amin allocated the Asians' businesses to his loyal soldiers, the puppets Nubians and Muslims who had no experience at all to operate the same businesses. The hullabaloo that followed was absolutely Amin's responsibility!

Some Western countries volunteered to take in the expelled Asians as refuge. Canada had at this time offered to take in some evacuees and many would eventually end up in that country. Britain also appealed to several other countries to help take in some of the departing Asians. Out of the 75,000 or so Asians who had been living in Uganda, historian A.B. Kasozi notes that Britain took in 27,000—the majority while 4,500 went to India. He goes on to say that, "[Some] 3,600 were put into refugee camps before resettlement in other countries. Another 20,000 were unaccounted for". (*Writes Kasozi in The Social Origins of Violence in Uganda, 1964-1985*).

According to Vali Jamal, in his book on Uganda Asians features: "On the very next day after the departure deadline, all remaining Asians were asked to assemble at the airstrip to validate their residency status. Between 6,000 and 7,000 people turned up. These were mostly people whose Ugandan citizenship had been confirmed by the Immigration Department during that three-month verification exercise. They were the ones who had opted to stay on—well, momentarily, because Amin came out with all his threats of the past three months. He said when addressing the Asians who were citizens of Uganda that: "Good you want to live here as citizens of Uganda, then you should be prepared to live as Ugandans; your daughters should be ready to get married to Africans. You will not be allowed to operate businesses in big cities. I shall send you to cultivate the soil in Karamoja!" Vali Jamal says that Haji Maki (Haji Adam's son) Abdurahman fainted on hearing this and he had to administer first aid to him. Eventually he managed to get himself to England via the refugee route "—and I met him once on Edgware Road in London where he was running a shoe store called Maksons, a derivative from his name Maki."

Some Asians who were not happy to be accorded the favor to live in Uganda as "citizens" went to the UNDP for help. Mr. Prattley was the Resident Representative. He advised them that if they were stateless, they could be helped as refugees. They took this hint and threw away their Uganda passport, thereby becoming "stateless". At least five thousand people did this. Refugee camps were set up for them at the Gurdwara and Patidhar Samaj. The UNHCR came in. Within a few weeks various countries in Europe—Italy, Switzerland, Belgium, Sweden, Malta and Spain—agreed to take a thousand each of these refugees. They were taken to camps in those countries. Some were absorbed there but for most it was a staging post for dispersion to more familiar countries. Many were accepted by Australia and New Zealand. The British relented and allowed those with family members to join them in Britain.

After expelling the Asians, Idi Amin handed over their shops to the *'mafuta mingi'* who had no experience in international businesses at all. Once they had finished the original stock, they could not restock but instead filled the shops with other local agricultural and industrial produces. For example a hardware store became a grocery retail shop or even a restaurant. For the first time goats were reared in storely buildings in the center of the city; the same facilities that used to be enterprises of the wealthy Asians became pastures to shelter animals.

The situation worsened when the donors imposed trade sanctions, which affected the donor-supported programs. Europe and America froze their aid to Uganda hoping that the economy would collapse. Uganda was hugely isolated. In the absence of foreign exchange, our currency was extremely devalued. The inexperienced dictator retaliated by ordering the Bank of Uganda to print more money (Ugandan Shilling). Out of defiance, he introduced his portrait on the currency. Because the foreign exchange issue became agitating, the illiterate Amin ordered the then finance minister to bring that "Mr. foreign exchange" to answer for his mischievousness. This was not the first time Idi Amin expressed his imbecility stupidity and shallow mindedness. The craziness of controversy used to accompany his often asymmetrically equivocal views! He is quoted to have called Entebbe Airport the bus parking for Airplanes. Also, he is quoted in his speech to call for the unity of East African Universities saying that Makerere University of Nairobi and Makerere University of Dar es salaam should join hands with Makerere University of Uganda. Just to mention a few blunders made by an uneducated dictator. I wonder how a sane, educated and intelligent person with a sovereign mind sat in his audience to listen to this baloney!

Essential commodities became scarce and were regulated and distributed by government officials. If you wanted fuel for example above five litres, you had to go to the district commissioner, who would then write you a letter authorizing the purchase. These were hard times that cannot be compared to today where one can spend at leisure. Essential commodities like sugar and salt were distributed by government official. The privileged people who had access to the big men received allocations of essential commodities on pieces of papers which they sold to traders with big margins of profits (*enjawulo*). The selling of non-existence stock to the gullible customers was akin to a daring 'air supply' (*empewo*). Some conmen became rich overnight.

Because the supply was by far greater than the demand, hoarding and black marketing was rampant.

Once every other week, you had to stand in the queue for the whole day in order to get a kilo of sugar, salt and a piece of washing soap. The military and Moslems were treated with preference to avert massive sufferings. The Moslems had an upper hand because they were handed packages of essential commodities after their weekly Juma prayers. Although not all Moslems perpetuated the nasty stereotype, most of them benefited from the regime. The government started providing for the army directly through goods ferried by a chartered aircraft. In order to finance these ad hoc transactions Amin started selling coffee on cash basis—with money paid directly to him.

The supply was by far greater than the demand. To mitigate the economic crisis, Amin allowed imports to enter free. Some greedy traders hoarded the essential commodities purposely to sell them on black-market. Counterfeit goods appeared on the market. For example motor oil packed as cooking oil; sand packed as sugar; a mixture of sand and ashes sold as cement, blocks of wood in cartons of washing soap and etc. Idi Amin ordered firing squad as counter offensive to traders who deliberately sabotaged the economy (economic bandits). He dealt with them in the same manner he dealt with militant dissents but this did not improve the economy.

Mention Egypt, people will first think of Pyramids but mention 'Uganda', the first thing you hear from any foreigner is the tyranny of Idi Amin. Amin is an enigma and a personification of terror. In the 1960s, after independence, Uganda was like a blooming flower laden with nectar. Naturally, all manner of insects; bees and wasps alike were attracted to it. Amin landed to deplete the flower of its life. The pollution is still well and alive today. The pinch of the economic turmoil has continued to be stroked up to today. Obote II could not change much. When Museveni came to power, the country was already in economic turmoil and his long term in office has not helped much. The group of people who are aptly labeled as Mafiosi (members of Mafia) who have hijacked our economy today are seeds planted by Idi Amin's corrupt regime.

Credit goes to President Museveni and NRM government for abandoning its initial Marxist economic policies that stressed a mixed private-state economy and steadily opening the economy up to private investment. The move ended the shortages of sugar, salt, cooking oil and medicine of the 1986-1990 period. In 1994, it was reported that Uganda had registered an annual growth rate of eight percent for the 1993-1994 period. The last time Uganda had felt this optimistic and confident in itself was in the 1960s and early 1980s. President Museveni (the "economist") decided that for the country to develop it needed a "middle-class". (For the record: one does not just create a middle-class; it arises out of sound economic-policies). Well, a "middle-class-of-sorts" was created, but the country is still wallowing in poverty and a long, long way from the 1st world target Museveni had in mind.

Idi Amin established Nagulu Public safety unity (PSU) headed by a notorious officer called [Kassim] Obura to deal with lawlessness and economic saboteurs. Rather than cracking down criminals, innocent law abiding citizens were victimized by the killing squads. Mzee Joseph Kimbowa had a big contractor that made his name in the 1960s and '70s through his firm, Kimbowa Building and Constructors, founded in 1950. He narrowly escaped death at the hands of Obura. He narrates the torture he went through at PSU in this way: "Two men were slapping me at the same time until I could not hear anything! They then put my head through the rim of a lorry and the beating started again. This went on for more than an hour until I passed out. The next morning when I regained consciousness the torture continued. I was made to stand in the open and look up into the sun with a finger pointed at the sun while moving in a circle. This lasted for some time until I lost stability and fell down."

Amin turned the State Research Bureau at Nakasero into a killing machine targeting his opponents and those with links to imperialists. Prisoners were brutally tortured before forced to meet their maker. The Christian denominations which were sponsored by the Western countries became an obvious target. During the times of Idi Amin, Moslems were the minority in Uganda making up less than 10% of the population. In his bid to expand the Moslem Empire down south of the Sahara, Idi Amin aggressively carried out the most vigorous persecution against Christians in the history of our country. Politically, the intensified intolerance and repression was intended to justify his failures. He was looking for political scapegoats to blame for the regime's difficulties and failures.

Idi Amin was the alpha and omega; he is remembered for issuing the most contentious and controversial laws since independence. The laws were originated ostensibly to regulate the exercise of the freedom of speech and freedom to assemble. The laws conspicuously lacked and in effect limited the enjoyment of those very liberties that are inherently granted, not just from a constitutional point of view, but from a divine order of creation.

Idi Amin suppressed the freedom of worship and religion. Freedom of worship means the right to pray within the confines of a place of worship or to privately believe, whereas freedom of religion is the right of the person to believe in the religion of their choice. Nina Shea, director of the Center for Religious Freedom and member of the commission says freedom of religion includes the right to raise your children in your faith; the right to have religious literature; the right to meet with co-religionists; the right to raise funds; the right to appoint or elect your religious leaders, and to carry out charitable activities, to evangelize, [and] to have religious education or seminary training.

In Amin's Uganda, the tyrannical factor was due to the flamboyant personality of Idi Amin and his capacity to attract international notoriety. His name often elicited jitters within the international press. By 1977 Uganda had become as much a case of sheer decentralized violence as one of purposeful tyranny. The severity and magnitude of the scorched-earth policy had reached proportions, which poisoned the minds of the people who were facing the onslaught, but without any possibility of retaliation.

A cunning dictator prefers underhand filthy methods to destroy those with divergent views. People who disagree with him are labeled as dissents deserving to be liquidated. The dictators ignore the fact that change, innovation, creativity can never be achieved if we all think alike. It is those that aspire to be different that bring change and improve lives. Those that have gone to the moon had to fight mediocrity and be different.

A dictator is insecure; he is even afraid of his own shadow. That is why dictators hate the elites. Amin was consistent in 'annihilating" the charismatic and truly patriotic Ugandans viciously opposed to him. It is this policy that sustained him in power. The thugs of the dictator derogatively referred to whoever didn't ideologically agree with them as *adui or Kipingamizi*. "Fighting ideological disorientation" means eliminating political opponents (*kipingamizis*), or those opposed to the dictators' ideologies. This is what Stalin did between 1936-37 with "the great purge" and it's the same thing that Hitler did with his "night of long knives". Pol Pot feared the educated class of Cambodia and eliminated two million people during the era of the Khmer Rouge.

Amin loved to be feared and to be hated. From a rudimentary, militaristic and barbaric point of view, it worked; from a professional and ethical it was sheer madness. Kahinda Otafiire said that, "Amin had actually not done anything bad to me personally. But as a student activist, I just did not like him. The fellow was so bad that he left you no option not to hate him—His functionaries were arresting people, throwing them in car boots, people were disappearing and the economy was in shambles with no sugar, nothing at all. Besides, the man's way of doing things was tomfoolery and he was such a buffoon. There was no government—just a bunch of buffoons marauding around".

Thomas Jefferson said that "When the people fear the government, there is tyranny. When the government fears the people, there is liberty." Idi Amin thought it safer to be feared than to be loved. No man is so egocentrically backward than this man. But it served his nasty ambitions. Ugandans are mediocre in critical analysis, but Amin silenced them! Generally speaking, Amin's strong sense of insecurity made all of the elites who were not members of his tribe and religion vulnerable. The killings cut across all sections of the population; the army, ordinary civilians, farmers, students, clerks, shopkeepers, government officials, imagined or real political opponents as well as religious figures, notably Janani Luwum, the Archbishop of the Church of Uganda. These victims were, according to historical accounts, shot or forced to club one another to death by the 'death squads'.

A former Tanzanian intelligence officer, Deusderit Kusekwa Masanja, who was detained in Makindye Military Barracks on accusation that he was spying for Tanzania, gave his account as he witnessed the Chief Justice murdered: "It was in September in 1972 when I saw the former Chief Justice of Uganda Benedicto Kiwanuka at night. He was wearing an army uniform. By that time he had lost weight, he was unshaven and barefoot. He looked very dirty. Some of the prisoners, especially the Baganda, recognised him at once and crowded around him to talk to him. By midnight he was taken out of the cell and taken into his own cell and instructions were given that nobody should approach him. On February 28, 1972, Kiwanuka was brought into the cells again and killed by a hammer as some senior army officers watched." (*Drum Magazine, April 1974*).

Different accounts have been given to the family with one stating that Amin pulled out a revolver and shot Kiwanuka twice through the head after he refused to sign the document. Reports indicate that authorities concealed Kiwanuka's body and all those who witnessed the shooting were also killed immediately. By this time, the smell of death and fright hung over Uganda. Unfortunately, we lived to witness such horrors unlike many who see them in movies. We can forgive but we cannot run away from our history as a nation, good or bad.

A great American philosopher once said: "Prize intellect above all else, for those who have intellect have true freedom." But Idi Amin debased the intelligent. He used the power of the gun to suppress the power of knowledge. Logic had no place in the day to day thinking. It was safer to swim with the tide and accept the backwards thinking of the illiterates. Eventually, Ugandans became used to the apathetic state of Uganda's abysmal leadership, such that the educated and merit driven Ugandan feared to contest into running the affairs of their country. Idi Amin comfortably rode on the back of irritates. The blame is not on the elite class alone. Take a look at today's situation.

We have a category of peasants who pride in sleeping even when jiggers disfigure their feet and they can hardly access basic services. The majority of the people would rather suffer silently than to wade into the murky waters. Until Ugandans appreciate and understand statesmanship, they will continue to elevate men of low degree.

Dictators hate to be accountable to anybody. Accountability is the fulcrum on which stewardship derives its very essence. A leader that run foul of controls that are meant to guarantee accountability in leadership is directly, and secretly too, encouraging fraud and mismanagement. Intriguingly, all dictators assume that they alone have the vision to rule their countries. The president of Equatorial Guinea, Nguema says that, he is only in power because "the people" have not found anybody better than him in the last 33 years. Obote had the same attitude; the people who asked him to cede office to his successors were often rebuffed by his customary rejoinder that he has not yet seen anyone with a vision to entrust the highest office to. Even Idi Amin, who was clumsy upstairs, going by all the bungled deals he made, aggressively insisted that Uganda cannot progressively develop without him! Whenever such comments are made by our leaders, the standard reaction of the elites is to be fretfully offended and insulted by the seeming slur. We are then opened to enraged long tirades about the sheer arrogance of implying that other Africans have no heads to think!

In order to achieve his nasty schemes, Idi Amin developed the puppet military force predominantly consisting of members of his tribe and religion (Muslims/Nubians) that caused mayhem. Among them, there was always a sucker desperately willing to take on the role of terrorizing the innocent citizens: Most notably the State Research Bureau, intelligent units and kangaroo courts chaired by Colonel Juma Ali, which were deployed to clamp down on criticism and dissenting voices. Amin persistently philosophized for them practically that their mothers were their guns. We were left at God's mercy as the lunacy prevailed. Some victims saw it necessity to rein themselves in so that they don't become vulnerable. I know many people who either joined the army or changed their religions to Islam to save their necks.

The puppets felt that they were willing partners in the regime's atrocities. This was one way of seeking the President's eye and securing rewards for loyal service. The puppets were promoted to occupy sensitive political and security offices as part of reward for their capitulation; a kind of vanity thing. The ranks in army and police did not go with a range of skills, experience and administrative responsibility required. Most of his officers were spineless sycophants ready to lick his feet; cowards ready to draw blood whenever they were instructed. Basically the Ugandan army and Idi Amin had a symbiotic relationship.

Idi Amin knew very well that when you deny the people their freedom of expression, you disarm them of their armor to fight for their liberty. Life, Liberty and Happiness are nothing without the means to defend them. Unarmed people make good corpses. There was bullying directly intended to silence the press. Many journalists like Fr. Kigundu were brutally murdered. The one role journalism is known for is the responsibility of holding leaders accountable. It is mainly because of this role that the media is known as the fourth arm of government after the Executive, the Legislature and the Judiciary. Every military state practices censorship. For example ministers in communist controlled Czechoslovakia had to submit sermons two weeks in advance before they could be preached. One Judge once wrote, "Censorship reflects a society's lack of confidence in itself. It is a hallmark of an authoritarian regime. Pontius Pilate was the first great censor and Jesus Christ the first great victim of censorship".

Although Idi Amin's armed forces and intelligence services were private armies, they were no longer porous. As the army grew extraordinary huge, it became increasing hard to be catered for; they would go on looting, killing and raping sprees with impunity. Some elements of the army, State Research Bureau (SRB) and police (PSU) became so powerful that they were their own masters and could call the shots without respect of the judiciary, legislature and even the larger executive. We were basically under martial laws. Pregnant women's bellies were cut open by bayonets; they displayed corpses with severed limbs to scare off people. The victims were picked by plain-clothed security personals and carried into the trunks (boot) of the cars like merchandises to the slaughter houses. Idi Amin cared less as long as his armed thugs scared people so that nobody dared to challenge him or retaliate to his intimidations. Amin achieved his objective of keeping people in a state of absolute fear because people continuously paid homage to his bullying. He intimidated all into submission. No one dared to remind the Emperor of his nakedness. You could poke the lion's eye at your peril! Lawlessness crept in and was fully fledged (full blossom).

Dictators are very good at using photo-ups to bolster their image. Occasionally, Idi Amin came out to address the press on the situation. He pleaded innocent saying that he would not kill an innocent person. He sarcastically said that the victims died because they stood in the way of his fired bullet. He warned the public that his bullet is fired; that they should never make a mistake of standing in its way. For a head of state to brag how he killed innocent civilians without remorse, one wonders whether Amin was not a deranged psychopath with a very serious psychological disorder.

The greatest fear was not the lawlessness itself but the absence of remedies to address it. No wonder people referred to Uganda as a failed state. As I said, Idi Amin deliberately failed to tame his soldiers, usually turning a blind eye whenever a case against them came up. He may not have ordered some of the killings but failing to prosecute and condemn those who did, was a sinful and evil mean oversight! The cost was enormously great. In less than a decade, they had slaughtered over 500,000 Ugandans!

Amin saw himself as a demigod! A nostalgic Field Marshall Idi Amin Dada claimed that he feared nobody but god (Allah). He killed in the name of his god who didn't care about the rest of Ugandans being ruled iron fistly. Idi Amin had a reputation of portraying himself as a super human being; he had power to give and to take life. He equated himself with the Son of God, the Giver of Life. He insinuated that he discussed with God concerning his day of death. He pretended to be the impeccable and the incorruptible. In the past such "accolades" were reserved for "leaders" like Stalin, Hitler, Mussolini and Saddam but now it was in our backyard right here at home. It was pathetic and scary!

Many of us who grew up during the times of the brutal regime of Idi Amin have fresh memories of the atrocities of the soldiers of Idi Amin. Most of the victims never recovered from the trauma. They are possibly held together by the sheer faith. We can forgive but not forget. I mean people who saw their beloved ones bundled up, exterminated and squashed like mosquitoes. I often want to puke whenever I read in our local newspapers some heartless people challenging others to prove that Idi Amin killed innocent people. Certainly Amin's soldiers were heartless, unsteady and emotionally vacillate, but who recruited and promoted the wicked officers? Amin trained them to be his killing squads and treated them with kid gloves, at the expense of the civilians!

The resilience is not just among the victims who lost their beloved but the impact of the tyranny is visible in all sectors of social life including the economy, politics and the moral behaviors of the people. The virus of Idi Amin's corruption has continuously infected our communities. It is noticeable among Ugandans at all levels of lives; from the highest echelons to the lowest organs, an invidious bloodline of toxins seems to drip through the entire state apparatus, spreading selfish interests, national irresponsibility and unabashed graft. Every spirit and vestige of concern for the population previously held to be sacrosanct in the epitome of the constitution of an independent state gradually diminished.

Idi Amin left a trail of economic mismanagement parameters that we have followed blindly. The culture of entitlement and the massive corruptions we see today are seeds which were planted by Idi Amin in his economic wars (*Magendo style*). An avid brief-case operator could amass huge fortunes without any declared accounts. It was all part of the chicanery or calculated impunity to maximize loot by deliberately evading the tax-man. If one got a government job and didn't divert the public funds to this personal pocket, then he was rated stupid or uncreative (*tayiiya*). The notion that people use their offices to become filthy rich while others scavenge for what to eat began during the times of Idi Amin; the number of destitute on our streets set against those who didn't even know how much wealth they had. The entitlement mentality blossomed during the time of Idi Amin.

People think that the government has to do everything by itself. The mindsets and attitudes of most people are obsessed with handouts or bailout (*okulembeka*) or simply look on with disinterest (*nfuniramu wa?*). Not to mention the materialism mentality: wanting what you can't get and getting what you don't want. Because of the sufferings inflicted on the hapless Ugandans, many people are hostages to the Stockholm Syndrome. The old adage goes, "You can't teach an old dog new tricks." The old trade that was started by Amin has never died. Trying to reverse it is like putting corn back on the cob.

Without doubt, Idi Amin is the most evil leader in the history of our continent. The saddest part is when some insensitive people parade Amin's pictures (with arrogant, smug grin face) on their websites in defiance. Keeping Amin on the front pages of our newspapers is a polite way of insulting our intelligence. Of course the perpetrators do not know the pain involved in losing your beloved one, and not being able to trace their dead bodies to give them decent burial. It is unfortunate that the story of Idi Amin is selling like hot cakes. Several comedies and movies have been produced about him to make money. I watched one of the movies and I was upset the way they dramatized the events to make it entertaining. It brought back baggage of memories and paradoxes. I think that the viciousness of Idi Amin and the effects of his rule are apparent without any need of re-inventing fictional instances. Intrudingly, greedy people make fortune out of it, whereas others smile about it, when in reality there is nothing to smile about. The epigram goes that, "a Black man can only cry when his heart is going to break". The heart of every caring African should be broken and our faces watered with tears.

My dad, Israel Kyeyune, was one of the countless victims of Idi Amin's regime, who disappeared between 1972-1979 and their bodies were never found. It was the same time that the archbishop of Uganda the late J. Luwum was murdered. Many people thought that Idi Amin had a genuine political war against dissents but only to discover that he had an axe to grind with Christianity. The idea that the Archbishop could hide boxes of bullets and weapons in front of his yard with intent of starting a rebel group easily exposed a clumsy propaganda effort by Idi Amin; the accusation was a fictitious creation by the government to victimize the clergy. Idi Amin used it as an excuse to crack down the monopoly of the Church of Uganda.

Many people including my dad were killed by Idi Amin because of their faith. My dad was the chairman of the board of the Church of Uganda at Namaliga Bombo. In 1977, the Church of Uganda was celebrating one hundred years since the Christian missionaries brought the light of the Gospel to Uganda (Centenary). The celebrations were the symbolic gesture of recognizing the influence of Christianity over the nation, something that did not augur well for the Muslim regime.

Archbishop J. Luwum, the spiritual leader of the Church of Uganda (Protestant Church), was vocal against the government excesses. He was right. "The church must be reminded that it is not the master or servant of the state, but rather the conscience of the state. It must be the guide and the critic of the state, and never the church . . . is not the master or servant of the state—and never its tool"—(Martin Luther King Jr.)

Other than being a Christian leader, Luwum's tribe was a liability. He belonged to the tribe that was considered to be hostile to the regime. Consequently, the Archbishop became the real cat among the pigeons, vulnerable to the sword of Idi Amin (*Kijambiya*). The country lost such a great hero of faith. But this loss was symptomatic of a wider national tragedy. The Church leaders were silenced and many other exterminated.

The sudden murder of the highest religious leader in one of the biggest denomination, in very macabre circumstances, as expected, electrified the nation to the point of outrage and bewilderment. It resulted into the bare-knuckled exchange between the Church leadership and the dictator. Of course after killing him, Idi Amin had to continue to kill and kill in order to disable the rumor mills of Katwe which were inexorably grinding out lots of conspiracies. There were trumped up charges against Christians that ended into numerous arrest and disappearances.

The persecution of my dad began with the psychological torture. Just a couple of weeks before my dad was abducted, Idi Amin's soldiers from Bombo barracks, went on rampage during broad day time vandalizing my dad's retail store. The whole battalion converged on my dad's retail store, roughed him up and carried with them almost everything from the shop without paying a penny. They left my dad bleeding heavily from the wounds inflicted on his head. When I came from school for lunch, the retail store was empty and my dad was writhing in pain after being severely beaten by soldiers.

A week before his abduction, my dad received a letter from Colonel Juma Ali Butabika (the rabid dog of Idi Amin) warning him to steer away from all the night rehearsals involving preparations for the Centenary. The crazy colonel indicated in the letter that it was a security precaution. My dad had a reputation of not mincing words. I heard him murmuring that, "Nobody tells us to pray but God." I knew my dad very well; he was always very bold and spoke his mind; he was not going to retrocede. It was another sign that he was made of sterner stuff and he could not be easily intimidated. Martin Luther King once wrote, "There comes a time when one must take a position that is neither safe, nor politic, nor popular, but he must take it because his conscience tells him it is right . . ."

After consulting the Church leadership, my dad refused to stop the Centenary activities but agreed to limit their gatherings to evenings; he shunned the night gatherings to elude suspicion and for transparence purposes. But the dictatorial regime was not satisfied. My dad paid dearly for his standing for the truth. He was abducted at the orders of Idi Amin by the notorious colonel called Juma Ali Butabika, who was the chief of the Military Tribunal and his life ended like a shooting star across a clear night sky.

The tragedy happened on the same day it was announced that our long awaited Ordinary Level Examination results were released by the ministry of education. On this historical day, the crazy colonel sent an invitation letter to my dad requiring him to attend an emergence meeting of reconciliation after the mysterious death of Archbishop Luwum. The same invitation was extended to various members of the ruling council of our local Church except for the treasurer (Micheal Nsubuga) and the Church secretary (Mr. Sentongo) who were already in custody. The emergency meeting was stage-managed to abduct my dad. It turned into a real virulent malaise that ate away the entire Church leadership.

On that fateful day, my dad asked me to attend to the customers in his retail shop so that he could go to attend the meeting. Before he left, he reminded me that our O—Level examination results were released. He promised me a gift of a new bicycle in case I passed with good grades to higher education (Advanced level). Unfortunately, he did not live another hour to know the status of my performance. Little did I know that the celebration I had anticipated would end in a mourning occasion for my dad by evening.

The level of panic by the government in handling the cases of the people who mysteriously disappeared was simply disenchanting. The close relatives of the victims were isolated in order to deter any leakage of information concerning the fate of their beloved ones. People were threatened not to associate with the immediate relatives of the victims. After the abduction of my dad, most of the family friends and our closest relatives avoided us out of fear of being labeled as sympathizers and collaborators. They did not want to be seen talking, hugging and crying with us. Sympathizing or associating with the immediate families of the victims bordered to treason. We mourned in isolation. These were my darkest moments. I give credit to Dr. Lwanga because he was there for me at this time of darkness. He regularly stopped over at my house on his way to work, and after work we prowled the night, to different places he used to frequent.

There are some family friends whom we trusted and who we expected to be there for us in such tough times of trials but they disappointed us by doing the opposite because politics stole away their consciousness and sense of reasoning. I guess they had empathy for the embattled victim, but no sympathy. Some were afraid to end up where my dad was ensconced whereas others were corrupted by the regime. They changed within a moment of time praising Idi Amin as their hero and labeling us as enemies of peace—albeit in a manner that is not very clear and largely built on assumptions. The culprits made intrusive comments without care that they offended us. They coughed the slogan "Amin oyee!" or barricaded Idi Amin, chanting, 'AL Haji,

ir actions removed doubt that
they were the dictator's demagogue apologists!

To put them in their place these were bootlicking self-fish sycophant.
Amin needed their impeccable articulation for his defense. Their
weakness like medical drug under-doze enabled the dictator to
militarily galvanize himself akin to the mutating HIV/Aids virus.
These were the Judas of our times. Judas Iscariot is known for his
devious kiss and betrayal of Jesus to the hands of the chief Sanhedrin
priests. To most Christians, Judas is seen as a traitor—the disciple
who betrayed Jesus to the Romans for 30 pieces of silver. After which
he hanged himself out of remorse and guilt. Even though Judas
showed penitence later, his name became a symbol of traitors and
turncoats throughout history. His motive seemed to be greed, but
some scholars speculate political desires lurked beneath his treachery.
From my understanding of the Bible, there are several explanations
as to why Judas betrayed Jesus. But the obvious explanation is that of
money, as it is the case with many these days. Henry Kyemba a former
minister in Idi Amin's regime wrote that, "I know many people in
our society who were interested in the properties of their relatives and
they connived with state agents to threaten and force them into exile."

Corruption is the major cause of dishonesty and hypocrisy. It is for
the same reason why Idi Amin recruited people from our tribes
(mores) to spy for him. They were comfortable with the dictatorial
regime as long as they were benefiting from it. They behaved like the
proverbial hyena which followed a drunkard hoping that his swinging
hands will loosen and drop off any time. The moles maintained their
undignified silence as Idi Amin continued to massacre other innocent
Ugandans. They were spooky quiet like the graveyard as long as they
were eating! They had a slogan saying that, "It is good mannered for a
Muganda not to speak when he was eating". "We cloak our cowardice
with the ill-fitting garment of political correctness."—Alistair Begg.

"Our civilization survives in the complacency of cowardly or
malignant minds—a sacrifice to the vanity of aging adolescents—
excess is always a comfort, and sometimes a career"—Albert Camus.

Idi Amin's regime was rotten to the core; literally chewing itself like a trapped fox, might chew its own leg in the bid for freedom! But because we lacked unity we let up in piling the pressure, on a rotten to the core system. Courage is contagious. When a brave man takes a stand, the spines of others are often stiffened. But very few had such courage to confront Idi Amin. Amin drew large crowds wherever place he was not because he was popular, it simply meant people were eager to see him. If you brought a monster at the place next to where Amin was, people would leave him and look at the monster. Curiosity in human beings does not mean popularity.

Like any other dictator, Idi Amin tactically used the divide and rule theory to secure himself in power. Amin was a graduate of the Orwellian Animal Farm (Stalin): He was akin to Napoleon taking away the puppies from their mothers, and turning them into menacing creatures against the rest of the animals on the farm. The central region in particular was deeply eaten up by disparity. The more we were divided the harder it became for us to come out of this quagmire and nightmare. The division among us gave Idi Amin more leverage and extended to the vicious dictatorial regime a lease of life. The most dangerous enemy is always the enemy from within the camp. The enemy from within behaves like a rat, which bites your foot at night and blows air on the bite so as not to wake you up.

The history of Buganda is characterized with betrayals and backstabbing. Politicians have a reputation of playing off leading tribesmen whenever the stakes are high. The dictators have successfully managed to manipulate some prominent Baganda people to hurt their fellow tribesmen. The problem with parochialism is that the President could appoint a fellow tribesman to an administrative office and we end up with a tribesman who is more chauvinistic than the non-tribesmen. Such characters sell out in exchange for cheap popularity and money. Their self-confessed political philosophy is that they would rather be a living dog than a dead lion.

Dogs usually live under the illusion that they are safe with the hunter whom they help to hunt down other animals for his choice of meat in exchange for a few bones and offal that will be thrown their way at the end of the day. A hunting dog is given preference treatment during hunting, after which it is mistreated as the rest of the animals. A dog's life is short, unpredictable and often brutalized! It could be poisoned once it is deemed rabid, thus dangerous to the hunter and his family. Odoobo C. Bichachi lamented, "That is the dog's life that many Ugandans and politicians are comfortable living simply because in their minds, they cannot figure out that a pack of dogs is actually more powerful than the hunter and can stand their ground anytime, anywhere. The hunter knows it but the dogs don't."

Blackmailing is the hallmark of a dictator. Idi Amin used undercover agent (moles) to terrorize us. It was hard to trust people and open up. Your closest companion could turn up to be the undercover agent spying for Idi Amin. The whole world became a small place; too small for even an insignificant roach like me to hide! We were in a risky situation compared to a roach crawling next to the beak of a rooster. We were betrayed by the very people we trusted. These are the very people who prematurely prejudged the victims, falsely accusing them to be saboteurs that recklessly provoked Idi Amin. One of the perpetrators looked straight in my face and bragged that my dad deserved to die because he trespassed by poking his nose into politics. How can one be a lazy thinker to come up with a heartless and insensitive statement like this with intent to insult and annoy the bereaved?

The handlers disparaged the Church with all kinds of unfortunate remarks because the Church remained docile when attacked. We were not allowed to profess our belief without ridicule or venom, or disparagement. The Christians tolerated the bashing without a hard hit-back because their hands were tied behind by their religious beliefs. They simply turned the other cheek. "Any fool can make things bigger, more complex, and more violent. It takes a touch of genius-and a lot of courage-to move in the opposite direction" (*Albert Einstein*).

The biggest problem in Africa is strangulation of serious debate. This has led to the dominance of intellectual space by self-seeking Sycophants, Self-defeatist opportunist and Self-seeking egoistic politicians without back bones who only sing praises to despots what is sweet for their ears. Like parrots, they say what the dictators say.

The people who follow politicians blindly are compared to a group of owls that have eyes but can't see. They are sycophants that usually say words of no substance but parrot like sounds heard from the masters in the junta. They are unscrupulous leaders shadowed by political myopia, pragmatism, untold greed and insensitivity to the common man. They are the reason for the flourishing of dictatorship. And for these men who are supposed to be our respectable leaders, to be factionalized like school prefects borders to a deranged mind. It leaves a lot of sour taste in the mouth, it is a big shame! It is because of their blindness that the dictators become arrogant, prompting them to think that they are immortals, and adorning themselves with distinguished medals and awards like VC, DSO, MC, conqueror of British Empire; then fantasizing in presidency for life. The balanced picture only emerges with their demise.

The perpetrators frantically try to out-do each other in a bid to prove their loyalty to the sickening dictators. They are willing to follow the dictators to the grave like the proverbial fly that refused to heed a warning. The Bible says that, "There is a way which seemeth right unto a man, but the end thereof are the ways of death" (Proverbs 14:12). One activist said that, "Two roads diverged in a wood, I took the one less traveled by and that has made all the difference."

Amin's henchmen used titles and nicknames other than their real names to evoke fear. These were not the official and real names of the people whom we treated as our national leaders but were hoods (phony). Most probably they suffered from a psychological disease called, national identity crisis and disorder syndrome; they did everything to be accepted and remain relevant. What would you expect of losers? I mean people who have no brains to talk of. They said rightly that they did what they did because they were following orders, not using their brains!

The regime was rotten to the core. Working for Amin had serious effects on people akin to a narcotic drug high that throws rationality out of the window and enters psychopath through the door clouding any reasoning. Therefore nobody worked in Amin's government had a clean record. Even the people who claimed to have a reputation of cleanness were accused of what amounts to influence peddling and political meddling. They were a bunch of morons who could not look straight in the eyes of Amin and give him a piece of their mind. They never did anything right because they were ever on the wrong side of everything.

Apparently, it was clear that Idi Amin was here to stay. It seemed as if the man was the only one arrogated to guide Uganda's future. Denying it was like living in self-denial. Self-denial is the refusal to take what one might have or to accept facts. Self-denial may result in self-sacrifice. This being the voluntary surrender of what one has; it may be an act, a habit, or a principle. "Self-sacrifice goes beyond self-denial in necessarily including the idea of surrender, as of comfort, inclination, time, health, while being also presumably in the line of a real duty."

Imagination of Uganda without Amin seemed to be day dreaming, the old suck was so adamant to the people of Uganda's plight. Most Ugandan reached the point when they surrendered to Idi Amin and accepted his abuses of human rights as a normal thing. The tyranny seemed to be here to stay. After all, he had declared himself the life president. Nobody expected him to go any time soon. He was determined to rule and stick there even when crawling on all fours (legs/hands). Our only hope rested on his health demise because he was a mortal man like any of us. The traditional adage says that, *"Enswasa Eteyanula Ereega Ngalabi"* meaning the alligator which over busks donates its skin to drum makers.

Dictatorship is a relational phenomenon. It takes two to tango; it takes a dictator and the people who promote the dictator for dictatorship to thrive. This fact made me hate the puppets of dictatorship more. I was occasionally dragged into an explosive mood but I was disarmed of all rights to express my emotions. I learned the hard way to zip my lips. Idi Amin's thugs monitored all of my actions and movements sniffing for an excuse to arrest me. Crying is a basic human emotion and a human right; but I was deprived of the same right too. Putting on a gloomy face made the culprits feel guilty. I resorted to putting on fake smiles. There is a saying that one smile hides a million tears. Psychologists agree with me that the people who smile, laugh and joke around the most are usually the unhappiest. My tormenters expected me to flash a smile all times; yet smiling could at times be interpreted as scornful in particular when it was directed at someone that hates you. I remember that I was rebuked for smiling at a soldier. He reprimanded me for behaving like a prostitute (*Malaya*) before him. Therefore pretending to smile was a quagmire—a catch 21, if you like, and quite disheartening.

The unexpressed hatred within me turned into bitterness. The bitter truth is that the world becomes an obvious enemy when you lose what you love and value most. When Idi Amin abducted my dad, he took away everything I wanted to have. This was the saddest moment in my life. I experienced hell on earth. I was reduced to a mere quivering mass of fear. I was bruised, heartbroken with shuttered dreams. My dad vanished during my sensitive years of adolescence when I was maturing from teen ages to young adulthood; at the crucial time when everyone needs a father to coerce him to do certain things.

We were tortured psychologically, physically and financially. The kind of selfishness and wanton abuse of power juxtaposed in Uganda during the regime of Idi Amin simply defeated rationale. As I said, just a couple of weeks before my dad's abduction, the soldiers ransacked and looted his business. To add pepper to the wound, as soon as he was abducted, Idi Amin's henchmen took him to his bank (the Libyan bank) and helped themselves with all the money on his account. As if it was not enough, the extortionists hatched plans to take advantage of the cash strapped family. For example Colonel Juma Ali's wife sent a messenger to me and collected from me huge amounts of money with false promises to release our dad. The witchdoctors also claimed their share. We were left penniless and stinking poor.

My dad was the sole bread winner for his family. Now that he was nowhere near, I was cast into the role of the head of the family, without the essentials of parenting. I had eleven siblings and a mother. My mother fled to unknown place with my siblings. Within a moment of time, the entire family was dismantled. We were looked at as a ship without a compass!

We tried all possible means to get my dad released but all of our efforts were frustrated. Idi Amin would not let go because killing a

Christian leader was a heroic act to his sponsors. He would endless kill and kill. He had a roster of faithful Christians belonging to different denominations ready to slaughter in exchange for oil money from the Arab world. The victims were like well-placed clients that boosted his business with the Arab world; the more he killed the more money flooded his account.

Idi Amin did everything possible to destroy evidences incriminating his thugs of killing innocent Ugandans. Many victims simply disappeared. For some lucky ones, like the late Archbishop Luwum, whose bodies were not deposed, Amin pressured the pathologists to doctor postmortem reports. Otherwise most people just disappeared without tracing their dead bodies. He either dumped the dead bodies in remote areas where they could not be identified or disfigured them beyond recognition with acid. Others were either buried naked with their heads cut off or burnt beyond recognition. Without exhibit of a corpse it was difficult to prove the homicide case. He then publicly justified himself, denying to kill anybody. In politics if something is rigorously denied, it is true.

It was tough for me to accept that my dad was dead. He was such a health man. Expectations of ever seeing him alive again were real, but at the same time it was having irreconcilable problems with reality. I was left in a dilemma not knowing what to do next; I lacked the capacity to act compared to an armchair warrior or a paper tiger. I was resigned to my fate. Those of you who have ever been in my shoes know that there is a deep-seated frustration coupled with that hopelessness of knowing that something ought to be done and yet you don't know what. I felt that way.

I was cagey about searching for his dead body even though it was necessary to give him a decent burial. Tracing his remains was even more problematic. We did everything within our reach but without positive results. There is an old African proverb saying that, "One cannot touch beyond his height limitation". One scientist warned that "If you scuffed your feet long enough without touching anything, you would build up so many electrons that your finger would explode."

I gave up the search after realizing that I was taken on a wild goose chase that will cost me more than the arm. It was scaring because most of the relatives of the victims of Idi Amin who ventured to look for their beloved relatives were forced to meet their maker at a record speed. It was overwhelmingly painful to lose my beloved one; but instead of mourning for him, I lived in fear for my life. Every morning I watched the sunrise but without assurance that I will see the sunset. I lost confidence in the very system that was supposed to protect me. It was like dancing along the razor's edge, any slight move and you are finished.

It is hard to build a life you didn't choose. Sometimes, I thought that I was hardened enough, but ended up buckled. Tears came rolling down my cheeks whenever I woke up and realized that I will never have a father around me anymore. I had sleepless nights recalling that the silent body of my dad lay dead in unknown place somewhere in the remote jungles. At times I had strange imaginations, seeing his remains left for the scavenging vultures or hyenas; it haunted me.

As I reflected on the entire situation, I was angry at myself. I thought that it was my fault that things went the wrong way, a scenario that may be familiar to many victims of abuse. Guilt became another monster taking a great toll from me. I lived in fear of having the monster within me. This was a very heavy burden to fall onto small shoulders.

Psychiatrists and psychologists have for long been intrigued by victims feeling guilty in order to justify abuses of other people against them. Such behavior is in particular common when the victims seek sympathy from the oppressors. It is of course worse if the victim actually develops a psychosis—where he/she increasingly loses touch with reality, and deteriorates into a life of delusions and hallucinations!

Idi Amin's soldiers and the fanatic Moslems looked at me suspiciously because I was born in a certain tribe and because I believed differently. These were errand boys raised to hurl stones at those from other ethnic backgrounds. I shuddered whenever I recalled the fate of the people who looked like me and who believed the way I did.

Unfortunately, I could not reverse the situation. I was hurt by their absolute incoherence. I thought that the world is very cruel, biased and selective.

Some people felt sorry for me but at the same time countered that they pitied me simply because they did not understand. It was like the positivity of the negativity. They wrongly reasoned because they were used to solving problems, but this was like a continuation of unwinding an endless sob story. My situation wasn't so clear-cut. In my case, there wasn't any clear resolution. Everything was shrouded in mystery. The contemplation of which kept my minds flabbergasted.

There is a saying that the future belongs to those who believe in the beauty of their dreams. Amin killed the innocence in me and scattered my dreams. I was hurt to the core of my nerves. I spent most of the time trying to solve the unsolvable puzzle. I consulted a couple of army officers of Idi Amin that used to chat with my dad, before his abduction, for a reasonable solution but they routinely feigned ignorance of what transpired under their watch! They took on a mystifying demeanor. I withdrew because I was too awe-struck and restrained to put them on spot.

One of the victims, called Sentego, who served with my dad as the secretary of the Church, escaped from the thugs of Idi Amin by opening the trunk of the car where he was locked, on the way to Nakasongola to be executed. He went underground, in hiding, but unfortunately he was killed by Idi Amin's thugs before the liberation of Kampala by TPDF. My dad never got such opportunity of escaping.

Later on it was confirmed that my dad was killed. According to reliable sources, he was tricked to think that he was released from jail. The same thugs that released him volunteered to drive him back to his house but they instead drove him to his execution. It is said that my dad was made to dig his grave, forced to lie inside it and then shot dead. Without evidence of the dead body and the grave yard it was still tough for me to acknowledge the death of my dad. Thirty years later, my dad's death and his subsequent burial place are still shrouded in mystery. It has been speculated that his remains lay in undisclosed grave somewhere around Nakasongola. Many bodies were buried in the area, especially between Muwaddwe village and Wajjala hill, during the 1970s. At best, I treat all of these as little iffy rumors or speculative rumblings that are devoid of empirical evidence.

I was troubled when they paraded hundreds of skulls on the streets of Luwero after liberation. I thought his skull might be one of them. I appeal to any person who has a definite location where the remains of my dad were buried to come forward with the information so that we can give him a descent farewell.

It bothered me and I did not understand why a person could stoop too low to kill somebody in cold blood because of his faith or his tribe. There is something about the tribes from northern Uganda that made them inherently violent and brutal. Ever since Uganda was declared to be a republic, the Northerners became the hunters, and the Southerners (Bantu) the hunted. Before NRA defeated UNLA, there was a myth of 'martial tribes' that only Luo and Sudanic speakers can fight, and that the Bantu speakers can't fight. We know that the domination of the army by the Northerners was not intentional from the start: It was initiated by the colonialists (British). The domination became intentional during the dictatorial regimes of Obote 1, Idi Amin, UNLF and Obote II; that is when the army was 90% dominated by the Northerners. These were blood thirsty war lords who were obsessed with wars without a possibility of cutting back on their adventures.

For a long time the Bantu tribes suffered abuses from the Northerners and West Nile including Sudanese, (Anyanyas). Generally, there was a popular belief or the conventional wisdom was that people associated with Amin's tribe were Anyanyas. Many Southerners are still experiencing Post Traumatic Stress Disorder because of the abuses melted on them by these thugs. Why should a person hate another human being to that extent? The cause of the hatred is not a mystery. You do not teach a child to crawl or a bird to fly: It is by instincts that a bird will fly. Killing is not provoked by these people; it is part of their livelihood. An angry Northern is more dangerous than an angry Southerner. There is ingrained hatred in the blood of the Northerners that demands rectification.

Generally, people from the northern region have a grim history full of frustration. They envied people from the south, east, west and central partly because most of them did not go to school or they went to school barefooted without shoes. They harbor an attitude that if they can't have anything, you will also not have it. This, plus teasing by stereotypes in some sections of the Ugandan community that associated them with, "low standards of hygiene, overcrowded homes, anti-social nature and predictability." This attitude reeks with envy and should be denounced.

Some people give shallow reasons like this one: The bigger problem is that the state was run by villagers who tried to live large. The people who embrace this theory say that the Northerners who grabbed power were not fit to rule. They did not represent the cream of the Northerners. This however, is only a microcosmic version of a people that have become so ingrained in the Ugandan social and economic set up. Given the fact, their suggestion is not lacking logic. We should take advantage of the young educated generation from all parts of the country to rehabilitate our nation. There is a cross-section of a young and ambitious people, a people hungry for skills and knowledge to transform their lives. Africa's challenges are two things: career politicians with little or no infrastructure related brain cells, who have no interest in development beyond their own compounds and stomachs, occupying seats meant for professional developers. Also an ill-educated populous with no idea of standards. Such people put their personal interests first before the interests of the nation; they are responsible for supporting dictatorship.

The other sound reason holding water is that people hate others because they are naturally evil; their hearts are darker than their skin! Whenever I look at Idi Amin, I see evil in action. This does not mean that all northerners are evil. It does not either mean that all southerners are perfect. Evil is in every person but to a different degree. Idi Amin massaged his ego and he became what he is—absolutely evil. His credentials in the kingdom of darkness are undisputable, proving that man is the cruelest animal.

I want to discuss killing in the name of religion. Islam has turned out to be a threat to peace loving people. Muslims masquerade-force others (non-Muslims) to do what they believe. Ugandans view Islam in Uganda as the legacy of British Colonial Power who brought the Sudanese people here to subdue Ugandans to obedience! After independence, the then administration went ahead and promoted the Sudanese immigrants like Idi Amin to high military positions allowing evil to blossom.

The savagery and barbarism we witness today take us back to the pre-historic times that predated the family, state and private property before we became civilized. This is a moral problem demanding a spiritual solution. There is only one escape route by repenting and embracing salvation. Jesus is the centerpiece of civilization; He is the superlative of all excellence. It is time we put to shame the devil and his works by demonstrating our timeless values of love compassion and solidarity through Jesus Christ.

This book is about Dr. Lwanga. He was God sent to help me to go through tough times. Idi Amin's thugs harassed us into being harmonious beings. Danger invisibly prowled us; there was no safe haven for me to hide. However as they say when the hunter learnt to shoot without missing, birds learnt to fly without perching. I knew I was being trailed and took precaution. To make the matters worse, the persecutions spiraled into unwanted rejections. At this crucial time, most people including my close relatives and fellow tribesmen ignored me as if I was a roadkill, someone deserving to be avoided rather than consoled. I was isolated and suffered a pariah status. The escalation injected in me bitter frustrations and triggered the boiling anger from within. Just to mention a few psychological challenges I had to grapple with.

It was tough to put a tragedy such as mine in the past without seeing justice done. I was in neutral without a possibility of spurring into positive action. I simply could not put the wrongs behind me to live like a normal human being. I was apathetically beaten down and confused young boy with dashed hopes. I was deprived of my basic human rights and I lacked the will to fight back. Inside my heart I felt clammy from a loneliness I neither wanted nor understood. I had nobody to run to but Dr. Lwanga stepped in to take over the place of my dad and the role of a credible counselor. He provided to me a shoulder to cry and to lean on in order to overcome my predicaments. "No one can innovate by themselves, one needs to work with other"— Prof. H Mlawa

I was left without a definite vision for my life. I drifted through life, resentful and feeling as if I was simply existing; life had short-changed me. I was left with two choices at my finger tips: I badly wanted to continue with my school in order to pursue my dreams. Also, I had the responsibility to take care of my siblings. Ironically, both options required money that I did not expect to fall from heaven like the proverbial manna. I kept my plans to myself. There are some things which are better not talked about but acted upon, in order to advance in your plans, rather than divulging your plans only to be scuppered!

Finally, I made up minds to move on with life by joining a Collage in eastern Uganda. I decided to talk to Dr. Lwanga about my pending plans. "No!" he interjected firmly before I could even complete explaining to him the whole story. Dr. Lwanga weighed in and advised me to give my siblings a chance to go school. He advised me to reopen my dad's business something that I reluctantly accepted because there was an issue of acquiring the commencing capital (*entandikwa*). Without hard cash on me, my chances of succeeding in business were slim. I accepted his counsel and simply believed in luck; but at that moment, the only luck I seemed to have was bad luck!

The little education I acquired gave me an edge over other businessmen. I, however, lacked the experience that those who had been in the business longer had. At first I lacked the financial clout to sustain me in business. Nobody donated to me hard cash but eventually God gave me ideas to make money. I want to talk directly to somebody seeking to succeed. Your living is determined not so much by what life brings to you as by the attitude you bring to life. Success is a journey and not a destination. The mistake most people make is aligning money with success. Money is only a medium of exchange and can never be measured side-by-side with success. Our greatest lack is not money for undertaking, but ideas; if ideas are good, cash will naturally flow to where it is needed. Money is like flowing water that always finds its way to flow.

All men dream, but not equally. A dream is a person's ambition to confront the challenges of life and overcome. Those who dream by night in the dusty recesses of their minds, wake in the day to find that it was vanity: Day-dreamers are dangerous because they may act on their dreams with open eyes, to make them come to pass. Dr. Lwanga opened my minds to think outside the box instead of focusing on my dreams selfishly. Eventually, my demeanor, mindset wise slowly but progressively changed. This became my "Red Pill" if you will. It was like waking up whereby you never wanted to go back to sleep. Dr. Lwanga was a thinking tank; you could ignore his advice at your peril!

Dr. Lwanga helped wholeheartedly; he helped all the way. He would give you a rope (advice) and holds a rope to sustain you as you go. A true friend is the one who makes you say that you can after you had decided you can't. He believed that in spite of setbacks a person can work his way from powerlessness to all powerful. He instigated the exploitation of the power by association, the power by achievement, and power by wisdom. His brilliant talk psychologically helped me to look at life more positively and instigated the faith and courage to follow my dreams through. I badly needed the experienced and compassionate hands for the speedy and rough down slope steering. Thank God that he did not deprive me of the same privilege. Albert Schweitzer said that, "Sometimes our light goes out, but is blown again into instant flame by an encounter with another human being."

It pays to hang around people with positive energy. The protection and in-charge aura they exude are motivating. I mean people who are not threatened to the extent of quaking in their boots, as many did during the times of Idi Amin. I had that feeling of security whenever I was standing next to Dr. Lwanga. You never know how strong you are until being strong is the only option you have left. "One who sees inaction in action, and action in inaction, is intelligent among men." ~ Bhagavad Gita

God used the late Dr. Lwanga to wake me up to harness my potentiality at the time when I was demoralized and discarded by the society. He polished my minds to keep my eyes open for opportunities for upward mobility. It was revealed to me that bad feelings are always going to there but it is better to think beyond the past. As one writer said that, "The world is a tragedy to those who feel, but a comedy to those who think."

I acknowledged that no matter how dirty my past is, my future is still spotless. I decided to pick up the broken pieces of my life, package them afresh and move on instead of feeling sorry for myself. Our greatest battles are fought in the minds. If your mind does not get destabilized, your body can adapt to any situation. You don't have to be great to start, but you have to start to be great. I decided to roll my sleeves, break a sweat and get the job done. After all no one ever drowned in their own sweat!

I want to talk directly to somebody going through rough times. It is possible to succeed in spite of the mishaps. Seneca wrote that, "It is not because things are difficult that we do not dare, it is because we do not dare that they are difficult". Paul said that, "I can do all things through Christ that strengthen me" (Philippians 4:13).

In the family of God there is no hate but Amin hated and taught others to hate. Surprisingly, Idi Amin had courage to be evil but not many good men had courage to be good. The fact is that both hate and love can be taught. Nelson Mandela said, "No one is born hating another person". People are taught, motivated and provoked to hate.

Dr Lwanga survived the odds of life because he was a "smooth operator"; he kept his cards close to his chest and his calculations were often hard for his foes to discern. The world we live in consists of people of different calibers. Some people make things happen, some watch things happen but fold their arms and look the other way, while others wonder at what has happened and do something about it. Then there are those who simply jump on the wagon without questioning. Harold R. McAlindon warned that, "Do not follow where the path may lead. Go instead where there is no path and leave a trail".

Dr. Lwanga was in his own class. He demonstrated that the love of the people must excel the love of self. He did not fake it; he was naturally and sincerely compassionate. Dr. Neuharth says concerning our human emotional nature that: "When you see another person being embarrassed, it humanizes that person and you feel a natural kinship." I agree with him but at the same time admit that not all people have the same human instinct. There are many people out there with inhuman instincts.

Scientists say that we are close to some animals. It is speculated that chimpanzees have a 97.8 per cent DNA similar to humans. Certainly, it is our moral instinct that makes us different from animals. Compassionate is a moral compass that makes us different from animals. Compassionate is not a skill you learn, but it is within human nature which makes you different from an animal that acts instinctively. Without it (compassion), you are likely to make many mistakes in life. A number of factors come to mind, but all working in tandem to, conveying the feelings the creator had in mind when creating His world in His image. A person with humility (*Obuntu bulamu*) is open and available to others, affirming of others, and does not feel threatened by others' differences, for he or she has a proper self-assurance that comes from knowing that he or she belongs in a greater whole and is diminished when others are humiliated or diminished, when others are tortured or oppressed.

After my dad's abduction I stayed with the Marijan family. In a society in which egocentricity, self-gratification, narcissism, and selfishness were glorified, it became more and more difficult for me to establish good relationships of any kind with anybody. The host family literally considered me to be part of their family. But I was skeptical regarding their sincerity for one reason, the people with whom I shared the roof, never bothered even one time to discuss the fate of my dad. I treated them to a prolonged silence in a bid to enable them sense my quest. Their failure to respond can be treated as: concurrence with my initial view that there was a conspiracy or guilt due to unabated paranoia. Ironically, they belonged to the tribe and religion of Idi Amin. Like any other person with the same ethnic background, they were Amin's close associates who had the capacity to influence his decisions but they did nothing about it. Inevitably, I was justifiably inclined to think that they saw no fault in Idi Amin because they benefited from the regime. They did everything possible to please the establishment; you may call it boot-licking.

In spite of their openhanded, it was hard for me to trust them. I suspected them to be some kind of Trojan horse. Their friends who worked in the killing squads of Idi Amin stopped over occasionally. It was hard to say anything because you couldn't tell who was in your vicinity. They had access to the highest office of the presidency but I dared not ask anything from them because it would be considered luring them to fight my personal war. Asking help from them was akin to a nun asking for solace from a witch-doctor. The same people could be sympathetic to you for a while but before the cock crowed thrice they would betray you. Such are like an irritating itch you cannot scratch, making your miserable life worse!

Idi Amin's tolerance of brutality and hostility betrayed the peace loving citizens to the bone. Candidly, during Amin's reign, most Nubians indulged in perfidy, they tried to turn history upside down and indulged what I would describe as ethnic chauvinism. They had an illusion of a better Uganda without Baganda and Christians. They epitomize precisely the wrong attitude harbored by some Ugandans today who promote sectarianism and crusade for disunity. We are a country with very low mentality citizens, exceedingly uncivilized, vulgar and uncouth. No wonder the country is moving backwards while other African countries are thriving. Our hope to move forward depends on people's willingness to embrace real change. We shall never taste true peace until our power of love overcomes the love of power. "A people that values its privileges above its principles soon loses both"—Dwight D. Eisenhower

Idi Amin encouraged xenophobia against Baganda. He rewarded his cronies with impunity. The culprits practiced bigotry and treated us as if we were sub-humans. Their mouths were venomous. They openly made sectarian statements putting down people who did not look like them. The determination and solemnity in their statements were unmistakable, just like the gaps in their cream teeth, created by a culture that plucks them out. Hatred was melted out to all indiscriminately like wild fire that could not distinguish between dry and green grass. They were skilled in mocking and undermining their opponents. For example feeding Christians with raw pork; making civilians eat their flip-flop sandals (*sapatus*) and stepping on people's tomatoes in market places. I have never witnessed such a bullish low level of intelligence being ably displayed at the world stage than these people did. Yet they boasted in their mild ignorance! God created man with a brain, and the problem is that most don't use it for anything more than a hat rack!

Tribalism has become the dirty that nobody in Uganda is likely to escape the splash of its dirty mud. There is nothing wrong to take pride in your tribe as long as you respect people from other tribes. We all have tribes and we must show allegiance to our tribes without biasness. But at times our skewed views on tribalism make whatever opinion we have on anything to be taken with a pinch of salt; in other words not to be judged as objective and reliable.

Thank God for some patriotic people who have relentlessly fought the anti-social sectarianism. Dr. Lwanga is one of them. In spite of the risks involved, he had his feet firmly planted on the ground. He did not join any of the armed struggles against the past regimes of terror but he positively fought with his brain. His cherished opinions were ever constructive and ideological. He practically demonstrated his message in his actions. He did not have to say it but he preached broad love in his actions. The village folks readily swallowed his message without much ado because it was not grounded in myth and fantasy.

It is a source of pride to know one's ancestry—a factor the Baganda people cherish and impart to their children. Dr. Lwanga was a proud African and a proud Muganda man who had both a cosmopolitan view of the world as well as a fiercely African identity. He was proud of his tribe but he had respect of people from different tribes. He practiced and liked to discuss the dynamics of his rich and quite restrictive culture. Also, he liked to learn from other cultures without a possibility of compromising his values. He was not like some whose views appeared to switch with emotions, perhaps the word enigma comes to mind; he was principled. Above all things he admired development. He never allowed the cultural differences to become barriers preventing growth and development. He believed that fanaticism causes our productivity and potential to become stifled.

Stereo types are a hidden cause of conflicts in Uganda. Ethnical and cultural stereotypes may seem humorous but they can harm people in the end. Racial and tribal stereotypes are automatic and exaggerated mental pictures that we hold about all members of a particular ethnical group. When we stereotype people based on tribalism, we don't take into account individual differences. Because our tribalism and racial stereotypes are so rigid, we tend to ignore or discard any information that is not consistent with the stereotype that we have developed about the ethnic group.

As a reader you may be aware, a stereotype is a generalized representation of a group by another such as an ethnic, religious, linguistic group, etc. When we have a stereotypical thought about a racial group or an ethnic group, we should follow it up with an alternative thought based on factual information that discounts the stereotype. We can obtain this factual information by leaving our comfort zones and exposing ourselves to people of different tribes and races. The bottom line is that we should do whatever it takes to reject stereotyping. The blaming game will not help; blaming our parents or our society for it will not cut. The buck stops with each of us individually. The only people we can control are ourselves.

Uganda has sixty-five tribes. It is considered to have the biggest number of tribes and languages in the world, followed by Liberia. When we think about a "tribe" we think about a group with common interests. On the positive side this group of people can focus on their common goal and work together to achieve progress or even change the world. But today self-deception has taken prominence. People in general are self-centered and sometimes lose focus of the actual goal and start to focus more on the power and money and other egotistical things in that matter. They would betray their own in a blinking of an eye in exchange for the mighty dollar. Without shame, they are likely to betray you and wash their hands as Pontius Pilate did! One writer warned that, "The deepest cycle of hell has been preserved for the betrayers!"

I salute the late Dr. Lwanga for being determined and resilient during such trying times of political turmoil, religious and ethnic persecutions. Many people would have given up but he kept going and going. Many elites decided to go to exile whereas others decided to join a clique of goons (the Muslims, army/state operatives) who had become untouchables because of their closeness to Idi Amin. They teamed up with the thugs to terrorize the rest of masses who were on the opposite side; who did not look like them and who believed differently.

The late Dr. Lwanga proved his uniqueness by standing firm with the victims of the brutal regimes (Idi Amin/Obote II), who were helpless and hurting. During the past military regimes, Bombo was a ghost town whose lonely inhabitants wandered around in a calamity stricken area trying to fulfill their boring and hopeless lives. It was the home town of Idi Amin and the military barracks commanded by the notorious Chief of the Military Tribunal called Juma Ali Butabika; the colonel whose rage was exactly like the one exhibited by mad people. Also, Bombo was in the heart of the Luwero Triangle during the massacre of Obote II and the Okellos regimes. Dr. Lwanga treated the sick bodies and the sick minds of the victims who were tortured and tormented by the military regimes of terror. He stayed close to his people and hobnobbed with the victims. He never betrayed their trust.

In spite of his generosity, he was not received with roses at all places. His compassionate, trustworthy, honesty and being down to earth bred him enemies. His popularity made some nervous. They retaliated by watching his steps closely. Some pro-Amin and pro-Obote supporters made 'defamatory publication' against him. The governments of a cartel of Mafias headed by the dictators hatched clandestine plots to finish him off. When your enemy resorts to violence it means you have won the battle of wits. Their nasty plans flipped because of his popularity among people, even among their own people; they reconsidered their plans because any attempt to handle him forcefully could backfire. Ultimately, those who hounded him seemed like unguided athletes who conceived a race against a slippery hill. Their evil efforts only boomeranged on them.

They say that all it takes is one bad day to reduce the sanest man alive to lunacy. Dr. Lwanga was occasionally persecuted. At a couple of occasions he narrowly escaped death. The intimidations were intended to blunt his growing clout. He was a wounded soul, but he focused on the petals of the rose rather than the thorns that surrounded it. In this way he managed to "stomach" his persecutors' shortcomings, with no confrontation at all and to prevail over adversity. Paying good for evil is biblical and an acceptable sacrifice to God. Jesus cautioned that the bulk of the human race won't understand it. They actually consider non-retaliation to be a weakness.

I said that it was hard to trust people during Amin's regime. Even those who appeared to be friendly could at times be moles paid by government to trap you. What if they were Amin's red herring? What if they were on the mission to gather information from you and report you to the military? Dr. Lwanga was like a lonely sheep surrounded by wolves in sheep skins but he showed the commitment and creativity that can deliver results even in the face of overwhelming state oppression. He was the type of person who weathered all harsh conditions; who melted even the harshest of his critics with his allure. He was protective with the words coming from his mouth because he knew that some spies were trailing him. "If you want to dine with the traitors, it is fit to use a long spoon for they may decide to hold your hand in the bowl and accuse you of stealing their food."

Dr. Lwanga survived the hostile environments by fighting with the power of the mind. With a psychological constitution like his, enemies were expected to rethink their motivations and come over to his way of thinking. In this way he turned his arch-enemies into amities. "When a man's ways please the Lord, he maketh even his enemies to be at peace with him" (Proverbs 16:7).

Time hides many things but at the same time establishes everything. When a man is chewing his food awkwardly you can tell there is sand in it. Sometimes the suffering got so unbearable that Dr. Lwanga wondered why he was born a Muganda. He deployed certain dynamics to counter the odds of life. The unpredictable circumstances forced him to turn to the bottle of beer as an escape line, in anticipation to beat his demons. This gives us a deep insight into the reckless decisions people make when pushed to the end of their emotional spectrum, and the disastrous far-reaching consequences that follow.

Despite the tribulations, he did not budge. There is no one single time when I saw Dr. Lwanga losing his cool or putting on a "grin face". He was ever a simple, quiet, soft-spoken, modest but serious gentleman; he was ever a warm amiable man. The thread of integrity commonly ran through his career and life. He always looked calmer when puffing at his favorite yellow pack of cigarettes (Crown). He became an ardent bar and nightclub regular and the life of the party. But when Idi Amin's thugs started to get involved in bar brawls, he withdrew from public places to private life.

A lot of good things are talked about the late doctor. This does not mean that he did not have monkeys on his back. He was a human being with flaws like any of us. We must not ignore the fact that addictive chemicals have long term biological side effects that are disastrous to our health. I want to talk directly to the pessimists; it is high time you appreciate the good things some Ugandans like Dr. Lwanga did for this country instead of picking at their bad things, after all, nobody is completely clean. I usually tell the members of my congregation that if you come to our Church as a detective inspecting for flaws in a pastor, it would take you less than one hour to see a couple of them because I am a human being with flaws like any of you. Like any other person, I need a Savior. It points to the fact that there is no respite from crisis when you are in the position of responsibility. That is why, at least in the hindsight we should be a bit understanding in the errors that leaders make. I am not trying to excuse deliberate mistakes but to drive home this bitter truth.

The life story of Dr. Lwanga is pregnant with beautiful examples and mind-boggling actions. As they say, it is only in the dictionary where success comes before work. It means that success doesn't just miraculously happen, but you have to put quite a lot of effort into enabling yourself or your projects to reach such a point. The challenge is, of course, that as a society, we have too many of the wrong role models and that needs to be addressed. It is in human nature to always want to advance to the next level. The problem is to look for success in the wrong places. Many people, in particular our politicians seek to succeed at the expense of others. Much of the public funds, whether generated internally or by donors, never reach the intended beneficiaries but are used amongst bureaucrats. There is unchecked massive corruption due to lack of proper supervision. No wonder President Museveni on his visit to Rwanda lamented that Uganda's government is full of thieves. Intriguingly, they steal and they get away with the loot.

I advise our poor citizens to subject the politicians to rigorous tests and whosoever is found to be lacking integrity or to have an unclean track record, like abuse of a public office be rejected. We need to get rid of the callous and insensitive personalities by voting them out of power. If we emphasize ideology and suitability, then we should not allow a person known to have been a poacher, or one who has previously advocated degazetting of game reserves for farming activities, to become a minister for wildlife!

While we are appealing to God to help our country to come out of the pit, we need to do our part. As O. C. Bichachi said that, "Increasingly, many Ugandans now think only an act of God will change the fortunes of this country. Unfortunately, that only provides anesthesia for the suffering and more momentum for the tormentors." The problem is that some people's motto is for God and my stomach. I heard some prominent politicians arrogantly saying that, "When we are eating, Don't make fusses" (*Temutufumuulira nfuufu..*).

We need to device means ourselves, as an all-out citizenry to clean up the mess. If Ugandans don't take courage to face our ugly past, the demons will continue to haunt us for many more years. We should silence the selfish politicians by voting them out of offices. When "chicken" have vices such as those of the greedy politicians, they are de-beaked, anyone up for the job? If greed is their moral driver we can stop them by our votes otherwise history will judge us. Remember that in democratic nations, people hold their leaders accountable by their votes. That is why democracy is the key to genuine change. "You can never have a revolution in order to establish a democracy. You must have a democracy in order to have a revolution." G. K. Chesterton

Your vote matters. In 1923, one vote gave Adolf Hitler's Nazi's party leadership. In 1875, one vote changed France from a monarchy to a republic. In 1776, one vote gave America English language instead of Germany. In 1649, one vote caused Charles 1 of England to be executed. Ugandans should be prepared for the unexpected by ensuring that every elephant that fights, should be made to suffer instead of the innocent grass underneath.

I want to end by emphasizing the need of unity. Unity is a central ingredient for the existence and continuity of any entity. In fact, we should not be calling upon our leaders to unite; unity should be a lifestyle to be lived every day. Communities should not only strive to achieve it but commit themselves to maintaining it always. The greatest problem of the people from central region is division. Professor Mahmood Mamdani, argued that Buganda is a majority with a minority mindset. In order to have meaningful unity there should be forgiveness. So let's bury the hatchet and forge a way forward for the good of our country.

Buganda is made up of over fifty clans that are united under their king. Betty Nambooze Bakireke made the following appeal concerning the necessity of a unified Buganda, "It is this principle that makes Obuganda from each Kaganda that unites with other Buganda to form Buganda regardless of each other's inclinations beyond Buganda. In the current situation, therefore, the call for unity is assumed to encompass the multiparty dispensation in which we are operating at the moment.

It is still worth noting that when we unite, it is for or against a situation, a person or an entity. This means that at one end unity could be abused while at best it can be [harnessed] for the good of each of the players and become a foundation for team spirit.

Unity, therefore, constitutes mutual understanding as a major ingredient on the part of each of the parties therein. Given that diversities are likely to [spring up] in between, unity could be toned down to such controllable terms as tolerance, compromise, sacrifice and cooperation from which we are required to choose a basis for our relationships with others—Preaching and calling for unity is a double-edged sword. Sometimes the thing that brings us together also pulls us apart. Sort of like a zipper".

Uganda's greatest asset is not only its resources, but its people and their diversity. Instead of being a force for division, diversity should be an asset of strength and a source of unity in the process of nation building. The unity must be intended to promote the values of democracy and human rights. We should be united behind the right leaders. We should read the lips of the politicians who spew lies. Somebody cannot lead the fight against corruption and banditry when he is culpable of the same vice. The people of Uganda have a reputation of supporting wrong characters to come into power out of emotional excitement. For example the masses supported Idi Amin because they were desperate. Most Ugandans celebrated several juntas, only to end up complaining that they were deceived. We should learn from our past (history).

Uganda was supposed to be a God fearing country. Our motto says that, "For God and my country". Our national flag has a crested crane being a symbol of gentleness, friendly and peaceful. Rebecca Kadaga said concerning the crested crane that its characters embody the spirit, of Ugandans because they are hospitable, happy and friendly. Incidentally, the Cranes mirror many things about Uganda, the Pearl of Africa. To be precise—the very epitome of brokenness. Unfortunately, in many aspects we have portrayed an unpolished Pearl of Africa.

We need a unified front in order to fight of dictatorship; this being the characteristic of a society that is not void of conscience. One writer said that, "The 'New International Moral Order' requires therefore at least three levels of conscience: the conscience of the individual be that person ruler or subject; the conscience of each society, be that society powerful or weak; and the conscience of the world community as a whole."

Odeke Benjamin wrote that, "We as human beings, are part of the whole called by us universe, part limited in time and space. We do experience ourselves, our feelings as something separate from the rest. A kind of optical delusion of consciousness. This delusion is a kind of prison for us, restricting us to our personal desires and to affection for a few persons nearest to us. Our task must be to free ourselves from the prison by widening our circle of compassion to embrace all living creatures and the whole nature in its beauty. We shall require a substantially new manner of thinking if mankind is to survive . . . . in days to come . . ."

I want to end by saying that we are always going to have opponents of peace. There will always be challenges but Uganda will rise and shine again. It is upon us to brand and rebrand The Pearl Of Africa. Civilization is the greatest treasure we have under our belt. As one columnist wrote that, to "Hate" is not a recourse. But to take back the land of our birth from the peddlers of hates in our midst. To hate our opponents is to agree with them, but to counter their insidious hatreds for opposing views is to announce to them, that we are able to; with the maximum power of educational outreaches, nullify their own ignorances with our own know-hows. Where they resort to guns and bombs; we fire back with the potency or re-education; facts and the strength of numbers. If this is going to work; if we must salvage what's left of our beautiful land for our kids and their own kids, please let us eschew sentiments, please let us numb the tongue to least utter the word 'hate' so they won't have to say, we are on the same level. I am not advocating folding hands and watch as the deceptive syndicate tsunami sweeps away our values, I am preaching the power of love that transcends any other force. Remember that the darkest places in hell are reserved for those who maintain their neutrality in times of moral crisis.

Spiritually, we are children of God united by God. When you look at your family you notice the stark differences between every person in it. Each of your children looks different, has a distinct personality, and likes different things than the others. Yet, despite the many differences they all belong. The same is true of the family of God. When we come together with other believers from different backgrounds, ethnicities, and walks of life, there's going to be some differences between us. But the unity we share in Christ is so much stronger than what divides us. We are all together the spiritual body of Christ. We are not human beings going through spiritual experiences but we are spiritual beings going through human experiences.

God used me to Reach-out to Dr. Lwanga at the Dawn of his Last Days:

In the past chapter I discussed how God used Dr. Lwanga to help many people to sail through the dark times of the dictatorial regimes. Some of us had given up on life. We thought that things will never change but in reality nothing stays the same forever. All things have their natural trajectory, and whoever tries to resist this natural course often loses. God had preordained timing for this piece of scum to depart from our midst. Indeed all things have an end. Even Idi Amin who sent hundreds of thousands of innocent people to meet their maker, sooner or later, went to have a rendezvous with the kind of fate reserved for people who do such things.

The old adage goes, "Every dog has its own day." Idi Amin weaved a web of deceit and control so tight such that he could not escape. When you have a tribal army, you are always going to have internal "clan" conflicts. Idi Amin was often described as walking a tightrope as he has sought to balance cracking down occasional internal mutiny and defending external aggression. The dictator needed to read the book called Art of War: "If you fight on many fronts you will definitely lose."

We discussed that the rumors of insurgency at the southern borders of the country ushered in the passive-aggressive presidency. With time power started to slip from Amin's hands. By 1978, his support base had greatly shrunk and his army was riddled with dissent, assassinations and desertions. The soldiers were marauding themselves as the dissents were gaining ground. The top leadership of the Uganda Army was worn out and seeking to reconcile themselves with their gods. It was basically a crumbling rouge regime with its leaders living in fear. Idi Amin occasionally came up to address the press with futile and sterile statements downplaying the internal disintegration. But there is a saying that when a bottle leaks, there must be a crack somewhere.

In 1978, Mustafa Adiris, who was the Vice President of Uganda was injured in a suspicious road accident along Kampala Jinja-Highway.

The accident reportedly led to a mutiny by troops loyal to him. The late President Idi Amin in return deployed troops to quell the mutineers that were fleeing towards the Uganda—Tanzania boarder. The incident reportedly sparked off the Uganda-Tanzania war in 1979.

The brutal regime of Idi Amin had a miserable end after Amin yielded to Col. Juma Ali Butabika's advice to attack Tanzania. Col. Juma Ali had under his belt a juicy docket as the chief of Amin's kangaroo courts. The Colonel was Amin's walking stick to whip those seen as a potential threat to his iron grip control to the built cult of personalization. He would do anything to ensure that the dictator 'superglues' himself in power. In a lightning speed record of twenty five minutes, Amin claimed Kegera region to be Ugandan territory. It was a counter offensive to neutralize the pro-Obote rebel forces based in Tanzania; the job he did with all the fierceness in the infamous Kagera Operation. The Tanzanians tested the excessive doze of Amin's wrath. This was a serious lapse of judgment on Amin's part. Like the Baganda say that *'akanaafa tekawulira bugombe'* literally meaning that an antelope that is destined to die ignores the sound of the horn of the hunter.

Manipulation of a people has a price and more often than not, it boomerangs with comeuppances. Idi Amin ridiculed and teased the Tanzanian and Zambian leaders. He insinuated that if Nyerere was a woman he would have married him. He mocked Kaunda that he was most qualified to cry as a baby. He ignored the Baganda's adage that goes: "*Akasajja akatono okanyomera mitala wamugga,*" (meaning, never despise the minor chief in his domain).

Amin and Nyerere had for a long time been involved in the dogs and cats lifestyle. The high stakes poker game continued, with each side keeping its cards close to the chest, probably saving the best for the endgame. A dog that wants to grab anything from any dog ends up attempting to grab a bone from its own reflection in a pond thus losing his bone. This is how Amin lost his bone. The invasion of Tanzania was the impetus that the then President of Tanzania, Muwalimu Julius Nyerere, needed to decide that it was time for Amin to go. While Amin was still wrapped up in his own ego and delusions of infallibility, Nyerere embarked on a task of an all-out attack to subdue him. Not only did he push Amin's demoralized and undisciplined forces back to the Ugandan border, but he pursued them all the way to Kampala and beyond to effect a regime change. Nyerere is the only man who had the requisite power and the dignity to effect change and save Uganda from the Abyss. Amin fled to Libya. For the majority of the people of Uganda who wanted to 'hang' Amin, we are thankful to Nyerere for having procured the 'rope'—and helped tighten the noose—around Amin's neck.

Idi Amin became a victim of himself; a victim of power, greed and terrorism—which progressed to the last level of human folly: the circumstances that made his end inevitable. At the end of the day he had to pay the piper (wages of sin). Brother Jim said that, "My case work as a homicide detective taught me something important: There are only three motives behind any murder (or any crime, or sin, for that matter). All crimes are motivated by financial greed, sexual lust (relational desire), or the pursuit of power."

I want to say that the tide of change is unstoppable. The resisting of a dictator is just good enough to buy him a short time. The wind of change is only invisible to fools. But people must come out to support the change. A Chinese proverb says that, "When the winds of change blow, some people build walls and others build windmills." There's nothing like free lunch. People earn their freedom by fighting for it. "There are no revolutionary institutions, only revolutionary people"— Terence Mckenna.

Efforts to liberate our country from the dictator had accelerated into passiveness until Tanzania moved in to end the Stalemate. Africa's internal conflicts though few compared to during the cold war, have become more complex. Internal conflict in Uganda, for example, was not just a Uganda issue but a global one. It took too long for the foreign countries to intervene allowing the conflict to take international dimensions. Thank God for the late Muwalimu J. Nyerere the former present of Tanzania for coming to our rescue. He proved tough enough to take the bull by the horns. Idi Amin failed to silence and to intimidate the late J. Nyerere, and failed to break our resolve to see a free country enjoying good governance. In the face of defiance, Idi Amin was like a fish swept ashore and grasping for air or a man drowned in the deep sea and holding on the water hyacinth for safety.

Idi Amin's army was a paper tiger that was only effective against unarmed civilians but proved no match to the disciplined TPDF. Amin's troops were well armed but poorly motivated and poorly led (by semi-literate generals), creaking under the weight of nepotism. It is for the same reason they were ineffective as a fighting machine. The Tanzanian People's Defense Forces were capable of fending off aggression and taking revenge for the noble blood of those who had fallen. "Victory at all costs, victory despite all terror, victory however long and hard the road may be . . ." Winston Churchill

In March 1979, our capital city and Entebbe airport were near the war front and constant infiltration from the porous "Masaka, Mpigi shoreline" rendered it unsafe to stay near the military barracks. Idi Amin thugs retaliated by killing more innocent civilians and looting. But at this moment we were not bothered because we knew these were the last kicks of a dying horse. A dying horse kicks indiscriminately everybody around it. We were ready for the ferocity and fury that came with the liberation. The old adage says that it is not advisable to scratch a wound that is healing. In the same way we were not bothered by the itch.

On April 11, 1979, the Tanzanian troops and forces of the Uganda National Liberation Front closed in forcing the dictator to flee the capital city. Two days later they marched into the city, overthrowing the proven rogue corrupt government of Idi Amin. Kampala fell and a coalition government of former exiles took power. On the day he was toppled, there were "celebrations", "celebrations" and more "celebrations" reminiscent of the ones that occurred when he took over power from Apollo Milton Obote in 1971. The visibly-liberated people jubilated with excitement like ordinary soccer fans whose team had inexplicably won the World Cup.

Idi Amin is despised as a bloodthirsty criminal by the world. He fled to Libya then to Iraq and later in 1981; he had to find sanctuary in Saudi Arabia where he was allowed to settle provided he stayed out of politics. He went to exile when still a very conceited man, without apologizing to the relatives of the victims of his regime, who bore the brunt of the chaos that descended on the country and had deep-seated apathy towards him. Human rights groups say as many as 500,000 people were killed during Amin's 1971-1979 rule over Uganda.

In 1989, his attempt to return by force through Zaire failed. Idi Amin remained in Saudi Arabia sending financial assistance to his brother Ramathan and six other relatives and friends plotting against the legitimate governments. Idi Amin died in August 16, 2003, at Jeddah, Saudi Arabia from a combination of hypertension and kidney complications. He left behind many children including Jaffar Amin, Taban Amin, Faisal Wangita, Ali Amin, Khadija Abria Amin, Mwanga Amin, Maimuna Amin, Hussein Amin, Moses Amin, Haji Ali Amin, Wasswa Amin, Kato Amin, Iman Aminu. The known spouses: Sarah Amin (m. 1975-2003), Madina Amin (m. 1972-2003), Nora Amin (m. 1967-1974), Kay Amin (m. 1966-1974), Malyamu Amin (m. 1966-1974).

People like Idi Amin give us a reason to believe in life after death because that is when people who die without getting justice and who die without paying for their crimes will face the music. One day the justice that we could not get from this world will be finally serviced. There is only one way to escape the divine justice. That way is by repenting and receiving Jesus Christ who paid the penalty for all kinds of sins.

The love of God is sacrificial. We are proud of the TPDF (*Wakombozi*) for sacrificing a lot for our sake. They fought for our freedom, human rights and erased extrajudicial massacring of civilians. The Tanzanians paid a high price for our freedom. Andrew M. Mwenda of the Independent newspaper praised the countries which did not go into hibernation when Amin was causing havoc. "For whilst Amin and his bandits were plundering our material resources, desecrating our cultural heritage and carrying out what was tantamount to a genocide in Uganda, the world—except for Tanzania, Zambia, Somalia, Botswana and Sudan—just sat by and watched." He went on to say that ironically, the so called civilized world swung into action to halt the horrors and atrocities committed by Hitler during the Second World War. Yet no leader of any major power, felt compelled to bring an end to similar atrocities committed by the monster in Uganda in the last quarter of the 20th Century. He praised a small nation, Tanzania, with meager resources to fight within her limitations and restore the conscience of the civilized world. (*The Independent by Andrew M. Mwenda*).

Unfortunately people did not enjoy the fruits of the liberation for a long time. Rochefoucauld warned that, "If we have not peace within ourselves, it is in vain to seek it from outward sources." Ugandans are to blame for the miseries which followed thereafter. The politicians and stalwarts were not ready to cast their difference aside and give this country a fundamental change. Changing the face can change nothing but "facing the change" can change everything. Some Ugandans were not ready to face the real change. As Morris D.C. Komakech insinuated that, "The real challenge is that we have failed ourselves by always opting for rather small pushes towards the windows of opportunity that beckon on us for a real change".

Rather than ushering in peace, the TPDF liberation turned out to be an advent to brood egocentric killing machines (The Obotes, the Okellos, the Lakwenas, the Konys and others alike). The post-Amin governments did not respect human rights; they were resentfully swollen with vengeances, the result of which was the persecutions of innocent civilians. The wars later spread over to Rwanda, Congo and Sudan with million lives unaccounted for. Not many people have a reason smile. The long awaited peace is still a pipe dream. Instead, we have been treated to unfortunate lamentations which I am sure make Nyerere shift uneasily in his final resting place in Butiama.

After the liberation, we had the ever shortest but sweetest regime of Professor Y. K. Lule (April 12, 1979 to June 19, 1979). In a moment of extreme elation, at his first public appearance and when he was sworn in as president of Uganda, Lule said in Luganda: "*Kyetwayagalizanga embazzi, Kibuyaga asudde*" (The tree for which we were searching an axe, the storm has unexpectedly brought it down). This evoked jubilation among his tribesmen who could not see beyond their noses. To their disappointment his reign lasted for just sixty-eight days.

Power slipped from his hands leaving traces of perforates just as of a hot knife through a mound of butter. The reason is because real power was not in the executive but in the UPC oriented military wing.

Power changed hands from Yusuf Lule to G. Binaisa and then to Paulo Muwanga. There emerged other oppressive military regimes which were no different from Amin's thugs. It was just a rotation of the same ideologies of oppression and tyranny: 'same monkey, different forest'. The opponents of peace tried to blow out the candle of peace by killing the peace loving citizens in Luwero Triangle. Also the massive arrests of people from central region in *Panda Gali* operation. These were years of suffering called '*mpawo atalikaaba*' (1980s). "Tyranny travels far when dressed as law enforcement officers"—Prof Calestous Juma.

Paul Muwanga rigged election and passed the mantle to his protégé—Milton Obote. Perhaps the most enduring words of Milton Obote were given during his speech on May 27, 1980 in Ishaka Bushenyi upon his return from exile. He warned Ugandans to recognize the need for self-sufficiency and to jealously guard our newly won freedom. The reappearance of Obote on the political arena defied logic. Obote left a mark on the history of Uganda as '*Ekitta ekitava ku sengejero*'. He ignored the adage saying that "*N'azina Obulungi ava mu ddiiro*" (even a good dancer comes off the stage). He became a "*Nakwale.*" *Amazina ga Nakwale* is a book written by Grace Semakula Musoke, based on a great dancer who was loved and admired for her great moves. But she never wanted to leave the stage and her dances turned into a nuisance, and eventually people hated her.

Obote II was a forceful return of Obote to rule the country with the iron hand. Luwero Triangle, the home area of Dr. Lwanga, became a battlefield littered with tens of thousands of human skulls who were mercilessly massacred by the soldiers. The slogan that, "the country is purchased by dead bodies" ("*ensi eguula milambo*") started during Obote II. One politician said, "Uganda had learnt nothing and forgotten nothing from its history of violence and it would soon be reminded through the only language the country and its politicians had mustered—violence".

During the period of the liberation of our country by the TPDF, I had accidentally become a successful business man in Bombo town. At the eve of the liberation of our country, I abandoned my home town (Bombo) and fled to the suburbs of Kampala, but Dr. Lwanga stayed behind in the ghost town throughout the liberation struggles from Amin, Obote II and the Okellos. I appreciate the strength and charisma he exhibited through these trying times. It is by the grace of God that he survived the wars of liberation that followed. Dr. Lwanga stayed with his people throughout the deadly wars because he cared for them. He was falsely accused to be aiding the dissents but his persecutors failed because it was all concoctions; there wasn't any muck to dig up. The persecutions made him more committed than breaking his will. One writer insinuated that, "Out of suffering have emerged the strongest souls; the most massive characters are seared with many scars."

Dr. Lwanga suffered the worst humiliation; he was squeezed between a rock and a hard place but he chose to die a principled death rather than sneaking away to safe haven. Some of us thought that his decision to stay was akin to choosing the kiss of death; but we were wrong. God allowed Dr. Lwanga to live through the hostile environments for a reason. He chose to make a statement by his perseverance. It was an endurance test for the human body, will, ambition, aspiration and desire to reassure us that we can excel to overcome social injustices. Many intellectuals betrayed our country by surrendering their souls to the dictatorship but he fought the dictatorial system not with guns but with minds. Unlike most of the highly respected intellectuals, he refused to be stripped of his intellect and schooling. Indeed he who fights with his betters and prevails is a man above all others. It is for the same reason he has my eternal admiration. The problem of Uganda is not lack of patriotism but lack of compassion for citizens and a true sense of nationalism.

Peace returned to Luwero after NRA took power on the 25th January 1986. Apparently 25th January coincides with the day Idd Amin took power in 1971. President Museveni proved to be a commander-in-chief who do not tremble before the fury of ordinary mortals. But it is still too early to roll out the drums and dance. It seems we have only won one battle in a never ending war!

In the past chapter I briefly discussed some of the physical, emotional and psychological torment that I experienced during the brutal regimes. You may find the details of the story in my book called *"Growing in the Spirit"* where I give my testimony in its fullness. I have been brief because I do not want my story to have prominence because this book is primarily about the fallen hero. I do not want to appear as if I am blowing my own trumpet. Regardless, I deemed it necessary for my reader to get acquainted with pieces of my testimony in order to know why I consider the late Dr. Lwanga to be my hero.

All I can say is that the abusive regimes had serious impact on me resulting into occasional emotional reaction with great acrimony. I had a fake smile from outside but I was a bitter and angry young man from within. I did not know how to vent my anger. My life was hanging on a rope; at a couple of times I even contemplated on committing suicide as a means of killing the other "bitter" half of me. But Dr. Lwanga stepped in; I harmonized his view with my situation to the best of my interest. He was God sent because I urgently needed somebody to talk to. It helped me to navigate the turbulent waters of the brutal regimes.

Those were my old bad days. My cheap rants predicted a fairytale dreamer. I had grown up to be a confused adult living a teenage life! Owing to an abusive and inconsistent youthful times, I suffered from hypermnesia being an abnormally sharp memories of the negative past events. I badly wanted to protect my space. That explains the paranoid and delusion I exhibited. I walked around like a mouse without a hole to sleep in. But thank God because I did not disappear into oblivion. Human resource eased and calmed the situation but could not permanently eradicate the misery. Even when my business potentiality invigorated and I started making lots of money, I ended up picking a reckless lifestyle like selling alcohol and running after young beautiful girls. But God did not give up on me. At His timing, He picked me from a furnace. He works in mysterious ways. He used the terrible circumstances that I went through to position me to receive his grace. The grace of God gave me a valid reason to rejoice in persecution with humility and humbleness.

God helped me to overcome my fears and the temptation of using my weaknesses (animalistic instincts) to demean others. Forgiveness is the most unnatural of human emotions in particular when your memories are like freshly opened wounds. God miraculously taught me to forgive my tormentors (enemies). After experiencing God's love, I realized that I had never known to love but rather had pity feelings for people. The old adage says that, 'pity is akin to love'. God injected true love in my heart for the first time. God helped me to love the very people I hated most. I saw the need to extend grace to them because God extended to me even much grace. For the first time I realized that whining and pulling out the "sectarian" card is moronic. Instead of seeking revenge, I resorted to praying for their salvation.

People who have easy life during their early times often never succeed. The Baganda's proverb says that *"Ekikula amangu, kiffa mangu"*, literally meaning that what grows quickly (not within the normal required time) dies quickly. Another proverb says that, "Better experience bad days in your youth than in the last days of your adulthood".

God is not the architect of our troubles but He can turn our trials into steps to bless us. Borrowing a leaf from the history of America, according to Hubbard, slavery was in the end a good thing for African-Americans: ".... the institution of slavery that the black race has long believed to be an abomination upon its people may actually have been a blessing in disguise. The blacks who could endure those conditions and circumstances would someday be rewarded with citizenship in the greatest nation ever established upon the face of the Earth" (*Pages 183-89*).

Without doubt slavery was a disgrace to the civilized world and a menace to Africa, far worse than any known hurricane in the history of the world, taking into account its effects to humanity. For example in Dakar, Senegal, the island called Goree was the famous slave house and export port. Over a period of nearly 350 years from 1486, about 26 million slaves were exported from Goree to the Americas and

Caribbean. A staggering 6 million of them died on the journey. Although slavery was bad, God turned the bad into good for the African Americans who are living in USA today. The infrastructure that we enjoy today in America was built on African sweat and blood. An average African American of today has an edge over an African living in the jungles of Africa.

Regarding my situation, God turned the evil plans of man into blessings. God allowed me to go through the trials of life for a purpose. God had a better plan for me. He eventually opened the way for me to know Him intimately. In early 1980s, I accepted Jesus Christ as my personal savior. Thank God for Richard Robert and Bishop G. Musisi whom God used to minister to me His saving grace.

It is after I surrendered my life to Jesus that I acknowledged my weaknesses and I accepted the weaknesses of others. According to the psychologists, once you recognize the specific bad behaviors that are holding you back, you can begin systematically to steer away from those behaviors. You can't start the next chapter if you keep re-reading the current one. God helped me to put the past behind. God helped me to realize that I did not have to live within the limitations of my past experiences. In Christ there is no guilt. My life changed forever. Some people who knew my past experiences wonder how I live happily in spite of my past trials. Fulfillment does not come from outside but from within. It is an internal spiritual transformation experienced after receiving Jesus Christ. Archbishop Orumbi made this profound statement: "For a corrupt person, nothing is enough. Therefore, corruption simply means what I have is not enough. The solution can only be in seeking salvation".

It was revealed to me that I was not an orphan because God is my Father. He is the father to the fatherless. All people are fatherless until they accept to be adopted into the divine family. The family of God includes all believers from different denominations (Catholics, Protestants, Baptist, SDA, Pentecostals and etc.), who accepted to be born again (be born of God) by receiving Jesus Christ in their hearts. They are committed to live the godly life by manifesting the life of Christ.

Some people confuse the need to be born again as a new religion. The reality is that Jesus redeems by restoring His new nature in us. To be born again is the core of the Christian faith. Jesus said that, "Very truly I tell you, no one can see the kingdom of God <u>unless they are born again</u>." Nicodemus asked: "How can someone be born when they are old? Surely they cannot enter a second time into their mother's womb to be born!" Jesus answered, "Very truly I tell you, no one can enter the kingdom of God unless they are born of water and the Spirit. Flesh gives birth to flesh, but the <u>Spirit gives birth to spirit</u>" (John 3:3-4). The Greek translation of again (John 3:3), also means from above; it means to be born from above (born of God). The Father is Spirit and those who are born of Him partake of the same nature as God. They are spirit. They share the same nature and character with God. They manifest the life of Christ. According to the laws of nature, everything gives birth after its kind. For example a cat gives birth to a cat. In the same manner, God is Spirit and his offspring are spirit. This is what it means to be born again or of God. The believers are adopted into the family of God by the Holy Spirit. They acquire the minds of Christ; their goal is to live the holy life. They are sinners under the grace. Their objective is to be holy but in case of sin, the grace of God covers their sins (past, present/future).

After I accepted Jesus Christ as my Lord and Savior, there was a dramatic change from a life of vigorous sin, contemplating suicide and perverseness to pure obedience, with hope and assurance of eternal life. My life took a positive turn forever. It does not mean the tough times are over. Jesus walks with me through tough times with such assurance of victory and hope. I would rather go through tough times with Jesus than having an idyllic life without Christ. Yes, temptation comes. There is no situation as dangerous as not being tempted. I have learned more about what I truly want out of life through the painful experiences than in times when everything is fine. God allows pain to humble us. As the old adage says, "Easy roads make sleepy travelers." The distressed soul does not sleep; it is after we enter into peaceful confidence and full self-assurance that we are in danger of slumbering. Old Erskine wisely remarked, "I like a roaring devil better than a sleeping devil."

The grace of God helped me to embrace the ethics with fundamental principle of morality. I started advancing my struggles against all sorts of immoral tendencies; the lumpens with infantile disorders, just to mention a few. With time God started to open doors for me. Later on He called me into full time ministry. Without prior arrangements, I went overseas to study. At this period of time, the process of clearance for young men to go to USA was more stringent. I am one of the blessed ones to get a visa with such ease. I did not go overseas as one of the fortune-hunters who ran away from unemployment (*Nkuba kyeyo*). I did not have to concoct stories in order to get a visa or to be accepted as a refuge, as many begin their lives in the Diaspora camps. Today, in a situation where there is no force, an African sells off all her/his property to go and work or sell themselves off as slaves. I wonder what verifies their action and reaction. Gone are the days of slave trade when our fore fathers were forced to leave their families behind to go abroad on other continents and work as slaves.

God opened my eyes to see His vision. Vision is a picture of the future that produces a passion for the future. I went for a Christian conference and later on returned as a Bible seminary student. Going to the Bible Collage all the way to university and earning graduate degrees was my dream coming true. It was the best thing that ever happened to me. I had always wanted to become a priest. At that time, the role models available to me in the village were priests. These are the people I looked up to as the cream of the cream; they lived the best life in society so that is what I looked forward to becoming. I went oversees because God called me on a special mission and I ended up pastoring a Church in USA and settling there. Although I am a citizen, I take pride in the roots and values of my Mother Land.

The grace of God opened my eyes to realize my stewardship responsibilities. We were created to manage this world on behalf of God the creator. We brought nothing into the world and we take nothing from the world. I gave up all the riches of the world that I had accumulated in order to focus on serving God. For the past twenty years I have been oversees faithfully serving God. God has helped me to shun the mentality of materialism; my desire is to serve God.

I often reminisce retrospectively at the scenario of life. I realize that there are a lot of things I could have done differently if only I could turn back the hands of time. My greatest regret is delaying receiving the gift of salvation. I often ask myself, "Why did it take me so long to acknowledge the truth?" The Bible says that there is a way that seems good to man but in the end it is destruction. One thing I don't regret is that I am saved. Two roads diverged in a wood, I took the one least traveled and that has made all the difference. I will never regret why I chose this path . . . I am glad I did!

At the end of last year (2011) I was privileged to visit my country after spending several years without going back. I was homesick because I missed my family, my mother and great friends like Dr. Lwanga. Homesickness is a feeling that instinctively features the attachment to a loved spot of one's upbringing. Betty Long Cap said that, "For man and beast, there is no place like home."

Clutching my old adage that the early bird catches the fat worm, as soon as I stepped on Uganda's soil, I made an appointment to meet Dr. Lwanga at his clinic at Bombo where he discharged his normal duties. Not that there was something important to discuss; it was just a premonition I had that I should check on him. I decided to go to where he was instead of him coming to my hotel because he was my elder. Due to some unavoidable circumstances, I was about three hours late for our appointment. You know that Kampala is such a car-crazed city where it is often quicker to walk to get a thing done than to drive on the traffic-choked roads. But he patiently waited for me outside his clinic in the darkness of the night.

I was over-excited to meet him. We exchanged hi-fives and hugged before resuming the discussions. The instinct to get as close as you can, eye-to-eye with the one you love, and hug each other is universal. He welcomed me with such great joy and enthusiasm. He was in a jovial mood; we were reunited and gelled together as one happy family. It never looked like there was an imminent implosion. He looked healthy and he was in high morale. Apart from limping in his limbs, he seemed he had no major health scares. Unfortunately, a couple of months later he succumbed to death. I can testify that despite his advanced years, he remained vital until the end. His death silenced a voice that one longs to hear again, especially in a country where oppression is still rampant. I will always remember him with a tender fondness.

Our meeting was enthusiastic. Except that our conversation was occasionally intercepted by telephone calls. At first he excused himself to answer a telephone call before resuming the talking. I did not blame him for not exercising phone etiquette because of the urgency of his work.

At his age, he radiated the amount of energy and passion that none of his contemporaries can easily show off. He was as motivating and inspiring as before. He showed great interest into what I was doing and he was itching to show me what he has been doing. To my surprise, all the talking was centered on spiritual matters. It seemed he had been deeply involved in religious study, in this evening of his life. He lectured to me why he believed that all religions lead to salvation. I gave him my view that Jesus is the only way to heaven as opposed to one of the ways to heaven. Before you accuse me of bigotry, we should put the blame where it belongs. Jesus said that He is the only way and truth (John 14:6). Any contrary belief makes Jesus a liar!

One man accused my professor of being narrow minded to believe that Jesus is the only way. My professor replied that, "May be God is narrow minded to make only one way to Him and to reveal that one way to us". If there were other ways to redeem the world why would God send His beloved Son to die for us? In the Garden of Gethsemane Jesus prayed to the Father that if there is another way take this cup from me (Luke 22:42). He partook of the cup of God's wrath (cross) because there was no other way to save man other than the way of the cross. Jesus chose not to save Himself from the cross in order to save us from our sins.

Christianity is not the only faith that proclaims to be the only way to heaven. When you study all of the world religions, each of them propagates that you cannot reconcile with God unless you embrace the teachings of their founding prophets. For example Islam teaches that nobody can go to heaven without believing that Mohammed is the prophet of God. His teaching condemns those of us who believe that he is a false prophet. The Quran teaches that it is a blaspheme for the prophet of God to die on the cross. We believe that the cross is central to Christianity, without the cross we are doomed. The Hindu believe that God has been incarnated hundreds of thousands of times. We believe that there is one unique event of incarnation involving Jesus that cannot be repeated; we cannot both be right! All religions cannot truly lead us to heaven because all religions do not agree that you can make it to heaven in your own way other than their way. The religions of the world do not agree on the truth. Either the entire phenomenon of religion is a hoax or one of them is true. I believe that the Bible is true. Jesus is the truth that connects mankind to God.

Some people falsely believe that the Jews are not supposed to believe in Jesus. As I said all of the twelve apostles and the majority of believers in the early Church were Jews. Cornelius was the first Gentile (non-Jewish) to receive the Holy Spirit (Acts 10). A Messianic Jew is a Jewish person who believes that Jesus (Yeshua) fulfilled the prophesies about the Messiah in the Jewish Scriptures, that he died to atone for the sins of mankind, and that God raised him from the dead on the third day. The Messiah is the ultimate Prophet, Priest and King! Examples of this title in the Tenach are found in Daniel 9:25 and Psalm 2:2. In the New Covenant, Yeshua claimed the title of Messiah (see Mark 14:61-62 and John 4:25-26). A Messianic Jew essentially is a Jewish person who believes that Jesus is the promised Jewish Messiah. He is the one who is born again.

The Messianic Jewish Alliance of America (MJAA) represents the interests of approximately 100,000 Messianic Jews in the United States. The MJAA is also affiliated with 15 other national Messianic Alliances through an International Messianic Alliance which represents the interests of up to 350,000 Messianic Jews world-wide (figures as estimated by the Jewish telegraph Agency 4/14/89). Today, there are approximately 8,000 Messianic Jews in Israel in 50 congregations! The Messianic Jewish movement is also growing in other countries. "As a child I received instruction both in the Bible and in the Talmud. I am a Jew, but I am enthralled by the luminous figure of the Nazarene . . . No one can read the Gospels without feeling the actual presence of Jesus. His personality pulsates in every word. No myth is filled with such life"—Albert Einstein

Judaism is not the end in itself. The Jews need Jesus as much as we need Him in order to be saved. The Bible emphasizes that the true Jew is the one born again (born of the Spirit): "For no one is a Jew who is merely one outwardly, nor is circumcision outward and physical. But a Jew is one inwardly, and circumcision is a matter of the heart, by the Spirit, not by the letter. His praise is not from man but from God" (Romans 2:28-29). Jesus called the Jewish religious people who did not believe in Him children of the devil: "If God were your Father, you would love me, for I came from God and now am here. I have not come on my own; but he sent me. Why is my language not clear to you? Because you are unable to hear what I say. You belong to your father, the devil, and you want to carry out your father's desire." (John 8:39-47). The religious Jews are physically descendants of Abraham and are sincere concerning their religious beliefs but without Jesus Christ they are lost and excluded from the spiritual promises of God.

The Church involves people (Jews/Gentiles) called out of the world into the kingdom of God. The word Church comes from two words. One word is *ek* which means out, and the other word is *kaleo* which means to call. The word is *ekklesia* and it means a called-out group. We are called out of the world to reach out to the lost world and to stand firm in the gospel presented to us by the apostles without a possibility of compromising. "But though we, or an angel from heaven, preach any other gospel unto you than that which we have preached unto you, let him be accursed" (Galatians 1:8).

This topic is about my reunion with the late Dr. Lwanga that took place the same year he died. The other thing I discussed with Dr. Lwanga is the assurance of our salvation. He still believed that we cannot for sure know that we are going to heaven until the judgment day. Remember his humor I discussed saying that, in this world we are like students taking their examination, who will never know their performance until the Day of Judgment.

The biblical truth is that we can have assurance of our salvation now. The Bible says that, "Believe in Jesus Christ and you will be saved"

(John 3:16; Acts 16:31). Let us examine the doctrine of 'assurance' from two perspectives: one is objective and the other is subjective. One has to do with something outside of us, the other has to do with something inside of us. That's what I mean by objective/ subjective. Objective considers that which is outside of us, subjective considers that which is inside of us. I am convinced that the Scriptures call upon both (that which is objective and that which is subjective, as the ground of our assurance). That is to say we look first to history and then to experience. Both are essential in assurance.

The objective ground is clearly indicated to us in statements like this, 1 John 5:1, "Whoever believes that Jesus is the Christ is born of God." Consider 1 John 5:11-13: "And this is the testimony: God has given us eternal life, and this life is in his Son. He who has the Son has life; he who does not have the Son of God does not have life. I write these things to you who believe in the name of the Son of God so that you may know that you have eternal life." Who is it that has the Son? It is those who have believed in Him and accepted Him (John 1:12). If you have Jesus, you have life. Not temporary life, but eternal. We can tell those who have eternal life. Jesus said that we shall know His disciples by their fruits (Matthew 7:20).

There is objectivity. You believe in the truth of Christ, therefore you are born of God. And in saying "believing that Jesus is the Christ," you are gathering up everything that is true about Christ, the true Christ, His work, His promises. According to 1 Corinthians 1:30, everything is yes and amen in Him. So the objective ground then is what you believe about Christ. To have assurance, you have to believe the right thing. Believing is receiving. The Bible says that, "But as many as received him, to them gave he power to become the sons of God, [even] to them that believe on his name" (John 1:12).

But secondly, there is subjective ground and that is internal. The subjective ground is the convicting, sanctifying work of the Holy Spirit in us. Romans 8:16, "The Spirit bears witness with our spirit that we are children of God." It is because we believe something outside of us, the historical fact concerning Christ, and it is because of the work of the Spirit inside of us, those two together produce in us assurance. And so in 2 Corinthians 13:5, we read what is essentially a call, a command, "Test yourselves to see if you are in the faith." The Scriptures call us to examine our faith. Peter wrote that, "Therefore, my brothers, be all the more eager to make your calling and election sure. For if you do these things, you will never fall" (2 Peter 1:10). Paul instructed us that, "Therefore, my dear friends, as you have always obeyed—not only in my presence, but now much more in my absence—continue to work out your salvation with fear and trembling" (Philippians 2:12).

Before we parted, Dr. Lwanga requested for my books. I handed to him a couple of copies of the old versions (unrevised books) which I wrote during my early times of the ministry. I was nervous thinking that he would not like them due some typing errors because they were published before doing proof reading and proper editing. Surprisingly, he understood the real world of writing and what it entails. After browsing through the memoirs, the late Dr. wrote to me a note complimenting my work and expressed his desire to have other books at his fingertips. He sent one of his sons to Nasaana (twenty five miles from his home town) to pick up other books. I could sense in him the spiritual thirsty to know the truth.

My books are not on the bestselling list but they provide a deep insight to biblical truth; they are good for personal devotions and home schools with outstanding curriculum built on a foundation of academic excellence and Christian character training. The gospel is central in all my books because we are called to preach the gospel.

Oakum Mario wrote that, "The ink of the scholar is better than the blood of the martyr" I am not a scholar but I write in anticipation of helping people to benefit spiritually and to evoke their thinking capabilities—to give uncannily-accurate interpretations that amplify a thousand-fold the power of the Word. Also an uncanny knack of foreseeing trouble in order to avoid it. My books are good for Christian apologetic. "Apologetics" comes from a Greek word used by Christian authors: πολογία (apologia). This word appears seventeen times in the New Testament, as either a noun or a verb. Most often, some form of the expression "make a defense" can be substituted for the term. Jesus, for example, tells his disciples that the Holy Spirit will help them "make a defense" (apologia): Luke 12:11-12—"But when they bring you before the synagogues, the rulers, and the authorities, do not worry about how you should make your defense or what you should say, for the Holy Spirit will teach you at that moment what you must say."

I began to write books not as a career but with mentality of promoting the reading culture, which is one of the wheels on which Uganda is being trolled. Basically, I have been writing in anticipation of selling ideas as opposed to selling books. My books and teaching materials reflect the very best in traditional Christian education, comprehensive curriculum, and eternal truths. My teaching is designed to "making a defense" or "making a case" based on various researches including the historical evidence, philosophical arguments, scientific investigation, and arguments from other disciplines of life. When we engage skeptics about the Christian Worldview, we are "making a case" for what we believe and acting as "Christian Case Makers". The materials in my books have turned out to be double edged—improving thinking, as well as crashing biblical illiteracy. I use numbers to draw pictures. Numeracy is a major priority for our school. Numeracy is the ability to reason and think critically, while biblical literacy is the ability to read for application and spiritual growth. My books are not substitutes for the Scriptures. I emphasize the need to read the Bible regularly because it is central to activating our faith.

It seems that my trip to Uganda, shortly before the death of Dr. Lwanga was not coincidental but it was in accordance to the divine plan. I was privileged to give back to the man who contributed much to my life. This reminds me of an African proverb in Runyankole— *"otaryeebwa omuhanda gwakuretsire"*; literally meaning—(never forget where you came from).

I met one of his friends and he insinuated that, "Dr. Lwanga's mind is never idle, he is ever reading and searching." Whenever I contemplate about it, I oscillate between tears and joy, believing that this was his turning point spiritually. It is as if he had a premonition of his imminent death. I reckon the last weeks following my dad's abduction were characterized with intensive spiritual thirsty; he spent most of his time reading the Bible. He was basically soaked in the Scriptures. In my own view, I think God weighed in at the eve of his death to ensure the soft landing. What passion; what commitment to get excited about Jesus Christ and be aflame with the spirit of God when death is at your doorstep!

I wanted to engage the late Dr. Lwanga with a spiritually mature person to guide him. The two powerful influences you need are the books you read and the company of people you keep. Before I left Uganda, I asked Dr. Lwanga to be the chairman of the building committee of our proposed Bible seminary in Luwero. He worked with Pastor Abraham Mulindwa who is a born again Pentecostal believer and Brother Expedito Kutesa who is a born again Catholic. Dr. Lwanga accepted the responsibility and served faithfully until he passed on. Paul insinuated that he who sows bountifully reaps bountifully (2 Corinthians 9:6). Dr. Lwanga sowed bountifully and reaped bountifully.

Paul compared this life to a race. He yearned to finish well without a possibility of disqualification. How we finish the race matters. God does not call us just to start the race but to finish well. It is my prayer that you run the race with intention of finishing well without a possibility of disqualification.

There is a popular saying that, "Death ends a life, not a relationship". After his demise, my relationship with Dr. Lwanga continued in the subconscious. When I was working on this book, I had a dream about the late Dr. Lwanga. In the same dream, he was distributing relief supplies to the needy. I approached him, and engaged him in a theological debate. We discussed the fulfillment of biblical prophecy. We discussed God's covenant with man (eschatology) when focusing on the Second Coming of Christ. At the end of the discussion I asked him if he still believe that Islam is one of the ways to heaven. The moment I asked that question he disappeared in rare; it was like pushing a delete button on the computer whereby you instantly lose the images on the screen. It seemed as if the question was offensive and disgusting to him. As for the skeptics, the Nigerians have a proverb saying that if the crocodile tells you that there is no more fish in the lake, believe it because that is where it lives.

I am still struggling to interpret the above dream. But inside me there is that assurance that Dr. Lwanga is in the right place. Whenever I think about it, I wonder at the amazing grace of God and I am pounced with a long sigh of relief. I am overwhelmed with an unspeakable joy. In life there are those moments of unutterable fulfillment which cannot be completely explained by those symbols called words. Their meaning can only be articulated by the inaudible language of the heart. This is one of such moments!

We must be ready all the times to meet our maker. The tragedy is that most people keep on postponing their spiritual preparation hoping that they have another day to live. The worst death is not dying from terminal sickness like Aids or cancer, it the death that strikes and takes us by surprise when we think we have many years ahead. I mean death from accidents, homicides, strokes, heart attacks and etc. People in this category do not get time to prepare themselves. The Bible advices us to be ready in seasons and out of seasons.

Our good works, religiosity, biblical illiteracy and rebellion won't get us very far. On the Day of Judgment God is not going to ask you the doctrine of your religion or what your priest told you but whether you obeyed the Word of God. It is important to read the Word and heed by applying the truth to your life.

Our salvation does not depend on our mental capability but on our spiritual transformation resulting from receiving Jesus Christ as our personal Savior. God saves us by recreating (regenerating) us into the image of His Son. He imputes on us the righteousness of Christ by His grace. The saved person is expected to manifest the fruits of salvation by obeying the commandments of God.

It takes the anointment of God to open our eyes to the truth. Jesus said that, "The Spirit of the Lord is on me, because he has anointed me to preach good news to the poor. He has sent me to proclaim freedom for the prisoners and recovery of sight for the blind, to release the oppressed" (Luke 4:18). The blind are not illiterates but anybody who has not known Jesus Christ intimately as his or her Lord and Savior.

The spiritual enlightenment happens when our minds are illuminated to understand the Scriptures by the revelation (unveiling) of God. The gospel opens our spiritual eyes to see the holiness of Jesus Christ. God is so perfect that the slightest scintilla of sin causes His wrath to react. He can do no other because He is perfect. We relate to Him within the perfection of Christ (imputed righteousness).

We are then convicted of our wickedness and we acknowledge our incapability to save ourselves from the same wickedness and be like Him. The Gospel opens our spiritual eyes to see the need of God to save us. We respond to the gospel by repenting our sins and ask Jesus Christ to come into our lives. We receive Him as our personal Savior by believing in His works on the cross on our behalf. We are saved from the eternal wrath of God by accepting the substitute death (punishment) of Jesus Christ at the cross. The spiritual rebirth involves the incorruptible nature of Jesus Christ that overcame death abiding in us to give us immunity over death. The same nature (spirit) returns to God upon natural death, waiting for the glorified bodies at resurrection.

A believer is the person that has been justified. Why is there a need for justification by God? We must not forget that human beings are born criminals (the Church euphemizes it as the original sin). We are all guilty before God—each and every one of us—because we've fallen short of His standard. And even if we have fallen short in only one area, we're guilty of breaking fellowship with Him and deserving eternal death according to His justice. That's exactly why we simply can't be saved by good works . . . because we really have no good works to offer, "For by grace you have been saved through faith. And this is not your own doing; it is the gift of God, not a result of works, so that no one may boast" (Ephesians 2:8-9).

Our good works (charity) without Christ end here on earth. Of course you can be nice but you will never reach the perfection demanded by God on your own. If you think you can go to heaven by being good, you don't understand the holiness of God. He is absolutely perfect, and His standard is perfection. So instead of trusting in your own goodness for your salvation, trust wholly in the righteousness of Jesus Christ, who can save you from eternal death if you will place your faith in Him. It is only the just (God) who can justify the unjust (sinner).

We receive His saving grace by putting our faith in the finished works of Jesus Christ at the cross. In His body justice is served because He paid the penalty for our sins. His righteousness was imputed on us. It means that God receives us in His very righteousness. His blood takes away the guilt of our sins so that we stand before God blameless.

Salvation involves believing, repenting and receiving Jesus Christ. This is done when a person is alive and mentally conscious. We decide our eternal destiny when we are still alive by accepting Jesus Christ as our personal Savior. There is no amount of prayer that can change a person's destiny after he or she is dead. You either have Jesus in you on this earth or you will never have Him at all! The Bible says that He who has the Son has life (eternal life).

The Father, the Son and the Holy Spirit work together to bring about our salvation. The Father opens our eyes to see the Son. The Son receives whosoever the Father sends. The Holy Spirit indwells those who have believed. The Holy Spirit works in us (transformation) and through us (sanctification). Jesus said that, "No one can come to me unless the Father who sent me draws him" (John 6:44). Also, "All that the Father gives me will come to me, and whoever comes to me I will never drive away" (John 6:37).

"But you are not in the flesh but in the Spirit, if indeed the Spirit of God dwells in you. Now if anyone does not have the Spirit of Christ, he is not His. And if Christ is in you, the body is dead because of sin, but the Spirit is life because of righteousness. But if the Spirit of Him who raised Jesus from the dead dwells in you, He who raised Christ from the dead will also give life to your mortal bodies through His Spirit who dwells in you" (Romans 8:9-11).

Jesus said that, "We worship what we do know, for salvation is from the Jews." (John 4:22). Worshiping God begins with salvation: In the Old Testament the presence of God dwelt in the mobile tent (Tabernacle). The Bible says that we are the (Temple) tent of God: "Do you not know that you are God's temple and that God's Spirit dwells in you?" (1 Corinthians 3:16). When a person is born again, God moves in and God is at home in the temple (tent) He made with His own hands. Like a mobile tent (Tabernacle), we move with Him wherever we go. He is in us purposely to guide us to places where He wants to be. His glory is established wherever He is and that place is marked by His name. What you worship determines where you go and what you do. We are caught up in worship wherever we are because God is worshiped wherever He is!

Enlightenment (or brightening) broadly means the acquisition of new wisdom or understanding enabling clarity of perception. Enlightenment is equivalent to Christian prayer, personal devotions and especially to Christian contemplation. Therefore Christians ought to pursue it. Christians do not pursue spiritual enlightenment in form of Eastern meditation, because their experience of enlightenment comes when wrapped in Eastern philosophy, or perhaps better said, Eastern reflections on the nature of the enlightenment experience, and these reflections may not be compatible with Christian belief. The Christians should pursue spiritual enlightenment in a Christian context as opposed to the secular context. Spiritual enlightenment in secular use, the concept refers mainly to the European intellectual movement known as the Age of Enlightenment, also called the Age of Reason referring to philosophical developments related to scientific rationality in the 17th and 18th centuries.

The comprehension of Scripture is not dependent upon worldly wisdom. What I am saying is illustrated in 1 Corinthians 2:14: "But the natural man does not receive the things of the Spirit of God, for they are foolishness to him; nor can he know them, because they are spiritually discerned." The Sanhedrin marveled at Peter and John, who were powerful and bold preachers in spite of being uneducated and untrained (Acts 4:13). In this Peter and John were part of a long line in which we might include John Bunyan, the tinker of Bedford, William Carey, a cobbler who became a great linguist and translator, and the uneducated shoe salesman D. L. Moody who turned up to be one of the greatest evangelist of the century.

As much as it is good to be intelligent, God reveals Himself to all men regardless of their intelligence or knowledge. The illumination of Scripture should not be neglected or treated as obscure or unimportant. You should consider it to be a blessing for you (a gentile or non-Jewish) to know God and to accept his only way of salvation through Jesus Christ. It is good to know Hebrew and Greek but intellect knowledge alone is not enough to get you saved. Remember that not all the indigenous Jewish and Greek people who spoke original Hebrew and Greek accepted God's way of salvation through Jesus Christ. This reminds me of the Ethiopian Eunuch. He was a Hellenistic Jew. He was a great man, well-educated and he was in charge of the treasury of his country. He was reading the Bible in his mother language (Hebrew) regularly but without proper understanding because he lacked the revelation of God. The Holy Spirit guided Philip to him to open his understanding to the Scriptures. The Bible says that, "The Holy Spirit said to Philip, "Go over and walk along beside the carriage." Philip ran over and heard the man reading from the prophet Isaiah. Philip asked, "Do you understand what you are reading?" The man replied, "How can I, unless someone instructs me?" And he urged Philip to come up into the carriage and sit with him" (Acts 8:25-32). God supernaturally opened his minds to understand the Scriptures and to receive the benevolence of salvation. This kind of understanding is different from intellectual understanding because it involves the spiritual revelation. (*In order to learn more about the Ministry of Philip please read my book called "The Acts of the Holy Spirit"*).

There are things that we cannot figure out with our brains. Supernatural is a word we often use for explaining things that . . . well . . . have no explanation! From the Latin super meaning "above" and "nature" these are often things that are "above nature" or can't be explained by the laws of nature as we know it. Mine is not to suppress any "rational reasoning" but rather to argue against the status quo that has muddled the mindsets of many and in one way or the other created a level of stagnation through the so called intellectuals who don't see any need of the supernatural but are preoccupied with the same old condescending "humanism" mindset even in matters pertaining to spirituality. Their religion is science, secularism and human rights; man is at the center of everything they do. They say that if a phenomenon is outside of the realm of nature (or science) then it cannot be experienced!

I want to warn that the need of the illumination of the Holy Spirit does not mean disengaging our brains. Trying to avoid rationalism, we may end up with an approach to the Christian faith that presents it as irrational subjectivism. I will elaborate on this in the chapters ahead.

Dr. Lwanga had the teachable spirit. He was open to learning. Open-hearted people listen, receive and flourish. The unteachable spirit is the greatest hindrance to spiritual maturity. The Spirit of God is evidently at work among the humble people who have the attitude of humility. It is good to be confident but not overconfidence to the extent of closing up to learning. There will always be some people who are so secure in the conviction that what they believe is a revelation from God or a Spirit-given interpretation of a passage that they are immune to any instruction. The spirit of deception is evidence in pride. I teach my student always to avoid familiarity to the scriptures. Always read the scripture with an open mind to learning as if you are reading it for the first time.

There are some people who expect a special private revelation as they are reading the Bible. It is common to hear people coming up with different interpretations of the scriptures claiming that the Lord told them. The Scriptures are divinely inspired and are divinely revealed. The Holy Spirit reveals the same truth to all believers. There is no unique interpretation that is uncommon to all. We should therefore allow the greatest teacher (Holy Spirit) to teach us. The Bible says that, "Above all, you must understand that no prophecy of Scripture came about by the prophet's own interpretation" (2 Peter 1:20).

The idea that the things of the Spirit are spiritually discerned is a glorious and comforting thought, but like so much in Scripture, it is something, which the ignorant can twist to their own destruction. We must allow the scripture to say what it means. It is a dangerous trend to make the scripture say something contrary to its intended meaning. Any revelation must open your minds to the truth to lift your burdens spiritually. A revelation allows you to discover the promises of God in the Scriptures. (*In order to learn more regarding the proper interpretation of the Scripture, please read my book called "The Spirit is the Crown of the Heart"*).

Dr. Lwanga's family members were staunch Catholics. Good Catholics are part of the large Christian family. The word "Catholic" means universal Church. The first Church was called Catholic before other doctrines stepped in like the Roman Catholicism. A good Catholic is the one who has accepted the full gospel and who has experienced spiritual transformation. He is not double minded but believes that Jesus Christ is the only way to heaven. He is transformed spiritually and he is converted into the likeness of Christ. The word Christian simply means Christ-like (Acts 11:26). The word Christian is used regarding followers of Christ (Acts 26:28; 1 Peter 4:16).

Faith lays hold upon the Lord Jesus with a firm and determined grasp. A double-minded person is a doubter. He is torn apart by different beliefs without necessarily sticking with one belief. James wrote concerning a doubting person in this way: "He is like a wave of the sea, blown and tossed by the wind. That man should not think he will receive anything from the Lord; he is a double-minded man, unstable in all he does" (James 1:6-8). The term "double-minded" comes from the Greek word *dipsuchos*, meaning a person with two minds or souls. It's interesting that this word appears only in the book of James (James 1:8, 4:8). To grasp the full meaning of this word, it is best to understand how it was used within its context. A double minded is a person who believes in Jesus and other false prophets. He believes that all religions lead to heaven. He discredits the truth by doubting the words of Jesus that He is the only way to heaven.

Relativism is the concept that points of view have no absolute truth or validity, having only relative, subjective value according to differences in perception and consideration. We must be careful with the propagators of relativism. When they say that there is no absolute truth, they are saying that there is no God because the sovereign God cannot exist without an absolute moral standard. There are also denying the authority of the Scripture. They are basically saying that man can believe as he wills. Yet, Jesus said that, "Thy Word is truth" (John 17:17). By denying the existence of absolute truth, the culprits are basically denying Jesus Christ to be the Son of God as the Scriptures proclaim. Mark Twain warned that, "The problem with most people is not what they don't know, but what they know for certain isn't true".

Tolerance means loving all people regardless of their religion without compromising the central doctrines of Christianity. Tolerance does not mean believing everything what others believe. Believing in God is an absolute conviction of the heart that His Word is true. Remember that obedience depends on yielding to the right authority. A soldier is obedient only when he implements the orders of his commander in chief. We have only one Lord (Master) whom we obey. His name is Jesus.

God gives us the free will to choose whom to obey. But we must be careful how we use the same freedom so as not to choose against His will. I like a quotation saying that, "Heresy is only another word for freedom of thought"—Graham Greene.

Our choices are limited to choosing Christ or Satan (light or darkness). Jesus said that, "Whoever is not with me is against me, and whoever does not gather with me scatters" (Matthew 12:30). Every choice made outside Christ is considered to be an aggressive rebellion against God. The will of a believer and the will of God are never in contradiction. God's will is for all to be saved. He does not wish that any of us should perish but that all of us should come to repentance. But you and I know that many people in our world will NEVER accept Jesus, never come to repentance, and simply will not be saved. So what's up with God's sovereignty? How can it be that something can be within 'God's will' (God can desire something) yet He seems to be unable to make that something happen? Without a choice between good and evil, we cannot prove our love for God. As much as God is willing to save all, He gave us the 'freedom' to love, obey and follow. Without 'free will', humans are simply robots who respond according to pre-programming rather than from a position of true love and obedience. The greatest favor you can do to yourself and the people around you is to accept Jesus Christ as your Savior.

I want to end by saying that it is not given to us to judge who is going to heaven but the Bible explicitly declares how to go to heaven and who can go to heaven. The Scriptures mean what they say regardless of our opinions. We are whistle blowers by virtue of the Great Commission (instruction to preach the gospel). Given the factor, we are called to encourage each other by sharing the truth rather than condemning them or even delighting in their errors. We are going to step on some toes in pursuit of our calling but we should remember that we are called to please God rather than men.

Dr. Lwanga Passed on the Legacy to his Brother

What is a legacy? It is what you will be known for in the future and with future generations. Right is never defined in terms of self-interest or expediency. "Doing the right thing" is the best legacy anyone can leave to his children. In "A Leader's Legacy", a book by James Kouzes and Barry Posner, the topic of leaving a legacy is explored. They make this statement: "By asking ourselves how we want to be remembered, we plant the seeds for living our lives as if we matter. By living each day as if we matter, we offer up our own unique legacy. By offering up our own unique legacy, we make the world we inhabit a better place than we found it." (Published by Jossey-Bass and available at www.amazon.com).

People are watching us. This world is like a theatre. Like all tragicomedies or pantomimes, the curtains finally get drawn down, either with the audience rolling in the aisles—handkerchiefs in their faces, or oscillating between tears and laughter. How you live and how you die matter. The fact that life is delicate with an expiration date makes every right-thinking person find their acts appealing rather than despicable. The priority of every person should be centered on creating a positive lasting legacy. I like this quotation: "The elderly are archeologists of their past, their preoccupation is digging in their past victories and failures to sum up their lives. The young are prophets of their future, their preoccupation is redeeming virgin opportunities that define their lives; novelty defines their sense of appreciation. Let vision and youthfulness kiss each other, Selah"

Passing on a legacy is preparing the transition of assignments before death. That includes the moral and monetary legacy. One of the more profound elements of moral principles resides in prudence, which is overall the quantitative and qualitative measuring stick for morality on the whole. It's the separating of "you" and "I" with an empathetic understanding for the freedoms that exist in between "us." The most incompressible thing about ourselves is that we are comprehensible. Live life as a monument to your soul. At the center of your being you have the answer; you know who you are and you know what you want. The world is looking for a person who has done something not a man who has great plans on papers. "Carve your name on hearts, not tombstones. A legacy is etched into the minds of others and the stories they share about you"—Shannon L. Alder

Alfred Nobel is remembered today by the great Nobel Prize. About a hundred years ago, he looked in the morning newspaper and to his surprise and horror, read his name in the obituary column. The news papers had reported the death of the wrong person by mistake. His first response was shock. "Am I here or there?" When he regained his composure, his second thought was to find out what people had said about him. The obituary read, "Dynamite King Dies." And also "He was the merchant of death." He was the inventor of dynamite and when he read the words "merchant of death," he asked himself a question, "Is this how I am going to be remembered?" He got in touch with his feelings and decided that this was not the way he wanted to be remembered. From that day on, he started working toward peace. Just as Alfred Nobel got in touch with his feelings and redefined his values, we should step back and do the same. Ask yourself, What is your legacy? How would you like to be remembered? Will you be spoken well of? Will you be remembered with love and respect? Will you be missed?

Benjamin Franklin recommends that: "Either write something worth reading or do something worth writing". We write our legacy during our life time. For example Obama's legacy is still being written but maybe one of his most enduring legacy will be that he erased the excuse that a black man—the term is used loosely to refer to all non-Caucasian peoples, cannot excel in a world dominated by white power and capital.

Passing on a legacy is biblical. God gave Moses an assignment to take the Israelites out of captivity. God instructed Moses to prepare Joshua for the next assignment of entering into the Promised Land. Moses handed Joshua the book of Law as his inheritance and instructed him to follow it faithfully. Moses understood that God worked through human leaders and so he wanted to make sure the people were in good hands. God commissioned Joshua with a responsibility to perform. He challenged him to be strong and courageous. The call of Joshua (1:1-18) highlights how this transition was choreographed and why it was effective.

Let us examine the legacy of Moses. The Bible says that Moses talked with God as a friend. The same statement was made in reference to Abraham (Genesis 18:20-33). Moses is the mediator of the old covenant. Moses followed strictly the book of the Law. The people of Israel regarded Moses the greatest man ever lived. They mourned for him for thirty days after he died.

God raised Joshua to lead the people into the Promised Land. Moses was a good influence to Joshua. Joshua worked under Moses for a long time. The name Joshua means Jesus (savior). Moses represents the Law that could not save us but that gave to us the awareness of the character of God. Joshua represents the grace which saved us and that teaches us to obey the Law of God. The Jewish God is the same as the Christian God. Jesus said that He was sent to the Jews first then to the Gentiles: "I was sent only to the lost sheep of Israel" (Matthew 15:24). Also read Romans 15:8-12 KJV. God provided salvation to whosoever believes through Jesus Christ (John 3:16). There is one way of salvation to all people (Jews/Gentiles). That way is through Jesus Christ. The Old Testament priesthood and the blood of animals temporary atoned for the sins of the people. They were symbolic of the blood and the priesthood of Jesus Christ that atoned for our sins once forever.

Why is the divine high-priesthood important? The priests could recognize leprosy but had no power to clean a leper. Jesus recognized leprosy and cleaned the leper. Leprosy is symbolic of our sins. The Law has mandate to show us the righteousness of God but has no power to affect the change of the soul into righteousness. The Old

Testament sacrifices had to be repeated over and over because they had no power to take away the sins permanently. But Jesus sacrificed for our sins once for all when he offered himself (Hebrews 10:12). Jesus has the power to clean the physical and spiritual leprosy (sin). That is why He is called the Savior.

A good leader is judged by leaving behind a good successor. I will use the example of Jesus. He finished the work of salvation but He left the dedicated authority to the Church to proceed with His work of establishing the kingdom of heaven on the earth (Mark 16:15; Matthew 24:14; 28:19-20).

Hezekiah was one of the best of Judah's kings, a man who passionately pursued pleasing God. Hezekiah ascended the throne when he was only 25. The young monarch smashed the pagan altars and images that dotted Judah's rolling hills (2 Kings 18:3-4). Hezekiah's reign was one of national religious reform and spiritual rejuvenation. He restored temple worship (2 Chronicles 29). God dramatically intervened in Hezekiah's life. Not long after Sennacherib's demise, the king of Judah grew deathly ill. The prophet Isaiah came to him and advised, "Set your house in order, for you shall die, and not live" (2 Kings 20:1). Hezekiah turned his face to the wall and wept bitterly. He pleaded with God to save him: "Remember now, O Lord, I pray, how I have walked before You in truth and with a loyal heart, and have done what was good in Your sight" (verse 3). But, before Isaiah had even left the palace, God answered the king's prayer. He instructed Isaiah to tell him: "I have heard your prayer, I have seen your tears; surely I will heal you . . . And I will add to your days fifteen years" (verses 5-6).

Did Hezekiah set his house in order as previously instructed by God? Ironically, Hezekiah, one of the most righteous kings had the most wicked king as his successor. **Hezekiah's son, Manasseh, was twelve years old when he became king**: This means that he was born in the *last fifteen years* of Hezekiah's life, the *additional* fifteen years that Hezekiah prayed for. Those additional fifteen years brought Judah one of its worst kings.

I am going use another example of lousy leadership without viable successor from outside the Scriptures. The example involves Muhammad the leader of Islam. From a historic viewpoint, with Muhammad's death in AD 632, disagreement broke out over who should succeed him as leader of the Muslim community. Umar (Umar ibn al-Khattab), a prominent companion of Muhammad, nominated Abu Bakr. Others added their support and Abu Bakr was made the first caliph. This choice was disputed by some of Muhammad's companions, who held that Ali (Ali ibn Abi Talib), his cousin and son-in-law, had been designated his successor. None of Muhammad's sons survived into adulthood, therefore direct hereditary succession was never an option. Later, during the First Fitna and the Second Fitna the community divided into several sects and groups, each of which had its own idea about successorship. Finally, after the Rashidun caliphate turned into Monarchies and Sultanates, while in most of the areas during Muslim history Sunnis have held power and Shias have emerged as their opposition.

People are going to remember you. You are most likely to be remembered for two things: The problem you solved and the problem you created. People become like the people they admire. Live your life as a dictionary so as to render meaning to those who refer to you. A legacy is what you will be known for in the future and with the future generations. Dr Martin Luther King Jr. said that "A man should do his job so well that the living, the dead, and the unborn could do it no better. A legacy built out of hard work and honesty never dies."

We learn something from everyone who passes through our lives. Some lessons are painful, some are painless. But, all are priceless. The history of bloodshed and dictatorship in Uganda is due to inherited sins; we have generations bending towards the evils of their predecessors. The explanation, as to why there are even young people still attracted to the Stalin—Leninism of the Marxists politics, can be attributed to the psychological phenomena of poor modeling by their elders. What more can we accept from off-springs of parents who are corrupt and bullies, etc, whose only response to their opponents is physiological and psychological 'torture'?

Dr. Lwanga lived an exemplary life. He was an exceptional gift to humanity. He was simply a great man. I cannot recollect anyone who knew him, even during the toughest times, questioning his integrity and steadfastness. He may not be here now, but he still communicates to us through his love. He will be remembered for his extreme modesty, discipline, dedication, sheer hard work, humility and honesty.

Dr. Lwanga deserved many awards during his lifetime. He worked under very hard conditions to serve our nation. He delivered services despite all odds against him. His success and passion has attracted more young men and women to a career that is traditionally a reserve for the tough and intellectuals, probably owing to the countless hardship and risks that come with it. He was a rare talent and professionalism. He died at the time when we needed him most. We needed him as the index of our values and as the embodiment of our aspirations. A man that had a strong back born as opposed to a straw back. We miss him a lot. With profound nostalgia his era shall always be remembered. It will take generations before this country chances on another man like him (R.I. P).

After Dr. Lwanga's death, people wondered who was going to fill the void he left behind. His death could cost the lives of his clients if no other doctor is brought to replace him. Thank God that Dr. Lwanga chaperoned his young brother Dr Vincent Kabuye Kawoya to take over his responsibility. Dr. Kabuye is not your usually alley cat, he is highly intellectual and ethical person. He grew up at the deceased's home where he was mentored, drilled through career related skills (exposed to some medical skills). Not that he never wanted to take up his current career and responsibility, but his upbringing in a medical field seemed to groom him for service at the earliest time of his life. From the beginning, he went to school with a clear vision of becoming a doctor.

This life is chosen driven; Dr. Kabuye did not become a doctor by the stroke of luck, he chose what he wanted to be and sacrificed dearly to achieve his ends. I watched him during his academic years; he slept less, worked hard and read more. He attended St. Mary's College, Kisubi, where he emerged as one of the best O-Level students. He did not let up in A-Level either, once again turning up to be one of the leading students at the same collage. I give him credit considering the conditions his generation studied under during the tumultuous decade of the Idi Amin presidency. He utilized the available opportunities to turn the tides against the odds of life. Optimism is encouraged when it does not border on delusion. "You are today a summation of your past choices. You will be tomorrow and into the future what you choose to do now. Lead Yourself First."—David Bernard-Stevens

Dr. Kabuye joined the best national medical school in East Africa (Makerere University) where he graduated as doctor. Today, Dr. Kabuye is one the promising young senior officers with very high ranks in the Uganda People's Defense Forces (UPDF), with such great future ahead of him. He is currently the Head of the Radiology Department at the General Military Hospital in Uganda. His astronomical rise in meaningful and respectful positions without having to lobby but on merit is applauded. He is real genius; all of us (Ugandans) should be proud of his achievements. I want to say that God has not finished with him. He is still working on him to be the finished product glorifying to Him.

Let us pry beneath the uniform and look at the man. Who is Dr. Kabuye? Dr. Kabuye never really forgot his humble origins. He still lives a simple but purposefully private life, in spite of his high rank in the army. It is interesting that the radical change from a private life into the full limelight has not had a serious impact on his good behaviors. When he approaches people, his face lights up with a contagious smile; he is ever calm, optimistic and humble. He has a warm heart for the people. The late Dr. Lwanga helped him to embrace the values and the apologetic legacy that have been instrumental for him to hold a public office. By association, he picked up the nuggets of wisdom of his late brother. His beliefs, alliances, aspirations, values, actions, ambitions, works and deeds project a promising ambitious humanitarian and activist.

I am privileged to highlight portions of Dr. Kabuye's achievements. You may call it an autobiography genre. I know it is better to write an autobiography at a somewhat ripe old age, when you look back at all your life's achievements. Alternatively Dr. Kabuye has achieved pretty much even at his earliest age. He is definitely at the height of his career.

I am not one of the court-jester writers whose cornucopia of anecdotes, jokes, quotations, epigraphs, and illustrations highlight the head honchos of history, and shining a more idiosyncratic, intimate light on figures of power and position for the sake of popping their aptitude. I have known Dr. Vincent Kabuye for a very long time; all the way since our youthful times. He is not the beneficiaries of history; he merits his achievements. He is a self-made man who has pulled himself up by the bootstraps.

Dr. Kabuye had a lot of huddles to overcome in order to be where he is. His childhood is described as "ordinary with nothing spectacular" though he was born in a relatively well-to-do family. He treaded a delicate path which could have seen him slip into the self-destructive pattern of many orphaned and poverty-stricken African children. He amazingly overcame all the limitations society placed on him intentionally or unintentionally. His survival was tagged to his brother, the late Dr. Lwanga. For a teenager, life was taking him on a rollercoaster of illusion and out of the world fantasies. Those of you who grew up in homes as dependents on family members rather than your biological parents know what I am saying. His youthful and academic years were very challenging but he remained focused on his Catholic faith as his brother gave him a hand of help. He has proved that with tenacity one can achieve anything.

Mirroring his father's footsteps, a youthful Dr. Kabuye chose to forego the beckoning comforts of an easy life, to join the national army that has ushered in the peace the country is currently enjoying. For him to quit the civilian life to pursue a military career, it was truly a leap of faith, but one that he has lived to relish. Not even in his wildest dreams did Dr. Kabuye expect to become a soldier. Not to mention that initially, his late brother Dr. Lwanga objected, but when it dawned on him that it was his destiny, he became very supportive. He defeated the mentality of the culture dictating that an educated Muganda does not join the army ("*ekyebeyi kyabeyi Omuganda takola busilikale*"). Being a Muganda and well educated in the army has not hindered him to achieve his dreams as the architects of phrase would want people to believe. Thank God that he has served faithful and protected the nation prestige even beyond the national frontiers.

Dr. Kabuye was always royal to his older brother (Dr. Lwanga); he always wanted to emulate him. The key to his success is loyalty to his superiors; to him loyalty comes before anything. His excelling performance is therefore not by luck or coincidence. He has established his own track record as a steady practitioner and an effective public servant. As a sign of approval of his abilities, he was assigned with an enormous task of being in charge of one of the most important departments of the military hospitals. In his capacity as a soldier and a doctor by professional, I can testify that Dr. Kabuye has not deviated from his late father's legacy and at the same time his mission is not at variance with his late brother.

Dr. Kabuye has shown himself to have organizational and strategic abilities. He is not numbered among the clique of a tiny echelon that has access to the national cake, only to divert the resources to personal enrichment and privileges. Thank God that he has successively protected the legacy of the Kawoya family. He has kept the 'Kawoya' name flying high in Uganda. He has saved the family an embarrassment of a son with appetite for shady deals and outrageous lifestyles, typical of the sons of the elites and politicians of today. I have witnessed in silent wonderment the murder of the record of many of our past heroes, by the very people who claimed to have inherited their legacies. Such are losers without any evidence of the qualities of the past heroes who created them. I mean qualities like characters, talents, integrity, organizational and administrative genius. They reflect little of the ideas, values and aspirations of the people they represent.

If Dr. Lwanga's life's achievements included building a healthy and well organized and articulate community, then his death proves the solidarity of his achievements. Dr. Kabuye plans to continue his brother's initiatives. Certainly, he has done his brother's legacy justice. Food for thought: "If you want to live under the shadow in your old age, plant a tree now by investing into somebody's life".

I encourage Dr. Kabuye not to think of where he is but where he is going. I can see in him a fighter who does not easily give up without achieving his goals. He walks the talk. He has followed the example of most of the old boys (alumnus) of St. Mary's Collage Kisubi; they are shining and impressive wherever they are.

Dr. Kabuye is social but he is selective regarding choosing his close associates. You can tell a man's ideas and ambitions by the company he keeps. He does not socialize to waste time. He is the Can-do person. I can read the following message in his eyes: "The time for high sounding words, slogans and clichés has come to an end. This is the time for concrete proposals and for action. We need to get back to work and improve our community".

Fred Allen, one of the popular American comedians said that "A conference is a gathering of important people who singly can do nothing, but together can decide that nothing can be done". The world today is looking for something real. It is tired of counterfeit spirituality, empty words of politicians, lifeless formulas that don't really work but just appealing to our emotions. Life is a shadow of what you believe. If you want something, create it by your practical living. Jesus did not preach something He couldn't do.

The army needs young officers of the ilk of Dr. Kabuye who worked hard to earn their promotions. According to one senior officer, "Promotion is recognition of excellence and a job very well done. It's a recognition that an individual deserves higher accolades that come with heavier responsibilities to the country." As much as Uganda has some of the best trained officers, the question, still lingering at the minds of many people is the symptomatic of the haphazard manner some of the officers were promoted to the higher ranks.

The bulk of senior officers in the UPDF were either Obote's or Amin's soldiers whose record has no background strength since they rode on the back of suppressive forces of the state, they rose to the ranks not because of their own doing and strength. Their inexorable rise in the army was clearly manipulated and chronicled. The past regimes' "often flawed" military appointments were premised on blinding loyalty rather than meritocracy. Often the lucky ones to rise to ranks had close ties to the higher echelons of the Uganda army. The past dictatorial regimes recruited private armies as opposed to a professional national army, whereby sons and relatives were handpicked for specialized training and meteoric rise to the top. The students of political science say that primitive army is the major cause of destruction. This arrangement is a clandestine usage of Public institutions like the army as personal ladder to personal aggrandizement and political hegemony.

Most of the officers from the past regimes have outlived their usefulness. They are old fashioned, corrupt bureaucrats polluted with the past errors. In Kiswahili there is a saying that: "*Usimkanie vyanda vitano*" (whoever has five fingers and he has stolen before, will do it again). They represent the change of guard that preserves the status quo and many of the past methods of work without a fundamental change and a system reset. The lawlessness we still witness today was cultivated a long time ago in the past regimes of terror; it's only now ripe for harvest. I suggest that the government retire some of these officers and re-employ them in the public service, that way the State's defenses are upped more. Rather than being left to create disharmony in the forces out of being disgruntled, the retirement option should be encouraged to create space for new, fresh and effective blood. If we continue to recruit and yet greatly limit exit from the military, the system will suffer suffocation or constipation of sorts.

J. Ikuya says that, "Undoubtedly, every period of the human race must constantly be replenished by the replacement of the old by the young. This is certainly necessitated by the very fact of natural attrition where human life, like all other forms, is mortal. It is also conditioned by the social process. In the rearing up of their offspring, humans nurture their young with a view of drawing them as they grow into their different forms of social activities embracing economic, social and cultural interests."

Dr. Kabuye is a new breed of Ugandan service men that are disciplined, moral, educated and good at the rule of law, who highly respect the country's constitution on which Uganda's hope's now lies. We need a top Brass that our soldiers can look up to, with credibility and respect. In any democratic state, a professional and disciplined army is essentially needed to protect the constitutional rights of the citizens because people vote for peace. We should borrow a leaf from developed countries where professional army officers train and go to space, emulating the highest knowledge in aeronautics, engineering, biology, etc. After celebrating the much-anticipated Uganda independence golden jubilee, as we chart our journey of the next fifty years, I join other Ugandans to wish our gallant fallen officers who have sacrificed their lives for the peace of our country. We say Alta Continua!

The army presents such great opportunity for the unemployed youth. At an annual growth rate of 3.2 per cent, Uganda's population has this year reached 34 million up from 26 million in 2006, indicating that more than 1 million people are added to the population every year. The State of the Uganda Population Report 2012 released recently shows that at least 56 per cent of the people are below the age of 18. In Uganda, the statistics say over 1.2 million children are born every year with less and less resources such as land available to sustain all of us. Currently about 83 per cent of the youth are unemployed and this, if not checked, could render this group of talented, energetic, illustrious and well educated young blood unproductive. If they are not put to work, it might lead to more social tensions in years to come. Scary isn't it? To make the matters worse, the aged civil servants who have reached retirement age are unwilling to retire in order to pave way for the fresh blood!

I think it is not just crazy and inhuman but equally antithetic to our common welfare when African governments keep spending billions of dollars on weapons and ammunition in the name of internal security when they fail to realise that the simplest and most effective way to check internal insecurity is to engage the youths productively. Do they need rocket science to know that youths need jobs?

When I advocate the replacement of the old guards by the youth, I am not suggesting that all of the young people are clean or all of the aged folks are useless deserving to be discarded. My concern is the officers who are polluted with the old yeast of the past regimes, not necessarily old in age. We should not ignore the fact that both the young and the old are on same side of the coin because they have been part of our ugly history that wrecked havoc our country. Some of the aged officers we have today were young officers during the past regimes. I recall that during Amin's regime, in the former Uganda Armed forces, there was a very young soldier whom they used to call Kadogo aka Mutukula, who used to stop over at my store and bragged about how he killed in cold blood. He used a slang term of capsules in reference to the bullets in his gun. Whenever he returned from the military operations, he bragged about the number of people to whom he prescribed his capsules (killed).

The young people can effectively serve side by side with the old folks who have experience at work. But they must have clean hands which are not tarnished by the innocent blood of the citizens. The current incompetence in the country can be averted only through painstaking work of sharing awareness and organizing it across the breadth of the whole of our society, the young and old, male and female, all united to exert strength to affect strategic stiff towards the interest of our people.

The battle should not be between the young against the old. People should be employed on credentials of their merits rather than on basis of their age difference. In fact in African traditions we have such great respect for our elders. As Brother James Ikuya said, "The slogan of 'fighting the old by the young' is a disrespectful ideology of reactionary opportunists replicating the very present-day selfishness that has stultified our political process—The claim that the young office seekers bring something new to our society simply because they announce that they are young is a farce, unless they indicate, for everyone's consumption, the horizon of an enriching ideological foundation. It is not the age or the gender of individuals that matters in politics, but the perspectives that they bring in shaping the future of this country."

Older folks (aged) have much to offer. They have stored wisdom and experience, yet they lack strength. Young people have maximum strength and swag but need to learn more from adults. What is the value of strength without wisdom? Theodore Bikel says, "All too often arrogance accompanies strength, and we must never assume that justice is on the side of the strong. The use of power must always be accompanied by moral choice." My interpretation of this is that strength and power are very useless without wisdom. Also wisdom without morality is disastrous. Both the young and old need one thing: Character is power that makes friends, draws patronage, support and open the way to wealth, honour and happiness. Somebody warned that, "We have always had that old age is the store of knowledge, this is because old age has many history stories but any one old who cannot remember the history and use it to solve the problems of now has an empty store."

The fastest runner doesn't always win the race, and the strongest warrior doesn't always win the battle. The wise sometimes go hungry, and the skillful are not necessarily wealthy. Enlightenment without discipline is void. We need the entire package in order to have ultimate peace. The problem begins with human heart. There is always conflict from within when our minds cannot agree with our hearts or when our feelings cannot agree with our minds and hearts. Conflict grows gradually to a level where we conflict with our surroundings. Jesus transforms the heart and renews the minds, bridging the gap between the heart and the minds. The greatest lie is that a person can change his attitude without experiencing the spiritual transformation. The bad attitude reflects the deception of the wicked heart.

Whether we love or loath the UPDF, police, Chieftaincy of Military Intelligence (CMI), Internal Security Organization (ISO), External Security Organization (ESO), Joint Anti-Terrorism Task Force (JATT) and many other over-lapping security organizations, the manifest fact is that they have become integral to our national lives—for now at least. All security agencies should be able to protect the people and the constitution without fear of being reprimanded. It is therefore necessary to revisit the past systems to ensure that we get the task force that represents the crème la crème and the officers who can command the respect of the people.

The cleanup I have been advocating in the military is necessary if we are to avert sliding back to the bad old days. Uganda has had a long history of profound military involvement in politics. The institution severely suffers from pollutions of the past regimes, yet the culprits are living in denial. In the past regimes there was an unconcealable frustration in the people of Uganda with the escalating acts of impunity and abuse by senior army officers. The current NRM government has tried to tame the soldiers to a certain degree but there is still much work needed. Recruiting young graduates with moral predisposition into the army will get us beyond the boiling, evaporating the past inconsistencies into thin air.

In course of building a nonpartisan national army, we should avoid the temptation of using the corrupt standards of the past regimes to measure efficiency. I contend that past membership in the army has never been and will never be on its own a viable asset for shaping our democracy without other pertinent attributes. The new bleed of the young elite officers, are viewed as a beacon of hope for a country whose future remains unpredictable. Their doctrine of immaterialism and sacrifice evoke nostalgia within the ranks of UPDF.

Ugandans have suffered a lot at the hands of the heartless monsters. I mean the armed personal of the past regimes made up of the 'functionally illiterate' officers of desperate job seekers on the streets. The men in uniform of today should prove the soldiers of the past regimes wrong. The crucial acid test for this generation's viability lies in its faithfulness to live in dignity, tribal respect yet considering, treating one another as a family belonging to one nation. They must resist being used by the corrupt politicians for their selfish ends. "We can't solve problems by using the same kind of thinking we used when we created them."—Albert Einstein

We need to encourage the moral, educated and talented youth to join the army, the field that lost integrity in the past times. The word integrity means at one in and out. People of integrity are supposed to be the same people in and out of uniform. Their characters are influenced by their internal transformation as opposed to their external makeover like uniforms and ranks. The Russian proverb says that, "When you meet a man, you judge him by his clothes; when you leave, you judge him by his heart".

True soldiers are judged by their respect for civilians. The consequence is a national army that protects the people and a people who respects the army! In such decorum the soldiers are humble and they acknowledge that they are mortal like any other person. In the past regimes, soldiers acted as if they were immortal and above the law. Whenever criminals got on the wrong side of the law, they put on military uniforms. People despised and scorned the military career holding it in the same regard as drug dealing; lucrative but immoral.

Decency is a virtue resulting from proper home training rather than mere comic performance. It cannot be stage-managed! Whereas it is true that we are all born with evil intents, some people are absolutely evil. This reminds me of a fable about the Scorpion and the Frog: 'A scorpion asking a frog to carry him across a river. The frog is afraid of being stung during the trip, but the scorpion argues that it will never hurt the frog because if it stung the frog, the frog would sink and the scorpion would drown. The frog agrees and begins carrying the scorpion, but midway across the river the scorpion does indeed sting the frog, dooming them both. When asked why, the scorpion points out that this is its nature.' Like the scorpion in the story, some people are naturally evil and they will never change. It is abnormal for them not to act evil!

I consider the discipline of any army to be the linchpin of patriotism. Uniform doesn't make or destroy the character, it reveals it. A soldier can be simple, honest, hardworking and committed to delivering quality output for his or her country without necessarily being mean and rude. I see the same qualities in Dr. Kabuye. I expect to see the same qualities in my son, Allan Semanda and many young officers.

All of us make mistakes. Willingness to accept mistakes is one of the qualities that make Dr. Kabuye a good leader. Apart from the grace, we are all vulnerable. The Psalmist said that "The Lord is my strength". It means that no one can stand without His grace. The moment Satan makes you believe that you can make it by your own strength; he has got you where he wants you. I have known Dr. Kabuye for a long time. Where there is a mistake he does not look for someone else to blame. Bad leaders make multiple errors but because of arrogance and sycophancy they ensure that those mistakes are repeatedly swept under the carpet. They cannot admit their own shortcomings, and will never have the benefit of learning from their mistakes. They are doomed to repeat the same mistakes until eventually those mistakes cost them their leadership positions.

I want to warn that deceit never pays off. In fact, it just might get you into more trouble when all the facts are made known. So live honestly. Be truthful in all your dealings. When you do, you'll have a clear conscience and be fully confident in your integrity. Remember that the righteous are bold as a lion. They have nothing to fear and to hide.

The term "Legend" is thrown around too loosely in the Modern day; the term is ubiquitous among most users. Dr. Lwanga fits the definition of a Legend. In the past chapter I gave a collection of values that personify his spirit. I discussed his personality and achievements. I said that he was a potential leader. Until his death he remained without a bliss on his character. He was a man of high integrity, with impeccable characters and lots of achievements. His consecutive years successfully catering for people with special needs left a mark in our history books. He lived a lawful and peaceful life and desired that all people lived in the same environment. He was assertive and you could never change his position and make him do something wrong. Dr. Lwanga's professionalism and personal trait were well suited to bring the much-needed harmony between people of different ethnical, religious and political backgrounds and to instill mutual respect and discipline within the community. Great leaders provoke followers. Well, if wishes were horses . . . the late Dr. Lwanga would require you and me to sustain this positive trajectory of things.

Dr. Lwanga was without question a remarkable visionary and the scope of his accomplishments is truly staggering. He was a mentor. His lasting legacy will be as a purveyor of constructive ideas. He will be greatly missed. Uganda would be a much better place today if the work he began is continued. Thank God for Dr. Kabuye who courageously moved in to fill the void. He has the set of values capable of standing the test of time. It is not coincidence that Dr. Kabuye is stationed at Bombo; it is by divine appointment that he is serving in the same area where his late brother served. There is a magnet attracting him to the place and to the people of Bombo. Dr. Kabuye's determination to continue the legacy of his late brother is the solid proof that Dr. Lwanga did not build his legacy on sand. If Dr. Lwanga's achievements included building a strong healthy community, then his death proves the solidarity of his achievements.

The Chinese say, a journey of 1,000 miles begins with a single step. Ever since we lost a great statesman in the person of Dr. Lwanga, his brother (Dr. Kabuye) has opened an avenue of constructive ideology. Let us emulate the only left living legend in the person of Dr. Kabuye. I know that many people are looking at Dr. Kabuye with such great expectations. I believe that we will get more than what we ever bargained for. I want to add that each of us has the same responsibility as Dr. Kabuye of continuing the late Dr. Lwanga's legacy. We should avoid the individual merit syndrome, by working together. Dr. Lwanga's legacy mirrors what Ugandans ought to be. God gave us potentiality to overcome the huddles of life. Inferiority complex is a worm that tends to deny us our abilities to excel. We were created to uplift one another. No man is an island to himself. We need each other. If the mountain had no pointed rocks and crevices you wouldn't have anything to grip on and to step on as you climb to conquer the heights of triumph!

Together, we can honor Dr. Lwanga (RIP) by continuing to pursue his vision. As one who had found his niche as a symbol of charity, humanitarian and statesman, Dr. Lwanga would surely turn in his grave if his legacy evaporated in thin air after his demise. Let us therefore remember him by aiming higher, being better and by pursuing success with the same kind of energy, grit, love and determination as he did.

Dr. Lwanga helped many because he didn't envy anybody. He helped people without taking advantage of them. His legacy lives on in perpetuity, inspiring countless generations. A Greek proverb says that "A society grows great when old men plant trees whose shade they know they shall never sit in". In order not to magnify the things that were trivial to the late Dr. Lwanga we should disdain envy. Godfery Nsubuga says that, "Envy always oscillates between stupidity and slothfulness of the mind otherwise there are things that are too inconsequential to deny us the opportunity to celebrate with the persons who have distinguished themselves as being better than us in those areas where we are not endowed with that special grace."

I know it's hard enough to make your mark without being compared to the person you are replacing. Considering the late Dr. Lwanga's influence, it won't be a herculean task for Dr. Kabuye to succeed. Taking into account the two brothers (Dr. Lwanga/Kabuye) have a lot in common. They are both loving and full of life and ideas. Dr. Kabuye is a man who pulled himself up by the bootstraps and knows thoroughly well pulling people out of their misery.

I compare Dr. Kabuye to Joshua who finished the work of Moses. Moses led the Israelites out of slavery from Egypt. Joshua led the new generation to their promise. Joshua, like Dr. Kabuye, had the military capabilities and he was a leader. Why do we need sharp military commanders in running the affairs of Uganda? The reason is because the past leaders militarized almost every Ugandan, right from a street man to a Bishop, man or woman. So, to reverse this trend, one has to use military methods. You cannot expect a civilian leader to lead a society which treats violence as the order of the day; where murder has become a crime of passion and both the law enforcers and the Parliament seem to have accepted it as a norm. Demilitarizing the country needs a military man or a leader with military training; and that is a fact we cannot deny.

God commanded Joshua to occupy the Promised Land without fear with a promise to be with him as He was with Moses: "As I was with Moses, so I will be with you; I will never leave you nor forsake you. Be strong and courageous, because you will lead these people to inherit the land I swore to their ancestors to give them. Be careful to obey all the law my servant Moses gave you; do not turn from it to the right or to the left, that you may be successful wherever you go" (Joshua 1:6-7).

God gave His Word to Joshua as the matching order and instructed him never to depart from the Word and the God of the Word. The Bible is the only book whose author is always present when one reads it. I have a word of encouragement to Dr. Kabuye: Read the Word of God everyday so that when you go through the valley, you have deposits of joy to draw from. Seek God earnestly. God is the majority. If God is for you, the majority is on your side (Romans 8:28-31). Norbert Mao said that, "Young and vibrant—should seek inspiration in the examples of towering Ugandans like Ben Kiwanuka who stood for truth against all odds. Truth does not require a majority. One person holding the truth is a majority. Multitudes glued together by falsehood are a minority".

The spirit of God is detectible in humility and humbleness. The Bible says that, "Better it is to be of an humble spirit with the lowly, than to divide the spoil with the proud" (Proverbs 16:19). God does not use mighty men but faithful men. The Bible says that, "Thus says the Lord, Let not a wise man boast of his wisdom, and let not the mighty man boast of his might, let not a rich man boast of his riches; but let him who boasts boast of this, that he understands and knows Me, that I am the Lord who exercises loving-kindness, justice, and righteousness on earth; for I delight in these things, declares the Lord" (Jeremiah 9:23-24).

All of our accomplishments depend on God. He gives us assignments and He accomplishes them through us. God gives us assignments with promises. God blesses what He has ordained. He fulfills His promises in us but it does not take away our responsibilities. Our commitment depends on our loyalty to Christ. Our loyalty to Christ depends on our obedience to His commandments. His commandments make us accountable to Him. We must consult Him in everything we do and we must do it in His way (according to the divine plan and will).

I am going to use the story Gideon for further illustration. God proved to Gideon that He does not need the mighty army and the mighty men to win His battles. The Midianites were camped north of the children of God near the hill of Moreh in the valley. The Lord said to Gideon, "You have too many men for me to hand Midian over to you. Israel might brag, 'Our own strength has delivered us.' Now, announce to the men, 'Whoever is shaking with fear may turn around and leave Mount Gilead.'" Twenty-two thousand men went home; ten thousand remained. The Lord spoke to Gideon again, "There are still too many men. Bring them down to the water and I will thin the ranks some more. When I say, 'This one should go with you,' pick him to go; when I say, 'This one should not go with you,' do not take him." So he brought the men down to the water. The Lord said to Gideon, "With the three hundred men who lapped I will deliver the whole army and I will hand Midian over to you. The rest of the men should go home." The men who were chosen took supplies and their trumpets. Gideon sent all the men of Israel back to their homes; he kept only three hundred men that defeated the huge and strong army of the Midianites (Judges 6:36-7:23).

When we come to the story of Gideon and his fleece, we are dealing with one of the most popular stories in the Book of Judges. The story of Gideon projects a situation when less is more. God wants us to die to our self-ego (self-denial) so that people might see Him in every inch of our accomplishments. The supernatural is not man-centered but God-centered. Everything that we do when God is not the motivation will evaporate in thin air after we cease to exist. The only good works that are rewarded are those treasured in heaven. Those works are done by Christ through us (Matthew 6:1). Christ must be the reason of everything we do. Everything we do must glorify Him. People should be able to see the love of Jesus in your eyes and works and give Him glory. All of our works are going to be tested by fire. The Bible says that, "Every man's work shall be made manifest: for the day shall declare it, because it shall be revealed by fire; and the fire shall try every man's work of what sort it is" (1 Cor. 3:13). The testing of fire is God's judgment. The believers are going to be rewarded for their good works. The nonbelievers are going to be condemned for every bit of their sins; rejecting Jesus Christ is rejecting God's grace.

Natural death is unavoidable in the natural world but choosing your eternal destiny and leaving a lasting legacy on the earth is optional: The decisions you make during your life time determines your destiny. I want to say that the goal of every person should be to live forever in the presence of God and leaving a lasting legacy to the next generation. Skills which are not put into practical application are wasted. We should put into practice the things we know and at the same time make the same knowledge available to others. An American writer Mark Twain summed up the idea of leaving a lasting legacy with the following statement: "Let us endeavor to live that when we come to die even the undertaker will be sorry."

Leaders leave legacies by serving people, helping others and teaching others. The ministry of Christ is about teaching the Word and serving others. People will remember you for what you have done for them, not what you have done for yourself. People who yearn to leave a legacy focus on serving the interests of the people of the next generation after they are gone. They do not selfishly focus on themselves. Everything we do should be aimed at shaping the destiny of the future generation. The test of our success is ultimately the improvement of the welfare and livelihoods of the generation of tomorrow.

Each of us has dreams. The issue is the nature of your dreams. "All men dream: but not equally. Those who dream by night in the dusty recesses of their minds wake in the day to find that it was vanity: but the dreamers of the day are dangerous men, for they may act their dreams with open eyes, to make it possible." ~ T.E. Lawrence

It is important to acknowledge that you have been given dreams for a reason, and much of that reason is to give you something to strive for. The dreams give you a vision to live for and to die for. The vision of every believer should be to know Jesus and to make Him known. Our goal should be to make a difference in the lives of others. The future belongs to those who give the next generation reason for hope.

All of us have unfulfilled dreams and hopes. We go through tough times struggling to implement certain ideas and register acknowledgeable accomplishments in life. For example there are places where we wanted to be in the past years or where we would like to be in the coming years. Success often comes by hard ways and sacrifices. The bottom line is that all of our dreams are available to us if only we're willing to take risks and make sacrifices. Bad dreams are self-centered whereas good dreams are centered on others. The good dreams involve a lot of sacrifices. At times sacrificing means giving up some of the things which seem to be important to you. In the economy of the world, success at times comes by downsizing your lifestyle.

It's a natural human tendency to come up with an ideal that we would like to fulfill in our futures. But what happens when the years go by and those dreams never come to fruition? What happens when we find ourselves, years later, in a situation that's so far removed from our ideal that we can only think that we've somehow failed, that we haven't accomplished our life's desire? It can be very devastating experience to see yourself failing in a field where others have excelled. Many people walk around with downcast attitudes because of their failures. Our memories of failure experiences can be really tormenting. It reminds me of the phase life some call the midlife crisis. We reflect on our memories and ask ourselves what have we done, how we could have done better and we envy those who have succeeded where we failed. We end up doing crazy things to create awesome memories only to find ourselves repeating the cycle.

The most important thing to consider, though, is your current situation and where you see yourself going if you stay in it. If you see yourself developing very little in or getting very little from your current situation, maybe it's time you examined those dreams of yours to see where they may be directing you. Revise your goals when pursuing your dreams. If you do not build your dreams, someone else will hire you to build theirs . . . Your time is limited, so don't waste it living someone else's life. Great dreams come from great discipline and inspiration. You can be inspired all day long, but if you don't have the discipline to advance your vision the inspiration is void. This time quit sailing in the sea of imagination and wishes; start dreaming big time and stick to your dreams.

Most people fail because of fear. Our lives are characterized with fear. At the very best the word for Fear, in all of its forms, is only listed 314 times in the Bible, in the original languages which includes words that have been translated into words such as terrible, dreadful, reverence, and terrible acts. There is positive fear yielding to safety and also negative fear resulting into failure. "There is only one thing that makes a dream impossible to achieve: the fear of failure"—Paulo Coelho

It is within human instincts to fear people of great achievements. It is scaring when we think of intellectual and famous people whose accomplishments in our community speak volumes. It hurts when we think about dying without seeing our dreams becoming reality. It is deemed as if we are useless to the communities. I have a tip for somebody who feels that he or she has nothing to offer and to be remembered of. This line of thinking won't do anything but make you a nervous wreck. Flip it and stop sabotaging Your Happiness. Truly we want to live a legacy but we need not to be stressed by the limitation of our capabilities. The key is to be willing and to try to do it.

Disappointment is the major cause of discouragement. The set back you are experiencing is most likely to be caused by discouragement. Peter denied Jesus because he was disappointed by Jesus. He rebuked our Lord for His intentions to die on the cross, and Jesus responded to Him that "Get behind me Satan". He fought the soldiers that came to arrest Jesus by cutting off the ear of the servant of the high priest but Jesus restored the ear and reprimanded him that everyone who uses a sword will be killed by a sword. Peter was a disappointed man when Jesus was crucified because Jesus frustrated all of his efforts to save Him.

Disappointment comes dressed in different fashions but most times we are disappointed by the unknown; by the hard things to figure out and get a grip on. At times these are the very things intended to benefit us. "All things are only transitory. Things are most likely to become worse before they become better. There are a good many ugly things there and the ugliest are the most pretentious. You have three choices: You can let the ugliness define you, or let it destroy you, or you can let it strengthen you."

Some external factors can influence the way we feel and think at any given moment but happiness is a decision we make. I can decide at any given moment how I feel about something, and we all have the ability to do this. Our emotions are motivated by our feelings and thinking. God created emotions in us for positive aspects but they can be easily manipulated to serve our corrupt nature. Most people treat their emotions as though they're purely incidental and sometimes even a hindrance in life. Emotions are often side-lined as impulsive and troublesome parts of ourselves that have to be controlled and are of little value to us. Actually, our emotions, both negative and positive, are all perfectly safe and healthy and serve us in incredible ways, especially when it comes to making important life decisions as long as the decisions we make line up with the Scriptures. Avoid reacting emotionally; pray about everything. Lizzie Velasquez who was dubbed to be the world's ugliest woman said that, "Some days life doesn't make sense," she writes in 'Be Beautiful, Be You': "You are called to change what you can, ask for help and pray about the rest."

It is impossible to maximize happiness. Happiness has eluded even those people who achieved their goals. Many people work hard to achieve what they believe will make them happy; but after they get there, they realize it wasn't the destination, it's the continuation of a journey with endless demands! There is no single person that has ever had enough of the happiness of this world. Even the people whom we envy depart from this world in despair. This universe is compared to a tree whereby we can enjoy some of the fruits and the leaves of the tree but we cannot eat the entire tree.

The world measures success with fat bank accounts. Money is not the source of happiness. Ms. Stevenson and Mr. Wolfers write in a study for the American Economic Review, Papers and Proceedings, Richard Easterlin's study in the 1970s that higher income does not equate to being happier. "We find no evidence of a satiation point. The income-well-being link that one finds when examining only the poor, is similar to that found when examining only the rich. We show that this finding is robust across a variety of datasets, for various measures of subjective well-being, at various thresholds, and that it holds in roughly equal measure when making cross-national comparisons between rich and poor countries as when making comparisons between rich and poor people within a country."

Success in this universe is compared to staircases whereby some are climbing up when others are climbing down. The people whom we admire today could be tomorrow's reproach. Success in this world is determined by the people around us, in particular the good things they say about our achievements. Have you ever wondered what heaven has got to say? Your living is determined not so much by what life brings to you as by the attitude you bring to life. Success is a journey and not a destination. The mistake most people make is aligning money with success. Money is only a medium of exchange and can never be measured side-by-side with success. Our greatest lack is not money for undertaking, but ideas; if ideas are good, cash will naturally flow to where it is needed. Money is like flowing water that always finds its way to flow.

The happiest people don't have the best of everything; they make the best of everything. A person wants three things to be happy in this world: someone to love, something to do, and something to hope for. But what we want is not truly what we need. You will never be happy if you continue to search for happiness outside what happiness consists of. True happiness is contained in the person of Jesus Christ; it is not discovered but it is experienced. Remember that happiness is not joy. Our joy depends on our internal fulfillment. As long as you are born of God (born again), you are blessed. All of the believers are children of our Father in heaven. He loves us equally. Our happiness comes from the joy of our salvation. This cannot be taken away, cease to exist, faked or even artificially manufactured. It is an experience resulting from our internal transformation. This is what is called spiritual fulfillment.

God blesses all of us equally by giving us equal measures of joy. Happiness is temporary but joy is eternal. The joy of the Lord is the source of our happiness. We were created to rejoice in the presence of God. David said that he delights in dwelling in the presence of God forever and ever (Psalms 23). This is the true essence of worshipping. The Joy of the Lord is not our initiation; it is given by God and deposited into the hearts of the believers. We are sustained in the same joy by the grace of God. The grace teaches us to obey. Obedience to God means subjecting our will to His will. It is denying the old ways and manifesting the new life of Christ.

God created us differently but He receives us evenly. God won't accept you because of your education, rank, looks, outfit, career, personality and etc., but because of your transformed heart. He receives Christ within us or within our hearts, this being our new born again nature. God gave us the same access to Him, through Jesus Christ. He gave us the same manual (Bible) as a survival kit in this world. He gave each one of us the same measure of faith that can grow depending on our obedience. He did not call the intellect but the faithful. But He called us to do different things. We are not all going to have the same accomplishments. At times we fail because our dreams do not constitute of God's plan for our lives. Pray to God and trust Him to put you where He wants you to be. You will be most effective when you are doing what God wants you to do rather than doing what you want. You will be most effective where you can do the most good, where you are able to serve others faithfully and where you can learn the most.

We must acknowledge this truth that God gave each of us the testimony of His life that indwells us. Every believer has a testimony to give to the perishing world. The testimony of the believer is the indisputable gift to the perishing world. The people of the lost world are waiting to see Jesus walking, touching and comforting them through us. On the contrary, most nonbelievers are frustrated and disturbed by the behaviors of many who call themselves "Christians," as Gandhi observed, "Your Christians are so unlike your Christ."

Again, God chose for us the kind of life to live. We live the same life (Christ's life) by manifestation. A sinner that needs to repent is your neighbor to love. Go where you will, you need not ransack the earth to find sinners, for they are common enough; you may find them in every lane and street of every city and town and village and hamlet. It is for such that Jesus died. Pastor Alistair Begg says that, "If you will select for me the grossest specimen of humanity, if he be but born of woman, I will still have hope for him, because Jesus Christ came to seek and to save sinners. Electing love has selected some of the worst to be made the best."

God chose for us two types of friends to behold. The vertical friends are those with whom we share the body of Christ. The horizontal friends are the nonbelievers whom we love dearly but also with prudence lest they dent our relationship with God. The vertical friends cannot be substituted by any natural means. They are our closest friends in whom we can freely confide. The priority of the believers is to win the lost world and to encourage others believers to stand. The blessing of those who are in Christ is that their good works go ahead of them in heaven. Their good works are remembered on earth and in heaven forever. This is the recommended legacy of each and every believer.

Dr. Lwanga/Dr. Kabuye in the Military Uniform

How to prepare our Beloved Ones to Die Honorably

This is an important topic because each of us has his own day on earth to be born and to die. Death is ultimate experience that cannot be explained even after experienced because dead people don't talk. That death is perhaps life's greatest mystery is not in doubt. That Dr. Lwanga was bound to die sooner than later was not in doubt either. Yet when it was announced, his passing hauled the world into a hardly-paralleled sense of loss. Death has no dimension, but it has one name. It will come different ways but it is still death. The reality is that death is strange to all. No one is comfortable with death. The good news is that Jesus defeated death on our behalf. Through Christ, God reconciled the world to Himself. He waits for your response. As the old saying goes: Surely, you cannot shake hands with a person whose fist is clenched!

Death came to us as a result of the curse of sin. Sin separates man from God. Jesus became a curse on our behalf to save us from sin. In the general sense, God is with all of us but experientially, He is with only those who are with Him (those who die in Christ). God sanctifies by separating His children from the rest of His creations. He is Jehovah Mekadesh: The Lord Who Sanctifies (Leviticus 20). All of us are born when separated from God and grow running away from God as fast as we can. However, we are like a racing car that at one point has to stop. The reality is that there is a point of time to stop and face the music. There is an appointed time for us to stop and face God, whether we like it or not. The Bible says that it appointed for man to die then judgment.

In the past chapter, we discussed that there are two appointed destines of man. One place is to live forever in the presence of God (heaven). The other place is to live forever when separated from God (hell). Emily Dickinson says that, "Parting is all we know of heaven and all we need to know of hell". Life goes on even after death; the naked truth is that death is not the end. I like this quotation: "The world is round and the place which may seem like the end may also be the beginning" (Ivy Baker Priest).

The kind of life we live determines our eternal destiny. The reality is that none of us has learned how to live until we figure out how to die. All of us should live as if today is our last day on this universe. We should be ready to die and we should prepare others for death. Pastor Alistair Begg asked that, "We prepare wisely to relocate, or go to college, or get married. But do we ever really plan for death?"

All of us need a will, a trust and a clear line of contingent beneficiaries on our term life insurance policy but this is not the primary aspect of preparation for death. Preparing for the grave takes far more planning than preparing the will, choosing a coffin and a plot (burial place). My primary concern is not about leaving a big fortune for your immediate families. As good as it may sound; it is not the subject of my concern. Sometimes we prepare our bodies for temporary things (material things) and we forget the main thing (soul). A person is never ready to die until he or she has assurance of the destiny of his or her soul.

The fallen nature opts for temporary fulfillment. It used to be that if it is good it sells; today it is if it sells it is good. Perhaps in the history of mankind, our generation scores the highest when it comes to embracing materialism. Materialism is never a solution to the basic need of humanity. There is a danger of holding on precious things loosely then end up losing them or holding on precious things tightly and lose them in the end. The material things cannot last forever. The main thing is the soul because the soul lives forever and ever either in the presence of God or separated from God. Being ready to die involves acquiring power over death. Paul full of assurance asked death that, "Where is your sting?"

All things will cease to exist and all people must die except God. We are all doomed unless God intervenes in our lives to save us. Jesus Christ overcame death and acquired immunity to death. All of the self-proclaimed prophets of the religions of the world are dead. None of them can claim the overcoming power over death when they are languishing in their graves. Jesus alone overcame death and has the key to eternal life. He extends to those who receive Him (believe in Him) the eternal life that is immune to death. God changes the heart in order to change the status of the soul. The redeemed heart (transformed) has the Spirit of Christ that is immune to death.

Christians can go through the sufferings of this world with assurance of victory. God saves us from corruption but not from the trials of the world. In the real world disaster cannot be avoided. Disaster will occur, whether you have prepared for it or not. This saying is referred to as "Murphy's Law."

God does not change your surroundings but He changes the heart so that you can cope with any disaster. The faithfulness of God is our guarantee that at the end of the day, His goodness is going to prevail against the deceptions of the world (Romans 8:28). Certainly pain will be swallowed in victory. God has no process without a purpose. God processes in us all things towards good. I am trying to say that it is not worth to pursue the material prosperity and ignore the spiritual things. Our corrupt bodies and their desires are temporary but the desires of the soul are forever. Therefore it is not worth to pursue the material prosperity and ignore the spiritual things.

It is a common phenomenon for people who have lost their beloved ones to send them off with this benediction: "May his soul rest in peace". The saying is most probably used as a sign of respect for the dead person rather than assuming the continuation of life in a better place. I want to say with confidence that a soul will be in a condition of restless until it rests in Christ. This kind of resting is not a result of wishful saying superstitiously but it is the decision a person makes during his or her lifetime to receive eternal life that Jesus alone can give.

The truth is that this life is not the end of the existence of the soul. This life is just a preparatory ground for another life that goes on forever. In a believer, the corrupt body is the veil that must be removed in order to reveal the spiritual nature. Death ends the physical life paving way for the spiritual life. I compare it to planting the corn or bean seeds; they must die (rot) in order for a new plant to come forth. A spiritual person lives even beyond the grave. The physical heart may lose its strength to beat, but the spiritual heart never loses its power to glow. We are born in this world when we are eternally separated from God. Eternal life in the presence of God begins now after receiving Jesus Christ and continues forever and ever. Jesus made a profound statement concerning Lazarus. He told His disciples that Lazarus sickness is not unto death (John 11:4). Jesus meant that the sickness of Lazarus includes death but will not end in death.

Life is a continuous journey with unending lessons. The most challenging ethical question is the issue of after-life. We are faced with the challenging 'decision-making' during life and at the end of life. It is painful to see our beloved ones die. I witnessed various end-of-life ethical dilemmas first-hand, and I could not abstain from reflecting on this challenging issues: Whenever you watch your beloved one breathing his last breath, your concern should be "The wages of sin is death". The reason is because every defaulting debtor to God is undoubtedly a sinner, and every sinner has put himself under the penalty attached to his sin. To speak precisely, men and angels are debtors simply because God has given to them His commandments, whether they be broken or fulfilled. A defaulted debt becomes a sin, and a defaulting debtor a sinner, when God is the Creditor. Being by nature and by practice hopelessly sinners and irretrievably guilty, we are lost unless saved by the grace of God. Deliverance comes to us from God because the penalty has been borne for us by the competent Substitute His own love had provided.

The dead person's identity is the body. People use phrases like: "Bring the body", "Lower the body into the grave", "Take the body to the graveyard", etc. People don't even call you by your name. The reason is because your name was attached to the soul that is dismantled upon death. Jesus said that, "And fear not them who kill the body, but are not able to kill the soul: but rather fear him who is able to destroy both soul and body in hell" (Matthew 10:28).

The resurrection of the soul takes place now by regeneration. Upon death, the body returns to dust (Ecclesiastes 12:7). According to science the soil (dirt) has seventeen elements as the body. The resurrection of the body is reserved for future judgment. The Bible says that "And as it is appointed unto men once to die, but after this the judgment" (Hebrews 9:27). Our death is "appointed." We all have an appointment with death. The Bible says that death is not a means of escaping the wrath of God but qualifying to face God to answer for your disobedience. After death there is assurance of judgment. This is called the second death. God made a way for us to escape death by acquiring eternal life through Jesus Christ. Jesus defeated death on behalf of the believers and made it ineffective. The dead in Christ will not be judged because they were judged in Christ; the wages of their sins were paid in full by Christ at the cross when He said "It is finished". But those without Christ will definitely pay the wages for their sins. The holiness and justice of God demand that we pay the wages of our sins, unless somebody pays the same wages on our behalf. Jesus alone qualifies to be the substitute sacrifice because the sacrifice must be perfect (sinless) in order to be acceptable to God.

Jesus is the perfect offering acceptable to God that takes away our sins and guilt. God was satisfied because debts are never forgiven, but they cease with death. Guilt disappeared in His perfectness. The Savior had to be God and man as well in order for Him to meet the requisites for our salvation. There is no human being that qualifies to be a substitute sacrifice because no human being is perfect. It is for the same reason that God gave His Son to put on human flesh, and lived the perfect life, and suffered death so that we are exempted from the consequences of our sins. The Bible says that Jesus was who was in the very nature of God (without sin) carried on himself our sins. God dealt with Him as such; He was made a curse for us, but it is never said guilty. Although He carried ours sins, God accounted Him to be holy (the Lamb without blemish) because He did everything in perfect obedience to the Father. God accepted his perfect sacrifice because He lived on this universe without breaking any of the commandments of God.

God does not take our salvation lightly. He paid for our sins dearly. Remember that it took His Son to come from eternity to the earth in order for us to become His sons. It is important therefore for us to focus on those sobering facts that draw us closer to God now and for eternity. Salvation is when God reaches out to the lost world to save a handful of People. The people of the Old Testament believed in the coming Messiah (Jesus Christ). The people of the old covenant looked at the future crucifixion of Jesus at Calvary. In the New Testament we put our faith in the finished works of Jesus Christ at the cross that happened over 2000 years in the past.

Remember that in accordance to the justice of God none of us deserved to be saved. That is why we consider our salvation to be God's amazing grace of God. Salvation begins now, in this life. The blessed ones are those who receive His only Son as their Savior. Those of us who are saved get what we do not deserve (grace). The rest of the people who never had opportunity to accept Jesus Christ or who rejected Him get what the sinner deserves (the justice of God). That is how the justice of God works.

Again, all of us deserved death according to the righteous judgment of God but by His grace, God reached out to the perishing world to save a handful of believers. The forgiveness of God is authenticated in the lives of the few believers who ask for it. Jesus warned that, "Enter through the narrow gate. For wide is the gate and broad is the road that leads to destruction, and many enter through it" (Matthew 7:13).

Remember that during the times of Noah, God destroyed the whole universe but saved just Noah and his family whom He declared to be righteous. Salvation for Noah and his family was by grace alone. But Noah and his family obeyed God by entering into the ark in order to be saved; in the same manner we are saved by the grace of God. But we are supposed to enter into the ark of salvation. The ark was the only means of escape and there was only one door to enter the ark (Genesis 6:16). Jesus used the analogy of the door to stress the fact that He is the only entrance into the Kingdom of God. Jesus said, "I am the door; if anyone enters through Me, he will be saved, and will go in and out and find pasture" (John 10:9). Eternal life begins now by acquiring the life of Christ and living it by faith. Eternal life can neither be silenced by death nor by grave. Eternal life is life spent in the presence of God here on earth and in heaven (forever). You can choose to live the same life now by faith.

This topic is concerning preparing our beloved ones to die. Life is a continuous learning without a possibility of graduation. It is not the years that you live in the life that matter but rather the life that we live in the years. Reflect before you act because it is the quality of the quantity that matters. They say that age is gold. As time chases us and age is stepping in, one of the advantages of aging is wisdom. Life is a wheel of fortune; it is your time to spin it.

Preparation for death is not only for geriatric and people with terminal sicknesses but for all people because we are all mortal men. Statics by mortality rate shows that one out of every 113 people died last year; there are about 107 deaths every minute, 6390 death every hour, and 56.0 million deaths every year. Every Sunset gives us one day Less to Live. Every minute, hour and day that passes project the time you will never be able to see again. While we are postponing, life speeds by. Those who wait to seek God on the eleventh hour always die at 10:59, one minute to the eleventh hour. There is no time like the present for postponing what you ought to be doing. The Bible says that, "Now is the time of God's favor, now is the day of salvation." (2 Corinthians 6:2). We should never take this life for granted. We are all vulnerable because we are all fragile vessels of clay (we were made from clay). This world is not our home; we are like people on a pilgrimage. Everyone has their own personal 'countdown' till we leave this world and are brought into the heavens above.

Jackson Putnam Professor of Neurology and Neuroscience at Harvard Medical School, and also the chairman of the Beth Israel Deaconess Medical Center Department of Neurology—explained that, there is a "biological clock ticking in each of us." No one can resist death. Tomorrow is not in our hands. It is therefore advisable to live every day as if it were your last. James Dean said that, "Dream as if you'll live forever. Live as if you'll die today." Death will certainly come.

But the trauma of the passing on of our beloved ones is much intensified if we were not prepared. Long time ago people used to look at old people scornfully and suspiciously because of their seemingly expired life span. In the past, there was a very fine line of demarcation which separated the generations. On one side were the old and aged whose end was presumed to be imminent and on the other side the young energetic youth, full of enthusiasm, who were expected to live many years ahead. Times have changed and so are our expectations. Today, young people are at a higher risk to die from unnatural causes like drinking alcohol, smoking, homicides and accidents.

Cancer is a giant killer of people of all ages. It is a leading cause of death worldwide, accounting for 7.6 million deaths annually, according to the World Health Organization (WHO). It has been said that 30% of cancer deaths are caused directly by poor lifestyle factors such as inadequate diet, obesity, low fruit and vegetable intake, lack of exercise, tobacco and alcohol use. Obesity increases your risk of getting cancer by as much as 40%. Cancers develop as a result of abnormal and uncontrolled division of cells. Other factors include: a diet high in red meat and low in fruits and vegetables, obesity and a lack of physical activity increase the risk; alcohol, especially beer, may increase your risk of suffering from cancer.

No one is immune to cancer but factors like smoking, boozing, working in places like mines and having it in the family increase the risk. The youth are more vulnerable in this area. Smoking is the major cause of lung cancer. Every year tobacco kills more Americans than did World War II—more than AIDS, cocaine, heroin, alcohol, vehicular accidents, homicide and suicide combined. Approximately 440,000 people die from their own smoking each year, and about 50,000 die from second-hand smoke annually. According to the Centers for Disease Control and Prevention 22,073 people died of alcohol, 12,113 died of AIDS, 43,664 died of car accidents, 38,396 died of drug use—legal and illegal—18,573 died of murder and 33,300 died of suicide. That brings us to a total of 168,119 deaths, far less than the 440,000 that die from smoking annually. As for the part about World War II, approximately 292,000 soldiers, sailors, airmen and Marines were killed in battle during World War II, according to a U.S. Census Bureau April 29, 2004, report in commemoration of the new World War II memorial in Washington, D.C. An additional 114,000 members of USA forces died of other causes during the war, bringing the total to 406,000 people.

Violence like gang related crimes kills many people today. The majority of the victims are young people below thirty years. The violent crime rate for England is 2300 in 100,000. The violent crime rate for the USA is 469 in 100,000. The problem is not because people have guns but because people are corrupt. Guns don't kill people. People kill people. You may not get shot, but instead you get stabbed and beaten to death.

The majority of the people who die prematurely are young people. There is a saying that the good ones die young. Hell is looking for the cream of the society. Given the fact, we are all vulnerable to death regardless of our age. We should be ready to die regardless of our age. Life expectance in Africa is still below fifty and in America just above sixty. Few people are expected to be one hundred years old. Georgia woman Besse Cooper, the world's oldest person, died this year on December 5th 2012, just after celebrating her 116th birthday recently. She became only the eighth person in the world and the fourth American to ever have been verified by Guinness World Records as having reached that age. It is amazing that she lived in 3 different centuries, the 1800's 1900's and 2000's. Still, Cooper fall sort of seven years to become the oldest person ever fully authenticated by Guinness. Jeanne Louis Calment from France lived to be 122 years and 164 days old before dying on Aug. 4, 1997, according to a Guinness spokesperson.

As I was revising this book it was announced that the oldest man died. Jiroemon Kimura celebrated his 116th birthday on April 19, 2013. He was born in 1897, in Japan. He died of natural causes in Kyoto's Kyotango city. He was well off the all-time record set by French woman Jeanne Calment, who died in 1997 at the age of 122, making her the longest living person in our history. Kimura live a healthy life: He did not smoke and only ate until he was 80 percent full, the local official told AFP. But still the unwanted visitor called death knocked at his door.

Before God judged the world by the floods people used to live beyond five hundred years. When sin mounted, God shortened life expectancy up to 120 (Genesis 6:3). According to the recent survey carried out, less than 50% of the people who participated expressed their willingness to live up to 120 years because of the burdens associated with aging. "Your spiritual destination is by far the most important decision you will ever have to face and make. If you think that this earthly life is miserable or long, eternity is over a million times longer than 120 years!"

God's plan for us is to live eternally, but how long we live in this world depends on our life styles: What we believe, where we dwell, what we eat and how we live. That is why God regulated the lifestyle of the Israelites when they were in the wilderness. He gave them the Moral Law (Ten Commandments) to obey in order to relate to God; the dietary laws (what to eat and not to eat) in order to be healthy; the civil laws (legal instruments) in order to be orderly. God gave this promise to the Israelites: "If you listen carefully to the voice of the LORD your God and do what is right in his eyes, if you pay attention to his commandments and keep all his decrees (statutes), I will not bring on you any of the diseases I brought on the Egyptians, for I am the LORD, who heals you." (Exodus 15:26). God guaranteed their freedom as long as they walked in obedience: "Now therefore, if ye will obey my voice indeed, and keep my covenant, then ye shall be a peculiar treasure unto me above all people: for all the earth is mine" (Exodus 19:5). God chose the Israelites to bless them in order to bless all nations.

As long as God is our protection we can live the lifespan God intended us to live happily. Given the fact, living longer does not mean living forever. The phrase "We are living longer" is therefore meaningless. Have ever asked yourself how "longer" is long? Definitely "longer" does not mean forever. Nobody lives forever in their corrupt bodies. Living one hundred years may sound good but it does not mean living forever. It is sad to know that eating healthy, thinking healthy and living healthy in the end still leads to death, it comes to us all. We might live longer by doing certain things but it is never long enough to our satisfaction. Solomon lamented that, "I have seen everything in this meaningless life, including the death of good young people and the long life of wicked people" (Ecclesiastic 7:15).

We come into this world crying and we leave it crying. We are born crying because of the trauma felt during childbirth and that is to follow in course of travelling the ambiguous journey of life in this world. Our bodies are prisons for our souls until liberated by death. In the same manner we left the wombs of our mothers, we leave our bodies and this world crying because of unfulfilled life lived and the torment of physical and spiritual death that separates a sinner eternally from the presence of God. This life is short and fast, we are born alone and without Christ we die alone. Life lived without Christ is life wasted. To such Jesus said that it is better if they were never born than to end up in eternal fires of hell (Matthew 26:24).

God demands that we live the life of faith. The life of faith is the fulfilled life of contentment. The life of faith cannot be lived outside Christ. The life of faith is full of hope; it is not limited by space and time. The Bible says that to God, one thousand years is like one day (Psalms 90:4; 2 Peter 3:8). These scriptures do not mean that there are two methods of reckoning time, God's way of time reckoning and man's way of time. The scriptures simply remind us of the faithfulness of God. What God has promised will come to pass. God is faithful and God is not slack concerning what He has promised. God is not limited by time. He sees the past and future as the present.

The true believers have eternal life: They have the quality and quantity of life, and the fulfillment of life. The fulfilled believers have responsibility to help other people who are not fulfilled to be fulfilled. God's expectation of the Church is to win the lost souls. Those who have not yet joined the family of God must be encouraged to do so for their own good. Jesus gave the Great Commission specifically instructing His disciples to preach the gospel as they moved around (go). "—go and make disciples of all nations, baptizing them in the name of the Father and of the Son and of the Holy Spirit" (Matthew 28:16-20).

We must be ready to sacrifice everything for the sake of winning our beloved ones to Christ. Paul said that "To the weak I became weak, that I might win the weak. I have become all things to all people, that by all means I might save some. I do it all for the sake of the gospel, that I may share with them in its blessings" (1 Corinthians 9:22-23).

Pastor Gram used the analogy below to illustrate the necessity of preaching the gospel and the manner of ministering the gospel to others: "Picture a winding road going up a hill. As you look at it, you notice its dangerous curves and foreboding cliffs. All of a sudden, you see cars navigating those curves, and most of those cars are driving off the edge of the mountain. So you're put in charge of helping reduce the number of people who are driving off the cliff. What would you do? Well, first, you might want to put up some guardrails. This would give them a warning that a dangerous cliff is ahead, and would probably help stop some of the cars before they actually tumbled over. Second, you'd probably create a good response team with state-of-the-art medical and rescue equipment like helicopters and ambulances, staffed with paramedics and doctors. While you might not save everybody, you'd save some. And while most of the world today is headed toward a Christless eternity, there are things we can do, like putting up guardrails—active, healthy Churches in communities around the globe. You can also bring in responders—those people who go out and take the message of Christ to the hurting and dying people of the world."

The task of taking the saving Gospel of Jesus to the ends of the earth is on us as the people of God. Winning the lost world is our spiritual battle; we are supposed to be on offensive proclaiming the gospel. This is the way we fight our archenemy (Satan). The Gospel is preached in words and deeds (godliness). So instead of playing it safe in Church on Sunday, get out and make an impact every day of the week for Christ! We must have a spiritual passion for pursuing God and reproducing that pursuit in others; this is commonly called discipling. Every believer is given a seed of Word to plant.

Wise sayings often fall on barren ground, but a kind word is never thrown away. You are a spiritual father because you are required to reproduce spiritual children. Until a spiritually mature man reproduces and disciples Christ-like maturity in others, he has no spiritual children and cannot be considered a spiritual father. A spiritual father reproduces spiritual children who have a passionate and intimate relationship with God the Father. The spiritual growth process of these children must continue so that they also become spiritual fathers who reproduce spiritual children too.

Jesus said that He came to seek the lost. Also He came for the sick. He finds us and then He uses us to minister to those who are still lost. So let us reach out to the hurting and dying around the globe! The gospel opens the eyes of man to acknowledge that he was created in the image of God. All people are like sheep going astray until they acknowledge this truth. Jesus Christ restores us to incorruptible nature of God.

Let us examine a couple of biblical characters who were ready to die. "So Joseph remained in Egypt, he and his father's house. Joseph lived 110 years. And Joseph saw Ephraim's children of the third generation. The children also of Machir the son of Manasseh were counted as Joseph's own. And Joseph said to his brothers, "I am about to die, but God will visit you and bring you up out of this land to the land that he swore to Abraham, to Isaac, and to Jacob." Then Joseph made the sons of Israel swear, saying, "God will surely visit you, and you shall carry up my bones from here." So Joseph died, being 110 years old. They embalmed him, and he was put in a coffin in Egypt." (Genesis 50:22-26).

Joseph had been grafted into the Egyptian life: He was a leader; he had married an Egyptian wife; but he did not settle for the present life in Egypt but looked forward to the future deliverance with hope. He promised his brothers that God will come to their rescue. He instructed them not to leave his bones in the foreign heathen land of Egypt when time for their redemption comes. The writer of the New Testament say that, "By faith Joseph, when his end was near, spoke about the exodus of the Israelites from Egypt and gave instructions about his bones" (Hebrews 11:22).

The Israelites were in Egyptian captivity for over four hundred years (Exodus 12:40-41). The promise of Joseph came to pass some three hundred years (three centuries) later, when God sent Moses to Egypt to deliver the children of Israel. Generations came and went but they all remembered to hold on the promise of God given to Joseph. They believed that it will come to pass as Joseph prophesized. Joseph's brothers left the legacy to their children, then the children to the grandchildren and so on . . . . They kept the coffin containing the bones of Joseph secure from generation to generation (for three hundred years) until the time of their deliverance. Joseph was ready to die by focusing on the future life after redemption.

Elijah the prophet wanted to die. Elijah had just been victorious in the showdown with the 450 prophets of Baal on Mount Carmel. Jezebel was filled with resentment, and resolved upon the destruction of Elijah. Elijah prayed to die. The Hebrew phrase is, "He requested for his life that he might die." There is life in death to the righteous. "It is enough." This is the language of disappointment. He looked for better fruit of his ministry than he found. He thought, surely this demonstration on Carmel will extinguish idolatry; but he finds Jezebel swearing against his life, and apparently in a position to carry out her purpose. "Now, O Lord, take away my life; for I am not better than my fathers." I am no more useful here than they have been who are gone hence. Let me join them (1 Kings 19:1-8).

I am going to use other examples of the people who were ready to die from the New Testament. Luke 2:25-32—Now there was a man named Simeon who lived in Jerusalem. He was a righteous man and very devout. He was filled with the Holy Spirit, and he eagerly expected the Messiah to come and rescue Israel. The Holy Spirit had revealed to him that he would not die until he had seen the Lord's Messiah. That day the Spirit led him to the Temple. So when Mary and Joseph came to present the baby Jesus to the Lord as the law required, Simeon was there. He took the child in his arms and praised God, saying, "Lord, now I can die in peace! As you promised me, I have seen the Savior you have given to all people. He is a light to reveal God to the nations, and he is the glory of your people Israel!"

Simeon occupies, in sacred story, a place peculiar to himself. He is kind of the Melchizedek of this transition-period—the connecting link between the Mosaic and the Gospel dispensations—telling by significant word and act, that "all old things" were "passing away" and all things becoming "new!" We may regard him, moreover, as the "representative man" of the pious remnant of Israel of that age. He had long been sitting, an earnest student, at the feet of the prophets who had testified of Christ, the Jewish Messiah. With the roll of Micah in his hand, and straining his eyes towards Bethlehem, he had been asking, in prayerful expectation, "Why His chariot has taken so long in coming? Why tarry the wheels of his chariot?"

But he can afford, also, to resign himself patiently to the will of God. This he knew, that great event waited for by all time, must be close at hand; for he had personally received a divine promise, that his eyes should not be sealed in death, until gladdened with the glorious vision which many saints and wise men of old had "desired to see, but were not permitted!" At length are his hopes and prayers gloriously realized. "The Desire of all nations, "according to the latest prophetic intimation, has "come." "The Lord," whom the devout Israelite had long sought, "suddenly comes to his temple," and, in the person of a little child, "fills it with his glory!" (Mal. 3:1.)

With the infant Babe in his arms, and the tear of joy and gratitude in his eye, he is permitted to take up the strains which for ages past had hung on the lips, and supported the faith of a waiting Church— "Unto us a child is born, unto us a son is given—and his name shall be called—Wonderful, Counselor, The mighty God, The everlasting Father, The Prince of Peace," the glory of his Church, the Consolation of Israel, the Light of the World! And now, the rejoicing patriarch, with the promised Savior in his arms, and salvation on his tongue, is ready to die. Simeon beheld, in these smiles of helpless infancy, the seed of a kingdom that would overthrow all others, and, yet, itself "never be destroyed;" a throne that was to be "established forever," and of "the increase of whose government and peace there was to be no end!" (Isaiah 9:7).

In Revelation chapter thirteen, verse eight, Jesus is referred to as, 'The Lamb slain from the foundation of the world. It means He was born to die for our sins. Jesus was announced as the Lamb that takes away the sins of the world (John 1:29). Throughout His three-year ministry, Jesus' death has steadily become an explicit part of His messianic mission. From this point on, it becomes the focus. From the ninth chapter of Luke 9, particularly verse 51: "When the days drew near for [Jesus] to be taken up, He set His face to go to Jerusalem." Jesus journeys toward His death in Jerusalem to offer sacrifice for the sin of the whole world. The phrase, "He set His face," sounds strange to our modern ears. But it is a good translation that alludes to Jesus' prophetic role. For God to "set His face" against a person or place is for God to show His wrath. The opposite is for God to "make His face shine on you and be gracious to you." But here, Jesus "set His face" to go to Jerusalem to become a blessing to humanity by becoming the perfect sacrifice on the cross. He is set to face God's wrath against the sins of the world. He is set to overcome all temptations and opposition to His mission.

Even as death draws near, Jesus does not turn in on Himself. He sends messengers into the villages along the way to prepare them for His arrival so that they might believe in Him also and be saved. Jesus prepared for His death in a spectacular way. At the end of His earthly ministry, Jesus headed to Jerusalem to be the sacrifice. He headed towards Jerusalem saying that His hour has come. Peter could not stop His move to be crucified. He celebrated his journey to Calvary by performing a miracle that nobody can do but God. He raised from death somebody (Lazarus) that was known by all people in his home area to have died (John 11:1-46). He proved that He has power over death. Death stalks and pounces on us but His death at the cross was a willing act of love to save the world.

When Jesus asked them to remove the stone, Martha hesitated saying that four days after his death, he must be stinking. She meant that there is nothing there; he is rotten! Jesus invoked His divine power at creation, when God spoke things into existence, and commanded Lazarus to come out of nothing (rot); and Lazarus did come out. Because of this miracle people wanted to crown Him as their King. But Jesus said that he did it for the glory of God. Jesus focused on the future glory. He said that what he did will be known in eternity. Theologians Moloney and Harrington view the resurrection of Lazarus as a pivotal miracle which starts the chain of events that leads to the Crucifixion of Jesus. They consider it as a "resurrection that will lead to death", in that the resurrection of Lazarus will lead to the death of Jesus, the Son of God, in Jerusalem which will reveal the Glory of God.

The very word "Testament" is translated "covenant," the Hebrew word berît, and the Greek noun diathēkē. A covenant is "a solemn commitment guaranteeing promises or obligations undertaken by one or both covenanting parties. Shortly before Jesus was crucified, He ate one final Passover dinner with His disciples which we refer to as the Last Supper. Jesus said, "And he said to them, 'I have eagerly desired to eat this Passover with you before I suffer. For I tell you, I will not eat it again until it finds fulfillment in the kingdom of God'" (Luke 22:15). At the Last Supper, Jesus initiated the new covenant where He demonstrated His eternal love for the sinners that was about to be accomplished at the cross. The Bible says that, "Now before the feast of the Passover, when Jesus knew that his hour was come that he should depart out of this world unto the Father, having loved his own which were in the world, he loved them unto the end" (John 13:1).

The Apostles were ready to die but they evaded capture in an effort to continue their personal ministries as eyewitnesses. The New Testament accounts describe men who were bold enough to maintain their ministry, but clever enough to avoid apprehension for as long as possible. As Brother Jim says that, "These early eyewitnesses were fully aware of the fact that their testimony would put them in jeopardy, but they understood this to be the consequence of their role as eyewitnesses rather than the goal." Likewise, we (Christians) must be ready to die but our priority is to finish our journey well on the earth.

The Apostles of Jesus were not afraid to die because they had assurance of after life in the presence of God. All of the twelve apostles of Jesus, apart from John suffered martyrdom. Paul is another biblical character who was ready to die. Saul became Paul after salvation. Paul lived the life pleasing to God. He lived for Christ and he was ready to die for His name's sake. Paul said that, "For to me, to live is Christ and to die is gain. Christ shall be magnified in my body whether it be by life or by death" (Philippians 1:20-21). Paul said that: "For I am already being poured out like a drink offering, and the time has come for my departure" (2 Timothy 4:6). Paul knew that beyond death is a much glorifying life. He felt it would be an honor to lay down his life for His Lord. And he eventually did die a martyr's death.

The word "martyr" comes originally from the ancient Greek legal term for "witness", for someone who gives testimony or evidence in a court of law. In the face of Roman persecutions of early Christians in the first three centuries of the Common Era, when Christian believers were put on trial for refusing to participate in state religious activities which were regarded as a civic duty incumbent upon all Roman citizens, the word took on an entirely new meaning. Witnessing to one's faith, giving testimony to one's most deeply held personal convictions in court under threat of torture and even death, became for these people the strongest calling that Christians could respond to and a way for them to directly imitate Jesus' suffering and death on the cross. Consequently, the martyrs who died giving public proclamations of their faith like this were immediately recognized as belonging to the very highest order of Christian saints in heaven and were venerated by their fellow Christians for the special relationship they had with God.

God made the way for all believers to become saints. The saints involve the living and dead Christians. Paul wrote to the believers in Rome calling them saints: "To all that be in Rome, beloved of God, called to be saints" (Romans 1:7). The goal of every person should be to become a saint. Everything including our lives belongs to God but God accepts only what is perfected in Christ. A saint is somebody who is dead to the old nature and is raised in Christ. Paul said that, "I have been crucified with Christ and I no longer live, but Christ lives in me. The life I now live in the body, I live by faith in the Son of God, who loved me and gave himself for me" (Galatians 2:20).

We are called to act saintly by presenting our bodies a living sacrifice, holy, acceptable to God. We do not change into a perfect and holy sacrifice overnight. It is a process of persevering with all steadfastness to present our bodies holy and acceptable to God. Begin transforming your body today by the renewing of your mind in Christ Jesus our Lord. A sacrifice was offered after it was killed. We must die daily to our old desires. Also, we must be ready to die for our faith. I, for my part, am committed not only to be a saint but a martyr as well. And having come close to death on several occasions, I know what it means to have your life back—and to make better use of our limited time on earth. I am committed to make Christ the center of my life in everything I do.

To be ready to die is to acknowledge the power of Jesus over death. This is not idle curiosity but knowing and acting on the revealed truth. It means receiving Jesus Christ and allowing Him to reveal the truth to you. There is joy whenever our beloved ones have assurance of their salvation before they depart from this world. This does not mean we do not miss our beloved ones when they die. We are deeply wounded because we are emotional animals but we have assurance of their soft landing in the presence of God. When Jesus visited the grave of Lazarus, He cried even when He knew Lazarus will live. He was emotional because of His humanity. Jesus knew that He was going to raise Lazarus from death. The crying of Jesus at the tomb of Lazarus had a spiritual significance. He grieved because the people around Him focused on the physical death and ignored the fact that He (Jesus) is eternal life (life forever). That is why He told the mourners that those who are in Him are immune to death: "And whoever lives and believes in me will never die" (John 11:26).

Although we are emotional, we must avoid living by our emotions. Living by emotions can lead to doing things out of necessity. Doing things out of necessity doesn't involve much thought, and most of those things we do out of necessity are basic animal instincts anyway. We must live by our convictions. God communicates to our spirit by His Spirit. When God speaks in a sound voice, the world trembles and things get dire. The voice of God is not necessarily a sound; it is not necessarily a thought or even a feeling. It is a conviction that happens when we meditate on His Word. At times His voice is offensive to our intellect because healing comes after we are offended by the very things that we naturally adore. It takes His Spirit to infuse His voice with deeper meaning. Every believer has an antenna to receive what the Spirit is saying. It is the inner voice that is contrary to human logic.

God gave us His written Word to guide us and wrote His Law in our hearts to regulate our desires and priorities. The desires of a person that is born of God (born again person) become the desires God. His conscience is programmed in the very righteousness of God. He does not deliberately violate his conscience. Virtue is a condition of the person (creature) that is in the presence of God, reflecting the behaviors of the Creator. The opposite of virtue is vice; it is a habitual, repeated practice of wrongdoing. We have no excuse for vice behaviors because God in his infinite wisdom, through Jesus Christ, demonstrated for us to fully perceive what He would want His people to be.

The Spirit of God convicts and reveals the truth. The believers are children of light; their eyes were opened to see the truth. The perishing world is blind to the truth; they are children of darkness; they are spiritually dead. The pathologist says that the confirmatory signs of death include bilateral dilatation and fixation of the pupils. "Here, no response is noticed from the pupil, for example, not even to sharp light." Likewise the spiritually dead have no ability to see the truth because they do not have Jesus, the light of the world.

The children of light can see what the children of darkness cannot see. It hurts us when our beloved ones cannot see what we see. Sometimes it is because of their stubbornness that they can't see; but most times it is because of the love of darkness (immorality). They enjoy the kind of life that is disgraceful to us and that is abomination to God. The Bible says concerning them that, "This is the verdict: Light has come into the world, but men loved darkness instead of light because their deeds were evil" (John 3:19).

Most people do not accept God's free gift of the grace because they see no need to be saved. The reason they don't see the need for the atoning death of Christ is because they don't have the concept of sin. Not until they have the concept of sin, as offensive and utterly repulsive before God and acknowledge their inability to untangle themselves from it, will they see the need for the Savior. That is when the death of Jesus Christ begins to make sense to them. It takes a spiritual revelation in order for them to have such experience.

Pastor Gram said that, "One question I'm often asked is why I preach so much about the ugliness of sin. And the answer is that if we don't have a right idea of what sin is, then we can never truly understand the Gospel and the grace of God." Our sin is repulsive to God. A non-repented sinner is alienated from God by his or her sin; He or she is completely separated from God. The Bible says that, "But your iniquities have separated you from your God; your sins have hidden his face from you, so that he will not hear" (Isaiah 59:2).

Yet in Christ, we stand face to face with God; we are completely forgiven and free from condemnation. So thank God today that if you're in Christ, you'll never face judgment for your sin! God loves a repented sinner but a non-repented sinner He will surely condemn. God provided Jesus Christ, our great High Priest, where we go to sacrifice for our sins by repenting. We do not need animals to sacrifice because He became our perfect sacrifice. Jesus is our Temple because the sacrificing cannot take place without the altar of the temple. He said that destroy this temple and I will build it in three days (John 2:19). Jesus was referring to His body that will be raised in three days.

Let me be clear: Believing in God won't save you. The Bible says that even the demons believe, yet they aren't saved (James 2:19). Throughout history people have believed in the existence of supernatural beings. Instead of asking, "Do I believe in God?" a more appropriate question is, "what kind of God do I believe in? What saves you is a personal relationship and faith in Jesus Christ—that He died on your behalf, rose again from the dead, and by faith in Him you can have eternal life. Jesus removes the only barrier (sin) that separates us from God. This is not casual or superficial confession because it must be accompanied with evidences of salvation (obedience to God's commandments). The affection for God constrains us to hate immorality.

We naturally see things from different prospective. It is true that some will never see the truth the way we see it. It is also true that the truth does not depend on the way people see things. The truth depends on God. A lie repeated often enough become the truth for some people. Our perceptions or memories of something can be changed or altered over time. This happens naturally or it can be intentionally manipulated. If something is said often enough, not only can you begin to believe it yourself, but other people hear it, or read it, and it merges into the collective consciousness. It is hard to accept the truth once the lies you were told were exactly what you wanted to hear. In this case the lie you want to hear becomes the truth to you. Well, in reality a fact or truth will never change—it is what it is regardless of your perception. True obedience is in reference to God's preference. God's way is the truth. Perhaps pride is the mother of all sins. Pride is an exaggerated self-evaluation. It is refusing to be what God intended you to be.

We've all heard countless times that we're living in a "secular age." We've seen the statistics saying that the number of people who don't identify with any religion is growing rapidly. While the statistics are true up to a point, we need to put them in context. What makes our age "secular"? The freedom and liberty to do as we want regardless of the divine 'will' makes the world secular. According to philosopher Charles Taylor, secularism is on rapid increase because the people of today treat belief in God as optional in ways that were literally unimaginable to people 500 or even 200 years ago. Ideas and cultural changes made this optional belief possible and, in turn, relegated religion to the private sphere.

The venue is set for people to embrace the false messiah (Antichrist). Jesus predicated the great falling away at the end times: "Because of the increase of wickedness, the love of most will grow cold" (Matthew 24:12). Also, "But when the Son of Man comes, will he find faith on earth?" (Luke 18:8). The seasons, ages and the people change but God never changes. St. Augustine wrote, "You have made us for yourself, O Lord, and our hearts are restless until they rest in you." Our age may tell us that belief is optional, (especially belief in God, the Father of our Lord Jesus Christ), but that does nothing for our restlessness.

Joe Loconte's fabulous new book, "The Searchers," is a kind of field guide to that restlessness. In Loconte's telling, many of us are in a situation similar to the travelers on the road to Emmaus in Luke 24. Our expectations have been, as the cliché goes, overtaken by events. The story we have invested in isn't likely to turn out the way we hoped that it would. For the disciples on the road to Emmaus, disillusionment came from a failure to understand how God intended to redeem Israel. They literally could not see the risen Christ until Jesus had "explained to them what was said in all the Scriptures concerning himself" and broke bread with them. The revelation ended the illusion. For our contemporaries, making faith in God optional made faith in a series of illusions possible. Loconte ticks them off one-by-one in a chapter entitled, aptly enough, "The End of Illusions." (*Regarding Loconte materials please visitBreakPoint.org.*)

The revelation leads to surrendering and is followed by commitment. Despite many decades of trying, psychology has not found much one can do to produce lasting increases in intelligence. Likewise we cannot induce a revelation. In order for someone to see the need for God's grace, God has to open his or her eyes to it (John 6:44). This can make us a bit uncomfortable. It's our own human inclination to think that we're in control. And that if we have the right words and the right inflection, we can open people's eyes to the Gospel. But the Bible is clear—only God can do that! I know there are some who feel frustrated by what I just said. Instead of frustration, it should create relief in knowing it's not up to us to save others. The God whom we trust in is the one who takes the initiative. He came to find us.

A fallen man has no affection for God. He may have affection for the false gods but not for one true God. When the Gospel is preached, God opens the eyes of the sinner to see Christ in order for the sinner to be convicted and repent. The sinner then asks for forgiveness; salvation takes place by receiving Jesus Christ as a personal Savior. The prayer of the sinner to God should be "Open my eyes to see you". Jesus is the light (vision) of the world to see God—"See Me see the Father" (John 14:7-11).

We should minister with such confidence that the love of God will reach out to the people whom we are ministering to. God is willing to make your house His home if you will let Him do it. When you do, you'll see your house transformed into a God-honoring home. God gave this stunning instruction to us: "Hear, O Israel: The LORD our God, the LORD is one. You shall love the LORD your God with all your heart and with all your soul and with all your might. And these words that I command you today shall be on your heart. You shall

<u>teach them diligently to your children</u>, and <u>shall talk of them</u> when you sit in your house, and when you walk by the way, and when you lie down, and when you rise." (Deuteronomy 6:4-7).

The first step to win our beloved ones to Christ is to pray for their salvation. Then go ahead to share with them the Gospel in words and deeds, with such confidence, knowing that only God can open their eyes to His grace. We are not sent to condemn the world because it is already condemned. We are sent to restore hope by preaching the Gospel. The Gospel is the Good News to all humanity that God saves the condemned people from condemnation.

Those who believe must know that they are saved by the grace of God. God loved us so much that He could not live us in our corruption. His grace made an exit of the narrow way for us to break from the broad way of destruction. Jesus said that, "Enter through the narrow gate. For wide is the gate and broad is the road that leads to destruction, and many enter through it" (Matthew 7:13). It means that the majority of people who are following other ways (not Christ) are destined to annihilation. You may say "it is not fair". Oh yes, you are right; fairness is not one of the attributes of God but just is. In accordance to His justice, God did not have to save any of us but He did it because of His unconditional love. God is justified to save whosoever He wills because His justice demands death to all of us (Rom. 3:23; cf. Isa. 59:2).

Apart from God nobody knows who is going to be saved. We are called to minister the gospel to all people in love. We should look at all people as potential candidates to salvation. Jesus gave the parable of the sower to demonstrate to us how we should preach the Gospel: "Behold, a sower went forth to sow; And when he sowed, some seeds fell by the way side, and the fowls came and devoured them up: Some fell upon stony places, where they had not much earth: and forth with they sprung up, because they had no deepness of earth: And when the sun was up, they were scorched; and because they had no root, they withered away. Other seed fell among thorns, which grew up and choked the plants. Still other seed fell on good soil, where it produced a crop—a hundred, sixty or thirty times what was sown." (Matthew 13:3-7). The handful of seeds are picked from the basket and are scattered massively, falling at different types of grounds. We are called to preach (sow) the gospel indiscriminately; different factors contribute to the growth of the seeds. The ones that fall on good ground are the minority who accepts Jesus Christ as their Savior. They are God's elects.

Loving God and neighbor is the greatest commandment. A neighbor is somebody next to you. Our relatives make a big chunk of our neighbors. Unfortunately some of us act like the people in the parable about the Good Samaritan, who found reason to avoid doing the needful. There are many Christians today who talk about love, but never do anything to show it. They know the doctrines of love and sing songs about it, but they fail to add actions to their words. That's not biblical love. Real love doesn't just sit on a Church pew. Real love has hands. Real love has feet. It hugs the widow and comforts the orphan. It gives to the poor and defends the downtrodden. Real love moves you into action. That's the love Jesus showed you, and it's the love you can show others!

Every believer is given a seed of Word to plant. Wise sayings often fall on barren ground, but a kind word is never thrown away. You are a spiritual father because you are required to reproduce spiritual children. Until a spiritually mature man reproduces and disciples Christ-like maturity in others, he has no spiritual children and cannot be considered a spiritual father. A spiritual father reproduces spiritual children who have a passionate and intimate relationship with God the Father. The spiritual growth process of these children must continue so that they also become spiritual fathers who reproduce spiritual children too.

True love involves giving value time to the people we love. In our daily lives, love is the best teacher. What you help a child to love can be more important than what you help him to learn. The good thing is that you don't have to go to college in order to learn to love. Our goal is to love as Christ loved. He demonstrated His love to us by stretching Himself on the cross. The good news is that you don't have to do the cross. Any measure of sacrificial love you give, He will not despise. Remember that Noah's ark was built by amateurs but the Titanic by professionals. Yet the Titanic never survived the much smaller storm!

It is important to spend value time with your loved ones. Remember that trust increases with intimacy. Quality with very little quantity isn't quality at all. No spouse or child will tell you in twenty years, "I wish you'd spent more time at work and less at home with us." But the sad reality is that many parents today are absent, spending quality time here and there, but not giving their spouses or kids the quantity of time they need.

Let all the decisions be made in the best interest of our people. As much as it is important to work, we must save value time for our family members or the people we claim to love. Give them the gift of your full attention. This gift alone will make others want to be around you and remember you. Unfortunately, this is a gift few people give. It is important to make a conscious decision, to choose time over money. It should be understood that the best investment of our limited time on earth is to spend it with the people we love. Time is our most precious treasure because it is limited. We can produce more wealth, but we cannot produce more time. When we give someone our time, we actually give a portion of our life that we will never take back. Our time is our life! Giving portions of our time to others is giving ourselves.

I want to emphasize that the people you love don't just need your quality time. They need quantity as well. It's the greatest gift you can give them. Spend time with your loved ones and you'll see God blessing your relationships in amazing ways. Investing time is like sowing. If you sow seeds, you will get some fruits. We all admire beautiful harvests but few people are willing to invest time and effort upfront. Be different. Plant healthy seeds in the lives of others in anticipation of harvests in greater measures. Quantity time becomes quality time when properly utilized to communicate love to your loved ones. Nicholas Sparks said that, "If conversation was the lyrics, laughter was the music, making time spent together is a melody that could be replayed over and over without getting stale."

I want to say that there is a need to reevaluate everything for efficiency purposes. Mahatma Gandhi gave what he called "Seven Deadly Sins": Wealth without work; Pleasure without conscience; Science without humanity; Knowledge without character; Politics without principle; Commerce without morality; Worship without sacrifice. As much as I don't agree with his dogma (religious doctrines), his saying holds some water.

True love is accompanied with responsibility. Our responsibility for each other changes with time. For example we are supposed to take care of our little ones all the way to maturity. In the same way, the children are supposed to take care of their aged parents. The culture of today has forsaken the same responsibilities. Parents take their children to day care facilities. Then children take their aged parents to nursing homes. As much as these facilities are important, they should not replace our responsibilities of taking care of our beloved ones.

This topic is about ministering the Gospel to your beloved ones. I am going to expound more on how to minister to our beloved ones. It is important to acknowledge that the family members are human beings first, then relatives. Therefore, keeping the flame in any relationship is a daily investment and there are no shortcuts! They are emotional too. We are called to minister the gospel in love. There are many people who claim to love their families and their extended families when in actual sense they do not know how to love. This is most probably the area where most of us fail. I am guilty of the same offence and I am working on making improvement in this area. There must be a good working relationship with your family members or close relatives in order for you to minister to them. Please take inventory of your relationship with the people whom you claim to love. Do you love in accordance to your standards or God's standard? God's standard does not justify unforgiving. We are called to love sacrificially. Sacrificial love gives without expectations of returns. The people of the world (nonbelievers) do not love sacrificially because they don't share in our values.

Becoming a Christian is likely to cost you friends and some family members. I know many people who were disowned by their family members after they embraced Christianity. Jesus described His mission on earth in this way: "Do not think that I came to bring peace on earth. I did not come to bring peace but a sword. "For I have come to 'set a man against his father, a daughter against her mother, and a daughter-in-law against her mother-in-law'; "and 'a man's enemies will be those of his own household" (Matthew 10:34-36).

The Lord Jesus predicted persecution to be encountered by those who choose to follow Him. Believers are ridiculed and despised mostly by their close relatives because of their faith. When people persecute you because of the truth it is because they are blind to the truth. Getting offended by them is like getting offended when the blind man steps on you. Remember that we are going to be vulnerable as long as we are carrying the light in the dark world. The light exposes the dirt of the world; this does not augur well for the worldly people.

We should expect persecution. Jesus was hated by the religious people of His time. They falsely accused Him to perform miracles by the power of Satan: "But some of them said, "By Beelzebub, the prince of demons, he is driving out demons" (Luke 11:14-15). Jesus predicted greater persecutions for His followers: "For if they do these things in a green tree, what shall be done in the dry?" (Luke 23:31). Also, "Behold, what manner of love the Father hath bestowed upon us, that we should be called the sons of God: therefore the <u>world knoweth us not, because it knew him not</u>" (1 John 3:1).

The Spirit of the Father and the Son dwells in us to make us overcomers. He has entrusted much to us; whatever He entrusts, He expects from us. God's blessings call for positive responses. We have no excuse for not witnessing to our family members. Successful evangelism should be fronted by committed personalities who are less prone to rocking the boat.

The greatest test for believers comes during the times of crisis. When you're trying to get to know a person, it is revealing to see how they respond under pressure. How they handle anger. How they respond under crisis. The Bible instructs us to turn the other check for the sake of winning others to Christ. The ungodly may ridicule your deep reverence for the Lord; but the prize of our high calling is sufficient consolation for us. God will reward us exceedingly.

The tremendous frustration for us is to be hurt by the people we trust most. The reality is that even the most sobriety minded person will back me up in saying, "We intentionally or unintentionally hurt the ones we love the most." Most times the people who offend us are our close relatives and friends who have not embraced the gospel. At times the very people whom we trust most are most likely to let us down.

It is unfortunate that families are increasingly becoming dysfunctional, and people are so heartless. People recklessly offend others without caring of the possible ominous repercussions of their actions. As a result many family members are increasingly at loggerhead. The causes are not necessarily the physical people but spiritual war because Satan targets families. As one brother said that, "It is not the dog in the fight but the fight in the dog!" The impact of conflicts among Christian families is even much greater. I want to warn that people are watching us. To the world you may be one person but to one person you may be the world. Satan takes advantage of the existing minor conflicts to destroy our credibility to witness the gospel.

It pains me to hear that so many adult siblings today harbor bitterness and hatred against one another. If that describes you, reconcile with your brothers and sisters. Tolerance is a vital tool for conflict resolution. If there is goodwill on one side, there will definitely be goodwill by the other side. The two sides need each other. You need their love and they need your love. That kind of love is so special, so don't lose it! We must establish channels to address the pending family crisis. It means having people whom we can turn to so that they in turn nonchalantly slot our grievances in positive discussions, mending the broken relationships.

Some people have what professionals call an "overly developed critical super-ego." In layman's terms, they are nitpicker extraordinaire. They pick on every little thing about others. Nothing you do will ever be quite right, in their opinion. The first thing to go after spending time with them is your self-esteem. Clearly, you're already a failure in their eyes—and if you don't look away from their judgmental gaze pretty fast, you'll see your own reflection there and internalize their damaging opinions as if they were your own.

We must exercise humility whereby self-control is encouraged and strengthened. Self Control is dominance over all desires. All of us have evil desires but we should never let the evil desires control us. In order to love people unconditionally we must admit that there is nothing like a perfect person. The Psalmist said that, "If You, LORD, should mark iniquities, O Lord, who could stand? But there is forgiveness with You, That You may be feared . . . ." (Psalm 130:3).

The fastest way to kill motivation is to expect absolutely no mistake. The military considers the 'zero defect mentality' to be dangerous. The reason is because such mentality runs from responsibility out of fear of making mistakes. We should stop being hypocritical, berating others for the same mistakes we are guilty of. Jesus said that he that hates is guilty of murder; he that lusts is guilty of adultery. The act of murder is hatred at its extremity of which we are all guilty. Adultery is the final stage of lust of which we are all guilty. His message is that we are all sinners and we all need a Savior. The difference is in the degree of sin. The consequence of sin is death. The only safe place for the sinner to be is under the grace of God. Remember that the mercies of God are as deep as His wrath towards sin. The choice is yours to take the grace of God extended to you through Jesus Christ or face the consequences of your sins.

Bitterness sucks. Such people think that they are mistreated by everyone. Their lives are characterized by never-ending series of unfortunate events—and you can't cure them, either. In fact, you'll be their next excuse for why things are going so horribly wrong in their lives. Bitterness is contiguous. Your real nightmare begins when you start to feel a little like them yourself, and your once-positive nature gets overwhelmed by others' perpetually gloomy outlooks and daily dose of misery. We must love people without compromising on our values. Paul wrote in 1 Corinthians 6:12—All things are lawful unto me, but all things are not expedient: all things are lawful for me, but I will not be brought under the power of any. Again the Apostle wrote in 1 Corinthians 10:23—"All things are lawful for me, but all things are not expedient: all things are lawful for me, but all things edify not".

The best way to win our beloved ones to Christ is by manifesting our transformed lives. The transformed life loves sacrificially. Our relatives know us better. They see us day to day and so are allowed a peek into our lives. They are acquainted with our little bad habits which we had before accepting Jesus Christ. After you are converted, the characters of Jesus Christ in your life become the non-contestable testimony to them. They may deny everything you say but they cannot deny what you do. When Jesus is the reason for everything you do, the people around you will be able to see Him at work through you everywhere and will be convicted. Jesus told us, "I am the vine; you are the branches. Whoever abides in me and I in him, he it is that bears much fruit, for apart from me you can do nothing" (John 15:5). Get that last part, folks, "a*part from me you can do NOTHING. NOTHING*". Everything you do that does not manifest the life of Christ is wasted. We can change the world by allowing Jesus Christ to work through us. Our good works are acceptable to men but the only works that are acceptable to God are the ones which Christ does through us. Remember that the evil people have their own standard of what is good but God's standard is only the perfect works of Jesus Christ.

We (believers) must love one another in order to win the lost souls. Confessing our sins to God and to each other is important even among believers. God is love. He is the mechanism that connects us together. When we are in Christ, we are one body (His body) regardless of our little denominations. We must focus on Christ who is the central pillar of our faith. It is not which Church you worship from or your religion, but Christ in your heart. If you don't have Christ in you, everything is vanity and vanity!

Christ in us is supposed to attract the nonbelievers to Christ. They must see Him in us in order for them to be convicted. He is the divine strength within us. We are fighting the spiritual battle and our enemy is spiritual. Christ fights our spiritual battles but we must put Him to work by crucifying the old self (killing the old nature). Carnal Christians neglect their spiritual weapons and use natural weapons to fight their spiritual wars. Paul warned that, "For to be carnally minded is death; but to be spiritually minded is life and peace" (Romans 8:6).

Certainly, spiritual transformation and growth comes with change but forcefully changing people by natural means, like shoving religion down their throats, is considered to be carnal minded. True change comes from inside to outside. God changes the hearts in order to change the ultimate desires. True change is becoming a person God wants you to be as opposed to a person you want to be. When you acknowledge that this world is a place where opportunities abound but not the end in itself then you are heading the right direction; you are having the purposeful minds and inspired destiny. Indeed there is real heaven to gain for those redeemed by Christ and hell for sinners who die without Christ. The decision regarding your destiny is made now in this world while you are still alive.

We should expect the people around us to change. However, change is essential but not necessarily easy, otherwise all would have embraced it. Remember that the Jews in the wildness saw numerous miracles but their hearts were still hardened by unbelief. Jesus performed amazing miracles yet He was rejected. Jesus was the best at evangelizing, yet His own brothers did not believe in Him until His resurrection (John 7:5).

At times the required change is secured by becoming comfortable with the uncomfortable. Meet the needs of the people you are ministering to. Hugh Martin says that, "If a man's religion does not affect his use of money, that man's religion is vain". The loving person is generous too. R. E. Phillips says that, "You only keep what you give away." The Statistics of the world indicate that the people who have the most live the longest. They say that no man can sincerely try to help another without helping himself first. Given the fact, sharing with the needy is a virtue. You can give without loving, but you can't love without giving. There are three kinds of givers—the flint, the sponge and the honeycomb. To get anything out of a flint you must hammer it. And then you get only chips and sparks. To get water out of a sponge you must squeeze it, and the more you use pressure, the more you will get. But the honeycomb just overflows with its own sweetness. Which kind of giver are you? "We make a living by what we get but we make life by what we give"—Winston Churchill

A family can survive without a nation but a nation cannot survive without families. Our problems do not originate from the White House (governments) but in our houses. The families designate values to the nation. God bestows honor to the nation by restoring values in families. Therefore the place to begin sharing God's truth is at home. That's where we're to live authentically by walking with God and showing others the grace He's given us . . . our spouses, our kids, our parents, and our friends. Start sharing the Gospel at home, testify of the Lord's goodness, and be a living witness to your loved ones of God's grace in your life. Family activities should be turned into gymnasiums to recruit family members to Christianity. For example meal times can be turned into social events to discuss the things that matter like spiritual aspects. Little things like praying for the food before eating and talking about the providences of God can make the difference.

It is unfortunate that families are increasingly becoming dysfunctional, and people are so heartless. People of the same family recklessly offend each other without caring of the possible ominous repercussions of their actions. As a result many family members are increasingly at loggerhead. Selfishness is the major cause of conflicts. Love of self, in the Christian sense, isn't selfishness; it isn't putting yourself first before everyone and anything else. On the contrary, love for self means that, upon realizing your own worth before God, you seek to live the best possible life, knowing that the results of such a life will be a benefit not just to yourself but also, and even more important, to those around you. The cultivation of a uniform courtesy, a willingness to do to others as we would wish them to do to us, would annihilate half the ills of life. The problem is not necessarily the physical people because we are fighting a spiritual warfare; Satan primarily targets families. As one brother said that, "It is not the dog in the fight but the fight in the dog!" The impact of conflicts among Christian families is even much greater; people are watching us. To the world you may be one person but to one person you may be the world.

The family is not only supposed to be the cradle of civilization but of morality. John B. made this comment, "I personally think immorality will only be terminated at family level by imparting moral education among our children as soon as they can begin to understand certain concepts." Like a former director of health services used to say, "Health is made at home and taken to hospital only when it breaks down." I want to pause and ask how much moral education are you investing in your family; how much moral education are families investing in our country Uganda? Remember that moral families make moral communities; moral communities make a moral nation. Plan to invest into your family wisely. Remember that if you fail to plan you plan to fail.

Neglecting our family members is therefore like cutting the branch we are seated on. As Achebe wrote that is when things start to fall apart. Helping our beloved ones to know God should never be taken lightly. There is a possibility of being separated from our beloved deceased ones forever. We can say farewell to those we love with hope that someday we will spend all time with them. Such assurance comes from knowing that our beloved ones accepted God's offer of salvation. The most important thing you can do to your family is to witness to them the Gospel. You must share your faith in Christ with them and they must see Him in your life. True preaching must be accompanied by true living. We are called to be orthodox believers and orthodox practitioners.

Remember that the power to save does not depend on our persuasive techniques but in the Gospel. The simplicity of the Gospel is that we were born into this world as habitual rebels against the creator of the universe. But God reconciled the world to Himself through Jesus Christ by forgiving our sins (2 Corinthians 5:19). We, who were guilty, can now walk to Him without guilt.

We are all candidates to God's grace. To be recipient of the grace is one of the most defining moments in life. We who have received grace must extend grace to others. We must show our love to those close to us even when we do not approve their lifestyles. Again, loving them does not mean to approve their beliefs and becoming partakers in their disobedient behaviors. It means loving them much by ministering to them the saving grace of Jesus Christ in love.

Grace is God's favor bestowed to us who didn't deserve it and who will never be able to pay back. We who have been forgiven need to forgive others. Forgiving is the condition of being forgiven. And being pardoned, every man should have a fair sized cemetery in which to bury the faults of his friends. Jesus loved us unconditionally and forgave us all of our sins. Preaching the Gospel is the solution to what we owe to God. Pastor Gram said that, "It's been said, "The Gospel has come to you because it's on its way to someone else." There's so much truth in that statement because the message of Jesus Christ should never terminate with the receiver. Rather, it should prompt the receiver to action!"

Most broken relationships are due to un-forgiveness. The biblical character Joseph left to us the legacy of forgiving family members who mistreat us. Joseph's life was anything but peaceful until he was sold into slavery by jealous brothers. Genesis 37:2 says he was seventeen when he was tending his father's flocks and was given the coat of many colors. Probably not long after that was when he was sold into slavery. He was later thrown into prison on false charges. Yet, he remained free of bitterness or regret and saw God as the "Great Engineer" behind even the worst of circumstances. It had been a long and very difficult rise to power, but Joseph, the son of Jacob / Israel, became the Prime Minister of Egypt (i.e. second only to the King / Pharaoh himself)—a nation of which Joseph, up to that time, wasn't even a citizen, but was merely a foreign slave and dungeon prisoner (Genesis 41:41-43 KJV).

In a final confrontation with his brothers, he graciously noted, "You meant it for bad; God meant it for good." Joseph acknowledged that what his brothers did to him was wrong and premeditated evil but God took what they intended to be evil and turned it into good for His glory (Genesis 50:20). Consequently, Joseph was able to save his brothers from famine and to uphold to the promises of God to Abraham.

It takes a revelation to see God in everything including the evil plans of others against us. If you are going through some rough times, that are no choice on your part, God is able to handle your situation. There is no problem that is too big to be worked out (Romans 8:28). In spite of the great devastations, God is in absolute control. At the end of the day the God of goodness will prevail; His plan for your life will be in the limelight. God has great prospection, way beyond our comprehensions. At every level of our life experience, the grace of God is at work even at times when it is not noticeable to our natural minds. God primarily focuses on our eternal destiny. Remember that there is a possibility of dying and ending up in hell.

It is difficult to forgive as long as we keep records of wrongs. Meditating on the wrongs of the people who offended us is the key to unforgiving. It is not easy to forget the past errors but you can let go of the past in anticipation of God's blessings. In order to forgive others you should be able to forgive yourself. Self-forgiveness enables the release of guilt, shame and fear, allowing you to move forward towards authenticity.

Aggressive defence is usually initiated by Guilt & Anger. It usually occurs in a situation where a defender is caught in a role reversal anomaly, usually associated with lack of discipline. It may also be a result of sullenness or deliberate or repeated failures in life. It can accelerate into passive aggressive behaviours. We should own our failures gracefully with awareness that we are all mortal and we are not exempted from flaws. C.S. Lewis once said that the problem with evil isn't that our desires are too strong, but that they're too weak; and what he meant by that was that people are fare too easily swayed emotionally. The sin that is defended and not repented of will definitely explode into a chain of reactions and multiple evils. Learn to accept your faults.

Our God is now God. He meets you as you are regardless of the past. You can embrace the present because God meets you by your current faith rather than what you did yesterday. There's no need to play the "what if" game. The past is forgiven and gone, and the future is in God's omnipotent hands; so you're free to focus on the present love of Christ extended to you: "Wherever you are, be all there," says Jim

Elliot. God wants you in the present because that's where his grace will flow.

Praying drives away fear and anxiety. Pray about everything. There is no little thing that does not require prayers. After praying, Quit worrying. An intimate man with God is never intimidated by man. When you kneel before God, you can stand tall before any man and against any situation. Praying invites God on board to tackle your adversity on your behalf. Remember that there is no failure more disastrous than the success that leaves God out.

We are part of the big family of God but also part of our earthly families. Home is the first place to win the lost souls. Islam is growing fast because the Muslims have big family members whom they recruit into their religion. Open your house to all people. Make others feel welcome. When you express warmth and genuine acceptance to others in the faith, you'll find genuine fellowship and grace that transcends any boundary!

We must be Bible oriented believers in order to be what God intended us to be. John Piper wrote that, "One of the great blessings of being a Bible-saturated Church with a Bible-saturated eldership and a Bible-saturated people is that the strange juxtapositions in the Bible of seemingly contrary emotions and emphases and truths prevent us from becoming a superficial, simplistic, lopsided people. For example, a superficial, simplistic, lopsided person might watch another person get angry at some sinful attitude he sees in a group, and draw the conclusion: This angry person is not a very compassionate person; he doesn't have a lot of empathy; he's not able to weep with those who weep. But the instincts of a Bible-saturated person would not draw this conclusion because over the years he has been deepened and broadened in his grasp of the complexity of godliness, by running into so many strange juxtapositions. He has been shaped by texts like Mark 3:5 where it says, "Jesus looked around at them with anger, grieved at their hardness of heart." And the superficial, simplistic, lopsided notion that godly anger and godly compassion cannot coexist in the same godly heart has been banished from the Bible-saturated mind forever.

Day after day, week after week, year after year, Bible-saturated minds and hearts are being formed by the hundreds of such deep and wonderful juxtapositions in the Bible. A people are being created whose instincts and inclinations are as complex as the Bible. And whose responses to situations are often as little understood as the Scriptures. Closer and closer to "the mind of Christ."

I want to emphasize that we are sent to minister and to evangelize the world including those people close to us (our close relatives/friends). Multiple opportunities avail for us daily, in course of conducting our daily activities, to minister to others. God sends people to us who need to hear the Gospel. It might be in your house, place of work, on the streets, grocery store and etc. A neighbor is somebody you have access to. Loving your neighbor means caring about their eternal destiny.

People often ask me the most effective method of evangelism. And I tell them, "The one that works!" And one that I've seen work very often is simply to invite others to Church. Not any Church but a Bible teaching Church. I mean the Church that teaches the Full Gospel. The Church that teaches the doctrine of salvation by faith and the sanctification of works. Why does it work? Because when lost people come to Church, they see the body of Christ authentically loving God and loving one another. They see real worship, hear real teaching, and feel real love by those who have the love of God in them. They experience the real presence of the Lord and they are convicted! It is our responsibility to inspire others to get involved in the ministry of our local Churches, where they can experience the love of God in and through the body of Christ. And above all else, let them see the love of Christ actively lived out in your own life every day. After the Holy Spirit adds them to the body (Church), involve them in worship, service and witnessing.

Pastor Gram says that, "When we read about the person of Jesus Christ, we have a photograph of God. That's because when we look at Jesus—how He loved others, obeyed God, and gave Himself for us—we get a clear look at the heart of our heavenly Father. But here's how what we have is so much more powerful than a photograph: God is in us if we are in Christ. He's given us the gift of His Spirit to lead and guide us all the days of our lives. So read the Scriptures and marvel at Jesus. When you do, know you're getting a clear glimpse of your Father in heaven and the Holy Spirit inside you!"

Should we use personal evangelism? Yes! Should we show Christ's love through serving others? Yes! These are wonderful ways to share the message and love of Christ with others. I pray we never neglect them! God called us (believers) to be His mouth piece and voice. We should not witness the love of God desperately but with such assurance that the world will end as God preordained. In heaven there are no surprises and there is no panic. God reconciled this world to Himself from eternity. The Bible says that, "Praise be to the God and Father of our Lord Jesus Christ, who has blessed us in the heavenly realms with every spiritual blessing in Christ. For he chose us in Him before the creation of the world to be holy and blameless in his sight. In love He predestined us for adoption to son-ship through Jesus Christ, in accordance with his pleasure and will—to the praise of his glorious grace, which he has freely given us in the One he loves" (Ephesians 1:1-6).

God executed His redemption plan from eternity for His own glory. Salvation is God's eternal plan focusing on His Son. Both the Old and New Testaments point unwaveringly to the One who will act as a mediator and Savior: the Lord Jesus Christ. God's intention from the very beginning has been for His Kingdom to be fully and finally fulfilled in Christ. While we have been waiting over 2,000 years for Jesus' return, the book of Revelation assures us that the wait will not continue forever. The world is progressing towards God's intentional conclusion where all of God's people will live in God's place under God's rule and blessing.

I want to end by saying that the people who are prepared to die primarily focus on the future healing as opposed to the present. I am not saying that God does not heal today. The gift of healing is available for all believers at His timing and will. Even those who experience the divine healing now are going to die because they are still mortal. Our immortality is in Christ. God's priority is to heal the soul. All believers will certainly be healed in future. God is not limited by time. He sees us in the glorified nature without sickness and death.

We can count on the promises of God for the divine healing of the nations. The Bible says that on the cross both our sins and healing were provided for. Isaiah prophesized that "—Surely He borne our grief and carried our sorrows, yet we did not esteem Him stricken, smitten of God and afflicted. But He was wounded for our transgressions, He was bruised for our iniquities: the chastisement of our peace was upon Him; and with His stripes we are healed (Isaiah 53:4-5; 1 Peter 2:24). Without doubt all believers are going to be healed at glorification because sin and sickness (corruption) will be rolled away. We shall all put on the incorruptible body that is not subject to death and the believers shall dwell in a new city coming down from heaven. The nonbelievers will eternally be separated from God. Therefore, your spiritual destination is by far the most important decision you will ever have to face and make because if you think earth life is miserable or long, eternity is over a million times longer than 120 years!

I want to end with these encouraging words: "Let us give up our work, our plans, ourselves, our lives, our loved ones, our influence, our all, right into God's hand; and then, when we have given all to Him, there will be nothing left for us to be troubled about"—Hudson Taylor

Building Monuments for our Beloved Ones

Egypt left a mark on history by building pyramids for their Pharaohs. The Great Pyramid of Giza (also called the Khufu's Pyramid, Pyramid of Khufu, and Pyramid of Cheops) is the oldest and largest of the three pyramids in the Giza Necropolis bordering what is now Cairo, Egypt, and is the only one of the Seven Wonders of the Ancient World that survives substantially intact. It is believed the pyramid was built as a tomb for Fourth dynasty Egyptian King Khufu (Cheops in Greek) and constructed over a 20 year period concluding around 2560 BC. The Great Pyramid was the tallest man-made structure in the world for over 3,800 years. A total of over 2,300,000 (or only 590,712) blocks of limestone and granite were used in its construction with the average block weighing 2.5 tons and none weighing less than 2 tons. The large blocks used in the ceiling of the King's Chamber weigh as much as 9 tons.

It is within human instinct to remember their heroes. In America there is a memorial day especially reserved to remember the fallen servicemen. It is imperative not only to read about the past heroes in history books, but also to designate a day for America to commemorate her great heroes' deeds. They are the reason for the peace we enjoy today. Americans are hardly unique in this type of communal recollection of a cultural memory. Throughout history, various societies have designated memorial days and monuments to remind themselves about the values and ideals they cherish most.

Kampala city, the capital of Uganda has monuments like Fort Rugard and the Clock Tower (Queen's clock) to mark the historical accounts of the colonial occupations. The name Kampala was delivered from

Impala. An impala (Aepyceros melampus) is a medium-sized African antelope. The city was built on a hill which was a hunting place for the king who used to hunt these antelopes. The name is historical and it evokes memories which are rich in history. In fact, the Bible records many instances in which God's people (and occasionally God himself) set up memorials to serve as a tangible reminder of God's faithfulness in the past and promises for the future.

In Genesis 28, the Old Testament patriarch Jacob heard in a dream God's promise to bless his descendants. Upon waking, Jacob established a monument to remind himself (and, presumably, those descendants) of the dream and of God's promise. At different occasion Jacob sets up a memorial pillar to serve as a reminder of his covenant with Laban (Genesis 31:43).

When the Israelites first crossed the Jordan River, they set up a stone monument for the specific purpose of reminding the future generations of the event: So Joshua called together the twelve men he had chosen—one from each of the tribes of Israel. He told them, "Go into the middle of the Jordan, in front of the Ark of the Lord your God. Each of you must pick up one stone and carry it out on your shoulder—twelve stones in all, one for each of the twelve tribes of Israel. We will use these stones to build a memorial. In the future your children will ask you, 'What do these stones mean?' Then you can tell them, 'They remind us that the Jordan River stopped flowing when the Ark of the Lord's Covenant went across.' These stones will stand as a memorial among the people of Israel forever" (Joshua 4:1-9).

God wants to be remembered and recognizes how people can easily forget. The shema (Deut. 6:4-9) is a liturgical prayer, prominent in Jewish history and tradition, that is recited daily at the morning and evening services and expresses the Jewish people's ardent faith in and love of God. This prayer was supposed to be hanged on doors, on foreheads and on wrists for memorial purposes (Deut. 11:18; Exodus 13:16).

A monument is a statue, building, or other structure erected to commemorate a famous or notable person or event. Monuments are biblical but they hold no spiritual significance. Physical monuments were a tangible reminder to God's people of their history and values— you might think of them as Biblical versions of the Washington Monument or the Lincoln Memorial, which serve a similar purpose for modern Americans. There are many accounts of such memorials being set up for that purpose.

America knows how to honor her heroes. All former presidents of USA have monuments in form of libraries. A Presidential memorial may have a physical element which consists of a monument or a statue within a monument. Its entire presence consists of a physical structure that is a permanent remembrance of the president it represents. Most well-known presidential memorials such as the Washington, Lincoln and Jefferson memorials have a physical element. There are also official presidential memorials that have a living element with only a minor physical presence. An example of a presidential living memorial is the Woodrow Wilson International Center for Scholars. Located in a wing of the Ronald Reagan Building in Washington, D.C., the Wilson Center has a small exhibit concerning President Wilson's life and work, but it is best known for its work to unite the world of ideas with the world of policy by supporting scholarship linked to issues of contemporary importance. In this way the living memorial perpetuates President Wilson's legacy of scholarship linked closely to international relations.

It is estimated that over 105 billion people have lived on this universe. In every generation there are a handful of people who have left a mark in the books of history. Various historical records reveal and recognize people who have been breaking ground, raising the bar and effecting meaningful change in the world. In England there are effigies marking the celebrities whose careers speak volume.

In our century, there are leaders with impeccable records whom we cannot ignore. I mean men and women making a difference in the realms of science, politics, business, finance, sports, entertainment and philanthropy. The true meaning of their ultimate sacrifice must be told through the buildings, infrastructures, libraries, charities, holidays and the stories of those whose lives they impacted. I am going to outline some of the characters with recognizable achievements.

Niels Bohr (1885-1962), a Danish physicist, was only 37 when he won the Nobel Prize for Physics in 1922 for his progress in understanding the structure of atoms (specifically his theory that electrons lived outside the nucleus in orbits of energy).

Enrico Fermi (1901-1954) responsible for discovering how to create a nuclear chain reaction, which led directly the creation of the atomic bomb. It was the atomic bomb that put an end to the Second World War.

Francis Crick (1916-2004) and James Watson (b. 1928) together discovered the double helix structure of DNA, the "blueprint of life." The discovery of DNA, the explanation of its construct, has been acknowledged as the most important biological work of the last 100 years, and the field it opened may be the scientific 'frontier' for the next 100. "In the 50 years since Watson and Crick revealed their DNA findings, the field of molecular diagnostics has flourished. The 1985 invention of polymerase chain reaction polymerase chain reaction (pŏl`ĭm⊠rās') (PCR), laboratory process in which a particular DNA segment from a mixture of DNA chains is rapidly replicated, producing a large, readily analyzed sample of a piece of DNA.

Jonas Salk (1914-1995) became a hero overnight when it was announced that he had invented a vaccine for polio. Polio attacks the nerve cells and sometimes the central nervous system, which can cause paralysis or even death. After being appointed head of the Virus Research Lab at the University of Pittsburgh in 1947, Dr. Jonas Salk devoted himself to finding a way to curb the devastating virus. Less than five years later, he invented a vaccine and decided to test it out.

Credit goes to the American researcher Robert Gallo and French scientist Luc Montagnier who both claimed to have discovered Human Immunodeficiency Virus (HIV).

Dr. Joseph E. Murray, who performed the world's first successful kidney transplant and won a Nobel Prize for his pioneering work. Since the first kidney transplants on identical twins, hundreds of thousands of transplants on a variety of organs have been performed worldwide. Murray shared the Nobel Prize in Physiology or Medicine in 1990 with Dr. E. Donnall Thomas, who won for his work in bone marrow transplants. Murray died at age 93 in November, 2012. He suffered a stroke at his suburban Boston home on Thanksgiving and died at Brigham and Women's Hospital.

Armstrong has been immortalized in human history as the first human to set foot on a celestial body beyond Earth. As one commentator complimented: "That's one small step for a man, one giant leap for mankind, he radioed back to Earth from the moon on July 20, 1969." As long as there are history books, Neil Armstrong will be included in them. Armstrong passed away Aug. 25. A U.S. Navy research vessel being built at a shipyard in Anacortes, Wash., will be named after Neil Armstrong. The ship is under construction at Dakota Creek Industries Inc. in Anacortes. The ship's construction is being funded by the Office of Naval Research and Armstrong's widow, Carol. It is scheduled to be completed in late 2014. The Auxiliary General Oceanographic Research ship, referred to as AGOR 27, will house acoustic equipment capable of mapping the deepest parts of the ocean. It also has onboard laboratories capable of a variety of oceanographic research.

I cannot forget to name some of the characters who left a mark on this universe by influencing morality. Back in the 1980s, First Lady Nancy Reagan spearheaded a campaign against drugs that was called Just Say No! I read some statistics recently indicating that this campaign was successful, lowering the use of recreational drugs significantly during that decade.

Mother Teresa was a very kind woman. She will be remembered because of her kind heart to people who aren't as fortunate as us (charity). For over forty years, she took care of needs of those without money, those who were sick, those without parents, and those dying in Calcutta (Kolkata), guided in part by the ideals of Saint Francis of Assisi. As the Missionaries of Charity grew under Mother's leadership, they expanded their ministry to other countries. By the 1970s she had become internationally well known as an advocate for the poor and helpless, due in part to a film and book, Something Beautiful for God by Malcolm Muggeridge. She was awarded the Nobel Prize for Peace in 1979.

We cannot forget Bill Gates the richest man in USA, and the richest woman in Silicon Valley, Laurene Powell Jobs, the widow of Steve Jobs for their support for the charities. They normally put their money where their hearts are. Bill Gates discovered Microsoft windows 7. Bill Gates has pioneered a crusade against the scourge of Malaria. Recently, the Bill and Melinda Gates Foundation, the world's richest charity, joined with the Rockefeller Foundation to launch a new development initiative for sub-Saharan Africa that they said would revolutionize food production and reduce hunger and poverty for tens of millions of people. Bill Gates agreed that the initial investment pales when compared with his contributions to the development of an AIDS vaccines. But he said that he expects the program to continue for decades. He has pioneered the fight against cervical cancer in Africa. Bill Gates says that he is happy that he is no longer the richest man in the world because he has donated most of his money to the needy around the world and he wishes other rich men can learn from him.

Of course we cannot ignore the impact of internet on the global social media. Mr. Zuckerberg the founder of Facebook said that his goal was to make "internet access available to those who cannot currently afford it". The group's statement said only 2.7 billion people—just over one-third of the world's population—had access to the internet. Adoption was growing by less than 9% a year, which was not fast enough. Potential projects include developing data compression tools, enhancing network capabilities to more efficiently handle data, building systems to cache data efficiently and creating frameworks for apps to reduce data usage.

The world rewards its own. Nobel Prizes winners and Oscars are rewarded after specifying the niche. Between 1901 and 2011, the Nobel Prizes and the Prize in Economic Sciences were awarded 549 times to 853 people and organizations. With some receiving the Nobel Prize more than once, this makes a total of 826 individuals and 20 organizations. Then there is the Nobel Peace Prize that is awarded to people who have done the most or the best work for fraternity between nations, for the abolition or reduction of standing armies and for the holding and promotion of peace congresses.

The only British prime minister to win the Nobel Prize for Literature, Winston Churchill, (1874-1965), saw action in many parts of the British Empire as war correspondent and soldier; he then became a writer of history and politician. Despite a lifelong speech impediment, Churchill was an inspirational public speaker and during the Second World War, unleashed the full power of the English language, breathing fire into a nation that was neither ready nor aware of the danger threatening it. John F Kennedy said that Churchill mobilized the English language and sent it into battle. As the fighting proceeded, the war of words proved vital. Churchill worked on the principle that he who tells the truth doesn't need to shout, and he never used a long word where a short one would do. Churchill's early life gave him many of the skills he would need to serve Britain in its greatest hour of need. Churchill is remembered to label Uganda as the pearl of Africa. (*The Wisdom of Winston Churchill*).

There are many Nobel Peace Prize winners even though I can't discuss all of them. The late Rev Martin Luther King Jr. merited the prize. It is impossible to listen to his speech without expressing my deep appreciation to the Nobel Committee of the Norwegian Parliament for bestowing upon him and the civil rights movement in the United States such a great honor. He is a real hero of the freedom struggle: His words were prophetic and still inspiring. He is a noble person who deserves the Nobel Peace Prize.

The Norwegian Nobel Committee decided to award the Nobel Peace Prize for 1993 to Nelson R. Mandela and Frederik Willem de Klerk for their work for the peaceful termination of the apartheid regime, and for laying the foundations for a new, democratic South Africa. Nelson Mandiba Mandela is considered, give or take, one of the world's living beacons of moral authority. He suffered greatly for the liberation of his people and after ascending to the highest office he reconciled with his tormentors. He said that even though he did not like [his predecessor] F. W De Klerk, he needed him for the sake of continuity of their nation. In August 2011, the South African government and sculptor unveiled a gigantic sculpture of Mr. Mandela at Howick, to mark 50 years since he was arrested on August 5, 1962. That arrest of course led to his imprisonment in Robben

Island, another internationally recognised site that is synonymous with the Nobel Peace Prize winner. The Eastern Cape Province is also home to the Nelson Mandela Bay stadium, which was constructed for $159 million ahead of the 2010 World Cup and sits 48,000 people. At least thirty streets and over thirty places in South Africa are named after Mandela.

Nelson Mandela born 18 July 1918, died of a lung infection at the age of 95 on December 5, 2013. When he passed away, all front pages of the local and internal news reporters combed corners of their memory to find the right words to describe him. Sekandi said that, "Mandela was an embodiment of humanity regardless of colour or social strata and stood as a giant and hero adding that his simplicity and statesman hood drew the world together to appreciate Mandela as a true patriot." 95 candles were lit during the funeral service to eulogize the global icon who died aged 95. Mandela's casket was buried at his family plot in his rural boyhood home of Qunu, watched by his widow Graca Machel, ex-wife Winnie Madikizela-Mandela, other family members and around 450 selected guests.

The award to Archbishop Desmond Tutu was motivated by the desire to make an extraordinary grant to an outstanding African civil society champion. Archbishop Desmond Tutu is and has throughout his life been one of Africa's great voices for justice, freedom, democracy and responsible, responsive government. In everything he stands for, says, and does, he displays a consistent determination to give a voice to the voiceless and to speak the uncomfortable truth.

Of course we cannot ignore the deceased African leaders who fought for the independence of their countries. There are freedom days celebrating the lives and contribution of some of the world's remarkable people conspicuously referred to as struggle heroes. It takes selfless effort and commitment to be inducted into this hall of fame. Also, the sincere liberators like Mawalimu Julius Nyerere who sacrificed a lot for the free world. He savoured being a teacher, that is why he carried the title Mwalimu (Kiswahili for teacher). Unlike many of his ilk, he abhorred gratification and self-aggrandizement. In January 1961, the late Mwalimu Julius Kambarage Nyerere made clear that he was willing to delay the independence of Tanganyika, to coincide with that of Kenya and Uganda—with the three new states later merging into a federation. This revolutionary spirit was to later inspire Nyerere's consistent militant support for the African liberation movement.

In Africa we have women with powerful stilettos who have the inspirational and transformational leadership qualities contemplated by the award criteria. I mean ladies like Ellen Johnson Sirleaf and Joyce Banda rocking our international media and leading their countries. Also Lady Justice Julia Ssebutinde presiding over the International Court of Justice which has given Uganda a lot of credibility. The Speaker of Uganda Parliament Rt. Hon. Rebecca Kadaga was among eight women from all over Africa who were awarded with the prestigious African Influential Amazon Award 2012. It was during the All Africa Women Leader's Dinner held in Nairobi Kenya. She was recently elected chairperson of the Commonwealth Women Parliamentarians International body. Margret Zziwa the first Ugandan female Speaker of the East African Parliament. Margret Mungherera is the first Ugandan female to chair the World Medical Council. Both of them have been awarded with honorary PhDs in recognition of their historical achievements. Their success projects that women are very particular and can execute well if given the right tools and support.

I want to take this opportunity to acknowledge some of the people who have influenced our communities even though they are not universally recognized. Nnabagereka Nagginda is considered a maternal figure for the Baganda. Ekisaakaate (Royal Enclosure) is perhaps the most popular program we have today. It promotes cultural values, leadership, spiritual and practical skills for the children from six to nineteen years. It is held as a two-week residential camp every year. She is the beacon of hope for the Pearl of Africa where almost everybody else thinks tribal, religion and what they will put in their pockets. The queen (Nnabagereka), has been central to giving back to society under her Nnabagereka Development Foundation with her main concern revolving around early childhood care and development, girl-child education, vocational training and employment for the youth, empowerment of women, health issues particularly regarding the prevention and cure of childhood diseases, nutrition, and sexual reproductive health including the prevention of HIV/AIDS.

Dr. Lwanga's name does not appear anywhere in the world renowned free encyclopedia, Wikipedia. He is neither an inventor nor a noble prize winner but he definitely scoops the man of the century's accolade; he demonstrated dedication to a cause that betters the world around him, or commitment to use his professionalism for a higher cause. The late Dr.Lwanga put an everlasting impression on the social scene in one of the most impoverished neighborhoods of the country. He was a gentleman of high esteem and value. We can learn from him that development is not about becoming a celebrated public figure but joining the poor in the village to cry with them. True humility is seeing the poor as those who represent God. God gives us an opportunity to know him more through the poor and those suffering. We must see the poor not as objects of charity, but people from whom we can learn.

Dr. Lwanga was successful as a person and he has much to show in terms of using his much celebrated professionalism to contribute to development outside his comfort. He is another wonderful role model for young people with larger than life aspirations. He is definitely an outstanding hero! An Inspiration for a Lifetime! I am privileged to be among multitudes mourning his passage. Indeed death is a bad harvester. May his soul rest in peace (RIP).

By the time I heard the news of his demise, I was at home. I flipped the pages of our national and local newspapers in search of script on the tragedy news but to my surprise none of the leading newspapers eulogized Dr. Lwanga. I was not surprised because today the moral people like Dr. Lwanga are not given space on the front pages of our news media. The media is obsessed with reporting the dirty of the societies rather than promoting the moral values. Real scholars are looked down upon while Crowd Pullers are eulogized and honored. It seems that the media is only highlighting what now appears as the accepted and glorified absurdities in society. The media has turned the worst of the societies into heroes; I mean the ilk of Gaetano, Bad Black, Maama Fina, Naalule and etc. No wonder immoral and rude behaviors in this country, across a wide spectrum of society seem to be on an upward spiral. I think it is worthwhile to bring awareness to the reader the decadence and its consequences but we must be careful not to recklessly promote the nuisance.

Whilst eulogizing our heroes, we should be sincere to use the same criteria (yardstick) of acceptable biblical morality. I like the tradition of burning the effigies in the likeness of the celebrities who end up living disgraceful lives. Towns across Britain light bonfires and set off fireworks on Nov. 5 to commemorate Guy Fawkes' failed plot in 1605 to blow up Parliament. The bonfires are traditionally topped with an effigy of Fawkes but have been decorated with contemporary figures over recent years. Previous Edenbridge effigies include comedian Russell Brand and soccer star Wayne Rooney. The fall from grace in less than a month of two icons of Sport—Lance Armstrong and Oscar Pistorius (both men who seemingly overcame unbelievable adversity) has disproved once and for all that sacred Nietzscheian canon: there is no superman. Man cannot rise above his base limitations. In other words, we may have wings of the finest gold, diamond hands and platinum heads, but these will always rest on feet of clay.

They is nothing wrong with being famous for the right cause. Some of us have attained widespread fame based on something noble (like Mother Teresa). Some of us have attained widespread fame because of something sinister (like Jerry Sandusky or Adolf Hitler who was the nastiest, most hate-filled, almost wickedest man in history). It's one thing to be famous, but another to be famously despised. The apostles were roundly despised by their Jewish culture as a consequence of their leadership within the fledgling Christian community. They were admired by even their persecutors because of their perseverance. In spite of hardship none of them recanted his testimony.

Dr. Lwanga was not insignificant, at least judging by the number of people who turned up in shovels to hold a vigil at his home and at his funeral to give him a hero's send off. Swarms of sympathizers camped outside his house bewailing. I have never heard somebody making a negative remark or writing a derogatory story about the life of Dr. Lwanga; not because Africans restrain themselves to publically make bad comments concerning a dead person but because he was naturally a resourceful and respected person. He was kind of man who adhered to the law and his professional code of ethics. He was principled. Principled people make a stand regardless, that's what Martin Luther King, Ghandi and Nelson Mandela did. "Happy are those who dream dreams and are willing to pay the price to make them come true".

Dr. Lwanga did not make astounding statements in press but his actions spoke louder than words. He deserves an establishment in memorial of his life. I suggest that we build a mausoleum to commemorate his life. I mean something that will evoke every person with fonder memories of the late Dr. Lwanga. This will help to teach the future generations that it pays to be an asset rather than a liability to the community. We have a generation of people who get mesmerized by the strength and mighty of others but who are indifferent to building their own. "The bravest know fear but they do not yield to it . . . . the world owes its progress to the men who have dared . . . . Men erect no monuments and weave no laurels for those who fear to do what they can"—Erick Ngilangwa.

Apart from the historical tombs of the kings, cemeteries may not be the most obvious tourist attractions, but they can provide a fascinating glimpse into the past. Cemeteries are great destinations for thrill-seeking travelers. They provide a peek into the past (history) and can hint at the deceased's legacy—all the while providing some great fodder for stories to tell.

People are looking for the final resting places of their heroes because they want to pay their respects to our nation's heroes. I want to caution that let us have an interest in visiting the cemeteries for historical purposes only rather than for spiritual fulfillment. The cemeteries around the country should provide visitors with unique, enriching, and occasionally spine-tingling adventures as opposed to haunted Gardens of Evil whereby you may have to dodge unearthly spirits as you wander among the historic headstones and monuments.

The teaching of future generations was the central purpose not only of physical monuments, but of the numerous memorable events and holy days. In 1942, at the height of the war in Europe, Mordechai

Shenhavi, a member of Kibbutz Mishmar Ha'emek, proposed to the board of the Jewish National Fund that a monument be erected to Holocaust victims. His proposal referred to commemorating the Holocaust that occurred in the Diaspora and the participation of the Jewish People in the Allied armies." Shenhavi also proposed the name Yad Vashem, which is taken from the Bible: "And I will give them, in My House, and within My walls, a monument and a name (yad vashem). Better than sons or daughters, I will give them an everlasting name which shall not perish" (Isaiah 56:5).

His suggestion was carried out only after the Knesset passed the Law of Remembrance of Shoah and Heroism—Yad Vashem in 1953, which inter alia decreed that a government authority be established to commemorate the Holocaust and its heroes. Israel is the only country to have a law requiring official commemoration of the Holocaust, evidence of the centrality of the Holocaust in the State's collective cultural experience. Yad Vashem, the Holocaust Martyrs' and Heroes' Remembrance Authority, is situated on Har Hazikaron (the Mount of Remembrance) in Jerusalem.

Today, some Jews have tattoos permanently inked on their bodies to remind them of the Holocaust, which was the systematic, bureaucratic, state-sponsored persecution and murder of approximately six million Jews by the Nazi regime and its collaborators. "All my generation knows nothing about the Holocaust," said Ms. Sagir, 21, who has had the tattoo for four years. "You talk with people and they think it's like the Exodus from Egypt, ancient history. I decided to do it to remind my generation: I want to tell them my grandfather's story and the Holocaust story."

God instructed the Israelites to observe certain days in remembrance for His works among them and His covenants established with them. The Sabbath is the seventh day (Saturday) in remembrance of resting after creation. Perhaps the most famous memorial "holiday" in the Bible is the Passover, which was commemorated annually to remind each Israelite generation of one of the most defining moments in their history—their redemption from the Egyptian slavery.

Jesus initiated the new covenant by celebrating the Last Supper on the eve of His crucifixion (On the evening before his death). Jesus observed his last Passover meal and after the meal, He instituted the 'Last Supper' (Mark 14:17-26; Luke 22:7-39). He asked us to celebrate Communion Service in remembrance of His perfect sacrifice on our behalf; also in anticipation of His Second Coming. Whenever we celebrate we proclaim His death and resurrection, this being the greatest way of preaching the Gospel.

So far we have discussed that it is biblical to build monuments for the people who inspired us and who contributed to the development of our communities as long such monuments do not become shrines to cater for the spiritual needs of the living people. Monuments can be established in memorial of the dead heroes and to recognize the living heroes. Monuments emotionally connect us to the accomplishments of our heroes. We cannot overlook the fact that history, like nature, celebrates only those that run to frontiers and horizons of glory.

Even the worst of the societies (notorious people) have monuments in their honor undeservingly. For example Gadhafi Mosque in Old Kampala, which is one of the biggest mosques in Africa, is a must see. It is a reminder of Uganda's notorious leader Idi Amin Dada, who initiated the idea of its establishment and his bosom friend Muamar Qaddafi of Libya, who completed its construction. If the worst of the society can be recognized, I am wondering why the cream of the societies (very important people) in particular the civil servants such as judges, doctors, teachers, civil right activists, and policemen, among others, their rewarding and remuneration remain sadly low despite offering great service to the nation. Don't we have obligation to remember them for their contributions to our communities?

I give credit to the town board of Bombo (my home town) for naming one of the streets in my home town after my dad (Israel Kyeyune). I suggest that the people of Bombo town honor the late Dr. Lwanga with a monument in honor for his contribution to the development of our area. Some of us (fairly independent—minded citizens) know the immense sacrifice he gave of himself to our communities, when he put his very life in harm's way. He used his professionalism to save the lives of many people. He inspired many people. He taught the people that suffering is not the end of life but you can make your dreams come true whatsoever through hard-work. I think I am not asking for too much; my enthusiasm is advocating something credible. Baganda people old adage says that, *"Ebirwa byerabirwa . . ."* simply put: "Today's events will long be forgotten tomorrow."

I know if Dr. Lwanga was alive, this would not sit well with his simple side of the man. He was kind of a successful individual who didn't take himself too seriously, and would shun any form of grandstanding or having his name plastered on things. But we must do it because we need his spirit and attitude of serving to linger. We can do something like a simple Dr. Lwanga charity or scholarship in recognition of the man's tireless efforts. Also, to inculcate in Ugandans the spirit of love and dedication to serving. This is how we can continue his legacy to live forever among every household for generations to come. Just a piece thought.

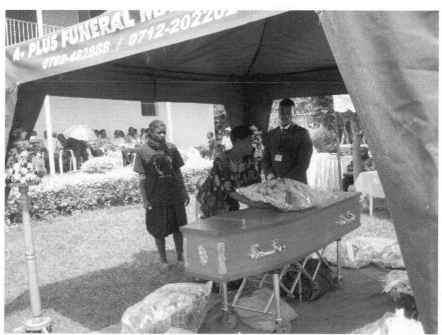

Widow Christine laying Wreath on the
Casket of the Late Dr. Lwanga

The Cocoon of Religiosity

The term religiosity should not be interpreted to mean religion or any one particular denomination. It is in reference to an attitude of doing things in a ritualistic manner without the sincerity of a clean and transformed heart. It is doing our little things hoping to earn salvation. Religiosity is seeking salvation in our own ways other than the prescribed way of God.

Every person (theistic or atheistic) is by nature religious in one way or another because every person with sound minds has something he or she believes in. People are programmed to look for things that coincide with their beliefs, leading to a perpetual biasness. Colloquially, people are looking to disprove the beliefs opposite of theirs, and are looking for explanations to apologetically defend what they believe without the proper tools. Others are just looking for something to believe in.

It is possible for any person including genuine Christian believers to slip off the track into the illusion of religiosity. The people who are consumed with the spirit of religiosity lack sincerity, unless when they are sincerely wrong. They believe that superstition has something to offer to the world. The spirit of religiosity is primarily detected in two groups of people: In the first group are people who think that they must do something in order for them to be accepted by God (legalism). They do things out of obligations rather than out of affection for God. In the second group are those people who think that after they become Christians they can live as they want regardless of the sanctioning of the Scriptures. There is no manifestation in their lives of piety. They think that the grace of God means deliberate disobedience to God with impunity. They ignore the commandments of God at their peril (for their destruction). There is no difference between their lives and the lives of the non-believers.

Religiosity causes people to confess Christ but when denying the transforming power of the Gospel. They might be regular Church goers, Bible hampers, radical fanatics and etc., but their lives do not reflect the character of God. There is no virtue in their lives. They claim to be Christians but detest the necessity to be born again. To be born again means acquiring a new heart that pulsates with life and affection for God.

The inherited sin causes us to rebel against God. We are not recruited into rebellion against God but we are born naturally rebels. We are all born with the same malady. Love for God (affection for Christ) is not natural to us unless it is born into us. We are born loving the corrupt world and the corrupt 'self' more than the creator.

Jerry Marcus, the famous brain scientists made this comment concerning the functioning of the minds: "The initial organization of the brain does not rely much on experience—nature provides a first draft, which experience then revises—'Built-in' does not mean unamiable, it means organized in advance of experience." (*Marcus, 2004*). If Marcus mentioned an assumption of being born with a "clean slate" it is not so. The Bible says that, "The heart is deceitful above all things and beyond cure. Who can understand it?" (Jeremiah 17:9). Man is born with a self-centered nature that is hostile to the divine. Except that God made the way for us to come out of our mess.

The neuroplasticity of the human brain means that no one has a static mind and all can overcome intellectual stumbling blocks if given enough time and care. I want to warn that it is improper to determine the spiritual status of man on the basis of human development paradigm. The corruption of sin had serious impact on our physical, psychological and spiritual capabilities. Natural growth makes us accountable for our mistakes but cannot rectify the spiritual defect; rules and experiences can restrain sin but none of these can eradicate the corrupt nature that causes us to sin. Only God can intervene to clean the heart by transforming it into a new nature.

A cleaned heart still rides in a corrupt body that has potentiality of influencing our decisions. That is why we are sneaky rebels with tendencies of hiding in our religions to do things in our own ways. There is a tendency of disregarding the conviction of the Holy Spirit through the Scriptures and then justify our rebellions to be sanctioned by the doctrine and dogma, the explication and officially acceptable version of a religious teaching. We feel secure to walk in errors as long as they are accepted by our religions. Religion is a matter of opinions rather than the truth.

I want to say that a person cannot be saved by his or her religion. Religion is a vehicle allowing us to embrace the truth but not the end in itself. A nonbeliever must be spiritually transformed by receiving Jesus Christ. The goal of every transformed believer should be to experience spiritual maturity. The spirit of religiosity hinders us to achieve the same goals. The spirit of religiosity is alive in the Church. You can attend Church regularly, read the Bible quite often, listen to sermons on tapes, read theological books, magazines and personal letters correctively but as long as you deliberately refuse to have open minds to the Scriptures and allow the Holy Spirit to teach you His Word, you cannot experience spiritual maturity. The spirit of religiosity is unteachable. The people victimized by the same spirit assume to know it all.

The spirit of religiosity follows blindly. It is possible to follow others when they are wrong. We should never allow others to tell us what to believe without checking them out. In this case others may be our parents, religious leaders, the majority and etc. Jesus promised to send the Holy Spirit to guide us into all truth. The truth is in the Scriptures. The Scriptures mean what they say. Thank God that we all have access to the Scriptures. Gone are the days when the priests claimed to have the sole access to the Scriptures, barricading the lay people the same access. Thank God for the Reformers that propagated changes sustaining the status quo.

Pope Francis I's papacy has proved to be liberal to its uttermost. In July, he told journalists that, "If someone is gay and is searching for the Lord and has good will, then who am I to judge him?" Recently the Pope said that atheists can go to heaven: "You ask me if the God of the Christians forgives those who do not believe and who do not seek the faith. I start by saying—and this is the fundamental thing—that God's mercy has no limits if you go to Him with a sincere and contrite heart. The issue for those who do not believe in God is to obey their conscience," he wrote in an open letter, to the founder of the La Repubblica newspaper, Eugenio Scalfari in September. He added, "Sin, even for those who have no faith, exists when people disobey their conscience." (*jabimanyi@ug.nationmedia.com*)

Suddenly, the Pope, it seemed had thrown a spanner in the works, at the possibility of countering plain scripture. It is okay if you did not believe in God, he said—as long as you are obeying your conscience. And by this, the Pope not only was he saying that atheists, who are true to their conscience, may indeed get to heaven, he was also implying that Christian believers, who are not true to their conscience, have no place in heaven. Now consider that the custodian of the biggest Christian sect on earth, the pope, whose opinion on Christian doctrine is unquestionable for many, thinks that it is actually okay for one not to believe in God. Certainly, it is possible for one's conscience to drive them to believe that there is no God or to believe in other gods. When writing in his epistle to Timothy in the Bible, Paul talks about those with a "good conscience, something that may point to the possibility of the existence of more than one form of conscience.

Most religious people claim to follow their hearts. It is possible to be sincerely wrong by following your heart. Just because you believe something does not necessarily make it to be true. The greatest lie of the devil is that your beliefs constitute the truth. The danger of such mentality is that we have everybody claiming the right of conscience without having the essentials constituting to the truth and without experiencing the discipline of the revealed truth. There is so much untruth being delivered to a bewildered world.

To most modern people, the idea that some things are true in all places and all times does not make sense. In fact it is considered to be narrow minded! I think to say that, "there is no absolute truth" is self-refuting because the statement is itself a claim of absolute truth. The reality is that the truth is absolute and is independent of our beliefs. We either embrace the truth as given by the Scriptures or we remain lost in our rebellion. If the truth was relative (depending on us) then there would have been no absolute standard of obedience because everybody could have been obedient in his own way. We believe that God has an absolute standard of righteousness; He is going to judge us by the same standard.

The true Christian faith is underpinned on the doctrine of a supernatural being (God) that oversees the creation of the universe up to Judgment day—when the world will supposedly end. I want to emphasize that believing in the existence of God is a requirement in order to become a Christian, but believing in the existence of God doesn't make you a Christian. You can admit that someone or something exists and still not be willing to have anything to do them. Believing must be accomplished by investing your faith in the finished works of Jesus Christ.

God predetermined the spiritual laws (truth) in the same manner He predetermined the laws of nature (gravity). We operate in this universe in accordance to the laws of nature, which we may violate at our peril. For example you cannot jump from the roof of the house believing that you will not fall down. The reason is because you are not God. God alone can naturally defile the physical laws of nature. Whenever God defiles the physical laws of nature we call it a miracle. Again, God set up natural and spiritual laws for us to observe when functioning in the physical and spiritual realms. The same laws depend on His sovereignty and character. We are called to obey God for our convenience.

Given the fact, God is not a dictator out there, forcing us to obey Him in order to hurt us. He is loving. He gives us commandments to obey for our own benefit. Truth and Love are synonymous. The world would have been the best place if all people lived in accordance to the commandments of God. By His love He reached out to us when we did not have a way out. There would have been no fear of any kind and no need of jails. The world is in mess because of our rebellions. We are naturally rebellious creatures trying to do things our own ways! The problem is that our ways are not God's ways, and our ways cannot save us. God provided the only way out of our miseries. The truth is God's providence that connects us to God to be like Him. We are regenerated in Christ who is the very image of God. No wonder Paul wrote that, "Nor height, nor depth, nor any other creation, shall be able to separate us from the love of God, which is in Christ Jesus our Lord" (Romans 8:39).

I want to say with confidence that nothing justifies rebellion. Before sticking to your beliefs, have you ever asked yourself what God wants you to believe? At the end of the day, God's will only will prevail. Remember that there is an appointed time when your body will be laying in the casket, without the ability to say yes or no even to an insignificant thing like a worm. At that moment you will be at the mercy of the creator; your believing in God or not won't make an iota of a difference. Thinking about death downsizes every one's ego. If you think that you are great, remember that cemeteries are full of the so called great intellectual men of this world. None of them resisted death. The only ones who have power to overcome death are the ones who have embraced God's plan of salvation.

It is delusional, to think that this life with its baggage is the only thing that counts. Also, it is a deception to think that everything rights itself in the end, without the intervention of the creator. The truth is that God created the universe because He has interest in what He created. He monitors what he created and He perfects what He created for His own glory. May be you say that, "I don't believe in that". It does not matter what you believe because your believing or not believing does not change the reality.

The truth is what connects man to God. This is a law to which there is no exception. Jesus said that He is the way, the life and the truth (John 14:6). There is an absolute truth because there is a sovereign and supreme God. This truth is not only truthfulness in word, but truthfulness in thought also, and not only the relative truth of our conception, but the Absolute Truth, the Eternal Principle that is God. There is a way to know God and there is a life of obedience manifested by those who know Him. That way is in Christ alone.

The redemptive aspect dictates that God provided the redeemer. The Bible says that, "For there is one God and one mediator between God and men, the man Christ Jesus" (1 Timothy 2:5). God chose the way to reconcile the world to Himself. His way is independent of human will and is not subject to discussion. There is no obedience outside His way. His way leads to spiritual transformation. Redemption involves recreation. In Christ we are new creatures (2 Cor. 5:17). None of the religious leaders of the world claimed to give eternal life; but Jesus claimed it and proved it.

I said, God's way is the truth. Jesus called it the narrow but the only way to salvation. It is narrow because only a handful of people find it. God is not restrained by numbers or majority: He destroyed the universe and saved just the family of Noah. He destroyed Sodom and saved just the family of Lot. It is either His way or no way. His way is open to people of all races, gender and classes. The Christians are not born Christians but they are converts from all religions of the world. God's way is not discovered by only the intellectuals but it is revealed to every person willing to obey; all of us have the same access to God through Jesus Christ; the same access is called the truth. God's way is at times a matter of no-sense to the wise people of the world. The Bible says that, "Where is the wise man? Where is the scholar? Where is the philosopher of this age? Has not God made foolish the wisdom of the world?" (1 Cor. 1:20). God gave us natural wisdom to use for His glory but His wisdom made way for even our foolishness to accept Him and be saved.

The Bible says that God is incomprehensible, but it also declares that God is knowable. To say that God is incomprehensible simply means that finite man cannot know everything there is to know about God who is an infinite being. We cannot contain the infinite God into our finite minds. To say that God is knowable means that, though incomprehensible, God can be known and man can grow in the knowledge of God, at least in a limited sense and to the degree that is needed for man to trust God and have a personal and growing relationship with Him.

To say that God is incomprehensible does not mean we should believe God's Word blindly without understanding. Nothing enrages and infuriates me more than the nascent insistence by some religious voices that we "must believe some things without understanding". Why would God create man with such sharp instincts if we were to disregard them? God gave us brains to facilitate our understanding but believing goes beyond natural comprehension into trusting God.

The life transforming nature of Christianity can't be credited to the strength of our belief but only to the power of the cross! If anything was ever antithetical to the "self esteem movement", the Gospel is. The spirit of religiosity admires the resurrection but rejects the suffering of the Cross. Emulation of Christ's life and teaching is possible only to those who enter into a new relationship with God through faith in Jesus as their substitute. Jesus said that we must take up our cross and follow him. We cannot get straight to the resurrection without the Cross. The cross is the heart of Christianity. The cross represents the temporary suffering we encounter with hope. If you lack the centrality of the cross all your theology collapses.

The Gospel is the greatest story ever told. We can know God because He has entered into our imperial phenomena reality. We can know God by intimately relating to Jesus Christ. This is the closest we can come to the knowledge of God. Jesus said that He came to reveal the Father (Luke 10:22). The Gospel reveals to us the loving Father. Apart from the Gospel, God is known as the merciless judge that righteously condemns the sinner. No one in sound minds would like to meet God when he or she is not in Christ because it means condemnation. God is a consuming fire: this is the kind of God all ways (apart from Christ) lead to. The way of Jesus leads to God the Father but all other ways lead to God the Judge.

A healthy relationship with God must begin with using our minds to acknowledge God (awareness). Every person was created with ability to acknowledge who God is. The awareness of God must progressively grow into seeking to know Him by His revelation, which then matures into a deeper personal experience of knowing Him intimately by receiving Jesus Christ.

Awareness of God is acknowledging the unknown creator. Mankind cannot discover God by natural means because God reveals Himself supernaturally to mankind. A non-regenerated man is dead in his sins. Dead means corpus; he is totally helpless; he cannot know God on his own (Ephesians 2:1; Colossians 2:13). The impact of sin disabled man's ability to know God. Without the help of God, man is doomed forever and ever. Without God opening our spiritual eyes we cannot see God. We end up worshipping the gods of our own imaginations. Our only hope is in heaven. We are doomed whenever heaven close up in silence. We are blessed when heaven opens up and speak to us. The Bible says that in the last days God has spoken through His Son to us (Hebrews 1:2).

The instruments for the quest of Truth are as simple as they are difficult. They may appear quite impossible to an arrogant person, and quite possible to an innocent child. Truth is found by those who are broken, humble and who have an abundant sense of humility. If you want to swim on the bosom of the ocean of Truth, you must reduce yourself to a zero. Self-denial is the principal doctrine of the manifesto of the kingdom of God.

Many people out there falsely claim to be the sole custodians of the truth. Various religions claim to know and to have the truth. The question is how do we separate the genuine from the false ones? The Bible says that we shall know them by their fruits. Those who have known the truth manifest the godly characters revealing the only one that is true, even our Lord Jesus Christ.

I mentioned that there is a tendency for a fallen man to find comfort in religions, like doing what others are doing without questioning the validity of their beliefs. They follow blindly without checking out their beliefs to see if they are biblical or not. Others blindly follow the religions of their parents without questioning them. Their loyalty is to a religious institution rather than God.

I want to say that we are all accountable to God individually. The security we have is in Christ alone. Other forms of securities like our religions which tolerate unbiblical values are temporary; they will not cover us when we stand before the throne of God. A successful search for Truth means complete deliverance from the dual throng such as escapism and religiosity. That is when a person focuses on Jesus Christ and His Word (Bible), for guidance. Don't get me wrong. I am not saying that it is wrong to belong to your denomination. It is ok to belong to your Christian religion as long as you embrace the full Gospel. I mean reading the Word of God in its totality without prejudice and heeding. God did not approve any one religion in the Scriptures. Jesus said that "whoever does the will of my Father in heaven is my brother and sister and mother" (Matthew 12:50). Jesus said that: "Not everyone who calls me "Lord, Lord' will enter the Kingdom of heaven, but only those who do what my Father in heaven wants them to do" (Matthew 7:21-22). The Christians manifest the fruits of salvation in their good works (godliness). Their characters point to Christ the Christian maker. They call Jesus Lord (Master) and obey His commandments.

I want to emphasize that the saving knowledge of God involves the intimate knowledge of Jesus Christ. It is impossible to know God intimately without the help of God. Throughout the history of the Church there have been anti-Christian ideas that have been recycled in our teachings. They did not come and go but came to stay. I am going to outline and elaborate on some of common anti-Christian beliefs within the doctrines of some denominations.

Theistic innatism: It is a belief that children are born believing in God or that every person is a theist until taught otherwise. It is a belief that the atheists are simply in denial. There is inconsistency in this teaching. Children have to reach the maturity age of accountability in order for them to acknowledge the existence of God. They must hear the Gospel in order to know God intimately and receive the saving grace. The Bible instructs us in this way: "Train a child in the way he should go, and when he is old he will not turn from it" (Proverbs 22:6).

Rationalism: In rationalism reason becomes the sole guide in discovering and learning about God whether in Scripture or in nature. The error of rationalism is that the supernatural is generally explained away by human reason. Rationalism, as a belief, is biased against the supernatural, i.e., the supernatural is irrational to the human mind and must be rejected. Although we can acknowledge the existence of God by our rational judgment, rationalism cannot yield to salvation.

In Matthew 18:3 Christ said, "I tell you the truth, unless you change and become like little children, you will never enter the kingdom of heaven" (NIV). Children humbly accept a lot of things as true by faith, but always because they have confidence in a person, parent, or teacher. So with faith all biblical facts are accepted because of an underlying faith in God's person and then in God's Word. Faith begins with someone higher and greater than ourselves where rationalism and empiricism do not. They begin and end with man.

Faith is the means by which we understand spiritual phenomenon. Spiritual phenomenon is an infinite subject beyond the experience and reason of man. But faith is an infinite means of perception which alone is able to grasp the infinite. By the faith means of perception, a person reads the Bible, sees a fact of spiritual phenomenon and accepts it by faith. This becomes spiritual fact or truth by which an individual operates and has confidence. Faith is the primary and Biblical means of perception (Heb. 11:3 "by faith we understand").

Does a person of faith has to disengage his brain in neutral? Is faith means of perception? Faith as a means of perception is not irrational, nor unreasonable, nor without evidence. So we read in Scripture that nature sings out the fact of God, giving constant evidence not only for the reality of God, but for something of the nature of God (Ps. 19:1-6; Rom. 1:19-20). The Bible holds fantastic evidence that its source is in God and that God has given us this book without error.

The Bible says that, "The weapons we fight with are not the weapons of the world. On the contrary, they have divine power to demolish strongholds." (2 Corinthians 10:4). The Greek word for "stronghold" is prison. To have freedom you must first acknowledge the bondage (slave to sin). The purpose and power of Scripture is to reveal Jesus to set the captives free. Unlike any other document in the world, the Word of God has the power to speak into our heart and transform our lives. But it's not what we know that changes us. It's who we know! (*For further study on this subject please read my book called "The Miracle at Prairie Avenue". Other books I recommend: Evidence Demands a Verdict, by Josh McDowell, Campus Crusade*).

<u>Secularism</u>: A concept related to the separation of state and religion. Secularity is the state of being free from religious or spiritual qualities. For instance, eating a meal, playing a game, or bathing are examples of secular activities, because there is nothing inherently religious about them. Saying a prayer or visiting a place of worship are examples of non-secular activities.

An approximate synonym for secular is worldly in the sense "this worldly", although from a Christian point of view, "secular" may be used as contrast to "spiritual". The root word of secular is saeculum, which in fact refers to the passage of time rather than a physical place or thing. Thus that which is secular can be more accurately thought of as taking place within time, rather than in relation to eternity.

Secularism has two distinct meanings. 1) It asserts the freedom of religion, and freedom from religion, within a state that is neutral on matters of belief, and gives no state privileges or subsidies to religions. 2) It refers to a belief that human activities and decisions should be based on evidence and fact, and not superstitious beliefs, however devoutly held, and that policy should be free from religious domination. For example, a society deciding whether to promote condom use might consider the issues of disease prevention, family planning, and women's rights. A secularist would argue that such issues are relevant to public policy-making, whereas Biblical interpretation or church doctrine should not be considered and are irrelevant. We are not supposed to be secular but we are trying to be secular. Relativism is the offspring of secularism.

<u>Liberalism</u>: Liberal Christianity, Progressive Christianity or Liberalism is movement of Christianity that is characterized by these points; diversity of opinion; less emphasis on the literal interpretation of Scripture; an intimate, personal, and sometimes ambiguous view of God; wider scope in their views on salvation (including universalist beliefs); non-traditional views on heaven and hell; an emphasis on inclusive fellowship and community; an embracing of higher criticism of the Bible. The conservatives believe in the church doctrine that says: "as it was, now is and forever, Amen". This statement is one of the fundamentals of idealism. It is a belief that the world was fixed by God to be as He intended it to be. Liberalism opposes idealism.

The liberals believe adjusting the scriptures to the emerging social and physical evolution.

We must be careful of the liberal theology and thinking that is aimed at promoting humanism at the expense of Christianity. The liberal thing revolves on the sense of perspective and the scrutiny of the world around them, anything that doesn't conform to the worldview is rejected. Among the Liberals, the "right" and "left" labels are swapped across the pond; just to make things more confusing. The liberal thinking is responsible for our drop in morality. Unfortunately, we are swiftly following the countries in Western Europe, where the educational systems are far more liberal. The Bible is increasingly becoming irrelevant to our values.

Dominionism: It is a tendency among Protestant Christian evangelicals and fundamentalists that encourages them to not only be active political participants in civic society, but also seek to dominate the political process as part of a mandate from God. This highly politicized concept of dominionism is based on the Bible's text in Genesis 1:26: "And God said, Let us make man in our image, after our likeness: and let them have dominion over the fish of the sea, and over the fowl of the air, and over the cattle, and over all the earth, and over every creeping thing that creepeth upon the earth." (King James Version).

The vast majority of Christians read the above text and come to conclusion that God has appointed them stewards and caretakers of Earth. However, some Christians wrongly interpret the scripture to mean that Christians alone are Biblically mandated to occupy all secular institutions until Christ returns. That, in a nutshell, is the idea of "dominionism." The belief originated in America out of fear that her greatness as God's chosen land has been undermined by liberal secular humanists, feminists, and homosexuals. I want to say that whereas it is true that political views should be shaped by morality and that it is the responsibility of the Christians to reclaim their countries back to God, we are called to do it through the gospel rather than politics.

<u>Humanism</u>: Humanism puts man at the center of everything, dethroning God the creator. Humanism sees no need for perfection. They claim to be faulty human beings but who need not a divine entity for guidance. Humanism promotes the power of ideas and how ideas came to permeate and influence the culture at large. One of the famous secular humanist, Paul Kurtz, died this year at the age of 82. Kurtz founded Prometheus Books, the first publishing company to print books exclusively for and about the skeptical world. Some of their books include George H. Smith's Atheism: The Case Against God and Victor Stenger's God: The Failed Hypothesis (the company's first New York Times bestseller). In addition, he founded the (currently named) Committee for Skeptical Inquiry, the Council for Secular Humanism, and the Center for Inquiry, organizations whose missions focus on spreading skepticism, reason, and Humanism.

<u>Universalism</u>: I meet many people today who are falling into the trap of universalism. The principle of "Available Light" (expounded at length by Moxey and Garrett, as well as the older Quaker concept of Inner Light) . . . that God evaluates each person's response to that truth which has been revealed to him/her. This idea basically says that no matter what you believe, you'll go to heaven as long as you are fully sincere in your faith. So whether you're a Christian, a Muslim, a Hindu, or any other faith, you'll go to heaven if you truly believe it.

Religious pluralism teaches that all ways lead to heaven. The claim of the religious pluralist is arrogant because it enforces its own belief on others. This can be incredibly arrogant, particularly if the person saying this hasn't studied all the world religions in depth and makes this blind assertion. All religions teach very different things about whom God is and how to reach Him. In fact, there is a lot of disagreement between the religions regarding the nature of God. Forcing all ways on them instead of their religious way is nothing but sheer arrogance.

And pure Universalists don't even think you have to have any belief at all. All you need is to be sincere in your own way. But here's the problem with universalism: What do you do with those who were sincere in their faith, but were sincerely wrong? Hitler was sincere in his faith that God created the white race as supreme. And the 9/11 terrorists were sincere in their faith that Allah would grant them paradise for killing infidels. So if you're truly a Universalist, you'd say those people would be in heaven.

Universalism breaks down on so many levels. So why is it so popular? Well, it's because in this postmodern age, people are afraid to claim their way is the right way. Here is my challenge to you: If someone thought drinking cyanide would make them happy, you'd have to tell them the truth that it would kill them. Why is speaking the truth to the perishing world hard? Simply speaking, the truth must be told when lives depend on it! Pastor Alistair Begg says that, "The work of preaching is the highest and greatest and most glorious calling to which anyone can ever be called." He goes on to say that "the most urgent need in the Christian Church today is for true preaching and as it is the greatest and most urgent need in the Church it is, obviously, the greatest need in the world also."

Agnosticism: This word comes from *a + gnosis* which means "not knowing." This school of thought does not deny the existence of God, but dictates that there are no sufficient grounds (i.e., rational proof or empirical proof) that God exists—or that if God does exist He can be fully known by natural brains. In reality it is an unwillingness to accept any of the sources of the knowledge of God (innate, tradition, nature, revelation), and an unwillingness to act in faith. Instead, it says I cannot know. An Agnostic says it is ok to search for the truth but as per now it is impossible to find the truth. The reason they say it is impossible to find the truth is because they do not want to submit to the truth.

Relativism: Relativism is the concept that points of view have no absolute truth or validity, having only relative, subjective value according to differences in perception and consideration. [1] The term is often used to refer to the context of moral principle, where in a relativistic mode of thought, principles and ethics are regarded as applicable in only limited context. There are many forms of relativism which vary in their degree of controversy. [2] The term often refers to truth relativism, which is the doctrine that there are no absolute truths, i.e., that truth is always relative to some particular frame of reference, such as a language or a culture (cf. cultural relativism).

Another widespread and contentious form is moral relativism. It's an argument agnostics have used for generations to discredit the credibility of orthodox Christianity. On the contrary, according to the Scriptures, there is absolute truth because there is a sovereign moral God. Truth is relative to right standard of measurement. Jesus is the ultimate standard of the truth because He is the standard of absolute morality.

Materialism: This is the system which tries to explain everything by physical causes which can be observed and understood. It denies and excludes any spiritual causes. Materialism is closely related to empiricism. It is preoccupation with or emphasis on material objects, comforts, and considerations, with a disinterest in or rejection of spiritual.

Empiricism: This is the system of pursuing knowledge through observation and experiment. In the empirical system, everything must be checked out through the senses. One must be able to smell, see, touch, hear, or taste in order to know or come to a bonafide conclusion. The empirical method or the empiricist is one who depends on experience or observation alone, without regard to theory or faith.

Christianity engages our faith. Faith involves trusting in the Word of God. Jesus is the manifested Word of God (John 1:1). True Christians put their faith in Christ. Salvation is "the gift from God." The Bible says that, "For the wages of sin is death: but the gift of God is eternal life through Jesus Christ our Lord (Romans 6:23)." Look at Ephesians 2:8, 9: "For by grace are ye saved through faith: and that not of yourselves: it is the gift of God: Not of works, lest any man should boast." Read Romans chapter five where salvation is called God's gift six times. Faith is complete confidence in someone or something expressed in a non-meritorious way. We invest our faith in the accomplished works of Jesus Christ at the cross. The Apostle Paul declares, "But God forbid that I should glory, save in the cross of our Lord Jesus Christ, by Whom the world is crucified unto me, and I unto the world" (Galatians 6:14). We are told in Titus 3:5 that, "It is not by works of righteousness which we have done, but according to His mercy He saved us."

We are not saved by works but true faith is proven by works. God is pleased by our faith. Faith without works is dead. Look at James 2:26, "For as the body without the spirit is dead, so faith without works is dead also." The knowledge (awareness) of godliness without experiencing and practicing it in the real life is empty and vain, like puffed up dry clouds of no value or usefulness (1 Cor. 8:1), (Jude 1:12). Knowledge alone can do nothing constructive until it is made alive in life experience. Knowing the Bible word without the Spirit's appropriation of it into the life is powerlessness. Intimately knowing the WORD, Christ Jesus, who abides within His people, is the source of the abundant kingdom of heaven life that is above and beyond natural life. It is the kind of knowledge that brings man back into the presence of God, where he or she is fulfilled. The same knowledge is brought about by the indwelling Spirit of God. The Christian life is Spirit led. Any knowledge without Spirit leads to hypocrisy.

I want to end by warning that some of the so called Christian denominations promote the traditions of men as opposed to the biblical doctrines. The leaders indoctrinate people into seeing what they want them to see only. The culprits read the Bible with prior beliefs and are not ready to be changed by the truth; they decided what to believe regardless of the truth. I advise you to read the Bible with an open mind. Check out various teachings before believing them. We must be aware that all of these denominations were started by men with flaw like any of us. These denominations (in error) are well funded to promote deception. "It is difficult to get a man to understand something when his salary depends on his not understanding it."—Upton Sinclair

Life after Death

Every living thing has life but God created human beings in His image and breathed into him His life. Life can be looked from the prospective of existence and living to fullness. The Greek word for "life" is zoe. This is the root of the English words "zoo" and "zoology." Zoe is used of the state of existing and being animate which is common to all mankind, whether saved or unsaved. For example, Paul says to the idol worshipping Greeks at Athens, "The God who made the world and all things in it . . . He Himself gives to all life (zoe) and breath and all things . . . for in Him we live (zao—the verb form) and move and have our being" (Acts 17:25-28). Zoe also refers to an individual person's life while on earth (Luke 16:25, Philippians 1:20, James 4:14). But in the Greek New Testament, zoe has a special meaning. It speaks of the life that is given by God through Christ Jesus to those who believe the gospel. In this usage, zoe is often modified by the adjective aionios [English: eon] which means "eternal", "everlasting", "of endless duration."

All living things have life. The prefix "bio" means life. That is why the term biology refers to the study of life. The Christian life involves much more than conscious existence. There is an experience of spiritual everlasting life that is above and beyond natural life. Scripture reveals that the source or fount of this zoe life is God the Father. Indeed, Jesus calls Him "the living [zao] Father" (John 6:57), indicating that zoe life is the very life that God has in Himself. Having life in Himself, the Father imparted this life to the Son: "For just as the Father has life in Himself, even so He gave to the Son also to have life in Himself" (John 5:26). In turn, the Son manifested this life to the world. Consider John's words: "In Him was life, and the life was the light of men, and the light shines in the darkness . . ." (John 1:4-5). Again, John says: "And the life was manifested, and we have seen and bear witness and proclaim to you the eternal life, which was with the Father and was manifested to us" (I John 1:2). Paul agrees with John's testimony. He says that God's purpose "now has been revealed by the appearing of our Savior Christ Jesus, who abolished death, and brought life and immortality to light through the gospel" (II Timothy 1:9-10).

The Bible promises life everlasting life either in the presence of God or separated from God: "Then he will say to those on his left, "depart from me, you cursed, into the eternal fire prepared for the devil and his angels." . . . And these will go away into eternal punishment, but the righteous into eternal life" (Matthew 25:41, 46).

Time in the afterlife is not an infinite for any of us. It is merely everlasting and there is a difference. God alone is infinite. He has no beginning and no end. Eternal life is life everlasting but not infinite life. Regarding eternal life, there is a beginning and the future that goes on and on without end, but it will never become infinitely long. So forever and ever means that it never comes to an end.

The physical life in this world is natural and has an end. It continues to get older and older but still has an age and therefore an end. Life goes on after the physical death of the body. A sinner will live forever in separation from God. Even though living forever and ever in this case does not mean living for an actual infinite amount of time. Hell is a place of separation, punishment to the point of none existence (II Peter 3:9-12). God has the power to destroy the soul. Jesus warned that, "And do not fear those who kill the body but cannot kill the soul. Rather fear him who <u>can destroy both soul and body</u> in hell" (Matthew 10:28). God has the right to destroy what He created. He destroys by judging.

Our natural minds cannot comprehend the extent measure of infinite with figures. The simple truth is, even though punishment in Hell is forever and ever, it can never become infinite because no one will ever endure an infinity of suffering because no one lives that long. Even though the condemned live forever and ever and ever and never die, no one suffers in Hell for an infinite amount of time. In the same manner the saved believers live eternally but not infinitely. No one enjoys Heaven for an infinite amount of time apart from God. There is no finite construction such as creation that could exist as an actual infinite. Infinite is synonymous with the divine. When we speak of the attributes of God, we are speaking of a qualitative infinite.

There is no way to fully understand the vast greatness of God. Infinity is the term man uses to describe something that cannot be counted or measured and God is surely immeasurable. Look at these scriptures: Psalm 145:3—Great is the Lord, and greatly to be praised; and his greatness is unsearchable. II Chronicles 2:5 & 6—And the house that I build is great: for great is our God above all Gods. But who is able to build him an house, seeing the heaven and heaven of heavens cannot contain him?

I think I need to explain more on the term infinite. Some people invariably dismiss the infinity to nonexistence simply because they can't understand it. Their attitude is like, "I cannot conceive in my mind of what an actual infinite would look like. Therefore, none exist." Others say "God is the infinite," without specification, the meaning would be pantheistic, equal to saying, "God is everything." I do not agree with both interpretations. I suggest that in using the word "infinite" we must always be specific. There is logic and biblical proof to support the theory of an infinite God, although I cannot offer any experimental proof in support of the theory.

Mathematicians accept that the concept of the infinite is useful in doing maths, but it's a different thing to say that an infinite set of things exist in the material world. In math, infinity is just a concept in your mind. Though the numbers we use to count may be potentially infinite, you and I are always working with finite numbers, not infinite ones. Our amounts are never equal because, no matter how much time we have neither of us can count to infinity. Every time we add one, we are still dealing with a finite number. We will never be able to get an actual infinite by adding one number after another.

Human life is within the context of finite. Human life without God is mere existence. The natural life or existence apart from God is empty and more like living death. Such life is vulnerable to natural and spiritual death. The natural death was extended to human life as a result of the divine judgment for sin. It is appointment for every living to die because of sin. The corruption of our bodies is the reality of death. The spiritual death is the separation from God brought about by sin. Emptiness is the evidence (reality) of the spiritual death. Without God, there is a void that nothing and nobody can do anything about. Emptiness is the lacking of hope because of the absence of connection to eternal life. If you asked a born again believer the meaning of emptiness, he or she will say that it is the absence of the passion of Christ in a human being.

This topic is concerning death. We discussed that sin brought the physical and the spiritual death to man. The Bible says that sin entered into the world by one man and death by sin; so death passed upon all men because of the disobedience of one man (Adam). Some people ask me this question: Where is the fairness of God to condemn the entire human race for the disobedience of Adam? The justice of God declared that eternal life should come to us by one man (Jesus Christ). The love of God imputed the righteousness of one man (Jesus Christ) to all people who believe in Him. We overcome death by acquiring the perfect life of Jesus Christ. Through Christ the immortality of God became the immortality of man.

I want to say that God is not fair but He is just and loving. Remember that even a monster can be fair in its own way. We can see the justice of God because death was imputed on mankind as a result of the sin of one man (Adam); Eternal life was imputed on man as a result of the righteousness of one man (Jesus Christ). The Bible says that, "The first man Adam was made a living soul; the last Adam was made a quickening spirit. Howbeit that was not first which is spiritual, but that which is natural; and afterwards that which is spiritual. The first man on earth is of the earth, earthly: and as is the heavenly, such are they also that are heavenly" (1 Corinthians 15:45-49).

Remember that we are not condemned because of the sin of Adam of partaking of the forbidden tree. But the inherited sinful nature of Adam (first sin) causes us to sin. We are all therefore sinners by nature deserving judgment. God saves us in spite of ourselves. Paul says that, "Christ Jesus came into the world to save sinners" (1 Timothy 1:15). We are born with corrupt intentions to sin. We are all condemned because of the broken laws of God (sins we commit).

But God provided a way out; it is by repenting and confessing our sins to Jesus Christ. The atoning power of the blood of Jesus Christ takes away our sins.

The death sentence was lifted. The Bible says that: "Therefore, there is now no condemnation for those who are in Christ Jesus" (Romans 8:1). The promise of eternal life was given to us who are living in this world, who are in Christ and who die in Christ. Jesus made this strong statement: "Verily, verily, I say unto you, If a man keeps my saying, he shall never see death" (John 8:51). The newly acquired life through Jesus Christ is God's life that is immune to death. The Bible says that, "Know you not that you are the temple of God, and that the Spirit of God dwells in you?" (I Corinthians 3:16). What? know ye not that your body is the temple of the Holy Ghost which is in you, which ye have of God, and ye are not your own? (I Corinthians 6:19). Also, "Whoever loves me (Jesus) will obey my teaching. My Father will love him and my Father and I will come to him and live with him" (John 14:23).

We need the human bodies to function in the physical world but our new nature is spirit because we are born of Spirit. Paul said that, "I have been crucified with Christ; and it is no longer I who live, but Christ lives in me; and the life which I now live in the flesh I live by faith in the Son of God, who loved me and gave Himself up for me" (Galatians 2:20). Because all humanity is bound up with Adam, so every human being has an earthly body just like Adam's. The Bible teaches that the body was created from the soil and it returns to the soil (Ecclesiastics 12:7). The Psalmists lamented that, "My soul clings to the dust; give me life according to your word" (Psalms 119:25).

Earthly bodies are fitted for life on this earth, yet they are limited by death, disease, depreciation and other weaknesses because of sin which was first brought to us by Adam. Sin does not dwell in our bodies. The heart of man is the seat for sin but our bodies were corrupted by sin. God told Moses that, "You cannot see my face, for no one may see me and live." (Exodus 33:20). Paul wrote that, "I declare to you, brothers and sisters, that flesh and blood cannot inherit the kingdom of God, nor does the perishable inherit the imperishable" (1 Cor. 15:50).

The good news is that believers can know with certainty that their heavenly bodies will be just like Christ's—imperishable, eternal, glorious, and filled with power. At this time, all are like Adam; one day, all believers will be like Christ (Philippians 3:21). The Apostle John wrote to the believers, "Dear friends, now we are children of God, and what we will be has not yet been made known. But we know that when he appears, we shall be like him, for we shall see Him as he is" (1 John 3:2). By His resurrection, Jesus turned physical death into a stepping-stone towards our glorification. The saving power is of God and the responsibility to keep us saved is of God. Pastor Alistair Begg says that, "If Jesus undertook to bring me to glory, and if the Father promised that He would give me to the Son to be a part of the infinite reward of the travail of His soul, then, my soul, until God Himself shall be unfaithful, until Jesus shall cease to be the truth, you are safe".

In the beginning God created man to live eternally. Adam had a beginning at creation but Jesus has no beginning because He is the creator rather than the creation: "For by him were all things created, that are in heaven, and that are in earth, visible and invisible, whether they be thrones, or dominions, or principalities, or powers: all things were created by him, and for him" (Colossians 1:16). Jesus existed before He came on the earth. He was with the Father in eternity. He came to reveal God to us. Jesus said that, "No man has seen God at any time; the only begotten Son, who is in the bosom of the Father, he has declared him" (John 1:18).

Jesus maintained His perfect relationship with the Father when He walked on the universe. When He died, He surrendered His Spirit to the Father: "Jesus called out with a loud voice, "Father, into your hands I commit my spirit. When he had said this, he breathed his last" (Luke 23:46). His spirit was immediately separated from His body. We know that His body was buried. After three days He rose from the dead. His Spirit was reunited with a new body. Paul said that in the same manner our bodies will be changed in the twinkling of an eye upon His return.

In Christ we earn an acceptable relationship with the Father. We are adapted into the family of God through Christ. "This prayer begins where all true prayer must start, with the spirit of adoption: "Our Father." According to the Lord's Prayer (Matthew 6:9), there is no acceptable prayer until we can say, "I will arise and go to my Father." This childlike spirit soon perceives the grandeur of the Father "in heaven" and ascends to devout adoration, "hallowed be your name." The child lisping, "Abba, Father" grows into the cherub crying, "Holy, holy, holy." There is but a step from rapturous worship to the glowing missionary spirit, which is a sure expression of filial love and reverent adoration—"your kingdom come, your will be done, on earth as it is in heaven."

Every inch of the glory that was lost in Adam is recovered in Christ. Jesus was the life giving Spirit at creation and He is the life giving Spirit at regeneration (Colossians 1:16). Christians are called witnesses to the glory of God because they have passed from death to life. Whenever we preach the Gospel we are witnessing to the power of resurrection which we have already experienced through Christ by regeneration (new birth). This is called spiritual transformation. It begins now when you are alive; when you decide to receive God's only offer to salvation (Jesus Christ).

By His death and resurrection, Jesus defeated sin which was the only hindrance to our eternal fellowship with God. In Christ we have eternity within us: The Bible says that God has "set eternity in the hearts of men" (Ecclesiastes 3:11). The human body is the veil that stands between us and the eternal glory. When physical death strikes, it simply unveils the glory behind the curtain of the human flesh. The Bible says that, "For we know that if our earthly house of this tabernacle were dissolved, we have a building of God, an house not made with hands, eternal in the heavens" (1 Cor. 5:1).

Paul said that, "—So now also Christ shall be magnified in my body, whether it be life, or by death. For to me, to live is Christ and to die is gain. If I am to go on living in the body, this will mean fruitful labor for me. Yet what shall I choose? I do not know! I am torn between the two: I desire to depart and be with Christ, which is better by far; but it is more necessary for you that I remain in the body" (Philippians 1:21-24).

In the above scripture Paul confirms that to be absent from this world is to be present with the Lord. According to Paul's words, the difference between the life here and death is not a difference between bad and good but it is the difference between good and much better. To be here is good but to be in the presence of God is much better. The main reason why Jesus wept at the grave of Lazarus is not because of grief. After all Jesus said that Lazarus was asleep and His sickness was not unto to death but for the glory of God (John 11:4). Jesus could not grief for Lazarus' death because He went with prior intention of raising him from death. Jesus wept because the mourners cared for this life and ignored the eternal life in Him.

Paul said that in Christ is the hope and the reason of his living. He was not scared of dying because it is more rewarding to die. Death means standing in the very presence of God forever. (Note) Paul does not say that to be absent from this world is to be present in heaven but rather it is to be present with the Lord. Our new life is in Christ. The Christian life is lived by faith. We must read the Scriptures and believe them as they are given to us even when we do not understand them fully. We are called to believe in things which are not seen and which cannot be figured out by our natural senses. We must have the conviction that everything will come to pass as it is written because of the authenticity of the Scriptures. My advice to the skeptics is that life is God's novel; let Him write it!

The Christian doctrine teaches that man is a spirit, soul and body: "Now may the God of peace Himself sanctify you entirely; and may your spirit and soul and body be preserved complete, without blame at the coming of our Lord Jesus Christ" (1 Thessalonians 5:23). On the contrary, philosophical materialism is a system of thought that you only believe in what you see. The theory denies the unseen matter like the conscience, spirit and soul. The questions this attitude should cause us to ask are, "Are material things really more important than anything else? Is material success the highest goal? If things are all there are, what's life all about? Why am I here at all? If life is really just about materialism, why should I even try to live a moral life? What does it matter how I treat others or how I live, as long as I have what I want? Why does what I believe about the origin of life matter? Man searches for justice in this world in vain; if there is no life beyond this world where and how will justice be served?

The vision gives us capability to focus on something bigger than ourselves and the world. Within mankind, there is a conviction of something bigger than this life; there is a conviction of justice beyond this world; there is a conviction of the source of life beyond this universe; there is a conviction of greater power than we have on this universe; there is a conviction of the perfect life that we haplessly try to imitate. The life of the people who live without Christ is characterized with emptiness. Emptiness is hopelessness. The people who commit suicide are convinced that dying is the only way of escaping the pain and emptiness of this life. We (Christians) believe that death is not a state of nonexistence. We are called to uplift each other. "Leadership is lifting a person's vision to high sights, the raising of a person's performance to a higher standard, the building of a personality beyond its normal limitations."—Peter Drucker

Paul said that, "Yea, and if I be offered upon the sacrifice of your faith, I joy and rejoice with you (Philippians 2:17). Paul rejoiced even when it means dying for the sake of the Gospel because his hope was beyond this world. He compared himself to a drink offering that is poured upon the altar, which immediately turns into vapor and rises up to God with sweet smell. The gap between heaven and earth was reduced to the blinking of an eye upon death: You close your eyes in death and you open your eyes when you are in the presence of God. Upon death, the spirit is united with the creator and the body goes into sleep until the resurrection day. Jesus dealt with the cause of death (sin) in order to eradicate the power of death. A believer is eternally united to God through Christ. Death has no power to separate a believer from God.

Here is a dilemma regarding the phenomenon of death: The dead in Christ are living whereas the living without Christ are dead. Some people whom the world considers to be dead are living whereas many of our friends whom we see daily breathing are dead. Real life is in Christ. The Bible says that: "He who has the Son has life; he who does not have the Son of God does not have life" (1 John 5:12). Also, "Whoever believes in the Son has eternal life, but whoever rejects the

Son will not see life, for God's wrath remains on him" (John 3:36). Jesus gave a true story of a rich man who was dressed in purple and fine linen and lived in luxury every day and at his gate was laid a beggar named Lazarus, covered with sores. The rich man had what he couldn't keep for ever (riches of the world) but the poor man had what could not be lost (eternal life in the presence of God) Luke 16:19-31.

Unfortunately some believers still consider death to be a curse from God released to torment them rather than a gift certificate inviting them into eternity. Often, I hear people challenging the love of God after losing their beloved ones in this way: "What sin did I commit against God for Him to take away my beloved one?" Or "why me?" Whenever you ask God such questions you are basically doubting the integrity of God. The Bible clarifies that we should trust God with all our heart and that we should not lean on our understanding (Proverbs 3:5). Questioning the integrity of God is doubting Him and leaning on your understand.

When David's firstborn son with Bathsheba became ill for days, David prayed and fasted. When the child died, David's servants were baffled by his reaction. Instead of mourning for the death of the baby, David got up, ate and worshipped God saying that he fasted hoping that God would spare the child's life but now that he is dead, he can praise God with hope to meet his son in eternity. David said, "I will go to him, but he will not return to me" (2 Samuel 12:15-24). David believed that in future he will join his son in heaven. He did not mean joining him in grave because in grave there is no consciousness. When David said that, "I will go to him" he meant a conscious reunion in the presence of God. David comforted Bathsheba and their love for each other was strong enough to overcome this tragedy. Later they were blessed with more children.

Death is a curse to a nonbeliever but it is no longer a curse to a believer because a believer has passed on from death to life (John 11:25-26). The benefit of death is our inheritance in Christ: We are co-heirs with Christ to the heavenly riches. We receive the same benefits here on the earth by faith. Jesus is not a distance source of eternal life but He is the eternal life (John 11:25; 14:6) that begins the very moment you receive Him. Every believer must have the reality of this conviction within his heart. The nonbeliever's hope stops at the grave but the hope of the believers goes beyond the grave even beyond decay (corruption). To a believer, physical death is permanent healing spiritually because death means resting in Christ and glorification at the resurrection.

One preacher said that whenever God takes a believer, it is because that believer is ready, in which case, death becomes a graduation. Simeon was not ready to die until he saw the consolation of Israel. The Bible says that, "Then he took Him up in his arms, and blessed God and said, Lord, now let thou servant depart in peace according to your word for my eyes have seen your salvation" (Luke 2:29-30). Paul said in that: "For I am ready to be offered, and the time of my departure is at hand" (2 Timothy 4:6). Departing has to do with moving from one location to another. The same word "departing" was used in reference to the transfiguration of Jesus. The transfiguration was intended to show Jesus in His glorified manner (Luke 9:29). The theme of the discussion was the departure of Jesus (ascension). The word departure (exodus) in the description of the theme of conversation between Jesus, Moses and Elijah; it is in reference to the resurrection of Jesus and His glorification.

The appearance of Jesus at the transfiguration is different from that one described after the resurrection. Mark gives an account of the ascension of Jesus in which the appearance of Jesus matches His appearance at the transfiguration (Mark 16:19). In Mark's account the place is same (Mount Olives), there is a cloud representing God's presence, there is the glory and Mark specifically mentions where Jesus is departing to—"at the right hand of God." In both incidences, there is preparation and readiness before the departure. In the same manner we (the bride) need preparations to meet our bridegroom (Jesus). In the real world, in any form of organization there are initiation rituals—orientation. Similarly, in the Ganda tradition before marrying off, a prospective bride is advised by "a senior lady" in matters relating to marriage. The Holy Spirit prepares us to present us a ready bride. Jesus was ready to depart in the same way believers should be ready to depart. The future coming of our Bridegroom is in future but will soon be highlighted in history because He is coming soon.

Jesus turned death into a gift certificate given to all believers to go into His presence. I am not trying to say that we should pray to die. I am saying that when death strikes or comes close to us we must be ready to handle it. Here is the blessed assurance: "Blessed be the God and Father of our Lord Jesus Christ, which according to His abundant mercy has begotten us again unto a lively hope by the resurrection of Jesus Christ from the dead" (1 Peter 1:3).

Regeneration means recreation. The corruptible (flesh) is consumed by the incorruptible (Spirit). Paul assured us that our real image is that of Christ: "If you then be <u>risen with Christ</u>, seek those things which are above, where Christ sitteth on the right hand of God. Set your affection on things above, not on things on earth. For you are dead, and <u>your life is hid with Christ</u> in God. When Christ, who is our life shall appear, then <u>shall you also appear with Him</u> in glory" (Colossians 3:1-4). In His high priesthood intercession, Jesus prayed that "Neither pray I for these alone but for them also which shall believe on me through the Word; That they all may be one; as thou, Father, art in me, and I in thee, <u>that they also may be one in us</u>" (John 17:20-21).

There are three persons in one God head. At creation, God made Himself known as Elohim. This name is in compound plural form rather than singular in accordance to the Jewish monotheisms. The name represents God the Father, Son and Holy Spirit working in harmony as a unit (one God) to create. When Jesus prayed that, "Let them be one as we are one" He was appealing to the union of the human spirit to the divine. Here is a mystery: He dwells in us (we are the temple of God); We are seated in the heavenly places with Him. His physical presence is at the throne in heaven but we are His spiritual body (Church) here on earth. Our life is hidden in Him; His life in us; our lives manifesting Him. This is considered to be a mystery. A mystery is something that is true but hard for the natural minds to comprehend. I do not need somebody to explain to me a mystery; I believe God's Word as He said it.

Paul told the people of Athens who worshipped the multiple pagan gods that God is as close as one's heartbeat, and at other times as far away as galaxy, yet always remains the one in whom we live and move and have our being. "God did this so that they would seek him and perhaps reach out for him and find him, though he is not far from any one of us. 'For in him we live and move and have our being.' As some of your own poets have said, We are his offspring" (Acts 17:27-28).

Paul wrote that, "For in Him dwelleth all the fullness of the God head bodily. And you are complete in Him which is the head of all principality and power: In whom you also you are circumcised with the circumcision made without hands, in putting off the body of the sins of the flesh by the circumcision of Christ: Buried with Him in baptism <u>wherein also you are risen with Him through the faith</u> of the operation of God, who has raised Him from the dead. And you, being dead in your sins and the un-circumcision of your flesh, <u>has he quickened together with Him</u>, having forgiven you all trespasses" (Colossians 2:9-13).

Salvation makes the union of God and man complete. We rule with Him in heavenly places now and we shall rule with Him after the resurrection in the new world. In Christ, our likeness with God was restored: We are the very image of God. I want to warn that the image of God in us does not turn us into gods as the New Age teaches. We are creations and we will never be God. Although Christ dwells in our temple (bodies), He retains His unique divine attributes which are foreign to mankind. He is God we are not: His sovereignty is never shared or even diminishes. He is omnipotent; He is omniscient; He is omnipresent. His attributes define who He is: His holiness is immutable; His justice is immutable; His love is immutable and etc.

God is neither a supreme being who is made up of the collective attributes added together nor is He composed of components of a little bit of every attribute. He is all together holy; all together justice; all together loving. He is a unified being. Within the diversity of the attributes there is unity because without unity (oneness) there is chaos. The fullness of God is not independent of His attributes: He is fully loving; He is full of grace; He is fully just; His holiness is perfect (complete). At the same time His love is holy and His justice is holy, gracious and immutable. God is one but with a variety of dimensions. There is unity of the variety rather than diversity. The fullness of God is portrayed in unity (oneness of God). Dr. R C. Sproul says that God is unity in diversity. He says that the word universe and university comes from a combination of two words (unity/diversity). Variety without unity means chaos or irrationality (meaningless). God is the transcendent point of unity that keeps the unity of all creation. The diversity of life and the unity of life find rest in the unity of God. Jesus is our resting place (Sabbath). We are whole and complete in Christ.

So far we have discussed that man finds his lost image of God in Christ. It is very important to know that a believer is a spirit rather than a soul. A soul comprises of the body and the natural life. A human spirit is part of us that communicates with the divine. The spirit of a fallen man was disabled by sin to communicate with God, unless we are regenerated. Believers are new creatures whose identity is in Christ.

I said that in a believer, Jesus is not the source of life but He is the very substance (eternal life). The source may be something beyond you. Jesus does not get life from somewhere and extends it to us. His Spirit dwells in us and His very presence in us is the eternal life we have: "But ye are not in the flesh, but in the Spirit, if so be that the Spirit of God dwell in you. Now if any man have not the Spirit of Christ, he is none of his" (Romans 8:9). He makes us one body (Church). He is the Bridegroom, We are His bride. The Bible says concerning such that the two are joined together to become one. The promise of eternal life is not in future but it is in present the moment you receive Jesus Christ into your heart (John 3:16). It is His resurrected life in you which has overcome death; it is His life in you that is not subject to death.

I mentioned that 'believing' is not just a formal awareness or trusting in information but it is receiving Jesus Christ into your life. The Bible says that, "But as many as received Him, to them gave He power to become the sons of God, even to them that believe on His name" (John 1:12). John 5:39, 40—"You search the scriptures, because you think that in them you have eternal life; and it is they that bear witness to me; yet <u>you refuse to come to me that you may have life.</u>

(Note) Jesus did not instruct us to come our religion but coming to Him. Religion should be a vehicle guiding you to receiving Jesus Christ. The Holy Spirit is the life of Christ in us. Obeying His Word activates His life in us.

Jesus said concerning the resurrection of the dead, "Have you not read that which was spoken unto you by God, saying, I am the God of Abraham, and the God of Isaac, and the God of Jacob? God is not the God of the dead, but of the living (Mat 22:31-32). The whole point of Christ telling the Jews that "God is not the God of the dead but of the living" is "now that the DEAD ARE RAISED . . ." They are "the children of God" only because "they are the children of the RESURRECTION" from the dead.

We have an intimate relationship with Jesus Christ that cannot be broken even by death. The teaching (doctrine) that after death a believer goes into sleep and he or she is temporarily separated from Christ for some time until the resurrection of the body is inconsistent. The biblical view is that of unbroken relationship with Christ or continuity of the personal conscious existence in the presence of Christ and in the presence of God. After regeneration, our consciousness of Christ is ever in place and cannot be broken, not even by death.

We are legally adopted into the family of God but the adoption has to be finally accomplished in future. The reason is because we have the problem of the un-redeemed body. We have to crucify it daily until God will finally change it with the resurrected immortal body. That is when we shall be removed from the presence of sin forever. Paul said that: "Because the creature itself also shall be delivered from the bondage of corruption into the glorious liberty of children of God. For we know that the whole creation groans and travails in pain together until now. And not only they, but ourselves also, which are the first fruits of the Spirit, even we ourselves groan within ourselves, waiting for the adoption, to wit, the redemption of our body" (Romans 8:21-23). Paul indicates that we are the first fruits of the Spirit (resurrected with Christ) but the final stage of adoption will take place when the corrupt bodies are glorified and the god of this world (Satan) is taken away. Our resurrected bodies will follow our spirit: There will be the new body, new world and no tempter. That is where we are heading.

Man is longing for that day when he is going to be crowned with the glory of God so that all his being will be a reflection of the glory of God (Romans 8:21). This is the same glory that was stripped of Adam after the fall and his nakedness exposed. When our Lord returns on earth all creations (the redeemed) are going to share in His glory. The lion is going to lay down with a lamb without fear. The dead in Christ wait in Christ to put on the new bodies (put off the corruption and put on the incorruptible bodies). But those who will be alive upon His return will be changed in a moment of time (1 Thessalonians 4:16-17).

Paul concludes by saying that: "For we are saved by hope: but hope that is seen is not hope: for what a man sees, why does he yet hope for?" (vs.24). Again the Christian life is that of faith. We have hope in the future but we live the future life now by faith. God placed eternity in our hearts. The Bible says that, "He has made everything appropriate in its time. He has also set eternity in their heart, yet so that man will not find out the work which God has done from the beginning even to the end" (Ecclesiastic 3:11).

Paul mocked death in this manner: "Where, O death, is your victory? Where, O death, is your sting?" (1 Cor. 15:55). Where is thy sting?— The word rendered sting (κέντρον kentron) denotes properly a prick, a point, hence, a goad or stimulus; that is, a rod or staff with an iron point, for goading oxen; (see the note on Acts 9:5); and then a sting properly, as of scorpions, bees, etc. It denotes here a venomous thing, or weapon, applied to death personified, as if death employed it to destroy life, as the sting of a bee or a scorpion is used. The idea is derived from the venomous sting of serpents, or other reptiles, as being destructive and painful. The language here is the language of exultation, as if that was taken away or destroyed.

O grave—ᾅδη hadē. Hades, the place of the dead. It is not improperly rendered, however, grave. The word properly denotes a place of darkness; then the world, or abodes of the dead. According to the Hebrews, Hades, or Sheol, was a vast subterranean receptacle, or abode, where the souls of the dead existed. It was dark, deep, still, awful. The descent to it was through the grave; and the spirits of all the dead were supposed to be assembled there; the righteous occupying the upper regions, and the wicked the lower; see the note on Isaiah 14:9. It refers here to the dead; and means that the grave, or Hades, should no longer have a victory.

The Bible says that, "The sea gave up the dead that were in it, and death and Hades gave up the dead that were in them, and each person was judged according to what he had done" (Revelation 20:13). I think this scripture is parallel to Isaiah 26:19. It says that, "But your dead will live; their bodies will rise. You who dwell in the dust, wake up and shout for joy. Your dew is like the dew of the morning; the earth will give birth to her dead". The scripture means the new bodies rising from the seas and dust. Consider Christ as the Speaker addressing his Church. His resurrection from the dead was an earnest of all the deliverance foretold. The power of his grace, like the dew or rain, which causes the herbs that seem dead to revive, would raise his Church from the lowest state. But we may refer to the resurrection of the dead, especially of those united to Christ.

Thy victory—Since the dead are to rise; since all the graves are to give up all that dwell in them; since no man will die after that, where is its victory? It is taken away. It is despoiled. The power of death and the grave is vanquished, and Christ is triumphant over all. It has been well remarked here, that the words in this verse rise above the plain and simple language of prose, and resemble a hymn, into which the Apostle breaks out in view of the glorious truth which is here presented to the mind. The whole verse is indeed a somewhat loose quotation from Hosea 13:14.

The world is worried about death but we (Christians) should never be worried of death. The only thing to worry about death is the manner we die. The manner we die matters; we must be ready to die and it must be a peaceful death. We must have assurance of our salvation. Also, we should be careful not to be taken by the worldly life in order to avoid to die prematurely and to avoid the cruel and painful death. Living right glorifies God and prevents early and painful death. A believer must live righteously in order to enjoy the fullness of the time that God prepared for him to live. I consider it to be an assault when

Satan takes somebody out of this life prematurely or before finishing the span of life that God prepared for him to live. Remember that God's sovereignty at times respects human will. God can allow us to destroy ourselves and cut our lives short of His intended time. God promised the Israelites the prosperity of life as long as they obeyed His laws. He pronounced the blessing in case of obedience and a curse in case of disobedience. The Bible says that, "If you falter in times of trouble, how small is your strength!" The choice is yours to falter or to remain strong. Whenever you choose to say yes to something, your 'yes' should be accompanied with 'no' to certain things.

It is important to acknowledge that this world is operating contrary to God's original plan. Dr. Jack Hyles said that, "Life is not a bump in the road, life is a bumpy road. If you do not believe that it is true just hang around a while and you won't be disappointed". The corrupt world is aggressively following the bad trait of the curse. For example drinking alcohol, casual sex, smoking which are the major health hazard. It is believed that every time you smoke a cigarette you reduce five minutes from your life span. There is now an exhaustive body of evidence—including hundreds of epidemiological, experimental, pathological, and clinical studies—to demonstrate that smoking increases the smoker's risk of death and illness from a wide variety of diseases. The U.S. Surgeon General has called cigarette smoking "the chief preventable cause of death in our society." The National Institute on Drug Abuse has estimated that in the U.S. alone, smoking is responsible for approximately 350,000 deaths per year.

Alcohol is hazardous. Alcohol, or ethyl alcohol (ethanol), refers to the intoxicating ingredient found in wine, beer and hard liquor. Alcohol arises naturally from carbohydrates when certain micro-organisms metabolize them in the absence of oxygen, called fermentation. Once swallowed, a drink enters the stomach and small intestine, where small blood vessels carry it to the bloodstream. Approximately 20% of alcohol is absorbed through the stomach and most of the remaining 80% is absorbed through the small intestine.

Alcohol is metabolized by the liver, where enzymes break down the alcohol. Understanding the rate of metabolism is critical to understanding the effects of alcohol. In general, the liver can process one ounce of liquor (or one standard drink) in one hour. If you consume more than this, your system becomes saturated, and the additional alcohol will accumulate in the blood and body tissues until it can be metabolized. This is why having a lot of shots or playing drinking games can result in high blood alcohol concentrations that last for several hours.

Gang related crimes are the major killer of teenagers in the western countries. In the most recent view, gangs are considered more pathological than functional organizations, so that the term has become almost synonymous with violent and criminal groups. Political persecutions, poverty and violence are the major causes of death in Africa. The most peaceful countries in the world like USA, drafted their constitutions from the Bible. Their motto is that, "In God we trust".

Promiscuity is the major cause of death among people of all ages. In the 1960s gonorrhea and syphilis seemed to be the only well-known STDs, and both of these could be treated with penicillin. Today there are over twenty-five different STDs, and some of the most common ones are without cures. Among the STDs that can be cured, some are becoming increasingly resistant to modern antibiotics. The "sex superbug," known scientifically as H041, and was discovered when a Japanese sex worker contracted gonorrhea in 2011. Unlike other strains of gonorrhea, which could be treated with some antibiotics, this new strain could not be stopped. Sub-Saharan Africa is more heavily affected by HIV and AIDS than any other region of the world. An estimated 22.9 million people are living with HIV in the region— around two thirds of the global total. In 2010 around 1.2 million people died from AIDS in sub-Saharan Africa and 1.9 million people became infected with HIV. Since the beginning of the epidemic 14.8 million children have lost one or both parents to HIV/AIDS.

Hepatitis B spread in the same way as HIV. Hepatitis B is more dangerous than AIDS. Studies have shown that Liver disease T is a hundred to 1000 times much more infectious than HIV/AIDS. HBV trojan is a lot small compared to HIV this means there are probably be a lot more contaminants of the virus in the offered amount of bloodstream. Alarmingly more people die from Hepatitis than Aids in India.

The world is corrupt and it is occupied by corrupt people. You do not have to search for evil because it is everywhere. Whereas I may agree that God has powers to stop anything including evil, I do not expect Him to work like an intermediary between your own nature and the evil that is parasitic to that nature. God is above that. We are the primary architects of our misery. God gave us the safe way to live and to overcome evil but we do the opposite. Even the atheists and communists, who do not believe in the God of the Christians, agree that embracing the moral values of Christianity is the safest way to live. The Bible lays out guidelines for prosperous living in this dangerous world. Those who live by faith the life of Christ in this world live eternally in the presence of God. God revealed Himself to Abraham, Isaac and Jacob as El-Shaddai, meaning God the All-Sufficient One, Almighty and the source of life (Genesis 17:1-5; Genesis 28:3). We have the power to resist death by receiving the only one who defeated death (Jesus Christ).

One of the most asked questions is that, "If God is all powerful, why does He allows evil?" Evil is the departure from the way things ought to be (God planned them to be). God created Satan but God did not create evil. Satan willingly became evil. I know some people argue that as long as God created Satan and gave him ability to become evil, then God is responsible for the mayhem caused by Satan. I want to pause and ask, "Is the man who invented the car (automobile) responsible for all accidents on our streets?" The answer is no! Accidents happen because of the reckless drivers. In the same manner God created Satan a perfect angel but Satan willingly became evil.

For everything, God created the positive and the negative. The plane cannot take off without the opposing gravity pulling it down. We cannot have electricity without the positive and negative. Resistance produces strength. That is why we go to the Gyms. We wouldn't have known the love of God without the cross. It is not amazing grace when God loves and reward the already righteous people. We call it amazing grace because God loved us even when we were yet sinners.

The greatest fear of evil is the consequence of evil, which is death. Remember that God created death but He designed it to work for mankind rather than against mankind. Adam was created and told eat plants which had life and died when cut down. In this case death was not against man. Man was never afraid of death until judgment as a result of sin. It is Adam who extended death to mankind because of his rebellion.

I said that all the negative things we experience were supposed to work for the proper functioning of the universe. Science says that it cannot rain without dust. We need the bacteria for our survival. For example digestion cannot take place without the presence of these microorganisms (bacteria). Several immunizations have been developed using some viruses (parasites).

Today, HIV is the most dreadful virus. Can something good come out the HIV virus? When I was writing this book, I came across this interesting article concerning little a little girl called Emma: "In April 2012, 7-year-old Emily "Emma" Whitehead was in the fight of her life following her second relapse of acute lymphoblastic- or lymphocytic-leukemia (ALL). The then 6-year-old's parents and doctors turned to an unlikely source to save the young girl's life—the HIV virus".

According to the article, the little girl had undergone two unsuccessful courses of chemotherapy at The Children's Hospital of Philadelphia that failed to achieve sustained remission. The treatment is similar to therapies being developed at other cancer centers around the U.S. Emma, with advanced leukemia, received the CT019 therapy (formerly called CART 19 therapy), underwent an experimental procedure involving a disabled form of HIV, the virus that causes AIDS. It is an experimental treatment that involves doctors reprogramming a person's T-cells—a type of white blood cell that plays a key role in the immune system—to search out and kill cancer cells. According to the experts, the experimental technique relies on help from a disabled form of HIV because the virus is adept at carrying genetic material into T-cells so they're able to kill off cancer cells. The experts say that the genetically altered T-cells go to work attacking cells in the body that play a role in the development of leukemia.

The patient is not afraid to contracting the deadly virus because the T-cells are removed from the patient before being bioengineered with the HIV virus. It is safe because the patient is not injected with the virus. It is more effective than chemotherapy, a drug that is one of the most common treatments of leukemia, which kills off all fast-growing cells in the body.

Emma's situation improved dramatically into remission three weeks after receiving the treatment at Children's Hospital of Philadelphia. A bone marrow test revealed Emma had achieved remission. Today, she's still in remission and thriving. However, her doctors caution the remission needs to be watched for a few years ahead in order to declare it a total cure. They are still careful not to use words like "cured." Researchers hope similar therapies that involve the reprogramming of a patient's immune system, may also eventually be used to fight cancerous breast and prostate tumors. (*http://health.yahoo.net/experts/dayinhealth/hiv-virus-possible-cure-leukemia*).

God created Satan and allowed him to prevail for such a time as this for His own purposes. God warned us not to mess with Satan and gave us immunity to his schemes. He did not leave us defenseless. He provided us with power to overcome evil. We act evil by our own will. We deliberately choose to mess with the devil, well knowing of the consequences. Adam knew the danger of disobedience and he chose to disobey. In the same manner we are warned of the danger of rejecting Jesus Christ and for some reasons we end up rejecting Him. If you are one of the few people who think that God is the cause of your problem because He created evil, I have the good news for you: God is not the cause of evil but He has a solution for evil. He made a way for us to overcome evil through Jesus Christ. "For whatsoever is born of God overcometh the world: and this is the victory that overcometh the world, even our faith" (1 John 5:4).

We must acknowledge that God is not the architect of our calamities. We are the major cause of our problems. People often ask me questions like this one: "Why does God bring cancer on people?" My answer is that God may allow bad things to happen to us but He does not bring bad things on us. Satan is the source of all kinds of evils. Most problems we encounter are due to our corruption. God is in control of this universe but we are in charge of our world. Man is the greatest enemy to mankind. We are the architects of the destruction of our world.

Today, we have polluted our foods and environment. We have chemicals added to our foods, reckless over eating with less time to exercise, cutting down trees without planting more trees, building in wetland, nuclear, chemical and biological warfare and etc., which are hostile to our lives. As Brother J. Ikuya said that, "Man is insanely using up all resources in voluptuous greed without care to address sustainability of doing so. We are recklessly destroying the earth's environment and eroding the ecological balance and health of the earth. A few people are amassing the entire globe to themselves whereas sense tells that their colossal fortunes are actually doomed."

The lifestyle of a person (what he eats, where he dwells, what he does and etc.) determines his physical wellbeing. It is estimated that every minute, four people die from heart attack. The number is equivalent to ten jumbo air plane crush every day. Most of the diseases and the problems which we encounter are manmade and are preventable. We plan every day's activities, and most times without consulting God and when our plans backfire, we blame God!

God's sovereignty made us stewards. His grace restrains evil and permits some of the evil things we initiate to happen but He does not plan evil against His creation because in Him there is no evil. When God gives up on a person, He simply removes His convicting power towards righteousness so that a person becomes absolutely evil. In this case a person manifests his or her true evil characters without any restraining power. God allows that person to be what he or she is (evil) as opposed to causing him or her to become evil. As I said, in God there is no evil and He does not cause somebody to be evil. He might allow us to go through some trials in order to test our faith. This does not mean He causes the evil things to happen. Satan is the architect of evil and he infected humanity with evil to fulfill his plan.

Evil is absolutely bad (evil) but when evil is sanctioned by the holy God, to test us, in this case evil becomes good because it is intended for good intentions. God tests us so that we can prove our loyalty to Him, in order for Him to bless us. God does not allow us to go through difficult things which we cannot handle. He gives us means of handling tough situations: "There hath no temptation taken you but such as is common to man: but God is faithful, who will not suffer you to be tempted above that ye are able; but will with the temptation also make a way to escape, that ye may be able to bear it" (1 Corinthians 10:13).

How we respond in tough times matters. One columnist said that, "The way in which a man accepts his fate and all the suffering it entails, the way in which he takes up his cross, gives him ample opportunity—even under the most difficult circumstances—to add a deeper meaning to his life. It may remain brave, dignified and unselfish. Or in the bitter fight for self-preservation he may forget his human dignity and become no more than an animal. Here lies the chance for a man either to make use of or to forgo the opportunities of attaining the moral values that a difficult decision may afford him. And this decides whether he is worthy of his suffering or not."

I said that the human sufferings and the geophysical catastrophes that frequently ravage our globe today cannot be attributed unequivocally to the direct action of God, but they can be traced ultimately to human rebellion, and the permissive will of the Creator. God allows evil to exist for His own reasons. Evil makes us responsible creatures. For example if fire did not burn painfully, many would have handled it recklessly until consumed but it without awareness. The burning pain warns us to move away.

God uses Satan to discipline His children in the same manner He used the heathen nations of Babylon and Assyria to punish His children (Israel). There are consequences of our rebellion. God is loving and merciful; but we must not forget that He is just. He will reward the wages of sin in accordance to His justice. One writer warned against taking God for granted in this way: "God wants to be wanted, to be wanted enough that we are ready, predisposed, to find him present with us. And if, by contrast, we are ready and set to find ways of explaining away his gentle overtures, he will rarely respond with fire from heaven. More likely he will simply leave us alone; and we shall have the satisfaction of thinking ourselves not to be gullible.

The test of character posed by the gentleness of God's approach to us is especially dangerous for those formed by the ideas that dominate our modern world". (*wienerdog*).

Like the earthly parents, God prescribes discipline to those He loves to correct. The Bible says that, "You have forgotten that word of encouragement that addresses you as sons: 'My son, do not make light of the Lord's discipline, and do not lose heart when he rebukes you, because the Lord disciplines those he loves, and he punishes everyone he accepts as a son.' Endure hardship as discipline; God is treating you as sons. For what son is not disciplined by his father?" (Hebrews 12:4-7).

However the paradigm of God as a "parent" may come under criticism when we consider the question as to whether a loving parent would subject their children to the kind of suffering or dangers which children of God have been subjected to. God told Abraham to kill his son, for example. To which Abraham complied, though God prevented him in the final moment from carrying it out. Yet God did subject his only begotten Son, Jesus, to circumstances leading to a painful and humiliating death. But then again He was a willing sacrifice, well aware of what was to come. But regardless, is God being too cruel to be reckoned a loving Father? I think the paradigm of "parent" is still appropriate and consistent if we increase our vision of the circumstances as much as God is greater than an earthly father, and what is spiritual is much greater than what is material. For example things that are material are temporary. Things which are spiritual are eternal. God primarily focuses on our spiritual benevolences which are eternal. In spite of the trials and evils of this world, God is in control. God planned to eradicate evil forever at His own timing. He sees His children glorified in Christ at His right hand because He is not limited by time. As per now, He does not forsake us. He walks with us through our hardship in the same way He was with Daniel in the furnace of fire. He walks with us in the valleys, in the swamps, on the mountain peaks—in all aspects of our lives. We can count on His provision and protection.

Certainly, we are in charge but we are not in control of this world. At the end of the day, the world is going to end up as God planned it to be. The reason is because God is sovereign. Never be discouraged when you are going through rough times or when you are not healed of a certain sicknesses. Remember that God looks at us within the context of eternity: We count in terms of years, months, days, hours and minutes but God counts in generations. He sees you in the context of a blessed generation pre-ordained from eternity. Every inch and aspect of your daily experience (what you are going through) brings you close to eternity. It is therefore important to value every minute and every second lived on this universe. We should not live for the present but for the future. Tomorrow is not in our hands but it works well when we put our trust in the God of tomorrow.

B.B. Warfield wrote that, "But, in the infinite wisdom of the Lord of all the earth, each event falls with exact precision into its proper place in the unfolding of His eternal plan; nothing, however small, however strange, occurs without His ordering, or without its peculiar fitness for its place in the working out of His purpose; and the end of all shall be the manifestation of His glory, and the accumulation of His praise."

We must live in this world with a conviction that we are not of this world; the world is not where we come from but where we came to. Our permanent home is eternity. The kingdom of God is a step that brings us close to eternity. Jerusalem is symbolic of the coming city from heaven. Jerusalem means the city of peace. No wonder the eyes of all people are focused at Israel today. Believers focus on the new city coming down from heaven.

The purpose of God for our lives will be fully realized in future. God sees us seated in heaven places. We must have the same mind of God. We should not live under the pressure of the circumstances of this world but over them, aiming high for the glory of God. God calls us to live by faith in spite of the present life's tragedies; we are supposed to live by faith in the future blessings now. Faith is not limited by time in the same manner God is not limited with time. By faith we can live today in the future hope of His glory. We were created to manifest the glory of God by dying to our old nature and manifesting the life of Christ. Nothing can withhold the glory of God. Not even death can eclipse the same glory. We lose nothing when we embrace the truth and die in Christ because death is the door way to the glory.

Solomon divided our life experience in times and seasons (Ecclesiastic 3). He said that there is time to do certain things and time to abandon other things. There is an appointed time for everything. And there is a right time for every event under heaven—a right time for birth, and another for death.

Ecclesiastes is a Greek word which can be translated "The Teacher". In this particular chapter he teaches us to live a purposeful life. The passage lists 14 "opposites," a common element in Hebrew poetry indicating completion. While each time and season may seem random, the underlying significance in the poem denotes a divinely chosen purpose for everything we experience in our lives. The familiar lines offer a comforting reminder of God's sovereignty.

The purposeful living puts trust in Jesus. Jesus said that not a single sparrow falls on the ground without the Father's consent. He said that, we, being of more value than the sparrows, we should not be afraid of anything (Matthew 10:29-31). Martin Luther used to take off his hat to the birds and say, "Good morning, theologians; you wake and sing but I, old fool knows less than you and worry about everything, instead of simply trusting in the heavenly Father's care." (*Quotation from: Report to Greco by Nikos Kazantzakin*).

Worry is one of the major causes of premature death. One doctor said that he has never seen a person dying from hard work but he has seen many dying from worries. It doesn't pay to worry because we can change nothing by getting worried. The world goes on its normality in spite of our worries. It works better when we trust in the one who made the world and who holds tomorrow. Death is the major cause of worry. The reality is that we can never live the perfect life in our corrupt bodies because life has an expiring date on it. None of us can live one minute beyond that appointed time. But we can enjoy living the fullness of the time that God intended us to live.

Satan uses our trials to tempt us into doubting the faithfulness of God. Unbelief is most likely to step in when we are faced with the trials of the world. That is when most people question their relationship with Jesus; things like what is wrong with my Christian walk? Or where was God? Unbelief can deter us from manifesting the glory of God. Unbelief was the greatest challenge to the earthly ministry of Jesus. Unbelief is equivalent to not believing: Unbelief is not necessarily doubt; it is absolute lack of faith. Jesus was not welcome as a deliverer (Messiah) because He did not match the Jewish expectations; they ended up missing to see the glory of God. The Bible says that Jesus did not do many miracles in His home areas because of the unbelief of the people. We called to invest our faith in God that transcend (exists above and independent from; to rise above and surpass) all things. Our faith should not be motivated by the circumstances surrounding us. When John the Baptist was languishing in jail he doubted the ministry of Jesus. He wondered if Jesus was doing His job as a deliverer. Jesus told John the Baptist's disciples to go and tell John that the blind receive their sight, and the lame walk, the leapers are cleansed, and the deaf hear, the dead are raised up, and the poor have the gospel preached to them, and blessed is he, whosoever shall not be offended in me (Matthew 11:2-6).

God allows the trials brought about by Satan to test our faith. We should be ready for such tests. Socrates once said that the unexamined life is not worth living. But unfortunately, many Christians go day after day and never seriously examine their lives before God. But not King David, who wrote in this passage, "Search me, O God . . ." The Hebrew word for search here means to dig down deep and mine the rich resources of a mine. And when we ask God to search us, it enables God to dig deep into our lives, remove those things that are wrong and bring out those things which are right. And not only did David pray, "Search me," but he also prayed, "Try me . . ." Now, this word was used in the context of a metallurgist who would take impure metal and remove the impurities. David is asking God to test him and remove anything that is impure in order to be stronger when the testing is over. In the Lord's Prayer, we humbly pray for holy perseverance, "Lead us not into temptation." It is an anxious desire for sanctification. "Lead us not into temptation, but deliver us from evil"—that is sanctification in its negative and positive forms. It is

God testing us to prove that we can pass the tests, and God protecting us from the snares of the enemy.

I want to conclude this topic by saying that our suffering should not be misconstrued to mean that God rejoices in our miseries. The problem of death was solved. Remember that living longer has never been a rewarding to our good works otherwise we would have men and women who are a thousand years old seated on the pews in our sanctuaries. We must remember that when death strikes, the numbers of years you have lived do not count. A man who died at thirty years old is as dead as the one who died at ninety. Christ alone makes a difference because He gives eternal life. This is life forever and ever.

We can tell those who have acquired eternal life. They are the ones manifesting the life glorifying to God. Neither do they take credit nor rewards for their accomplishments but they give credit to Jesus for every inch of their accomplishment. For example the apostles suffered for the sake of the gospel but were determined to take the glory of God to the known world. Not a single one of them lived longer because of their testimony. Not a single one benefitted financially or relationally. They treasured in heaven their good deeds. "Divine good works" emanate strictly from God through Christians who are under the leadership [fullness] of the Holy Spirit. On contrary, "human good works" are those works that emanate from any source other than God. Individuals who are "lost" [without Christ], as well as "carnal" Christians, are capable of such good works. But the believers manifest the works of Christ.

Again, we cannot get saved by being nice (good works) because we cannot be perfect at all times. But God demands our good works as evidences of our salvation. The grace of God helps us to live the perfect and acceptable life to God. It is like scoring eighty on the test but the teacher adds twenty to make it one hundred. The grace of God adds on where we lack to make it perfect obedience.

The blood of Jesus atones for our sins. The biblical writers used the powerful metaphor of the blood of Jesus to help Christians grasp the treasures Jesus secured for them in His death on the cross. His blood is symbolic of the life of Christ. The New Testament uses the blood of Jesus as often as the cross and His death. I want to emphasize that life is so precious. We can use multiple allegories to explain the afterlife but nothing can bring hope as the historical death and resurrection of Jesus Christ. If He rose from death, we too have hope to rise (1 Thessalonians 4:14).

I want to end by speaking directly to you. You need a reservation in order to go to heaven. Hell does not need reservation because by nature we are all heading to hell. The grace of God stepped in to save a handful of people who did not deserve salvation. The saved ones escaped God's wrath towards sin in hell. The question is that, "Are you numbered among the few who are never going to see God's wrath?" Allow me to warn you that it is scaring to fall into the hands of an angry God! God's love is without measure and so is his wrath towards sin.

(Part of this information is taken from my book called "The New Generation of Worshippers in the 21 Century", Revised Version).

God's Solution to the Decaying Culture

Culture is the way of behaviors that shapes our perception and informs our investment decisions. We grow up into certain cultural settings and traditions which we embrace as our ways of life and moral aptitudes. It is within human instincts to do what we see others do. We often hear statements that we ought or should do certain things. Ethic is descriptive of the values of a given society whereas morality is imperative or commands expected to be observed by the society. In our communities, the ruling ethic is determined by statistical morality. If the majority of people approve the values, they are deemed to be normal. In accordance to the morality of the Christians, what is right depends on the transcendent God. The life of Christ produces in us true enlightenment. We have come to grasp the grace that God works His way down to us, dies for our moral and religious failures and offers us His perfect life.

Culture is how we live, what we do, what we say and how we survive in our environments. Culture is the backbone and the greatest foundation of the stable societies. Culture is a function of worldview, the sum total of our beliefs about the world and about life. Unless born again, worldview directs our daily perceptions, thoughts, words, and actions. It is the philosophical framework out of which culture flows. Different cultures have transformed with time in order to cope with the changing world. We are bombarded with change from every direction. Many historians, sociologists and journalists have expressed concern in recent years about the rapid change in our society. In Uganda we seem to have lost appreciation of culture hence our society is currently undergoing a state of gross moral decadence.

Throughout history, there are many genius people who contributed to the values we embrace today. Some of them were teachers, philosophers, religious leaders and etc. But none of them did us like Jesus. He is the most influential man ever walked on the universe because the destiny of all people who ever lived on the universe depends on Him.

Different cultures have transformed with time. We keep on changing our values depending on the circumstances. In Uganda we seem to have lost appreciation of culture hence our society is currently undergoing a state of gross moral decadence. The virtues of the Bible never change with time. The challenge of the Christians is to counteract the ever changing culture of the world with the non-changing Word of God.

People behave and act in certain ways because of the influence of their cultures. Various cultures are influenced by various factors including environments. Generally speaking, we are habit keeping creatures. Aristotle, analyzed that an individual that is born in the wilderness and left to live with the animals of nature would predominately adopt and conform to the primary source the individual encounters. For example, if the individual encounters wolves as his or her primary source, then the individual will undoubtedly conform and take on the disposition of the wolves, thus conforming to that which is known. He or she would walk on all fours; communicate as the wolves do through howling, yet the same individual can learn to imitate and adapt to a new environment, for example: if you took the individual away from the wolves and placed him in a new environment he or she could learn and change his or her pattern of thought.

You are not shaped so much by your environment as you are by your perception of your environment. The environment is not the key, for the individual is able to change, grow, and eventually differentiate or evaluate the options at his fingertips—choosing what he or she finds to be acceptable, pleasing, or simply the manner in which he or she finds himself or herself most accustomed to.

There is a true story involving a baby boy who was adopted by the monkeys in the jungle of Africa (Uganda). In 1985, Mayanja was rescued by NRA from the monkeys which had adopted him. By the time he was rescued he was about five years old. He used to behave (eat, walk and make noise) like monkeys. He was adopted by Jennet Museveni's children home (UWESO), and later on by L'ARCHE in 1991. Today, he is thirty years old and has made tremendous improvement although he retains some of the behaviors of the monkeys. In particular he cannot speak like a normal human being.

According to Henry, "Ethics deals with the voluntary conduct of individual man insofar as it is judged to be good or bad in reference to a single, inclusive, and determinative principle of moral value grounded in and validated by ultimate reality". (*Henry Stob, Ethical Reflections, page 24*).

While all law is based in ethics, behind civil law is a power that intends to enforce it, while ethics is "voluntary" (as mentioned above). That is, the rule of law under the civil government carries the "power of the sword." Thus, civil law is "involuntary," that is, "enforced." The large part of this enforcement is functionally voluntary (for the Christian, this obedience is a duty under God), as a police force is not stationed in every home or with every individual.

Christians are called to value the rights of others more than their own rights. Civil rights are rights that are bestowed by nations on those within their boundaries. A civil right is a right or privilege that can be enforced by an individual. This means that if a person violates another's civil rights, it gives the later a right to an action for injury. Examples of civil rights are freedom of speech, press, and assembly; the right to vote; freedom from involuntary servitude; and the right to equality in public places. Violations of civil rights occur in instances of discrimination against an individual solely because of his/her membership in a particular group or class. Statutes have been enacted to prevent discrimination based on a person's race, sex, religion, age, previous condition of servitude, physical limitation, national origin, and in some instances, even sexual preference.

Whereas there are universally acceptable civil rights, the violation of the same rights is apparently common in many countries. In many countries, citizens have greater protections against infringement of rights than non-citizens; at the same time, civil and political rights are considered to be universal rights that apply to all persons. Not to mention that civil rights have not penetrated deep enough to uproot some of the abusive cultures. The cultural issue is a sensitive area that calls for the cooperation of the natives involved.

The truth is that we live under the same sky, but we don't all have the same horizon. In the secular world there is no right universal culture and there is no uniformity of morality. The standard of what is morally acceptable varies from one ethical grouping to the others. It is compared to beauty. Beauty lies in the eyes of the beholder; if you don't like somebody, there is someone who admires him or her. The criteria for rejecting or accepting certain values depends on people's opinions, religious back ground and culture rather than merits and demerits.

The metaphor of salvation is God's gravity snatching us from the void of eternal separation of the corrupt world. Jesus replaced the civil laws with the Sermon on the Mountain. The Church has mandate to manifest the unconditional love of God. In a God fearing nation, the main focus when choosing and implementing the societal values ought to be on consolidating the people's relationship with God. Also, on bringing out central issues that bond people together or disaffect them rather than just the highlight on the purely individual traits.

Human beings are what we are. Being created in God's image, we have free-will that God respects to certain extent. We have considerable freedom to choose how we live and express ourselves. We even have freedom to cut ourselves loose from the metaphorical strings that seem to tie us down. Granted, there are false and illusory bonds, from which we really ought to free ourselves, but there are cords of reality too, and if we cut them we will fall. Real freedom is to be who and what God made us to be. Failure to do so is self-deceit, self-deception, self-delusion and succumbing to muted ecstasy and reverie. This must be so, because being created in God's image, our freedom is not absolute. We were not made for ourselves. We were made for a purpose, and we have been made to be what we are in relation to other realities: people, the rest of creation, and especially God.

We live in a free culture. I mean the culture that holds religion hostage. 'Freedom' is one of the most frequently used word in our times and it has been redefined by the secular world. Biblically, there are two kinds of freedom corresponding to the inner and outer aspects of life. Outer freedom is freedom of action, political or social freedom. Inner freedom is freedom of the mind, freedom from the bondage of ignorance of human nature and its potentialities. Jesus provides our freedom from inside to the outside. Right now He rules at the hearts of the believers, giving them spiritual freedom from the bondage of sin. He will return to rule the world (in the Millennium kingdom), giving the world the political and social freedom it has never experienced before.

In modern culture (secular world) the emphasis is on freedom of the outer aspect of life, freedom of choice and action. The individual is not allowed the inner freedom to act from conviction and internal harmony. Freedom has been misinterpreted to mean doing what you want irrespective of God's way and without considering the right of others to freedom. And there is indeed a cliff looming for our culture as it seeks to loose itself from the cords of reality.

According to Christianity, God defines our freedom in Christ. In Him we win our freedom primarily from sin and worldliness (corrupt system of the world). He defines how to love Him and our neighbor. Unfortunately, many Christians succumb to worldly trappings and fall into a mixed world view; professing a belief in Jesus, but living secular lifestyles: "Secular" means "denoting attitudes, activities, or other things that have not religious or spiritual basis."

If God's ways get in our way, it is because the way we've chosen leads toward a precipice. Christians who resist culture's headlong rush may seem to be standing against freedom as prescribed by the secular world. In reality we aren't. We're standing for the freedom to be who and what humans really are, as God made us. It is the freedom to be real. It is the only real freedom. To be 'UPRIGHT' means to be right with God; it means to be up and to be right. You can't be right and not stand up for what is right!

We are called to champion the causes for a society in which development goes hand in hand with equity, modernity that does not trample the good traditional values, which do not contradict the morality of the Scriptures, and progress that does not leave the vulnerable—young generation behind.

The worldviews of most contemporary intellectuals are outgrowths of various types of naturalism. They share the assumption that there is nothing outside the physical world, so people, and everything else in life, are nothing more than matter and energy interacting. An atheist is a person who does not believe in the existence of God the creator of the universe.

We do not have to prove that there is God. The burden rests on the shoulder of the atheists to disapprove the existence of God, in spite of the overwhelming evidences available. For example the moral argument is the argument from the existence or nature of morality to the existence of God. There can be no morality without a moral creator. That is why everyone has a tendency of feeling guilty in case of wrong doing. Two forms of moral argument are distinguished: formal and perfectionist. The formal moral argument takes the form of morality to imply that it has a divine origin: morality consists of an ultimately authoritative set of commands; where can these commands have come from but a commander that has ultimate authority? The perfectionist moral argument sets up a problem: how can it be that morality requires perfection of us, that morality cannot require of us more than we can give, but that we cannot be perfect? The only way to resolve this paradox, the argument suggests, is to posit the existence of God.

The atheists who believe in the nonexistence of God at all believe that this world is a result of some cosmetical accidents. The atheists are aware that it is impossible to convince somebody with sound minds that the sophisticated human organs like the brains, nerves, lungs, heart, liver, kidneys and eyes assembled themselves by accident without a master mind to design them and their functioning. For example the human nervous system is the most sophisticated. The sophistication enables humans to acquire language, cultural transmission, and abstract conceptual representation, among other unique qualities that distinguish humans from other animals.

Nervous system can be defined as an organic system that contains specialized cells networked together. The nervous system has three main functions: sensory input, integration of data and motor output. Sensory input is when the body gathers information or data, by way of neurons, glia and synapses. The nervous system is composed of excitable nerve cells (neurons) and synapses that form between the neurons and connect them to centers throughout the body or to other neurons. These neurons operate on excitation or inhibition, and although nerve cells can vary in size and location, their communication with one another determine their function. These nerves conduct impulses from sensory receptors to the brain and spinal cord. The data is then processed by way of integration of data, which occurs only in the brain. After the brain has processed the information, impulses are then conducted from the brain and spinal cord to muscles and glands, which is called motor output. Glia cells are found within tissues and are not excitable but help with myelination, ionic regulation and extracellular fluid.

The total length of your circulatory system stretches an amazing 60,000 miles. That is more than twice the distance around the Earth. The central nervous system is connected to every part of the body by 43 pairs of nerves. Twelve pairs go to and from the brain, with 31 pairs going from the spinal cord. There are nearly 45 miles of nerves running through our bodies. Intelligence is the only known cause of complex functionally integrated information processing system.

It follows once again, that intelligent design stands as the best—most causally adequate—explanation for this feature of the cell, just as it stands as the best explanation for the origin of the information present in DNA itself. In "Signature in the Cell", Dr. Meyers walks us through what information is and the different ways information is defined, created and discovered. He also goes into great detail on probability theory and the history of scientific reasoning. He then lays out the history of origins of life research including a fascinating exposition of the discovery of the DNA double helix, and the surprise of specified information that lies within. Dr. Meyers argues why the current OOL theories fail to explain how the first cell could have arisen by chance alone due to the insufficient probabilistic resources (temporal as well as physical) of the universe. He further argues why self organization/bio-chemical predestination models do not provide an adequate explanation for the origin of life. He also explains why the RNA world and other current models fail to explain the OOL, or what Dr. Meyers calls the "DNA enigma"

"Signature in the Cell" is not "Creationist Tripe", but a 600 page argument. Dr. Meyers does not necessarily argue for a God as the intelligent agent behind the OOL, but that an intelligent agent is the most likely cause of the specified information in the double helix and information processing systems of the cell. Dr. Meyers argument is not that "It is way too complicated to understand so therefore God did it" but an appeal to what we know about how information is created and that information comes from minds, or agents. As some like to say and I'm paraphrasing several ID opponents here . . . Let's not kid ourselves, we all know who Dr. Meyers means when he says an intelligent agent, he means God.

Well maybe, or if your ontology will allow, probably, but both Richard Dawkins and Francis Crick believe in, or are at least sympathetic to an intelligent agent as the cause of life on earth. They just believe that the intelligent agent was or could have been extra-terrestrial. The panspermia theory too has its problems, and ultimately pushes back the OOL or "DNA Enigma" to an earlier time and certainly from what we know of the universe, one is stopped by the previously mentioned wall of probabilistic resources.

In the epilogue Dr. Meyers opens the door to some of the latest discoveries of the hierarchical nature of DNA information storage. Quite interesting really, Super folders, folders within folders in optimized locations for efficient retrieval. He also touches briefly on what used to be thought of as "Junk DNA" or non-protein coding regions of the DNA molecule. What was once considered to be only leftovers and redundancies from transcriptions can now be shown to work as a sort of operating system. It will be interesting to see what comes from the ongoing research.

Dr. Meyer concludes the book in Appendix B with solid critique of multiverse theories and in chapter 17 provides a very powerful answer (rebuttal) to the ubiquitous "Who designed the designer?" question (challenge). There IS an answer to the DNA Enigma, and Dr. Meyer's positive argument is that life on earth was caused ~3-4 billion years ago by an intelligent agent, most likely God. Perhaps he is correct. (Signature *in the Cell: DNA and the Evidence for Intelligent Design, by Dr. Stephen Meyer*).

The human body has about 100 trillion cells. Every living cell in the body is capable of sustaining, repairing and reproducing itself because of the intelligent creator. Engineers design appliances that have no capability to self-sustain, self-repair and reproduce. No car can repair itself in case of breaking. You cannot leave your car in a garage and the next morning you find a new motor engine in it unless somebody installed it. In the same manner you cannot find your car having three other small cars reproduced by any natural means.

Harbert Spenser was a renowned English philosopher and sociologist known for applying evolutionary theory to the study of creation. He came up with an idea that everything in the universe can fit in the five knowable categories namely: Time, Force, Action, Space and Matter. I wish he knew that his idea was the first verse in the Bible. Genesis 1—"In the beginning God created the heaven and the earth". (In the beginning—time, God—force, created—action, heaven—space, earth—matter). But in our case it is not force creating but the persons of the God-head (Father, Son and Holy Spirit). The reason is because energy produces nothing of intelligence. Intelligence alone has capability to create information and ideas. That is why John writes that in the beginning God the Word (idea).

Jesus declared that, "I am the light of the world: he that followeth me shall not walk in darkness, but shall have the light of life" (John 8:12). Light sustains life. Light is the only solution to all issues of your life. God designed humans in a much more sophiscated manner. For example the human eyes see things upside down and the brains turn them upright. Animals see better at night because they can't see colour as we do. The thicker the darkness, the brighter the light, and remember, light shines brightest at source. Jesus is the light for us to see even the invisible things to the natural eyes and minds. Without Him we are left in absolute spiritual blindness. He is the source of light. It means we are not manufacturers but distributors.

Christians are the light to the darkened world (Matthew 5:14-16). Unfortunately, some of the so called Intellectuals (atheists) regard Christianity to be the world's greatest problem as opposed to the solution. Occasionally, some leading scientists (atheists) convene in conferences and discuss what they consider to be an urgent need to clip the wings of the growing clout of Christianity. The idea that the evils of this world could be greatly minimized by eliminating Christianity has been loudly articulated in recent years. Books against Christianity proliferate are quite popular. "The world needs to wake up from its long nightmare of religious belief," declares Nobel laureate and physicist Steven Weinberg. I can imagine the world without Satan but I can't imagine the world without Christians. "People living in the vanity of their own mind not only destroy themselves, but far too often, they bring destruction to others around them."

The atheists hate the Christians because they hate God. They hate God because they cannot survive in the righteous world. The righteousness of God exposes the immorality of the world. It is the same reason the Pharisees, Sadducees and Scribes hated Jesus. The righteousness of Jesus was like a white background that exposed their dirty. They hated Him because their own religious righteousness could not match His own righteousness. The purity of Jesus made them look bad in the eyes of the people.

The atheists are not against false gods but they are against the God of the Bible. They openly confess that they hate God. This is self-contradiction because it is impossible to hate somebody who does not exist. By hating God, they basically acknowledge His existence. There can be no narrative of the story without the existence of the story! I suspect that they are in cognitive dissonance.

The deception of the atheists is evidently seen in the contradiction of the concept denying the existence of God. Some atheists say that believing in God is a delusion. Other atheists say that even if there is God, there is no evidence to prove that He exists. He left nothing pointing to His existence. Other atheists falsely believe that god is in everything and everything is god. They believe that anything or person can qualify to be god depending on somebody's faith. Pantheism is the belief that God is everything. Although they do not agree about the basic epistemological principles, all of the worldviews share one thing in common: They lack a source of hope.

The atheists disagree on a number of issues in their arguments against the existence of God. In spite of their disagreement, they have formed a united front against Christianity purposely to get rid of the gospel. They forget that before the gospel came we were pagans, and if the gospel goes we are left to worship ourselves. It seems some of us are on the highway to destruction because we are denying and repudiating the fundamental thing about our very being—that we were created by the loving God in His image.

The reason the atheists reject the object truth is because there can be no object truth without the supreme God. They deny the existence of God not because they can't acknowledge Him but because they can't stand the God whom they already know (Romans 1:19).

The atheists deny the truth and yet believe that their denial is truthful. A believer confesses with confidence that there is God and there is objective truth. If there was no objective truth, we couldn't have a way to define what is good, much less a reason to believe that good will triumph. If the fate of society rests on achievements purely based on human resources like political goals, there is no way to be sure that these goals will be achieved, since there is no Providence to bring them about. If life is pointless and meaningless, death is ultimate, so any good things in life are doomed to be destroyed. Then we can as well embrace the height of moral degeneration that is sinking our communities.

The atheists use science and philosophy to support their views but the laws of science are not in their favor. According to science, the law of matter states that man can neither create nor destroy matter. The same law points to God alone that can create and destroy matter. The fundamental principle of God's creation is: The total amount of matter and energy in God's creation always remains the same.

Scientists have unsuccessfully tried to create and destroy matter and energy; they can only affect the chemical changes or reactions. After affecting the chemical reactions the atoms that God created are preserved. The process of preserving the atoms is labeled as the "Conservation of Mass Law".

One atheist tried to prove that he can create something but every time he tried his creation experiment, he began with materials already created. He failed miserably because he was challenged not to use any material thing in order to be a creator. Creativity is different from creating because creating brings something out of nothing. God created by bringing things out of nothing. He spoke things into existence.

Christians have an answer to the question of creation. Since matter cannot be created or destroyed by any other matter, then the only alternative is that matter came into existence by the creator who is self-existence. He does not need anything beyond Himself to exist. He was, He is and He will be. God is an infinite God. He has neither beginning of days nor end of life.

The teleological argument is the argument from the order in the world to the existence of a being that created it with a specific purpose in mind. The universe is a highly complex system. The scale of the universe alone is astounding, and the natural laws that govern it perplex scientists still after generations of study. It is also, however, a highly ordered system; it serves a purpose. The world provides exactly the right conditions for the development and sustenance of life and life is a valuable thing. That this is so is remarkable; there are numerous ways in which the universe might have been different, and the vast majority of possible universes would not have supported life. To say that the universe is so ordered by chance is therefore unsatisfactory as an explanation of the appearance of design around us. It is far more plausible, and far more probable, that the universe is the way it is because it was created by God with life in mind.

If God exists then there is the purpose of this universe. Life is with objective purpose. Rebelling against God means rebelling against the purpose of God for this universe. God fine-tuned this universe to operate on certain cosmological laws which we can violate at our peril. The cosmological argument seeks to demonstrate, among other things, that God is a metaphysically necessary entity. He is related to His creation ethically.

The late Francis Schaeffer wrote of the significance of one's world view, which, in the final analysis, represents one's doctrinal perspective about God and life: There is a flow to history and culture. This flow is rooted and has its well spring in the thoughts of people. People are unique in the inner life of the mind—what they are in their thought world determines how they act. This is true of their value systems and it is true of their creativity . . .

People have presuppositions, and they will live more consistently on the basis of these presuppositions than even they themselves may realize. By presuppositions we mean the basic way an individual looks at life, his basic world view, the grid through which he sees the world. Presuppositions rest upon that which a person considers to be the truth of what exists. People's presuppositions lay a grid for all they bring forth into the external world. Their presuppositions also provide the basis for their values and their basis for their decisions.

"As a man thinketh, so is he," is really most profound. An individual is not just the product of the forces around him. He has a mind, an inner world. Unfortunately, most people catch their presuppositions from their family and surrounding society the way a child catches measles. But people with more understanding realize that their presuppositions should be chosen after a careful consideration of what world view is true . . .

It is important to realize what a difference a people's world view makes in their strength as they are exposed to the pressure of life. That is why the Christians of the early Church who were able to resist religious mixtures, syncretism, and the effects of the weakness of Roman culture speak of the strength of the Christian world view. This strength rested on God's being an infinite-personal God and His speaking in the Old Testament, in the life and teaching of Jesus Christ, and in the gradually growing New Testament. He had spoken in ways people could understand. Thus the Christians of the early

Church not only had knowledge about the universe and mankind that people cannot find out by themselves, but they had absolute, universal values by which to live and by which to judge the society and the political state in which they lived.

A follower of Jesus is called a disciple because he or she is under instruction to be an overcomer and to be effective in changing the world. Our challenge as Christians is to counteract the ever changing culture of the world with the non-changing Word of God. The metaphor of salvation is God's gravity snatching us from the void of eternal separation of the corrupt world. Teaching is for believing and application; but it must be the right teaching of the Word. The many references in the New Testament to doctrine or teaching (83 times these words are found in the NASB New Testament) make it clear that doctrine or theology is not a cold and impotent force, but a vital element to the spiritual, moral, and social being of mankind (1 Tim. 1:3; 4:6, 16; 2 Tim. 3:10, 16; 4:2-3). Indeed, it is the difference between life and death, a sense of significance and happiness, and joy and peace. It is the doctrines of the Bible which bring people into a factual knowledge of the "true and living God" which must form the basis for knowing God personally. Only then can people turn from all the false gods of the world to the one true and living God (1 Thess. 1:9). We become Christlike in the measure that the Word prevails in us—E.W.Kenyon

We have no excuse of not believing. But we live in a culture that has, for centuries now, cultivated the idea that the skeptical person is always smarter than one who believes. You can be as stupid as a cabbage, as long as you doubt. The fashion of the age has identified mental sharpness with a pose, not with genuine intellectual method and character. Only a very hardy individualist or social rebel— or one desperate for another life—therefore stands any chance of discovering the substantiality of the spiritual life today. Today it is the skeptics who are the social conformists, though because of powerful intellectual propaganda they continue to enjoy thinking of themselves as wildly individualistic and unbearably bright.

Christians should not be regarded as dumb. God does not call us to leap into darkness but into light. Christianity advocates using human capabilities including intellects to the maximum as ordained by God. Anti-intellectualism is hostility towards and mistrust of intellect, intellectuals, and intellectual pursuits, usually expressed as the derision of education. Christianity is not anti-intellectualism. Throughout history, there are many elites who have been confessing Christian believers. I am going to outline some of the famous scientists who were or are followers of Christ.

Nicholas Copernicus (1473-1543) who was the Polish astronomer who put forward the first mathematically based system of planets going around the sun was a Christian.

Sir Francis Bacon (1561-1627) was a philosopher that is known for establishing the scientific method of inquiry based on experimentation and inductive reasoning was a believer in Jesus Christ.

Johannes Kepler (1571-1630) who was a brilliant mathematician and astronomer was a follower of Christ. He did early work on light, and established the laws of planetary motion about the sun.

Galileo Galilei (1564-1642) is often remembered for his conflict with the Roman Catholic Church. His controversial work on the solar system was published in 1633. It had no proofs of a sun-centered system (Galileo's telescope discoveries did not indicate a moving earth) and his one "proof" based upon the tides was invalid. It ignored the correct elliptical orbits of planets published twenty five years earlier by Kepler. Since his work finished by putting the Pope's favorite argument in the mouth of the simpleton in the dialogue, the Pope (an old friend of Galileo's) was very offended. After the "trial" and being forbidden to teach the sun-centered system, Galileo did his most useful theoretical work, which was on dynamics. Galileo expressly said that the Bible cannot err, and saw his system as an alternate interpretation of the biblical texts.

Rene Descartes (1596-1650) was a French mathematician, scientist and philosopher who has been called the father of modern philosophy. His school of studies made him dissatisfied with previous philosophy: He had a deep religious faith.

Blaise Pascal (1623-1662) was a French mathematician, physicist, inventor, writer and theologian. In mathematics, he published a treatise on the subject of projective geometry and established the foundation for probability theory. Pascal invented a mechanical calculator, and established the principles of vacuums and the pressure of air. He was raised a Roman Catholic, but in 1654 had a religious vision of God, which turned the direction of his study from science to theology. Blasie Pascal wrote of this mystical experience "I have found him, not the Holy Spirit of a cold church building. I have found him, the Holy Spirit in the Bible."

Isaac Newton (1642-1727)—In optics, mechanics, and mathematics, Newton was a figure of undisputed genius and innovation. In all his science (including chemistry) he saw mathematics and numbers as central. What is less well known is that he was devoutly religious and saw numbers as involved in understanding God's plan for history from the Bible. He did a considerable work on biblical numerology, and, though aspects of his beliefs were not orthodox, he thought theology was very important. In his system of physics, God was essential to the nature and absoluteness of space. In Principia he stated, "The most beautiful system of the sun, planets, and comets, could only proceed from the counsel and dominion of an intelligent and powerful Being."

Robert Boyle (1791-1867)—One of the founders and key early members of the Royal Society, Boyle gave his name to "Boyle's Law" for gases, and also wrote an important work on chemistry. Encyclopedia Britannica says of him: "By his will he endowed a series of Boyle lectures, or sermons, which still continue, 'for proving the Christian religion against notorious infidels . . .' As a devout Protestant, Boyle took a special interest in promoting the Christian religion abroad, giving money to translate and publish the New Testament into Irish and Turkish. In 1690 he developed his theological views in The Christian Virtuoso, which he wrote to show that the study of nature was a central religious duty." Boyle wrote against atheists in his day (the notion that atheism is a modern invention is a myth), and was clearly much more devoutly Christian than the average in his era.

Michael Faraday (1791-1867) was the son of a blacksmith who became one of the greatest scientists of the 19th century. His work on electricity and magnetism not only revolutionized physics, but led to much of our lifestyles today, which depends on them (including computers and telephone lines and, so, web sites). Faraday was a devoutly Christian member of the Sandemanians, which significantly influenced him and strongly affected the way in which he approached and interpreted nature. Originating from Presbyterians, the Sandemanians rejected the idea of state churches, and tried to go back to a New Testament type of Christianity.

Gregor Mendel (1822-1884) was the first to lay the mathematical foundations of genetics, in what came to be called "Mendelianism". He began his research in 1856 (three years before Darwin published his Origin of Species) in the garden of the Monastery in which he was a monk. Mendel was elected Abbot of his Monastery in 1868.

William Thomson Kelvin (1824-1907) was foremost among the small group of British scientists who helped to lay the foundations of modern physics. His work covered many areas of physics, and he was said to have more letters after his name than anyone else in the Commonwealth, since he received numerous honorary degrees from European Universities, which recognized the value of his work. He was a very committed Christian, who was certainly more religious than the average for his era. Interestingly, his fellow physicists George Gabriel Stokes (1819-1903) and James Clerk Maxwell (1831-1879) were also men of deep Christian commitment, in an era when many were nominal, apathetic, or anti-Christian. The Encyclopedia Britannica says "Maxwell is regarded by most modern physicists as the scientist of the 19th century who had the greatest influence on 20th century physics; he is ranked with Sir Isaac Newton and Albert Einstein for the fundamental nature of his contributions."

Lord Kelvin was an Old Earth creationist, who estimated the Earth's age to be somewhere between 20 million and 100 million years, with an upper limit at 500 million years based on cooling rates (a low estimate due to his lack of knowledge about radiogenic heating).

Max Planck (1858-1947) made many contributions to physics, but is best known for quantum theory, which revolutionized our understanding of the atomic and sub-atomic worlds. In his 1937 lecture "Religion and Naturwissenschaft," Planck expressed the view that God is everywhere present, and held that "the holiness of the unintelligible Godhead is conveyed by the holiness of symbols." Atheists, he thought, attach too much importance to what are merely symbols. Planck was a churchwarden from 1920 until his death, and believed in an almighty, all-knowing, beneficent God (though not necessarily a personal one).

Both science and religion wage a "tireless battle against skepticism and dogmatism, against unbelief and superstition" with the goal "toward God!" Here is a testimony of one of the scientists of our times, from the most outstanding university in USA. Dr. Eben Alexander has taught at Harvard Medical School and has earned a strong reputation as a neurosurgeon. And while Alexander says he's long called himself a Christian, he never held deeply religious beliefs or a pronounced faith in the afterlife. But after a week in a coma during the fall of 2008, during which his neocortex ceased to function, Alexander claims he experienced a life-changing visit to the afterlife, specifically heaven. He says, "According to current medical understanding of the brain and mind, there is absolutely no way that I could have experienced even a dim and limited consciousness during my time in the coma, much less the hyper-vivid and completely coherent odyssey I underwent," Alexander writes in the cover story of this week's edition of Newsweek.

So what exactly does heaven look like? Alexander says he first found himself floating above clouds before witnessing, "transparent, shimmering beings arced across the sky, leaving long, streamer like lines behind them." He claims to have been escorted by an unknown female companion and says he communicated with these beings through a method of correspondence that transcended language. Alexander says the messages he received from those beings loosely translated as: "You are loved and cherished, dearly, forever." "You have nothing to fear." "There is nothing you can do wrong." From there, Alexander claims to have traveled to "an immense void, completely dark, infinite in size, yet also infinitely comforting." He believes this void was the home of God.

After recovering from his meningitis-induced coma, Alexander says he was reluctant to share his experience with his colleagues but found comfort inside the walls of his church. He's chronicled his experience in a new book, "Proof of Heaven: A neurosurgeon's journey into the afterlife," which will be published in late October.

"I'm still a doctor, and still a man of science every bit as much as I was before I had my experience," Alexander writes. "But on a deep level I'm very different from the person I was before, because I've caught a glimpse of this emerging picture of reality. And you can believe me when I tell you that it will be worth every bit of the work it will take us, and those who come after us, to get it right." (*By Dr. Eben Alexander*).

We can conclude that Christians are not non-thinking, anti-science, anti-intellectual, superstitious and gullible people. Christians believe that science was ordained by God to study and to improve on nature. Science should therefore not be used to disapprove the Scriptures. Science should not be in conflict with the Bible. Science should be in agreement with the Scriptures. I am going to us the example of the first person who discovered that the earth is round. History has conflicting accounts regarding the first person who discovered that the world is round. It is taught that Columbus set out to prove the world was round. If he did, he was about 2,000 years too late. Ancient Greek mathematicians had already proven that the earth was round, not flat. Pythagoras in the sixth century B.C. was one of the originators of the idea. Aristotle in the fourth century B.C. provided the physical evidence, such as the shadow of the Earth on the moon and the curvature of the Earth known by all sailors approaching land. And by the third century B.C., Eratosthenes determined our planet's shape and circumference using basic geometry. In the second century, Claudius Ptolemy wrote the "Almagest," the mathematical and astronomical treatise on planetary shapes and motions, describing the spherical Earth. This text was well known throughout educated Europe in Columbus' time.

The Bible projected that the earth is round, before any person discovered that the earth is round. Take a look at this scripture in the book of Isaiah: "He sits enthroned above <u>the circle of the earth</u>, and its people are like grasshoppers. He stretches out the heavens like a canopy, and spreads them out like a tent to live in" (Isaiah 40:22). The book of Isaiah was written between (circa) 740-680 B.C., toward the end of the reign of King Uzziah and throughout the reigns of King Jotham, Ahaz and Hezekiah.

Whosoever created the universe understands it perfectly. For example a very interesting verse to consider is Job 26:7 which states that God "hangs the earth on nothing." This might evoke an image of God hanging the earth like a Christmas tree ornament, but hanging it on empty space. He did not wait for science to discover it in order for Him to write it in His holy book.

The Bible says that this world expands, "God stretches the universe" (Isaiah 40:22). Science agrees that this world is expanding. Most astronomers today believe that the universe is expanding. This expansion is a very natural result of the physics that Einstein discovered—general relativity. At the same time they (Atheists Scientists) believe that the earth is eternal. They falsely believe that it was not created by an eternal God. Their argument contradicts their theory because in order for something to expand it must have a beginning. The earth cannot therefore be eternal. There is a time when it was not. It was created by an eternal being (God). The economy of creation dictates that the creator owns everything He created. (*Regarding science and the scriptures please read my book called "The Miracle at Prairie Ave"*).

Science cannot prove or disapprove the existence of God. There is no telescope powerful enough to see God sitting on His throne in heaven. Science demands experimental facts in order to prove something. However, the experiment to prove the existence of God is non-existence. We can tell the existence of God by examining others sources provided by God. The evidence of nature is the non-disputable proof of the existence of God. I want to say that some explanations do not need explanation in order to be valid. For example in case you walked on the moon and you found an abandoned well assembled machine, it would be self-explanatory that somebody walked on the moon before. Definitely, somebody took time to create everything that exists. Some African tribes call Him simply the unknown creator (*Katonda or Omutonzi*).

This reminds me of Paul when he was in Athens. He saw the people having several altars to multiple gods including the unknown creator. The Bible says that, "Then Paul stood in the midst of Mars' hill, and said, Ye men of Athens, I perceive that in all things ye are too superstitious. For as I walked around and looked carefully at your objects of worship, I even found an altar with this inscription: TO AN UNKNOWN GOD. Now what you worship as something unknown I am going to proclaim to you" (Acts 17:22-23). Paul was not debating mythology; he was debating basing his argument on historical truth that happened less than twenty years ago, a couple of hundred miles away.

Jesus said that He came to reveal the unknown God. He said in a very confrontal way that no one can know God except through the Son: "Now this is eternal life: that they know you, the only true God, and Jesus Christ, whom you have sent" (John 17:3).

The law of science says that nothing can exist by itself. According to Christianity, the self-existence God created all things. The same God was not created. He is His own sufficient reason; but He is not cause of Himself. By sufficient reason in the full sense I mean an explanation adequate for the existence of some particular being.

Christianity is faith oriented. It is about believing even without seeing. One of the leading scientists of our times made this pound statement "*We don't question the things we "see." We're so innately programmed to assume that "seeing is believing," that we forget our minds can play tricks on us. We never stop to question our brains. We never stop to consider the fact that images and sounds are nothing more than electrical impulses and waves of pressure translated by other electrical impulses in our brain.*" Although this guy is not a Christian, he seems to agree with the Christian principle of not trusting the minds but the heart (faith).

Christians are pro-science. They are for scientific discoveries that do not exclude God. They have a reputation of encouraging those scientists whose discoveries are grounded on moral grounds. October 22, 2012, according to*LifeSiteNews.com*—Pro-life advocates were debating the awarding of the Nobel Prize for medicine to Dr. Shinya Yamanaka, the discoverer of induced pluripotent stem (iPS) cells, with some outright condemning the work and others calling it a boon that will advance ethical medical technology.

In 2007, Yamanaka, a researcher at Kyoto University, published a paper in the journals Nature and Stem Cell announcing that his team had created embryo-like stem cells from the skin cells of mice. The process he developed, using a set of four genes to re-program the cells, was hailed around the world as a possible solution to the unethical use of living human embryos to obtain "pluripotent stem cells"—i.e. cells that can be induced to become any type of tissue in the body.

Until this discovery, the scientific world was largely convinced that adult stem cells were limited and only embryonic stem cells could be malleable enough to produce the many different tissue types needed for medical applications.

If you're like me, you have non-believing friends who claim that Christians are biased. They know that we, as Christians, believe in the existence of God, so they assume that we are unable to evaluate the evidence properly. Non-believers are convinced that Christians start out with a presupposition that clouds our judgment. In truth, however, many of our "rational", "science based" friends are far more constrained by their presuppositions.

Remember that ALL of us have a point of view, but this does not necessarily mean we are unfairly biased. Bias has nothing to do with holding a viewpoint. Bias occurs when this viewpoint eliminates certain forms of evidence and evidential conclusions before we even begin the investigation. And while atheists may argue that Christians have this kind of bias, a quick examination of the culture's reliance on science reveals that just the opposite is true. I bet you've heard a friend say something similar to: "I am a science and evidence person. Truth can only be determined empirically, and science is the only way to really know truth." When people make statements like this, they may be revealing something more than a point of view; they may be exposing a rigid bias that is grounded in an over-reliance on science. There are three dangers in over estimating the ability of science to determine truth: Over-Reliance on Science is Self-Refuting. When people make the claim, "Science is the only way to really know the truth," simply ask them if they "really know" that this statement is true. If they do, ask them how science helped them come to this conclusion. It turns out that the statement, "Science is the only way to really know the truth," cannot be derived or verified by science! This statement is a philosophical proclamation that defies its own claim: it cannot be verified or confirmed as "true" through any scientific examination or method. It turns out that, for people who make this claim, there is at least one truth they can know without the benefit of science: the fact that science is the only way to really know the truth! See the problem here?

An Over-Reliance on Science is Inappropriately Limiting. There are many things that we know without the benefit of science. The previously mentioned philosophical claim is just one example. But there are more:

1. Logical and mathematical truths: these must be accepted as foundational presuppositions in order for us to engage in any scientific study, so we clearly can't use science to determine the logic and math facts that precede science.

2. Metaphysical truths: some truths about the nature of the world (such as whether or not the external world is real in the first place) cannot be determined through the use of science.

3. Moral and ethical truths: science cannot tell us what is morally virtuous or vile. It may, on occasion help us to know what "is" (related to the material world), but science can never tell us what "ought to be" (related to moral judgments).

4. Aesthetic truths: science cannot help us to determine or judge what is beautiful or what is ugly.

5. Historical truths: perhaps most important to the study of the Christian worldview, science cannot determine what is true historically. Science can tell us nothing about who won the Oscar for best picture last year, and in a similar way, science can tell us nothing about the ancient claims related to the historicity of Jesus or the historical reliability of the Bible.

If we are going to reject all categories of truth that can't be determined or verified scientifically, we are going to have to reject all truths related to logic, mathematics, morals, aesthetics, history or metaphysics. The most important claims and assertions of life would have to be ignored as untrustworthy.

An Over-Reliance on Science is Prejudicially Biased. For example, the Bible predicted an increase of nature hostility at the end times. As much as science is important, our protection does not come absolutely from science. Can you imagine that even the avowedly greatest country of the world cannot resist the rampage of Mother Nature? What I mean is that nobody (apart from God) can insulate us against the ravages of the hurricane, earthquake and other hostile climates.

More importantly, an over-reliance on science eliminates explanatory options on the basis of bias. There is a difference between the scientific method (a rational process of testing) and scientism (an irrational commitment to philosophical naturalism). Philosophical naturalists refuse to consider anything outside the natural world as an explanation for the events they observe. Christians, on the other hand, are better able to let the evidence take them where it leads. If natural laws and processes can account for a particular phenomenon, so be it. If natural laws and processes fall short of providing an explanation and the evidence points to the existence of something supernatural, that explanation is still on the table. Philosophical naturalism rules out an entire category of supernatural explanation even before it seeks to determine if anything supernatural exists!

It turns out that the Christian worldview has the ability to embrace natural explanations without rejecting the supernatural ones out of hand. An over-reliance on science (often described as "scientism") causes us to reject anything supernatural before we even begin to investigate an explanation. Which of these two approaches is most prejudicial? Which is least tolerant of the variety of explanations that are available to us? An over-reliance on science has blinded our culture to the rich explanatory possibilities. It's no wonder that many post-enlightenment "truth seekers" have so much trouble finding what they seek.

I want to end by discussing the impact of the so called first world (developed nations) on the rest of the world. The backlash of capitalism is an open market for all things including immoral values. Sandel recently summarized his ideas about capitalism in the Atlantic. In "What Isn't for Sale?" he writes: "Without being fully aware of the shift, Americans have drifted from having a market economy to becoming a market society . . . where almost everything is up for sale . . . a way of life where market values seep into almost every sphere of life and sometimes crowd out or corrode important values, non-market values."

We cannot ignore the impact of science on our communities in particular in the area of modern technology and communications. The number of web users in the world is high rocketing. By January 2014, in China, the number has surged to 618 million, a government agency said, underscoring the rapid growth of online connectivity in the country with the world's largest Internet population. New ideas are travelling at the speed of lightning. They have contributed to a lot of developments but at the same time there are some setbacks which cannot be overlooked. In these modern times where information travels at light speed, copy and paste have become the order of the day, in an era where time means money and information is quiet available it is somehow cheap to copy and paste. It is for the same reason we are jammed up with new ideas (immorality) shooting from all corners of the world. You don't have to hunt for them; they meet you wherever you are even in your sitting room. Most of them are very destructive to our morality. The young generation in particular is confused not knowing what to pick and what to discard.

America, the world power is infecting the world with secularism in the name of tolerance and democracy. Civility is necessary for democratic discourse. But it's also sadly lacking in our countries today. Rejecting immoral people is considered to be undemocratic. In fact President Obama said that the people who hate homosexuals have old ways of thinking. He used the term 'old ways of thinking' to mean old days racists. It is unfortunate that most politicians today behave like celebrities, known to promote immorality. One columnist insinuated that psychologists slot politicians into personality types, one being the "Type T Personality". The 'T' is for 'Thrill', which could account for straying and general unscrupulousness. Like celebrities, politicians are surrounded by indulgent sycophants who give an impractical belief that they are above normal morality. They falsely believe that they're the masters of their fates and captains of their souls. Politics is nothing more than a contest of egos, or the domain of special interests. It is pursuing self aggrandizement.

The role of the developed countries is helping the weak economies of our countries (third world) to grow. Unfortunately, the rich nations use their aids as baits to trap us into their immorality. There are attached strings on the aids given. Strings like tolerance of others' value even when such values contradict the morality of God. Aid was once described as being similar to prostitution; money being offered in return for favors with no love in between. We don't need to beg and sell our morals like some paupers do in exchange of the mighty dollar.

Addressing delegates in May 2011, Cecilia Ogwal said, "Practices that are against African culture are now classified as human rights. I am forced to accept homosexuality. That is wrong and should be condemned, it cannot be accepted."

Convinced that advent of homosexuality in Uganda must be attributed to the activities of global gay lobby, one young man said: ". . . The gay lobby is a satanic movement whose leaders deserve to be executed." An older gentleman, probably in his mid-late fifties, also weighed into the anti-homosexuality diatribe and said: ". . . In Bushenyi where I come from, if such a man was caught sodomising a teenage boy, I can tell you people will chop off his penis and make him eat it before they turn to his body and cut it into pieces for dogs to eat." (*Uganda Correspondence, newspaper, Dec. 11, 2012*).

And if you thought that is the usual homophobic bravado you would expect from testosterone filled semi intoxicated African men, then here this: A middle aged woman, who seemed to be only drinking soft non-alcoholic drinks, also declared her deep phobia of homosexuality: ". . . My own son, whom I carried for nine months and shed blood to bring to this world—and I find another man sodomising him, you are joking: I will stab that bustard straight in the heart with my kitchen knife and walk straight to police and say I have killed a biological mistake." (*Uganda Correspondence, newspaper, Dec. 11, 2012*)

I am not trying to advocate violence against homosexuals. I am trying to show that although Western countries consider homosexuality a human right, homosexuality is anti-African culture. These countries fail to understand that Africans build and groom a society based on defined values. I don't believe that some people are naturally born homosexual. I believe that homosexual is a sin like any other sin. All sins need to be repented and forgiven. It is wrong for an adulterous heterosexual to point a finger to a homosexual when both of them are swimming in the same pool of God's judgment and wrath. The pedophiles are both heterosexual and homosexual; their perversion is rooted in their evil lustful desires, lust for power and dominance. Again, all sinners need to repent. Mr. Lund insinuated that, "It does not help when the country claims a moral superiority by contemplating capital punishment for "aggravated homosexuality". The contrast to the reports of large scale theft euphemistically called corruption is too much to swallow so Ugandans appear as world champions in hypocrisy" (*Daily Monitor, December, 18, 2012*).

Nobel Laureate Archbishop Desmond Tutu on Tuesday (Dec. 4) urged Uganda to scrap a controversial draft law that would send gays and lesbians to jail and, some say, put them at risk of the death penalty. He said that the law will be akin to discrimination (racism). I want to say that Homosexuality is not a human right, but a human vice and God detests it. Equating an act of sodomy to human rights defeats logic. What about the rights of our innocent children who are manipulated and recruited into homosexuality? I mean our children who are being recruited into the vice by giving them a lot of money and other goodies! The mission of the Secular Western powers is to de-moralize the universe in the name of tolerance. Homosexuality should never be compared to races either. Otherwise people addicted to drugs will also be justified to seek their rights. Freedom should not be interpreted as the right to do as you want. Otherwise it becomes part of a suspect quasi-theology, sweet-named as "freedom." And isn't pedophilia, prostitution, and even rape an individual's way of exercising their rights and freedoms?

The gays are not just looking for simple recognition but they are looking for preference treatment of dignified promiscuity. Homosexuality is sexual perversion and not orientation. It is a choice that a person makes. I agree with President Mugabe who said that if the dogs can know the difference and they do not have half of our intelligence, what about human beings. I may not agree with his political policies but I agree with him on this one. God created us in his image: with the dual male and female characteristic. He also created the animals, with the same male and female dual characteristics; for purposes of procreation. Even plants have the male & female characteristics (stamen & pistil) in the flowers). In the animal kingdom, acts of homosexuality are only witnessed in animals that are being removed from their natural habitats.

The greatest favor we can do to the homosexuals is to help them to be delivered from their immorality and its consequences (flames of hell); but they must admit that they need our help. I know somebody might say I am judging them. I want to say that we are allowed to judge others as long as we are not judgmental (judge with ill intents). The Bible says that, "Hate the evil, and love the good, and establish judgment in the gate: it may be that the LORD God of hosts will be gracious—" (Amos 5:15). Do you know that the Gospel is preached in form of judgment to the world? Oh yes, receive Jesus and be saved or reject it and perish in your sins.

Africa has become a dumping ground for many unwanted things including the trash cultures! How long are we going to allow the moral filth to be dumped on us in the name of tolerance? If we are not careful we might be as well surrendering our continent to scavengers. Our moral values need to be sterilized and preserved. We must put a stop to all this and claim our continent back! All people (not just

Christian people) should know intuitively that if we continue on our current course, our culture will further degenerate and decay into greater selfishness, hedonism, and immorality. Any moral society enunciates what social values it espouses for society as a basis of its organization and protects the same values from the encroachment of anti-social foreign values.

Civilization is neither westernization nor exclusive to other climes. It is building a society on values and institutions with respect to the Moral Creator. The standard of morality is determined by the Scriptures. We must protect the values which are not in contradiction to the scriptures. We should never be afraid of the perpetrators of immorality. Americans think that it's OK to simply shout down their opponents, malign their motives, or, when all else fails, make vicious personal attacks. The state cannot stand by and watch as the family institution is torn apart by Western vices such as homosexuality, equal rights, and women emancipation amidst the abject poverty in which our people wallow.

There are those moral values which make us Africans, which we cannot afford to lose. James Ikuya says that, "Although humans are biologically similar, the societies and communities in which they live are distinct by their geography, history, products, language, etc. There are qualities and activities which make people French, English, American, etc."

Every bit of behavior we embrace influences the norms of our culture. While fetishes and rituals are part of culture, they are only the ceremonies of the much more deep-rooted things and values that embody human activities. Our meaning of culture is the diverse values necessary to motivate and pollinate the creativity of every society. Each culture has obligation to shield its community from domination by another; it promotes its independence by permeating it with its pride. Without such pride, all people would be dissolved and overrun by others. In most African cultures, there are certain aspects of life that are covered by a veil of shame and silence. These are commonly known as taboos and they are presumed to be inviolable. These unwritten laws are the filtering mechanisms mostly addressing the morals of a society. It is disturbing that taboos in Uganda are no longer respected. This has perpetuated immorality. Sexual morals, for instance, have been disregarded. Immoral acts such as sodomy, defilement, lesbianism, prostitution, indecent dressing and the use of vulgar language are openly embraced with pride!

I want to talk directly to our cultural elders. When leaders don't stand for something, their people will fall for anything. The restitution to rectify the deficient is not getting new or innovative ideas into the minds of the people but getting the old ones out. We need to revisit our old values lest we remain caricatures and cartridges of a false tradition or humanity forever. Elders used to play an important role in educating our youth and in promoting our values but today the impact of their guidance has diminished. We have lost our priorities because there are a lot of obstructions out there. We seem to be locked in surreal behavior akin to the taxi drivers in Kampala's traffic-choked roads whereby the adhering to the driving rules by the exasperated drivers is done only under the feared watch of the traffic cops. As soon as the cops are deemed to be gazing the other way, the reckless drivers zoom off the wrong way unlawfully blocking other road users. Those of you who have ever been in my home city know what I am talking about. Everybody seems to be seeking to gain momentary personal advantage over the other. Likewise, the elders have lost parental control. Consequently, we have a generation of loose morals who cannot control their libido.

Ironically, during the pre-colonial era, we (Africans) were too naked, openly sexual, and too savage for their (Whites) liking. Thank God for the coming of the missionaries who brought light to the Dark Continent. But after two world wars, Europe liberalized—nudity became an accepted way of life. They prefer walking naked on the beaches and in nude club as we used to do. Women in society are accepted to do things which were formerly reserved for men. Bestiality and zoophilia are common practices. The cancer of immorality is spreading like wild fire. Liberalism and secularism have partly become the original version of us. The kind of moralism that drove the missionaries to come to our rescue has evaporated in thin air.

I want to emphasize that all cultures have flaws. There is no such a thing as a perfect culture. One writer compared culture to a piece of raw meat sitting in the sun. That meat will decay. Similarly, every culture ever known has over time decayed. The decay is due to the corruption of sin. Sin corrupts our lives individually and cooperatively as a community. It is only the blood of Jesus that can eliminate the weed of immorality (*Regarding culture and Christianity please read my book "Shaping the Society"*).

Now I want to talk directly to the Christians. See clearly where the road is leading, and you won't be bothered by the rocks and pebbles over which you must travel. Jesus Christ is Lord regardless of what most people may say. So stop worrying about the status quo and trust what you know to be true. And one day when your faith is made sight, you'll rejoice as you see your Savior face-to-face. When this blessed day will dawn, how wonderful it will be to gaze on that blessed face forever, and without a cloud rolling between, and never have to turn our eyes away to look on a tired and sinful world.

Jesus is not just a teacher of morality but He is the Savior. Throughout history there have emerged many teachers of morality who are not Christian but their teachings did not go deep enough to save. In fact, apart from Christ, none of the great teachers of the world and leaders of the religions of the world was able to live the quality of life that they preached. Jesus alone did everything that He preached. He preached the cross and He died at the cross. He preached eternal life and He resurrected to eternal life. The empty tomb is the undisputable evidence of the resurrection of Jesus. It is historical truth because all of the Apostles (apart from John) testified to the resurrection and became martyrs for the same cause. These folks were either crazy or committed, certifiably nuts or certain about their observations.

Dr. Thomas Arnold, professor of history at Oxford, said a number of years ago, "I know of no fact in the history of mankind which is proved by better and fuller evidence of every sort, to the understanding of a fair inquirer, than the great sign which God hath given us that Christ died and rose again from the dead."

Along the same lines, noted attorney Sir Edward Clark said, "As a lawyer I have made a prolonged study of the evidences for the resurrection . . . To me the evidence is conclusive, and over and over again in the High Court I have secured the verdict on evidence not nearly so compelling."

Pastor Gram says that the evidence that Jesus Christ is alive is indeed compelling! To deny that is to deny the most reasonable conclusion of the eyewitness accounts. So stand firm in your faith, knowing that what you believe is as provable as any fact in history. The evidence is on our side.

Paul said that, "For I delivered to you as of first importance what I also received: that Christ died for our sins in accordance with the Scriptures, that he was buried, that he was raised on the third day in accordance with the Scriptures, and that he appeared to Cephas, then to the twelve. Then <u>he appeared to more than five hundred brothers at one time</u>, most of whom are still alive, though some have fallen asleep" (1 Corinthians 15:3-6).

We are not here by accident but in accordance to the divine plan. We are the preservatives (salt) of this world. If the culture is rotting, don't blame the culture—it's natural. Blame the lack of salt. God's expectation to change the cultures of the world is in the Church. Jesus said that He came to glorify the Father (John 8:54). God has positioned the Church in His righteousness and established in her a vital and dynamic interconnection with Christ and the Father through the empowering presence of the Holy Spirit purposely to glorify the Father and advance the heavenly kingdom on the earth (John 14:23-24).

The mission of Jesus Christ on the earth is to seek the lost world: To save those who are not saved from eternal condemnation (hell) and to save those who are saved from themselves (old Adamic nature). Only the dead in Christ can live forever in the presence of God. We all have a choice to make. We find favor with God whenever we make choices glorifying Him by manifesting the life of Christ. This must be the priority of each and every believer. The moral God demands morality patterned after His very character. Our morality is our godliness.

We must be aware that the moral decay will intensify as we are approaching the end times. Paul warned Timothy that the last days will bring an intensification of evil: "Now the Spirit expressly says that in later times some will depart from the faith by devoting themselves to deceitful spirits and teachings of demons" (1 Timothy 4:1). The Apostle Peter's minds did not differ from Paul. He prophesied that, "Scoffers will come in the last days" (2 Peter 3:3). Jude predicted the same: "In the last time there will be scoffers, following their own ungodly passions" (Jude 1:18).

Given the fact, sin will not prevail forever. God predetermined how this world will end. The Second coming of Christ involves the judgment of the sinners to purge sin from this universe. We (believers) are promised to experience heaven on earth when our Messiah returns. But the skeptics will definitely face the wrath of God. An apocalypse (Ancient Greek: ποκάλυψις apocálypsis, from πό and καλύπτω meaning 'un-covering'), translated literally from Greek, is a disclosure of knowledge, hidden from humanity in an era dominated by falsehood and misconception. A prophetic revelation, especially concerning a cataclysm in which the forces of good permanently triumph over the forces of evil.

Recently a group of youth scientists (non-Christian) warned that unless there is a change in man's attitude (repent), our civilization will cease to exist in the next hundred years. I like Brother J. Ikuya's comment. He said that: "Although scientific notions are generally reputed to be diametrically distinct from religious dogma and beliefs, there are amazing occasions when there appears to be a convergence in their standpoints. The Christian faith and other religions are underpinned on the doctrine of a supernatural being (God) that oversees the creation of the universe up to Judgment day—when the world will supposedly end.

There are visible signs in nature like massive earthquakes predicting the end of times. On 3rd November 2013 a total solar Eclipse passed over West, Central and East Africa, including the countries Equatorial Gabon, Congo, Uganda, Kenya and Ethiopia. It is a hybrid eclipse which is the rarest of the four types of solar eclipses. It is believed that the last time it happened was some 500 hundred years ago. It is not likely to happen again in less than 150 years. It is one of the many wonders of the world.

The earth is immense in size, about 8,000 miles in diameter, with a mass calculated at roughly 6.6 x 1,021 tons. The earth is on average 93 million miles from the sun. According to science, as the earth moves farther from the sun in its orbit, the sun's gravitational force on the earth decreases. Gravitational force is inversely proportional to the radius. If the earth traveled much faster in its 584-million-mile-long journey around the sun, its orbit would become larger and it would move farther away from the sun. If it moved too far from the narrow habitable zone, all life would cease to exist on earth. If it traveled slightly slower in its orbit, the earth would move closer to the sun, and if it moved too close, all life would likewise perish. The earth's 365-days, 6-hours, 49-minutes and 9.54-seconds trip around the sun (the sidereal year) is consistent to over a thousandth of a second! Certainly, the earth is not eternal, it will one way or another come to an end. But we worship an eternal God that created the universe and in His wisdom sustains it in right place in space without visible poles.

According to religious teachings, on Judgment day, humans will be called from the dead to face trial for their sins. The righteous ones, according to the teachings, shall be rewarded with heavenly, everlasting life while sinners will be whisked to hell. On their part, scientists predict that in five billion years from now, the sun that provides our earth with energy and light will begin to 'die.' As a star, the depletion of the sun's hydrogen that fuels its incandescence and fission will result in its gradual fading from its present brightness to a red glow that will finally turn into a shrunken dark matter. It is perceived that the 'dying sun' will kick up huge flares into space, dilating its reach over twenty times its present size. The flames will then engulf the orbit of some planets like the earth, gobbling and consuming them up into nonexistence.

Somehow, in this portrayal by the scientists, we find the ingredients of the everlasting fire preached by the Christian faith. So science agrees that this world will definitely come to an end and there is no scientific remedy to avert the disaster! It turns out that the forecast of science is even more apocalyptical and remorseless than the religions which, at least, offer the solace of continued life [for the non-sinners in heaven].

Science has no answer to sustain life beyond the death of the sun but they are desperately searching for solutions through conceived emigration to other planets and some other stratagems. "The measure of human stupidity is not the failure to establish a city on Planet Mars but the failure to recognize the fact that human civilization will ever amount to nothing irrespective of the innovativeness and inventiveness if the lordship of Christ is not at the pinnacle of all our endeavours." Godfery Nsubuga

It is important to acknowledge the following facts: The geophysical catastrophes that frequently ravage our globe today cannot be attributed unequivocally to the direct action of God, but they can be traced ultimately to human rebellion, and the permissive will of the Creator. The whole earth waits for its redemption. There will be no global holocaust before the return of our Lord. The Bible promised that He will come back the same way He ascended to heaven (Acts 1:9-11). There will be people on earth and every eye will see Him (Revelation 1:7). He is coming to set up His kingdom on earth (Revelation 20). His Kingdom is the climax; it is the culmination of redemptive history, as it unfolds in this world. And so we're really reaching the climax, the culmination of all of human history. This is a day that was described by the prophet Jeremiah in chapter 23 and verses 5 and 6.

Certainly, this world is not eternal because it will come to an end as predicted by the Scriptures: "I saw a new heaven and a new earth, for the first heaven and the first earth passed away" (Revelation 21:1). Our hope is not in the sun but in the Son. The coming of the Son of God in the flesh is the turning point in redemptive history, which is in the outworking of God's plan for rescuing His fallen world. It marks a decisive divide between all that came before and all that God does from that crucial point onward.

I want to end this book by this scripture. It is quoted by three of the four Gospels: "What good will it is for a man if he gains the whole world, yet forfeits his soul? Or what can a man give in exchange for his soul?" (Matthew 16:26; Mark 8:36; Luke 9:25). This is the profound truth: Man is restless in this world regardless of what he or she has because this world is hostile to our true nature. Politics, cultural ideologies, our careers, money, kids, and even romantic love—all of these have failed to quell our restlessness. We remain restless until we rest in Jesus Christ.

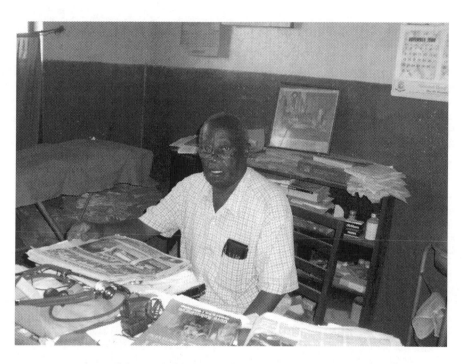

Our heartfelt condolences to the Kawoya family, friends and all concerned Ugandans. Dr. Lwanga, your legacy lives and Uganda stands to learn from it. You were a gift to our country. You will be greatly missed.

Index